STUDIES IN CHRISTIAN HISTORY AND THOUGHT

A Sure Ground on Which to Stand

The Relation of Authority and Interpretive Method
in Luther's Approach to Scripture

STUDIES IN CHRISTIAN HISTORY AND THOUGHT

A full listing of all titles in this series
will be found at the close of this book.

STUDIES IN CHRISTIAN HISTORY AND THOUGHT

A Sure Ground on Which to Stand

The Relation of Authority and Interpretive Method
in Luther's Approach to Scripture

Mark D. Thompson

Foreword by Alister McGrath

Wipf and Stock Publishers
199 W 8th Ave, Suite 3
Eugene, OR 97401

A Sure Ground on Which to Stand
The Relation of Authority and Interpretive Method in Luther's Approach to Scripture
By Thompson, Mark D.
Copyright©2004 Paternoster
ISBN: 1-59752-734-3
Publication date 6/5/2006
Previously published by Paternoster, 2004

This Edition Published by Wipf and Stock Publishers
by arrangement with Paternoster

Paternoster
9 Holdom Avenue
Bletchley
Milton Keyes, MK1 1QR
Great Britain

STUDIES IN CHRISTIAN HISTORY AND THOUGHT

Series Preface

This series complements the specialist series of *Studies in Evangelical History and Thought* and *Studies in Baptist History and Thought* for which Paternoster is becoming increasingly well known by offering works that cover the wider field of Christian history and thought. It encompasses accounts of Christian witness at various periods, studies of individual Christians and movements, and works which concern the relations of church and society through history, and the history of Christian thought.

The series includes monographs, revised dissertations and theses, and collections of papers by individuals and groups. As well as 'free standing' volumes, works on particular running themes are being commissioned; authors will be engaged for these from around the world and from a variety of Christian traditions.

A high academic standard combined with lively writing will commend the volumes in this series both to scholars and to a wider readership.

Series Editors

Alan P.F. Sell, Visiting Professor at Acadia University Divinity College, Nova Scotia, Canada

David Bebbington, Professor of History, University of Stirling, Stirling, Scotland, UK

Clyde Binfield, Professor Associate in History, University of Sheffield, UK

Gerald Bray, Anglican Professor of Divinity, Beeson Divinity School, Samford University, Birmingham, Alabama, USA

Grayson Carter, Associate Professor of Church History, Fuller Theological Seminary SW, Phoenix, Arizona, USA

For Kathryn

Contents

Foreword	xiii
Preface	xv
Abbreviations	xvii

Introduction
The Unaccommodated Luther — 1

Chapter 1
Luther's Inheritance — 11

Holy Scripture: The Central and Critical Testimony	12
The Nature and Use of Scripture in the Patristic Period	17
The Christian Use of the Jewish Scriptures	17
The Emerging Canon of the New Testament	18
The Threat of Heretical Interpretations of the Scriptures	20
Interaction with the Graeco-Roman Thought-World	22
A Growing Commitment to Allegory	24
The Church as the Guardian of Scripture	28
The Nature and Use of Scripture in the Medieval Period	31
A Fundamental Commitment to the Patristic Inheritance	31
A Renewed Emphasis on the Academic Study of the Scriptures	34
A Developing Ecclesiastical Positivism	35
A Growing Concern for the Plain Historical Meaning	38
The Rediscovery of Aristotle	43
The Emergence of the New Learning	44

Chapter 2
The Very Words of God? Luther on Inspiration and the Origin of Holy Scripture — 47

God as the Author of Scripture	53
The Human Writers as the Authors of Scripture	61
Dual Authorship	67
The Word of God	68

Chapter 3
Divine Words? Luther on Inspiration and the Nature of Holy Scripture — 91
A Theory of Inspiration? — 91
Inspiration, Incarnation, Accommodation, and the Cross — 103
The Extent of Inspiration — 112
Inspiration and the Authority of Scripture — 119
  Luther's Questions about the Authorship and Date of Particular Biblical Books — 123
  Luther's Statements about the Canonical Status of Particular Biblical Books — 124
  Luther's Explorations of the Problems of Biblical Chronology — 125
  Luther's Evaluation of Particular Biblical Books — 130
  Luther's Treatment of Prima Facie Error in the Biblical Texts — 138
Inspiration and the Interpretation of Scripture — 141

Chapter 4
A Focused Text? Luther on the Unity of Holy Scripture — 147
Unity in Terms of Origin — 150
Unity in Terms of Content — 152
  Christ as the Centre of Scripture — 152
  A Common Predicament and Solution — 163
  Letter and Spirit — 167
  Law and Gospel — 171
The Relationship of the Old and New Testaments — 177
Unity and the Authority of Scripture — 183
Unity and the Interpretation of Scripture — 184

Chapter 5
An Intelligible Text? Luther on the Clarity of Holy Scripture — 191
The Emergence of the Issue in Luther's Writings — 193

The Importance of the Clarity of Scripture according to Luther	205
What is Clear?	213
Two Types of Clarity	228
Clarity and Translation	235
Clarity and the Authority of Scripture	239
Clarity and the Interpretation of Scripture	241

Chapter 6
Sola Scriptura? Luther on the Sufficiency of Holy Scripture — 249

Scripture and Tradition	252
Scripture and Reason	265
Scripture and Experience	271
Sufficiency and the Purpose of Scripture	274
Sufficiency and the Authority of Scripture	276
Sufficiency and the Interpretation of Scripture	279

Conclusion
Luther's Confidence in Scripture as the Authoritative Word of God — 283

Bibliography — 289

Alphabetical Index of Luther's Works Cited — 307

Chronological Index of Luther's Works Cited — 317

Scripture Index — 327

Subject Index — 331

Author Index — 335

FOREWORD

Martin Luther's understanding of the place of Scripture in Christian theological reasoning is of major importance to both the church historian and the theologian. As the large body of scholarly literature to deal with this debate makes clear, it has not proved easy to offer a precise account of what Luther meant when he famously declared that his 'conscience is captive to the Word of God'. Yet the importance of the question means that it cannot be overlooked. Luther scholars have long recognized the need for a serious engagement with this issue.

Mark Thompson's lucid and informed study of Luther's approach to the Bible is easily the most important to have been published in the last decades in the English language. Showing himself to be a master of both Luther's own writings and the vast body of literature relating to them, Dr Thompson develops an approach to the question which makes sense of many of the difficulties encountered by Luther scholarship. Setting Luther's thought against its backdrop in the late Middle Ages and Renaissance, he argues that it possesses an inner coherence and strength which has not been fully appreciated by his interpreters. This erudite and persuasive book will be of compelling interest to all concerned with the fundamental themes of the Reformation, the development of Luther's reforming theology, and the continuing discussion of the authority and interpretation of the Bible within the church. Though scholarly rigorous, Dr Thompson's work has been written in a very accessible style, which will ensure that this book has a wide and appreciative readership. I warmly and sincerely commend this book as an important contribution to Luther scholarship, and to the wider task of the church today, as it seeks to ground itself in the truth of the Scriptures which inspired Luther's life and work.

Alister McGrath
Professor of Historical Theology
Oxford University

PREFACE

In the almost seven years since the research presented in this volume was completed at Oxford University, the torrent of Luther studies, examining almost every aspect of the Reformer's life and thought, has shown no sign of abating. Indeed, in the last few years very significant contributions have been made and new investigations into old questions have shed much valuable light on the remarkable character and theological legacy of this sixteenth century German Christian. However, none of this work has convinced me that the basic lines of the present study are in need of revision. I am as convinced as ever that much twentieth century Luther scholarship misread him under the pressure of modern theological, philosophical, and ecclesiastical concerns. What is more, I remain committed to the view that best use is made of Luther's legacy only when it is taken seriously on its own terms. We do ourselves no favours and we do not deal with Luther fairly, when we describe his theological convictions in terms he himself would not recognise. To play somewhat on the title of Philip S. Watson's influential study of Luther's theology from 1947, we might simply say that all parties are best served when we 'let Luther be Luther'.

The research that lies behind this volume was made possible by the generosity and support of many people. The librarians and staff of a number of libraries gave invaluable assistance: Bodleian Library, Oxford; Taylorian Library, Oxford; Wycliffe Hall, Oxford; University Library, Cambridge; Tyndale House, Cambridge; and the Löhse Memorial Library, Luther Seminary, Adelaide, South Australia. Special mention should be made of Mr Kim Robinson, Chief Librarian at Moore Theological College, Sydney, Australia. Mr Robinson's willingness to search for material which could not be found anywhere in the United Kingdom made the task of engaging with a wide range of Luther scholarship possible.

The then Principal of Moore Theological College (now Archbishop of Sydney), Dr Peter F. Jensen, was a particular encouragement throughout the three years spent studying Luther's legacy in the city of spires. Dr Jensen ensured that personal, financial, and spiritual support were readily available for Kathryn and myself. Indeed, correspondence with him was one of the many joys of our time in the United Kingdom. We are very grateful to him and the Moore College Council, in particular the Bursar, Mr Doug Marr.

Many other people have read parts of this thesis and have made helpful suggestions. Amongst those who deserve special mention are Mr Mark Baddeley, Drs Peter Bolt and Andrew Shead, Revd Dominic Webb, and the late Professor Heiko A. Oberman. I remain in their debt.

Most assistance, of course, was provided by my supervisor in Oxford, Professor Alister E. McGrath. Professor McGrath ensured that those years of research were fruitful both personally and academically. His constant encouragement and advice, enriched by his own extensive knowledge of Luther and Reformation theology, remains greatly appreciated. Our appointments to discuss Luther's theology were always stimulating. Futhermore, his kindness in giving me the opportunity to teach alongside him on the staff of Wycliffe Hall, Oxford during the second year of my studies provided further stimulation in my thinking about Luther and Scripture.

As valuable as the academic stimulation of Oxford proved to be, it was the spiritual support and nourishment provided by the congregation of St Ebbes which has had the most lasting influence. Rarely have we experienced such rich fellowship and genuine Christian care. We remain particularly indebted to the then Rector, Revd David Fletcher, his assistants Revd Vaughan Roberts (now the Rector of St Ebbes), Revd David Gibb, and Miss Annabel Heywood, together with their families.

However, this research could not have been undertaken, nor would it have been brought to this conclusion, without my wife Kathryn. She bore much of the burden of our sojourn to the other side of the world and at every point enriched it by her presence. Her encouragement, questions, and constant interest, not to mention her perseverance in proof-reading and collating the thesis in those final days, were almost overwhelming. I thank God for her. Since that time in Oxford, God has blessed us with three delightful daughters, Elizabeth (born 1999), Anna (born 2001) and Rachel (born 2002). However, I am sure that, if they ever should read this book, they will agree it is only fitting that their mother remain the person to whom the published version of this work is dedicated.

Soli Deo Gloria

ABBREVIATIONS

CC   *Corpus Catholicorum. Werke katholischer Schriftsteller im Zeitalter der Glaubensspaultung,* various editors, 43 vols to date (Münster: Aschendorff, 1919-).

CCSL   *Corpus Christianorum Series Latina,* various editors, 176 vols to date (Turnholt: Brepols, 1954-).

CR   *Corpus Reformatorum*, ed. W. Baum *et al.*, 101 vols to date (Berlin/Leipzig/Zurich, Theologischer Verlag, 1834-).

CSEL   *Corpus Scriptorum Ecclesiasticorum Latinorum,* ed. Johannes Bauer *et al.*, 90 vols to date (Vienna: Hoelder, 1866-).

EA var. arg.
   D. Martini Lutheri Opera Latina Varii Argumenti ad Reformationis Historiam Imprimis Pertinentia, ed. Heinrich Schmidt, 7 vols (Frankfurt & Erlangen: Heyderi & Zimeri, 1865-73).

LW   *Luther's Works,* ed. Jaroslav Pelikan & Helmut T. Lehmann, 55 vols (St Louis/Philadelphia: Concordia/Fortress Press, 1955-86).

PG   *Patrologiae, cursus completus, series Graeca,* ed. J.P. Migne, 162 vols (Paris: Migne, 1857-66).

PL   *Patrologiae, cursus completus, series Latina,* ed. J.P. Migne, 221 vols (Paris: Migne, 1844-64); *Supplementum,* ed. A. Hamman (Paris: Migne, 1958).

WA   *D. Martin Luthers Werke: Kritische Gesamtausgabe, Schriften,* ed. J.K.F. Knaake, G. Kawerau, *et al.*, 66 vols to date (Weimar: Hermann Böhlaus Nachfolger, 1883-).

WABr D. *Martin Luthers Werke: Kritische Gesamtausgabe, Briefwechsel*, ed. J.K.F. Knaake, G. Kawerau, *et al.*, 18 vols (Weimar: Hermann Böhlaus Nachfolger, 1930-85).

WADB D. *Martin Luthers Werke: Kritische Gesamtausgabe, Die Deutsche Bibel*, ed. J.K.F. Knaake, G. Kawerau, *et al.*, 12 vols (Weimar: Hermann Böhlaus Nachfolger, 1906-61).

WATr D. *Martin Luthers Werke: Kritische Gesamtausgabe, Tischreden*, ed. J.K.F. Knaake, G. Kawerau, *et al.*, 6 vols (Weimar: Hermann Böhlaus Nachfolger, 1912-21).

Journal abbreviations conform to the convention set out on the website of the *Journal of Biblical Studies:*
http://journalofbiblicalstudies.org/Abbreviations.htm

INTRODUCTION

The Unaccommodated Luther[1]

Four hundred and fifty years after his death, Martin Luther's life and thought continue to attract both public and scholarly interest. He remains almost as controversial as the day on which he stood before the Holy Roman Emperor and the representatives of the Roman curia, excommunicate and under the threat of an imperial ban. Though he left behind him a literary deposit almost unrivalled in the history of Western theology, the debates continue to rage over many of the central tenets of his theology. His writing has stimulated vastly divergent interpretations, and in the twentieth century alone he was blamed for everything from the holocaust to the introspective conscience of the West.[2]

---

[1] This title reflects my critical appreciation for the work of Richard Muller, especially his attempts to extract Calvin from the 'modern accommodations' which dominated Calvin scholarship in the latter half of the twentieth century. Richard A. Muller, *The Unaccommodated Calvin: Studies in the Foundation of a Theological Tradition*.

[2] Peter F. Wiener, *Martin Luther: Hitler's Spiritual Ancestor;* Krister Stendahl, 'The Apostle Paul and the Introspective Conscience of the West', *HTR*, 56 (1963), 199-215.

During the last hundred years a particular focus of attention has been Luther's approach to Holy Scripture.[3] This is hardly surprising for above all else he was a student and teacher of the Bible. By any assessment, he remains a figure of extraordinary significance in the history of biblical interpretation. Furthermore, in the twentieth century debates over the origin, nature, and function of the Bible, he was cited by those on every side. Such attempts to claim Luther's support for various modern positions often led to distortion, as one particular array of Luther texts was set up against another, sometimes with little or no indication of their literary and historical context. Luther the fundamentalist was countered by Luther the forefather of biblical criticism, or both were rejected in favour of Luther the existentialist.[4] Partly as a consequence, an immense secondary literature has arisen, eclipsing the massive critical edition of Luther's own work itself. However, there is as yet no genuine consensus on Luther's approach to Holy Scripture.[5]

Any serious attempt to analyse Luther's thought in this area must deal with a number of factors which threaten to confuse the picture. The first of these is the need to place Luther firmly against his own background both historically and ideologically. Luther's thought did not emerge in a vacuum. Even at the points at which he is most creative and insightful, there are echoes of the centuries which preceded him.[6] His own contribution to biblical interpretation and the

---

[3] Ernst-Wilhelm Kohls even suggests that the key to understanding Luther lies not simply in his doctrine of justification but most importantly in his resolute dependence upon the scriptural word. Ernst-Wilhelm Kohls, 'Die Lutherforschung in deutschen Sprachbereich seits 1970', *Luther-Jahrbuch* 44 (1977), 28–56.

[4] For example, John W. Montgomery, 'Lessons from Luther on the Inerrancy of Holy Writ', in John W. Montgomery (ed.), *God's Inerrant Word: An International Symposium on the Trustworthiness of Scripture*, 63-94; Jack B. Rogers and Donald K. McKim, *The Authority and Interpretation of the Bible: An Historical Approach*, 76-88; Lennart Pinomaa, *Der existentielle Charakter der Theologie Luthers: Das Hervorbrechen der Theologie der Anfechtung und ihre Bedeutung für das Lutherverständnis*; Gerhard Ebeling, 'The New Hermeneutics and the Early Luther', *TToday* 21 (1964), 34-46.

[5] Eugene F. Klug, 'Word and Scripture in Luther Studies since World War II', *TJ* 5 NS (1984), 3-46; Scott Hendrix, 'American Luther Research in the Twentieth Century', *LQ* 15/1 (2001), 1-23.

[6] This remains the case notwithstanding David Steinmetz's convincing argument that 'Luther is always more than the sum of the parts of his theological heritage'. David C. Steinmetz, *Luther and Staupitz: An Essay in the Intellectual Origins of the Protestant Reformation*, 141; cf. Walther von Loewenich, *Martin Luther: The Man and His Work*, 21; Heiko A. Oberman, *The Reformation: Roots and Ramifications*, 3.

articulation of a Christian doctrine of Scripture exists within the context of a long history of both, stretching from the biblical period right through to the emergence of Renaissance humanism in Northern Europe. His writing displays an extraordinary familiarity with the biblical text, the patristic inheritance, and the ecclesiastical and theological ferment which dominated so much of the intellectual life of the Middle Ages. These provide him with more than merely basic categories of thought and terminology. Luther himself argued that his whole approach to Scripture was thoroughly orthodox and could be found in the writings of many who had preceded him. Yet what is lacking in many modern studies is an appreciation of the degree to which Luther builds upon the exegetical and theological inheritance he had received. Instead, some have attempted to account for his achievement in terms of his upbringing and psychological profile, though not without generating significant dissent.[7]

A second complicating factor is the figure of Luther himself. Luther the man keeps breaking out of the categories used to describe him. He was both a pastor and a scholar, a controversialist and a man plagued by the question, 'Are you alone wise?'[8] He was determined to let the Word do it all and yet he bordered on workaholism, maintaining a regimen of teaching and writing that is almost incomprehensible even in the age of computers. On certain issues he was prepared to change his mind, as on the issue of allegory and its place in biblical interpretation. On others he was not prepared to alter one syllable, as is evident in his debate with the Swiss over the words of institution at the Last Supper. In addition to all of this, the modern student of Luther is faced with the sheer volume of his literary output. That which kept printers working at a frenetic pace in the first half of the sixteenth century makes a comprehensive statement of his theology, or even one component of it, a challenging task in the twenty-first.[9]

A particular difficulty arises from the fact that Luther left no full-length treatise devoted to the nature and use of Holy Scripture, despite precedents from the pens of Augustine of Hippo and Hugh of St.

---

[7] Erik H. Erikson, *Young Man Luther: A Study in Psychoanalysis and History;* Heinrich Bornkamm, 'Luther und sein Vater: Bemerkungen zu Erik H. Erikson, *Young Man Luther*', *ZTK* 66 (1969), 38-61; Paul Reiter, *Luthers Umwelt und Persönlichkeit;* Ulrich Becke, 'Eine hinterlassene psychiatrische Studie Paul Johann Reiters über Luther', *ZKG* 90 (1979), 85-95.

[8] 'Bist du allein klug?' *Vom mißbrauch der Messen* (1521) *WA* VIII, 483.2 = *LW* 36, 134.

[9] Lewis Spitz has observed that Luther wrote the equivalent of one or two treatises a month from 1516 until his death in 1546. *LW* 34, 281.

Victor, among others.[10] Yet no serious interpreter of Luther doubts that he was interested in the subject. Three pieces of evidence in particular ensure such a conclusion. In the first instance, Luther described himself as one bound by oath to give his life to the exposition of the Bible. Through circumstances he did not control, he had been placed in the position of a Doctor of Holy Scripture and required to address the world from its pages. He included a testimony to that fact in his 1530 commentary on Psalm 82.

> I was forced and driven into this position in the first place, when I had to become Doctor of Holy Scripture against my will. Then, as a Doctor in a general free university, I began, at the command of pope and emperor, to do what such a doctor is sworn to do, expounding the Scriptures for all the world and teaching everybody. Once in this position, I have had to stay in it, and I cannot give it up or leave it yet with good conscience, even though both pope and emperor were to put me under the ban for not doing so. For what I began as a Doctor, made and called at their command, I must truly confess to the end of my life.[11]

The second piece of evidence is Luther's talk of being captured by the teaching, and indeed the text, of Scripture. This is Luther's famous *Knechtsgestalt* ('servant stance') before the word of God. On a number of occasions he professed an inability to change his opinions because

---

[10] Augustine, *De doctrina christiana* (*CCSL* XXXII, 1-167); Hugh of St. Victor, *De scripturis et scriptoribus sacris* (*PL* CLXXV, 9-28); Hugh of St. Victor, *Eruditionis Didascalicae* (*PL* CLXXVI, 741-838).

[11] 'Ich bin aber ynn solch ampt erstlich gezwungen und getrieben, da ich Doctor der heiligen schrifft werden muste on meinen danck. Da fieng ich an als ein Doctor dazu mal von Bepstlichem und Keiserlichem befelh ynn einer gemeinen freien hohen schulen, wie einem solchen Doctor nach seinem geschwornen ampt gebürt, für aller wellt die schrifft aus zulegen und yederman zu leren, habe auch also, nachdem ich ynn solch wesen komen bin, müssen drinnen bleiben, kan auch noch nicht mit gutem gewissenn zuruck odder ablassen, ob mich gleich Bapst und Keiser drüber verbanneten, Denn was ich hab angefangen als ein Doctor aus yhrem befelh gemacht und beruffen, mus ich warlich bis an mein ende bekennen.' *Der 82. Psalm ausgelegt* (1530) *WA* XXXI-I, 212.8-18 = *LW* 13, 66. cf. *Glosse auf das vermeinte kaiserliche Edikt* (1531) *WA* XXX-III, 386.30-387.15 = *LW* 34, 103; *Ein Brief D. M. Luthers von den Schleichern und Winkelpredigern* (1532) *WA* XXX-III, 522.2-8 = *LW* 40, 387-388. Studies of Luther's 'doctor consciousness (*Doktoratsbewußtein*)' include Hermann Steinlein, *Luthers Doktorat: Zum 400 jährigen Jubiläum desselben (18./19. Oktober 1912)*; Brian A. Gerrish, 'Doctor Martin Luther: Subjectivity and Doctrine in the Lutheran Reformation', in P. N. Brooks (ed.), *Seven-Headed Luther: Essays in Commemoration of a Quincentenary 1483-1983*, 2-11.

Scripture made this impossible. 'I have been conquered by the Scriptures adduced by me and my conscience is captive to the word of God', he declared before the world at Worms.[12] Such statements presupposed a powerful commitment to the authority of Scripture and confidence that its meaning could be determined. This is also why Luther was prepared to endure attacks upon his person but was, as he himself said, 'more cutting and passionate when defending Scripture than some can stand'.[13] The third piece of evidence is quite simply the phenomenon of Luther's literary deposit. The sheer bulk of exegetical material, whether in his commentaries, lectures, and sermons or in his more polemical and occasional work, highlights his commitment to the exposition of Scripture as fundamental to the theological task. Luther was first and foremost, and self-consciously, a biblical theologian.[14]

Nevertheless, this absence of a treatise devoted to the doctrine of Scripture or interpretive method has important consequences for any reconstruction of Luther's views on those subjects. What Luther thought about the origin, nature, and function of the biblical text, and the principles underlying its use, must be gleaned from a variety of contexts. Sometimes the pertinent comments are merely incidental to the argument he is pursuing in the document at hand; at other times he launches into a sustained treatment which reveals that his commitment to a particular perspective on Scripture played a crucial role in the development of other facets of his theology. Therefore, if we are to understand Luther properly, care must be taken to give due weight to the context of each statement, to recognise the development in his

---

[12] '[V]ictus sum scripturis a me adductis et capta conscientia in verbis dei' *Verhandlungen mit D. Martin Luther auf dem Reichstage zu Worms* (1521) *WA* VII, 838.6-7 = *LW* 32, 112. cf. *Eyn brieff an die Christen zu Straspurg widder den schwermer geyst* (1524) *WA* XV, 394.19-20 = *LW* 40, 68.

[13] 'Sie fechten mich auch nichts an, ich hab mir nie furgenommen, mich an denen zurechen, die mein person, mein leben, mein werck, mein weßen schmehenn, ich weyß selbs fast wol, das ich nit lobens werd bin: das ich aber scharffer und hitziger byn uber die schrifft zuerhalten, wen etlich leyden mugen, sol mir niemant billich vorweysen, ich wils auch nit abgahn.' *Von dem Papstthum zu Rom wider den hochberühmten Romanisten zu Leipzig* (1520) *WA* VI, 323.11-15 = *LW* 39, 103.

[14] 'Luther ist Schrifttheologe. Die heilige Schrift ist die Quelle, aus der seine Theologie sich speist; sie ist die Norm, der alle Theologie sich zu unterwerfen hat; sie ist die lebendige Autorität, durch die allein Theologie und Kirche lebensfähig sind.' Friedrich Beisser, 'Luthers Schriftverständnis', in Peter Manns (ed.) *Martin Luther, Reformator und Vater im Glauben,* 25. Cf. Paul Althaus, 'Die Bedeutung der Theologie Luthers für die theologische Arbeit', *Luther-Jahrbuch* 28 (1961), 13.

thinking or conversely its consistency over the course of his teaching career, and to let him address his own issues in his own terms.

The resulting picture may not be as tidy as some suggest or even as some modern ecclesiastical or theological positions demand. Yet neither should it be assumed *a priori* that Luther was prepared to live with a fundamentally fragmentary, incoherent or self-contradictory doctrine of Scripture. Luther's basic education involved rigorous tuition in logical analysis. In the light of this it is surely legitimate to operate with the working assumption that Luther believed himself to be consistent and to attempt to understand how that might be so.

In addition to these complications, the intervening centuries make it difficult for modern students of Luther to produce an accurate assessment of his theological thought. This difficulty operates on three levels. Firstly, between Luther and the present day stand such influential movements of thought as Protestant Orthodoxy, Pietism, Romanticism, Existentialism, Liberalism, Fundamentalism, Neo-orthodoxy, Ecumenism and Inter-faith Dialogue. In one way or another, each of these is capable of skewing a modern presentation of Luther's theology, either in part or in whole. Secondly, Luther remains an important contemporary resource and the use made of him by figures as diverse as Barth, Bultmann, and Moltmann can obscure his own concerns and theological conclusions. Thirdly, the renaissance in Luther studies which began with the quatercentenary of Luther's birth in 1883 is itself a contributing factor here, as highly influential studies of the past assume an orthodox character of their own and make a fresh examination of the evidence both imperative and yet controversial.

This volume represents such a fresh examination of the evidence for Luther's approach to Holy Scripture. It is justified by both the present unresolved debate on the issue and the continuing significance of Luther for modern theology and hermeneutics. Further, it will suggest that underlying much of the modern literature on the subject is a series of assumptions and prejudices which is rarely subjected to scrutiny on the basis of Luther's own statements and practice. In a few important cases, inconsistencies and outright error in translation, as well as a neglect of the literary and historical contexts, have exacerbated this problem. Only a determination to re-examine the primary sources in detail and in context, combined with an emphasis on the actual words Luther used, will prevent the faulty conclusions of one study from becoming the insupportable foundations of the next.

More particularly, this study is an exploration of the relation of various elements in Luther's approach to Scripture. It is therefore primarily a theological investigation, though one circumscribed by the historical particulars of his background, life, and writing. It examines the way his convictions about the nature and origin of the biblical text shaped his interpretive practice. It also identifies connections between both of these poles of Luther's approach to Scripture and other important elements of his theological thought. However, the historical dimension of our investigation remains significant, especially since we cannot simply assume that Luther expressed himself identically or even consistently on this subject throughout his life. What is appropriate in one context might be counter-productive in another.

The key questions with which we are concerned surround Luther's confident and insistent movement between statements about Scripture and the use of Scripture. At the outset it is important to realise that the language of 'confidence' or 'boldness' is actually Luther's own. He often spoke of his attitude toward Scripture in this way.[15] He even told his students in 1516 'you will not be bold or very confident without Holy Scripture'.[16] This confidence was clearly not an incidental feature of Luther's approach since it allowed him both to challenge the structures of church and empire and to insist upon a particular interpretation of individual passages of Scripture. Yet how is this boldness to be explained? How are these two features of it related: that is, how are Luther's statements about the authority of Scripture related to his interpretive method? What characteristics did Luther see in Scripture which justified such a connection?

Since this investigation aims at an understanding of Luther's own terms and categories, it begins with a brief survey of Luther's background. The first chapter outlines the *prima facie* teaching of Scripture itself, a number of the key developments affecting the patristic articulation of the nature and function of Scripture, and the various influences on Luther's immediate context, i.e. medieval scholasticism and the emergence of Northern humanism. These provide us with a glimpse of the broad contours of the pre-understanding with which Luther approached his own exegetical and theological work.

After this survey Luther's own contribution is brought into focus. In successive chapters his statements on Scripture are classified according to their bearing on its inspiration, unity, clarity, and sufficiency. The use of these categories to aid our analysis is not as arbitrary as it may

---

[15] E.g. 'confidentia' in *Luther an Jodokus Truttfetter in Erfurt* (9 May 1518) *WABr* I, 171.72; 'fiducia' in *De votis monasticis Martini Lutheri iudicium* (1521) *WA* VIII, 597.3 = *LW* 44, 282; 'mag ichs künlich wagen' in *Ein unterrichtung wie sich die Christen ynn Mose sollen schicken* (1525) *WA* XVI, 385.28 = *LW* 35, 170; 'certissime ac securissime ausit dicere' in *In epistolam S. Pauli ad Galatas Commentarius* (1535) *WA* XL-I, 133.29-30 = *LW* 26, 67.

[16] '[N]on sis audax aut nimium confidens sine sacra scriptura' *Praelectio in librum Iudicum* (1516-17) *WA* IV, 534.36-37.

at first seem. In the first place, given the often scattered nature of Luther's comments, some classification is clearly necessary. Any analysis will involve the identification of similar statements and an attempt to relate them to each other as well as to other groups of statements.[17] Further, the four categories that have been employed here reflect the basic issues addressed in a Christian doctrine of Scripture: the origin of these texts, their relation to one another, their accessibility and intelligibility, and their relation to other putative sources of theological authority. These are not just the concerns of conservative historians and theologians at the beginning of the third millennium. As the first chapter will demonstrate, these concerns emerge in much of the patristic and medieval discussion, and they are addressed in the pages of Scripture itself. They also reflect Luther's own language, for he speaks of *inspiratio* (*Eyngebung*),[18] *tota scriptura*,[19] *claritas scripturae*,[20] and *sola scriptura*.[21] There are indeed other relevant issues, such as the truthfulness of Scripture and its efficacy, and these are touched upon as they arise. However, it will become evident that the four basic categories which provide the basic structure for our investigation do in fact make possible a productive exploration of those ideas which explain Luther's movement from his affirmations of Scripture's authority to his distinctive interpretive method.

The approach adopted here differs from the norm in its extensive use of Luther's own words.[22] An accurate analysis of Luther's thought cannot avoid this and must not become preoccupied with the later

---

[17] The danger that such synthesis will distort the material is always real. However, while this danger cannot be entirely avoided, the present study seeks to minimise it by careful and self-aware methodological reflection (see below).

[18] *Predigten über das 2 Buch Mose* (1524-27) *WA* XVI, 82.25.

[19] *Disputatio I. Eccii et M. Lutheri Lipsiae habita* (1519) *WA* II, 302.1.

[20] *De servo arbitrio* (1525) *WA* XVIII, 609.4 = *LW* 33, 28.

[21] *Vorwort zu den Annotationes Philippi Melanchthonis in epistolas Pauli ad Romanos et Corinthios* (1522) *WA* X-II, 310.12-13.

[22] Indeed, the title of this volume alludes to the disputed words attributed to Luther at Worms: 'Here I stand, I cannot do otherwise. So help me God. Amen (*Ich kan nicht anderst, hie stehe ich. Got helff mir, Amen.*)'. *Verhandlungen mit D. Martin Luther auf dem Reichstage zu Worms* (1521) *WA* VII, 838.9 = *LW* 32, 113. Indeed, Luther's earlier preface to his published lectures on Galatians, suggests that Christians should 'flee for refuge to the most solid rock of Divine Scripture [*ad divinae scripturae solidissimam petram confugere*]'. *In epistolam Pauli ad Galatas commentarius* (1519) *WA* II, 447.11-12 = *LW* 27, 156.

scholarly discussion.[23] In many cases it is only as the structure of his argument at a certain point is appreciated that the true import of a well-known quotation becomes clear. Too often a neglect of the context has led to faulty conclusions. In addition, the consideration of quotations in context aids our study of the connections of Luther's thought. They reveal the use made of the doctrine of Scripture by Luther in polemical and non-polemical settings.

A brief justification for yet another monograph on Luther and Holy Scripture seems in order before we proceed. In the first instance this study provides a theological examination of Luther's views which seeks to be sensitive to the historical particulars of each affirmation he made. It offers a critique of some influential interpretations of Luther's thought on Scripture and uncovers the poor evidential base of some frequently repeated conclusions. In addition, it explores the range of Luther's writing, both polemical and non-polemical works, his letters and sermons as well as his lectures and tracts, and does so across Luther's entire career. This allows one to distinguish more accurately between those elements of Luther's approach to Scripture which are incidental and those which are more fundamental, and to assess the degree of continuity and/or development in his thinking. Further, at key points Luther's attitude towards Scripture is related to the larger themes of his theology as a whole, especially where Luther makes this connection explicit. Finally, the pages which follow seek to do justice to Luther's own categories and terminology and to avoid the projection of modern concerns upon the writing of a man who lived in a very different world. As significant as any other factor in Luther studies is an appreciation of him as a sixteenth century man.[24]

---

[23] This conviction should be evident in the pages which follow. Nevertheless, each subsequent chapter in this volume will begin with a brief survey of scholarly conclusions about the concept under view, only embarking upon sustained interaction with the secondary literature in order to highlight significant insights into or potential misreadings of Luther's theology. The critical factor in each phase of the discussion remains a detailed examination of Luther's own writing.

[24] It is, of course, impossible to remain completely unaffected by the modern debates about Scripture which appeal to Luther's views in one way or another. These debates have proven so critical for the task of theology as well as its content that no one writing serious theology in the first decade of the twenty-first century can write as if they had not occurred. However, a sustained attempt to use Luther's own language and to follow the course of Luther's own arguments — across the breadth of his writings and the length of his teaching career — should minimise the distortion such modern debates may create.

A final methodological footnote: in this volume we follow the emerging convention of citing Luther in translation in the text and in the original language in the footnotes (I have not followed this practice in the case of the patristic and medieval authors in chapter one). The most accessible English translation is that found in the American edition edited by Jaroslav Pelikan and Helmut Lehmann (cited as *LW*). Where this is available, I have chosen to use it with modification only at those points where comparison with the original suggests this is necessary.[25] The original text used is that of the *Weimarer Ausgabe* (*WA*), the standard critical edition of Luther's works. Luther's at times idiosyncratic spelling is retained.[26]

---

[25] However, it will be noted that quite a number of the comments which are critical for our purposes are found in writings which are not translated, either in the American edition or elsewhere.

[26] The *Weimar Ausgabe* is not beyond criticism, as Kenneth Hagen has shown. Kenneth Hagen, *Luther's Approach to Scripture as seen in his "Commentaries" on Galatians 1519–1538,* 1–12. Nevertheless, it remains a highly significant and reliable critical edition.

Chapter 1

Luther's Inheritance

On 22 October 1512, Martin Luther was officially received into the theological faculty of the University of Wittenberg. Three days later he began his duties as *lectura in Biblia* and the rest of his life would be spent in biblical exposition and theological reflection. He had been equipped for this task by more than five years of graduate theological study which had brought him into contact with almost fifteen hundred years of Christian thought based on the Bible.[1] Indeed from one point of view what we find in Luther's writing is a critical and constructive engagement with the exegetical, theological, and hermeneutical tradition which he had received through his monastic and university studies. Certainly he did not see himself as introducing novelty to theological discussion, as witnessed by his constant appeal to the Scriptures and his less frequent, though no less significant appeal to the teaching of the Fathers and the doctors of the Church. Therefore if his own work is to be understood properly, it must be placed firmly against this background.[2]

---

[1] The most direct influences on Luther's theological formation have been explored by Martin Brecht, *Martin Luther: His Road to Reformation 1483-1521*, 23-174; Walther von Loewenich, *Martin Luther: The Man and His Work,* 35-105; Heiko A. Oberman, *Luther: Man between God and the Devil,* 50-206.

[2] This is not to say that Luther made extensive use of the biblical passages referred to below or that he had a precise knowledge of the specific contributions of each person mentioned (though there is ample evidence of a first-hand knowledge of the writings of Origen, Augustine, Gregory the Great, Jerome, Aquinas, Hugh of St. Victor, and others). Nevertheless, the text of Scripture and the writings of those mentioned below created the culture of biblical interpretation into which Luther was inducted in 1512. Even when he

Holy Scripture: The Central and Critical Testimony

The most fundamental component of Luther's inheritance was the teaching of the Scriptures themselves. His theological training took place in a monastic context in which the Bible played an unusually prominent role.[3] He would later recall that even before his formal theological studies began, he had carefully worked through the little red Bible he had received as a novice.[4] Further, Staupitz had arranged for him to be assigned the task of Bible memorisation, a task at which he apparently excelled.[5] When he finally left the monastery it was to take up the life of a biblical scholar, a life dominated by detailed engagement with the biblical text, through preaching, lecturing, writing, and translation. On top of all this, Luther himself testified that it was his custom for many years to read through the entire Bible twice a year.[6] 'The Holy Scriptures are a vast and mighty forest', he explained, 'but there is not a single tree in it that I have not shaken with my own hand (*sed nulla arbor est, quam manu non pulsavi*)'.[7] It is inconceivable, given this background, together with his own strong statements about Holy Scripture as the sole source of the articles of faith, that the teaching of the Bible itself should have had no significant influence on his approach to Scripture.

It is important to remember the form which Luther's training in the Scriptures would have taken. The world into which Luther was born, while not entirely devoid of 'critical thinking' in the modern sense of the word, rarely applied such methods to the teaching of Scripture. Pre-critical exegesis took place in the context of pre-critical presuppositions.[8] Wrestling with the meaning of the text was commonplace, and an awareness of its literary history was indeed emerging,[9] but the *prima facie* evidence of the biblical texts generally

---

made mistakes about the source of particular ideas he remained acquainted with those ideas themselves.

[3] Brecht, *Road to Reformation*, 86.

[4] *Tischreden* #116 (1531) *WATr* I, 44.16-45.3 = *LW* 54, 13-14; Brecht, *Road to Reformation*, 85.

[5] J. Otto Scheel (ed.), *Dokumente zu Luthers Entwicklung (bis 1519)*, 203-205; Oberman, *Luther*, 136.

[6] *Tischreden* #1877 (1532) *WATr* II, 244.20-23 = *LW* 54, 165.

[7] *Tischreden* #674 (1531) *WATr* I, 320.9-10 = *LW* 54, 121.

[8] For a modern appreciation of pre-critical exegesis, see David C. Steinmetz, 'The Superiority of Pre-Critical Exegesis', *TToday* 37 (1980), 27-38; Richard A. Muller and John L. Thompson, 'The Significance of Precritical Exegesis: Retrospect and Prospect', in Richard A. Muller and John L. Thompson (eds.), *Biblical Interpretation in the Era of the Reformation*, 335-345.

[9] E.g. Luther's comments on the composition of Jeremiah (*WADB* XI-I, 193.10-17 = *LW* 35, 280-281) and Hosea (*WADB* XI-II, 183.14-16 = *LW* 35, 317).

played a much more important role than it does in many modern approaches to the subject. Therefore, if we are to sketch the biblical background to Luther's thinking, rather than to our own, we must give the *prima facie* evidence full weight.[10]

The framework for Scripture's teaching about itself is the dynamic of God's verbal address of his people and their response of faith. This is demonstrated in the early chapters of Genesis, where the momentum of the narrative is associated with the words 'And God said (ויאמר אלהים)'. Abraham provides the pattern for a right response to the words that God speaks: ' and he believed (והאמן) the LORD; and he reckoned it to him as righteousness'.[11] This dynamic was not materially altered by the inscripturation of God's words at God's command. Moses 'wrote (יכתב) all the words of the LORD (כל־דברי יהוה)' and when these were read to the people they responded with 'All that the LORD has spoken (דבר) we will do, and we will be obedient.'[12]

The writing and reading of God's words remains a significant feature throughout the Old Testament. At God's command, Moses writes the words which form the basis of the covenant between the LORD and Israel.[13] Moses also records God's instruction that the future kings of Israel should write for themselves a copy of the law of God as one of the first acts of each reign and read it regularly.[14] The prophets too are conscious that they are writing the words of the LORD. Their extensive use of the expression 'Thus says the LORD (כה אמר יהוה)' is reinforced by specific references to God's command to write.[15] The presupposition is always that God is capable of effectively communicating with his people through the medium of these human words. He has provided a lamp (נר) and a light (אור) which is able to impart understanding to the simple (פתי).[16] The words which God has spoken are not beyond the reach of his people, they are both accessible and intelligible.[17] Nor are they in need of supplement, either from the wisdom of the surrounding nations,[18] or from the imagination of the prophets themselves.[19]

---

[10] David H. Fischer, *Historian's Fallacies: Toward a Logic of Historical Thought*, 132-135.
[11] Gn. 15:6; Is. 66:2b; Mk. 1:15; Jn. 16:20; Rom. 10:17.
[12] Ex. 24:4,7.
[13] Ex. 34:27.
[14] Dt. 17:18.
[15] Is. 8:1; 30:8; Je. 30:1–2; 36:1–32.
[16] Ps. 119:105, 130.
[17] Dt. 30:11, 14.
[18] Dt. 13:1 [12:32].
[19] Je. 23:22.

The New Testament emerges within this prophetic framework. Both the Gospels and the epistles emphasise the fulfilment of that which was 'promised beforehand through his prophets in the holy Scriptures (ἐν γραφαῖς ἁγίαις)'.[20] Jesus himself challenged the Jewish religious leaders about their refusal to believe the testimony of Moses and the prophets who spoke of him.[21] After his resurrection, he walked with two of his disciples towards Emmaus, and 'beginning with Moses and all the prophets, he interpreted (διερμήνευσεν) to them in all the scriptures (ἐν πάσαις ταῖς γραφαῖς) the things concerning himself (τὰ περὶ ἑαυτοῦ)'.[22] Paul insists that 'Christ is the end (τέλος) of the law' and 'all the promises of God find their "Yes" in him (ὅσαι γὰρ ἐπαγγελίαι θεοῦ, ἐν αὐτῷ τό Ναί)'.[23] The epistle to the Hebrews develops a typological relationship between the Old Testament priesthood, sacrifices, and response of faith on the one hand, and Jesus, his death, and faith in him on the other.

The New Testament is never presented as the necessary supplement to a deficient Scripture, any more than the later books of the Old Testament suggest a lack in the earlier ones. Prior to the coming of Jesus, no other word was necessary. Nevertheless, with the life, death, resurrection, and ascension of Jesus, we enter a further, final stage in God's self-revelation which is both proclaimed and explained in the New Testament.[24] The Old Testament certainly remains critical for a proper understanding of what God has done in the last days, yet the New Testament exposition of the gospel and its consequences exercises a reciprocal interpretive function: what has been revealed in the past takes on a new significance in the light of Jesus Christ.

There can be little doubt that for the writers of the New Testament the expression 'the Scriptures (ἡ γραφή)' principally refers to the Old Testament. However, the evidence also suggests a growing awareness of the authority of the emerging New Testament itself. Three factors contribute to this development. The first is the conviction we have already identified, namely that God's self-revelation has continued, and indeed reached its fulfilment, in Christ. In an important sense Jesus himself is the Word of God — the full and personal expression of the mind and purposes of God.[25] The second factor is Jesus' promise to send the Spirit after his death and resurrection, to remind his disciples

---

[20] Rom. 1:2.
[21] Jn. 5.39–47; cf. Jesus' question to the Pharisees, 'Have you not read (οὐκ ἀνέγνωτε) in the Scriptures...?'
[22] Lk. 24:25–27; cf. 24:44.
[23] Rom 10:4; 2 Cor. 1:20.
[24] Jn. 1:14–18; Gal. 3:23 – 4.7; Heb. 1:1–4.
[25] Jn. 1:1–18; Heb. 1:1–3; Rev. 19:3.

of the things he has taught them. The proclamation, and by extension the writing, of the apostles is intimately associated with the Spirit of Christ.[26] Thirdly, Jesus' commission of the disciples, his prayer for them and those who would believe through their word, and in particular the Damascus Road conversion and commission of the apostle Paul, are foundation stones for an authoritative addition to the Hebrew Scriptures.[27] The apostolic gospel and its explanation, in its oral and written forms, is recognised as the powerful, living Word of the powerful, living God.[28] This is why Paul is able to insist that the Corinthians acknowledge that what he writes to them is 'a command of the Lord ($κυρίου$ $ἐντολή$)'.[29] For this reason he also expects his letters to be read in the churches.[30]

The two passages which most directly address the origin and nature of Scripture are properly understood in this larger context. In 2 Pet. 1:20–21, concluding an argument in defence of his teaching about 'the power and coming of our Lord Jesus Christ', Peter speaks of the unique dual authorship of Scripture:

> First of all you must understand this, that no prophecy of Scripture ($προφητεία$ $γραφῆς$) is a matter of one's own interpretation ($ἰδίας$ $ἐπιλύσεως$), because no prophecy ever came by the impulse of man, but men moved by the Holy Spirit ($ὑπὸ$ $πνεύματος$ $ἁγίου$ $φερόμενοι$) spoke from God ($ἐλάλησαν$ $ἀπὸ$ $θεοῦ$).

Three observations are important in this connection. Firstly, Peter insists that Scripture is not adequately understood without recourse to its ultimate origin in God himself. It is this divine origin which differentiates Scripture from the 'cleverly devised myths' of verse sixteen and the 'destructive heresies' which he mentions in the beginning of the next chapter. Whatever else might be said about Scripture, it is a word from God ($ἀπὸ$ $θεοῦ$). Secondly, Peter affirms there is a definite and objective meaning to Scripture. Precisely because these words are God's words, their meaning has an anchor outside of the experience of the interpreter. In this particular context, that anchor is located in the heavenly attestation of Christ as the beloved Son of God in the midst of the transfiguration.[31] Manipulation of the prophetic words, no matter what the motive, must fail because God has something to say. Thirdly, Peter speaks here of a work of the

---

[26] Jn. 14:25–26; 16.:2–15; Acts 4:8, 31; 7:55–56; 13:9; 1Cor. 2:6–13.
[27] Jn. 17:8, 18; Acts 1:8; 2 Cor. 5:18–21; Jn. 17:20–21; Acts 9:1–22; Gal. 1:11–24.
[28] 1 Thes. 2:13; 4:2; 2 Thes. 2:15; Heb. 4:12; 1 Pet. 1:23; 2 Pet. 3:2, 15–16.
[29] 1 Cor. 14:37.
[30] Col. 4:16; 1 Thes. 5:27.
[31] 2 Pet. 1:16–19; Mt. 17:5.

Holy Spirit which enables the human writer to speak this definite word of God. While this is the closest the New Testament gets to a description of what might be called 'the process of inspiration', in reality it does little more than indicate the principal players in the process (the Holy Spirit and the human author) and the result of the process (they spoke from God). By using the theologically neutral word φέρειν, Peter leaves the process itself somewhat vague. However, what is not vague is that this is something that happens to the human author.

The perspective is quite different in the other key passage, 2 Tim. 3:16–17. Here the emphasis is not on the writer, or even on the process in which the writer is involved, but on the product of that process, the Scriptures themselves:

> All scripture (πᾶσα γραφή) is inspired by God (θεόπνευστος) and profitable (ὠφέλιμος) for teaching, for reproof, for correction, and for training in righteousness, that the man of God may be complete, equipped for every good work.[32]

Several observations are pertinent. Firstly, the subject under discussion is 'all Scripture'. Paul does not differentiate here between primary and secondary material within Scripture. His use of the adjective 'all' ensures the widest possible application of this description. Thus, in light of the comments made above, there is every reason to include the emerging New Testament in this description, while granting that first and foremost the apostle would have intended to refer to the Old Testament.[33] Next, while θεόπνευστος is a *hapax legomenon*, its meaning is not difficult to determine. The derivation of the word, from θεός and πνέω, yields the meaning 'breathed by God'. This is supported by the context, in which the origin of the Scriptures is integral to the point being made. Paul contrasts the Scriptures, which have originated with God, with the deceitful teaching of 'evil men and impostors'.[34] So, in 2 Tim. 3, Paul is determined to present the most intimate connection between God and every biblical text. These words have come from God, indeed, they have been carried by the breath of God. Further, precisely because this is so these words are profitable and purposeful. The goal of this divine provision is the thorough equipment of the believer for life and ministry in the world. Timothy

---

[32] It is from the Vulgate translation of θεόπνευστος (*divinitus inspirata*) that the term 'inspiration' became the standard category for talking about God's relationship to the text of Scripture.

[33] The use of ἱερὰ γράμματα in verse 15 and the transition to πᾶσα γραφή in verse 16 also points in this direction.

[34] 2 Tim. 3:13.

will not need the religious resources promised by those Paul calls 'deceivers and deceived'; this written deposit, the Old Testament and the apostolic writings, is all that he needs.[35] The utility and sufficiency of Scripture are thus brought into close relationship with its divine origin.

This complex of ideas formed the basis of reflection upon the origin, nature, and use of Scripture from the apostolic era until well after the time of Luther. Even when it was not articulated in detail it constituted an important part of the pre-understanding with which biblical scholars approached their task. However, over the centuries a variety of challenges and external influences would also play an important role.

The Nature and Use of Scripture in the Patristic Period

The profundity of Luther's direct engagement with Holy Scripture ought not to obscure the fact that he had an intimate and extensive knowledge of the works of the Church Fathers. Not only Augustine, but Origen, Jerome, and Gregory the Great feature prominently in his writings, and there are scores of references to others. There can be no doubt that the teaching of the Church Fathers also represents a significant element of Luther's theological inheritance.[36] Certainly this was the case when it came to reflection upon the origin, nature, and use of Scripture. In fact the patristic period witnessed extended discussion of these issues, influenced by a number of important developments.

The Christian Use of the Jewish Scriptures

In the years following the destruction of Jerusalem in AD 70, the heightened antipathy between Jews and Christians fuelled a debate about the meaning and use of the Jewish Scriptures. The New Testament appeal to these in its exposition of the Christian gospel had established the pattern for successive generations of believers. With a few heretical exceptions, Christians continued to accept the 'Old Testament' as the Word of God. However, Jewish leaders refused to accept Christian expositions of the sacred texts and were incensed by the way these were used to support the claim that Jesus of Nazareth was the Messiah.

This debate gave particular prominence to the question of a Christological reading of the Old Testament. It became increasingly important for Christians to demonstrate that these texts were

---

[35] On the alternative to the Scriptures, see 2 Tim. 3:3–5, 13.

[36] Jaroslav Pelikan, *Obedient Rebels: Catholic Substance and Protestant Principle in Luther's Reformation*, 27-104.

fundamentally about Jesus. Conversely, they charged Jewish exegetes with manipulating or ignoring the intended meaning of the divinely inspired writers. Such a charge presupposed the accessibility of this intended meaning: not only does the Old Testament witness to Christ, it *clearly* witnesses to Christ. If this was the case, then the Jews did not find Christ in their Scriptures because they refused to believe what was written there. Justin Martyr's discussion of the testimonies to Christ in his *Dialogus cum Tryphone Judaeo* provides one of the earliest surviving accounts of this kind of reasoning:

> Are you acquainted with them, Trypho? They are contained in your Scriptures, or rather not yours, but ours. For we believe them; but you, though you read them, do not understand (οὐ νοεῖτε) the sense in them (τὸν ἐν αὐτοῖς νοῦν).[37]

Justin here laid claim to the Jewish Scriptures on behalf of the Christian Church. He insisted that these texts cannot be understood without a sensitivity to their inherent Christological witness. In the light of this, the result of Jewish exegesis must be a skewed interpretation ('not understanding the sense in them') because Jewish presuppositions fight against the texts themselves: texts about Jesus are not allowed to speak of Jesus. Justin located the problem of misunderstanding in the reader rather than in the text. Others would take up this same argument. The patristic period was littered with treatises berating the Jews for an incompetent handling of their own quite intelligible Scriptures.[38]

The Emerging Canon of the New Testament

The emergence of the New Testament as a collection of sacred texts coordinate with the Hebrew Scriptures, raised similar issues.[39] There is considerable evidence that individual apostolic texts were recognised in this way from a very early date.[40] There is also early evidence that the various apostolic writings were gradually being gathered into a

---

[37] Justin Martyr, *Dialogus cum Tryphone Judaeo*, 29 (*PG*, VI, 537).
[38] Jaroslav Pelikan, *The Emergence of the Catholic Tradition (100-600)*, 15. For a survey see A. Lukyn Williams, *Adversus Judaeos: A Bird's Eye View of Christian Apologiae until the Renaissance*, 3-150.
[39] On the details connected with the canonicity of the New Testament documents, see David G. Dunbar, 'The Biblical Canon', in D. A. Carson and John D. Woodbridge (eds.), *Hermeneutics, Authority, and Canon*, 315-342; Bruce M. Metzger, *The Canon of the New Testament*.
[40] *Sancti Barnabae Apostoli Epistola Catholica*, 4.14 (*PG*, II, 734); Polycarp, *Epistola ad Philippenses*, 12.1 (*PG*, V, 1013-1014); Justin Martyr, *Apologia*, I.67.3 (*PG*, VI, 430).

collection and that thereby an overarching unity was being claimed for them. Irenaeus quotes from the New Testament almost as frequently as he does from the Old Testament and seems to have a concept of 'Scripture' which brings together the Old Testament and the apostolic writings.[41] However, it is Clement of Alexandria who was the first to use the word 'testament ($\delta\iota\alpha\theta\eta\kappa\eta$)' of the New Testament writings.[42]

Whether individually, as parts of small collections, or together as the 'New Testament', these writings were quickly recognised as the work of the Holy Spirit. Irenaeus argued that the use of the word $X\rho\iota\sigma\tau\acute{o}s$ rather than $I\eta\sigma o\hat{v}s$ in Matthew 1.18 was the result of the Holy Spirit's concern to prevent future deception.[43] John Chrysostom was convinced that God's intimate involvement with Scripture gave significance to even its most trivial details.[44] Augustine considered both Old Testament and New Testament to be gifts of the Holy Spirit by way of the sacred writers.[45]

Nevertheless, consensus on the precise limits of the canon did not come easily. By the time of Hippolytus many were convinced that the canon was closed, and argued such in response to the claims by some of new or private revelation from God. Yet the question remained as to just what was the content of that which had been closed. The Muratorian Fragment appears to be an annotated list of the books of the New Testament, which describes them as 'sacred in the esteem of the Catholic Church (*delictione in honore tamen eclesiae catholice*)', and distinguishes them from those writings which 'cannot be received into the Catholic Church (*in catholicam eclesiam recepi non potest*)'. However, the list omits Hebrews, James, 1 and 2 Peter, and 3 John, and it appears to endorse both the Book of Wisdom and the Apocalypse of Peter.[46] Eusebius of Caesarea records a clear distinction between $\tau\grave{a}$ $\acute{o}\mu o\lambda o\gamma o\acute{v}\mu\epsilon\nu a$, those books which were universally accepted, and $\tau\grave{a}$ $\acute{a}\nu\tau\iota\lambda\epsilon\gamma\acute{o}\mu\epsilon\nu a$, those books which were disputed,

---

[41] André Benoit, *Saint Irénée: Introduction à l'Étude de sa Théologie*, 105-106; Denis Farkasfalvy, 'Theology of Scripture in Irenaeus', *Revue bénédictine*, 78 (1968), 319-333.

[42] Hans Freiherr von Campenhausen, *Die Entstehung der Christlichen Bibel*, 339. Eusebius also quotes an anti-Marcionite in this connection. Eusebius, *Historiae Ecclesiasticae*, V.16 (*PG*, XX, 465).

[43] Irenaeus, *Contra Haereses*, III.16.2 (*PG*, VII, 921).

[44] John Chrysostom, *Homilia in illud, vidi Dominum*, II.2 (*PG*, LVI, 109-110).

[45] Augustine, *Enarrationes in psalmos*, CIV.27 (*CCSL*, XL, 1547); cf. *De Civitate Dei contra Paganos*, X.1.2 (*CCSL*, XLVII, 272); Augustine, *De consensu Evangelistarum*, I.35 (54) (*CSEL*, XLIII, 60). A. D. R. Polman, *The Word of God According to St. Augustine*, 41-43.

[46] MS 10ᵃ, line 19; MS 11ᵃ, lines 4-5 in S. P. Tregelles, *Canon Muratorianus*, 19, 20.

presumably because the earliest Fathers did not refer to them. It is a distinction he traces back to Origen.[47] Outside of this was of course another category, those books which were universally rejected. It is not until Athanasius' Festal Letter of AD 367 that we have anything like an official pronouncement of the current twenty-seven New Testament books as alone canonical.[48] It is his list that was confirmed by the Council of Carthage in AD 397.

The Threat of Heretical Interpretations of the Scriptures

The early Christian approach to Scripture was also challenged and refined by the rise of heresy from within, and in particular that brand of heresy which appealed to the same Scriptures in support of its ideas. This is a phenomenon anticipated by the New Testament itself; indeed, theological dispute of one kind or another actually played a critical role in the emergence of a number of the New Testament documents. Nevertheless, it was in the ensuing centuries that Holy Scripture became a battlefield, with conflicting interpretations of particular biblical passages raising the possibility that Scripture was obscure. In such a context, the Patristic explanation for the reality of heterodox and heretical teaching followed the apostolic pattern, as when Irenaeus accused the Valentinians of wilfully distorting the Scriptures:

> They try to adapt to their own sayings in a manner worthy of faith, either the Lord's parables, or the prophets' sayings, or the apostles' words, so that their fabrication ($\pi\lambda\acute{a}\sigma\mu a$) might not appear to be without witness. They bypass ($\acute{v}\pi\epsilon\rho\beta a\acute{\iota}\nu o\nu\tau\epsilon\varsigma$) the order ($\tau\acute{a}\xi\iota\nu$) and the sequence ($\epsilon\acute{\iota}\rho\mu\acute{o}\nu$) of the Scriptures and, as much as in them lies, they disjoint the members of the Truth. They alter ($\mu\epsilon\tau a\phi\acute{\epsilon}\rho o\nu\sigma\iota$) passages and rearrange ($\mu\epsilon\tau a\pi\lambda\acute{a}\tau\tau o\nu\sigma\iota$) them; and, making one thing out of another, they deceive many by the badly composed phantasm of the Lord's words that they adapt.[49]

For Irenaeus, perversity was a sufficient explanation for divergent biblical interpretations. Proper interpretation, in contrast, would be sensitive to the form of the text, observing its order and sequence, as well as its central witness to Christ.

Tertullian attacked the heresies of Marcion along the same lines. For him, heresy was undoubtedly a result of the abuse of Scripture rather than a defect in it. He expanded Irenaeus' explanation of heretical

---

[47] Eusebius, *Historiae Ecclesiasticae*, VI.25.3 (*PG*, XX, 582).
[48] Athanasius, *Epistulae Festales*, 39 (*PG*, XXVI, 1438).
[49] Irenaeus, *Contra Haereses*, I.8.1 (*PG*, VII, 521).

interpretive practice to take into account both the complication and the simplistic reduction of Scripture:

> In this manner heretics always either wrest (*rapiunt*) plain and simple words (*nudas et simplices voces*) to any sense they choose by their conjectures, or else they explain (*dissoluunt*) conditional and reasonable [words] (*condicionales et rationales*) in a simple manner (*simplicitatis condicione*).[50]

Tertullian identified the same abuse of Scripture amongst those who diluted the moral commands of Scripture. In his Montanist work *De pudicitia*, he attacked those who appeal to the text of Scripture to support an unconditional reception of others who have lapsed into unchastity:

> But this is the custom of perverse and ignorant heretics, indeed of the carnal generally, to be armed with the opportune support of some ambiguous text (*alicuius capituli ancipitis*) against an army of decisions (*exercitum sententiarum*) about the whole document.[51]

The text in question is 1 Corinthians 7, and in particular Paul's concession to those 'burning with passion' in verse nine. The use made of this text by those calling for leniency was described by Tertullian just a few lines earlier as 'a false testimony from the apostle (*falsum testimonium de apostolo*)'. Yet how could Tertullian be sure this was so false if he had no access to 'a genuine testimony from the apostle (*sincerum testimonium de apostolo*)'? Tertullian developed his own argument, confident that the meaning of this text is accessible to all:

> [Paul] does 'permit', to be sure, not adulteries, but marriages. He does 'refrain', to be sure, not from marriages, but from debaucheries. He tries to overlook not even natural things; would he flatter every sin? He takes pains to restrain the sacred sexual union, lest the cursed sexual union be excused.[52]

The struggle against heretical abuse of the Scriptures, and in particular the insistence that such abuse arose from wilful distortion rather than honest confusion, presupposed access to the intended meaning of the texts in question. In this way the question of Scripture's clarity became an important one early in the life of the Church. The same struggle would in time make necessary a more extensive treatment of orthodox interpretive method.

---

[50] Tertullian, *Adversus Marcionem*, IV.19.6 (*CCSL*, I, 592).
[51] Tertullian, *De pudicitia*, XVI.24 (*CCSL*, II, 1314-15).
[52] Tertullian, *De pudicitia*, XVI.24 (*CCSL*, II, 1314).

Interaction with the Graeco-Roman Thought-World

These developments took place within a church which from the very beginning was committed to engagement with the world around it. Not only did effective communication of the Christian message necessitate some attempt to understand the intellectual environment into which it was spoken, but successive generations of Christian leaders actually emerged from within that environment and were almost inevitably influenced by it. This is most telling in the way affirmations of the *fact* of biblical inspiration began to involve attempts to explain the *process* of biblical inspiration.[53] As these multiplied, terms, concepts, and examples from outside of the Scriptures proved almost irresistible.

Some writers began looking to classical mythology for analogies to biblical inspiration. Theophilus of Antioch compared the Hebrew prophets and the Greek Sybils.[54] In doing so he laid emphasis upon the passivity of the human medium. This in turn opened the way for an ecstatic or 'mantic' view of inspiration which appeared in a most extreme form among the Montanists of the late second century.[55]

A similar result was obtained by those who sought analogies to biblical inspiration in the composition and performance of music. Athenagoras described the prophets as men who were guided by the Spirit and who spoke both of God and the things of God. This much was entirely orthodox. However, his explanation of just how this happened went further:

> But, since the voices of the prophets confirm our arguments — for I think that you also, with your great zeal for knowledge and your great attainments in learning, cannot be ignorant of the writings of either Moses or of Isaiah and Jeremiah, and the other prophets, who, lifted in ecstasy above the natural operations of their minds by the impulses of the Divine Spirit (οἳ κατ ἔκστασιν τῶν ἐν αὐτοῖς λογισμῶν, κινήσαντος αὐτοὺς τοῦ θείου Πνεύματος), uttered the things with which they were inspired (ἃ ἐνηργοῦντο ἐξεφώνησαν), the Spirit making use of them as a flute-player breathes into a flute (συγχρησαμένου τοῦ Πνεύματος, ὡσεὶ καὶ αὐλητὴς αὐλὸν ἐμπνεῦσαι).[56]

---

[53] Bruce Vawter, *Biblical Inspiration*, 8; John N. D. Kelly, *Early Christian Doctrines*, 60-64.

[54] Theophilus of Antioch, *Ad Autolycum*, 2.9 (*PG*, VI, 1064).

[55] Epiphanius, *Adversus Haereses*, II.1.48.1 (*PG*, XLI, 856).

[56] Athenagoras, *Legatio pro Christianis*, 7, 9 (*PG*, VI, 904, 905-908). Hippolytus would later speak of the prophets as instruments of music which were moved by the Word operating 'like a plectrum (ὡς πλῆκτρον)'. Hippolytus, *De Christo et Antichristo*, 2 (*PG*, X, 728-729).

This language too would be discredited in the light of its use by the Montanists. Nevertheless it survived into the early third century when Clement of Alexandria, drawing on the Old Testament picture of David and Saul, spoke of the Holy Spirit reducing human body and soul to harmony, so as to use his chosen 'instrument of many tones (τό πολυφώνον ὄργανον)' to express his own chosen melody.[57]

A third approach spoke of the process of inspiration in terms of the everyday world of the scribe whose job it was faithfully to record the words dictated to him by another. Indeed, many who were concerned to protect the inspiration of the actual words of Scripture seem to have found it difficult to conceive of the process without some element of dictation. Gregory the Great was particularly fond of this language, not only describing each biblical writer as merely a 'pen (*calamus*)' of the Spirit, but also equating divine authorship with dictation: 'Therefore the one who dictated what was written is the one who really wrote these things (*Ipse igitur haec scripsit, qui scribenda dictauit*)'.[58]

Two of these approaches are to be found in the writing of Augustine. He could draw lines of connection between biblical inspiration and pagan mythology. In his *De Ciuitate Dei* he claimed that the Erythraean Sibyl wrote some passages which openly refer to Christ (*quaedam de Christo manifesta conscripsit*).[59] Elsewhere he could adopt the language of dictation. In a letter to Jerome he made clear that the Holy Spirit not only gave (*donante*) these writings but dictated (*dictante*) them.[60] The dictation analogy may also explain his regular practice of using the ablative case for the Spirit and the preposition *per* for the biblical writers.[61] Nevertheless, unlike so many before and after him, Augustine could also emphasise the genuinely human origin of the Scriptures. One striking example is found amongst his sermons:

> After the resurrection, the Lord Jesus appeared to his disciples in many ways. They had [the source material] from which the Evangelists might write as divine inspiration furnished to them the recollection of things to write about (*sicut eis subministrabat spiritus recordationis rerum quas scriberent*). One Evangelist related one incident, another told something else. Any of them could omit what

---

[57] Clement of Alexandria, *Cohortatio ad Gentes*, 1 (*PG*, VIII, 60).
[58] Gregory, *Moralia in Job*, praef. 1.2 (*CCSL*, CXLIII, 8); cf. Ambrose, *Epistulae*, VIII.1 (*PL* XVI, 912); Jerome, *Epistulae*, 120.10 (*PL*, 22, 997).
[59] Augustine, *De Civitate Dei contra Paganos*, XVIII.23.1-2 (*CCSL*, XLVIII, 613).
[60] Augustine, *Epistulae*, 82.2 (*CSEL*, XXXIV, 353); *De consensu Evangelistarum*, I.35 (54) (*CSEL*, XLIII, 60).
[61] Augustine, *Enarrationes in Psalmos*, 8.7 (*CCSL*, XXXVIII, 52); 104.27 (*CCSL*, XL, 1547). A. D. R. Polman, *Augustine*, 51.

was true; but he could not put in anything false. Consider that one person said all those things, for One truly did say them, because there was one Spirit in all the Evangelists.[62]

As well as providing terminology and illustrative material for early Christian explanations of the process of biblical inspiration, interaction with the Graeco-Roman thought-world raised questions about the sufficiency of Holy Scripture. At times the attempt to demonstrate the rationality of Christian doctrine in terms intelligible to the pagan world led to the acknowledgement of truth, even some theological truth, in the wider literature. Justin Martyr argued that Christ had been known, at least in part, by Socrates.[63] Theophilus suggested the Greek Sibyl and the Hebrew prophets 'have all spoken things consistent and harmonious with one another ($\phi\acute{\iota}\lambda\alpha\ \dot{\alpha}\lambda\lambda\acute{\eta}\lambda o\iota s\ \kappa\alpha\grave{\iota}\ \sigma\acute{\upsilon}\mu\phi\omega\nu\alpha$)',[64] and Augustine could even find a place for the Erythraean Sybil in the City of God.[65] Nevertheless, the evidence will only stretch so far. There can be no doubt that the Fathers were committed to a view of the Scriptures as unique, authoritative, and sufficient.

A Growing Commitment to Allegory

One of the most enduring contributions of the patristic discussion of the nature and use of Scripture was the development of an allegorical approach to biblical interpretation. This approach had been employed by the New Testament writers themselves,[66] but it took on a new significance in the face of the early Christian debates with both Jews and heretics. Through the employment of allegory, it could be shown that the Old Testament spoke of Christ at almost every point. This in turn reinforced the Christian charges that the Jews had refused the testimony of their own Scriptures and that their rejection of the apostolic writings was perverse. Similarly, the heretical attempt to drive a wedge between the Old Testament and the New from the other direction, including the wholesale repudiation of the Old Testament by Marcion, could be dismissed as a failure to understand the allegorical significance of the Old Testament text.

The latter second and early third century witnessed an ever-widening application of allegorical method by Christian exegetes, particularly those associated with the Catechetical School of Alexandria. Clement, who headed the school from about AD 190 to

---

[62] Augustine, *Sermones,* CCXLVI.1 (*PL,* XXXVIII, 1153).
[63] Justin Martyr, *Apologia,* II.10.8 (*PG,* VI, 461); II.8.3 (*PG,* VI, 457).
[64] Theophilus of Antioch, *Ad Autolycum,* 2.9 (*PG,* VI, 1064).
[65] Augustine, *De Civitate Dei contra Paganos,* XVIII.23.1-2 (*CCSL,* XLVIII, 613).
[66] E.g. Mk. 12:1-12; 1 Cor. 9:9-10; Gal. 4:24; Heb. 9:23-24; 1 Pet. 3:21.

202, argued that each biblical text contained hidden 'layers of meaning'. The key to understanding these was familiarity with 'the secret traditions of true knowledge (αἱ ἀπόκρυφοι τῆς ἀληθοῦς γνώσεως παραδοσείς)'.[67] Clement explained that the hiddenness of Scripture was necessary in the light of its subject matter. Religious language cannot be plain and open, because truth about God, by very definition, can only be conveyed 'in enigmas (αἰνίγμασι), in symbols (συμβόλοις), in allegories (ἀλληγορίαις) in metaphors (μεταφοραῖς), and in similar figures (τοιουτοισί τισι τρόποις).'[68]

Clement's successor at the Catechetical school, Origen, built upon his approach. He explained that Scripture ordinarily has three senses corresponding to the tripartite constitution of a human being: body, soul and spirit. This allows the simpler person to be edified by the 'flesh', those 'somewhat more advanced' by the 'soul', and the mature by the 'spiritual law which contains "a shadow of the good things to come"'.[69] While he was convinced this three-fold pattern holds for most of Scripture, he was willing to concede that there are some passages where the obvious, literal sense is totally unedifying. In such cases, he suggested, it is proper to seek only the soul and spirit of the passages.[70]

Origen's method drew a new line of connection between the spiritual condition of the reader and the nature of the text. This was to become a familiar way of holding together the surface intelligibility of the text and the benefits of the allegorical method. Scripture contains a hierarchy of meanings which stands parallel to a hierarchy in Christian experience or spiritual development. However the undeniable concomitant of this approach was an admission that the deeper, more profound meanings of the text are not normally accessible to every reader. It is in this connection that Origen and his successors spoke of 'obscurity (ἀσάφεια)' and 'the dark sayings (οἱ σκοτεινοί λόγοι)' of Scripture.[71]

---

[67] Clement of Alexandria, *Stromata*, I.12 (*PG*, VIII, 753). Clement's appreciation of many of the structures of Gnostic thought is obvious at this point. R. P. C. Hanson, *Allegory and Event: A Study of the Sources and Significance of Origen's Interpretation of Scripture*, 117.

[68] Clement of Alexandria, *Stromata*,V.4 (*PG*, IX, 41) See the discussion in Anthony C. Thiselton, *New Horizons in Hermeneutics*, 166.

[69] Origen, *De Principiis*, IV.1,11 (*PG*, XI, 364-365).

[70] Origen, *De Principiis*, IV.1,12 (*PG*, XI, 368).

[71] Origen, *De Principiis*, IV.1,10 (*PG*, XI, 361, 364). There were, of course, dissenters from this general trend towards an ever increasing use of allegory and appeal to the multiple senses of Scripture. Most of these were associated in some way or other with the Catechetical School in Antioch (e.g. Diodore of Tarsus, John Chrysostom, Theodore of Mopsuestia, and Junilius). Robert M.

However, it was possible to view even 'obscurity' in a positive light. This became evident in the work of those Latin writers credited with installing a modified form of the Alexandrian method as the standard exegetical approach of the Western Church.[72] Undoubtedly the most important of these was Augustine. In his *Confessiones* he recalled the expositions of Ambrose, and in particular his use of 2 Cor. 3:6: 'for the letter kills, but the spirit gives life'.[73] It was this text which was to provide an extraordinarily productive framework for his own understanding of Scripture. On one level, it was simply another way of expressing the law/grace dichotomy which underlay the relationship of the testaments; on another, it pointed beyond the literal meaning of any particular text to its figurative or spiritual meanings:

> For that doctrine by which we learn the command to live temperately and properly is 'the letter that kills' unless it is accompanied by 'the spirit that gives life'. Certainly that is not the only way we must understand what we read: 'the letter kills, but the spirit gives life'. [We are also meant to understand it in such a way] that we might not take something written figuratively, the proper sense of which produces nonsense (*cuius est absurda proprietas*), just as it sounds literally. Rather, as we observe that it indicates something else, we nourish the inner man by [our] spiritual understanding (*spiritali intellegentia*), because to think according to the flesh is death, on the other hand to think according to the spirit is life and peace.[74]

To say a biblical text was 'obscure' was, for Augustine, to say that its plain and literal meaning yielded only nonsense. However, far from bringing the interpretive task to an end, such an observation was in fact only its beginning. Augustine actually argued that difficulties in the text were part of the kind provision of God. Christians would be puffed up with pride if everything was laid bare before them in the Scripture and they would despair if the biblical texts were totally impenetrable. God had therefore designed the Scriptures for the benefit of all believers:

Grant and David Tracy, *A Short History of the Interpretation of the Bible*, 63-72.

[72] Beryl Smalley identified two main 'channels' through which 'Alexandrian exegesis penetrated to the Latin middle ages': 'indirectly through the Latin Fathers and directly through translations of Origen's works'. Beryl Smalley, *The Study of the Bible in the Middle Ages*, 13; cf. Gillian R. Evans, *The Language and Logic of the Bible: The Earlier Middle Ages*, 114.

[73] Augustine, *Confessiones*, VI.4 (6) (*CCSL*, XXVII, 77).

[74] Augustine, *De spiritu et littera*, VI (*CSEL*, LX, 157-58).

However, no one is uncertain (*ambigit*) now that everything is learned more willingly through the use of figures (*similitudines*), and that we discover it with much more delight when we have experienced some trouble in searching for it. Those who do not find what they are seeking are afflicted with hunger, but those who do not seek, because they have it in their possession, often waste away with their pride. Yet in both cases we must guard against discouragement. The Holy Spirit, therefore, has generously and advantageously planned (*modificauit*) Holy Scripture in such a way that in the easier passages (*locis apertioribus*) He relieves our hunger; in the more obscure (*obscurioribus*) He drives away our pride. Practically nothing is dug out from those obscure texts (*obscuritatibus*) which is not discovered to be said very plainly (*planissime*) in another place.[75]

Yet according to Augustine the complexities and obscurities of Scripture were not only beneficial, they were necessary. The epistemic consequences of the Fall have made it impossible for human beings to understand the truth about God in a direct manner.[76] If God is to be truly known by sinful men and women, then he must not only make himself known (i.e. *revelatio* must begin with God), but he must do so in a way that is adapted to the human mind (i.e. *revelatio* must involve *accommodatio*). For Augustine, grace in the face of human sin and its consequences is the most basic explanation for the distinctive form of Scripture.

Augustine's own exegetical method involved distinguishing four different types of meaning in Scripture.[77] A similar method was espoused by his near-contemporary John Cassian, whose terminology and explanation would dominate the exegetical tradition for centuries to come. Cassian spoke of one historical sense and three kinds of spiritual knowledge (*spiritalis scientia*): 'allegory (*allegoria*)', in which the person, word, or event 'prefigures (*praefigurat*)' another mystery; 'anagogy (*anagoge*)', in which the spiritual mystery points to the 'more august secrets of heaven (*sacratiora caelorum secreta*)'; and 'tropology (*tropologia*)', the moral teaching in which is given instruction concerning the amendment of life and the practice of asceticism.[78]

---

[75] Augustine, *De doctrina Christiana*, II.6 (8) (*CCSL*, XXXII, 36); *De Civitate Dei Contra Paganos*, XI.19 (*CCSL*, XLVIII, 337-38).
[76] Gillian R. Evans, *Augustine on Evil*, 36, 62-65.
[77] Augustine, *De Utilitate Credendi*, III (5) (*CSEL*, XXV, 7-8).
[78] John Cassian, *Collationes*, XIV.8 (*PL*, XLIX, 962-63).

The Church as the Guardian of Scripture

One further development of the period is relevant to our investigation. This was the growing insistence that the Church, embodied in the succession of bishops and given voice in the teaching of the councils, was not only the proper context for all biblical interpretation, but also the guardian and guarantee of *correct* interpretation. Irenaeus was one of the first to argue that the teaching of the Church is critical to the interpretive endeavour precisely because the Scriptures had been entrusted to the apostles and through them to those bishops in apostolic succession. Their guardianship had a divine origin and guaranteed both a genuine text and a proper understanding:

> True knowledge is [found in] the teaching of the Apostles ($ἡ\ τῶν\ ἀποστόλων\ διδαχή$), the ancient system of the Church ($τὸ\ ἀρχαῖον\ τῆς\ Ἐκκλησίας\ σύστημα$) with reference to the whole world, and the mark of Christ's body according to the successions of bishops, to whom they committed that Church, which is in every single place. [The Church] carefully and continuously comes to us without pretence, [providing] a very full handling of the Scriptures (*Scripturarum tractatio plenissima*), and a legitimate exposition according to the Scriptures (*secundum Scripturas expositio legitima*), careful, accepting neither addition nor subtraction, reading without falsification, without danger, and without blasphemy.[79]

It is significant that Irenaeus stressed that the Scriptures are inviolate and that the authority of the Church does not extend to adding or subtracting from the biblical text. Irenaeus was seeking to avoid the suggestion that the Church, rather than the Scripture, is the ultimate theological and hermeneutical authority. Yet he also wanted to insist that this authority necessarily operated within the fellowship of believers.

This argument for the indispensable role of the Church in the hermeneutical enterprise would be developed in the ensuing centuries. Augustine spoke of how he had come to believe 'in the Holy Scriptures, which the authority of your catholic church commends (*scripturis sanctis, quas ecclesiae tuae catholicae commendaret auctoritas*)'.[80] It is in this context that his well known declaration on this subject needs to be understood:

---

[79] Irenaeus, *Contra Haereses*, IV.33.8 (*PG*, VII, 1077). Only a fraction of this section is preserved in Greek, the rest has come to us in Latin translation.

[80] Augustine, *Confessiones*, VII.7 (*CCSL*, XXVII, 100).

> Indeed I would not have believed the Gospel (*Evangelium*) except the authority of the Catholic Church roused me to action (*commoveret*).[81]

Augustine was not suggesting that the authority of the Catholic Church is greater than that of Holy Scripture, nor did he consider Scripture to be somehow inadequate or insufficient for Christian living or the formulation of Christian doctrine. Certainly he recognised the Church as the authoritative context for biblical study, as well as her authoritative direction to believe what is written there. Nevertheless, one extraordinary difference separated Scripture and the teaching of the Church. In his treatise *On Baptism*, Augustine explained:

> However, who does not know that the sacred canon of Scripture, both of the Old and New Testament, is contained within its own established limits, and that it is to be preferred to all later letters of bishops to such a degree, that it ought not to be possible to doubt or dispute at all, whether anything established as written in it is true or right (*utrum uerum uel utrum rectum sit quidquid in ea scriptum esse constiterit*)? But on the other hand, the letters of bishops which have been written or are being written, since the closing of the canon (*post confirmatum canonem*), may be refuted if there be anything in them which by chance deviates from the truth (*forte a ueritate deuiatum est*).[82]

The foundation of his argument here is the assumption of a closed canon and therefore an unalterable body of biblical material. In contrast he reminded his readers that the teaching of bishops remains susceptible to refutation by other more learned people, by more experienced bishops, or by the authority of Church Councils. Further, even the authority of universal councils is relative. Their decisions can be altered by other, later councils. Only Holy Scripture stands above and beyond contradiction or correction.[83] Augustine was remarkably consistent at this point, even insisting that anyone who reads his own work should be 'not only a pious reader but a free corrector (*non solum pium lectorem sed etiam liberum correctorem*)'. He followed these words with a warning: 'Do not desire to serve my writings as [you would] canonical Scripture (*Noli meis litteris quasi scripturis canonicis inseruire*)'.[84]

---

[81] Augustine, *Contra Epistolam Manichaei Quam vocant Fundamenti*, I.5 (6) (*PL*, XLII, 176).
[82] Augustine, *De Baptismo contra Donatistas*, II.3 (4) (*CSEL*, LI, 178).
[83] Augustine, *De Baptismo contra Donatistas*, II.3 (4) (*CSEL*, LI, 178).
[84] Augustine, *De Trinitate*, III. pr. 2 (*CCSL*, L, 128).

The Vincentian Canon emerged in this context. It took its name from the classic statement in the *Commonitorium* of Vincent of Lérins, who vigorously opposed Augustine's soteriology. He too emphasised the need for adherence to the authoritative interpretation of the Church as a protection against idiosyncratic and heretical interpretations of Scripture:

> Here someone may possibly ask: Since the canon of the Scriptures is complete (*cum sit perfectus Scripturarum Canon*), and is abundantly sufficient for every purpose (*sibique ad omnia satis superque sufficiat*), what need is there to add to it the authority of the Church's interpretation (*Ecclesiasticae intelligentiae auctoritas*)? The reason is, of course, that by its very depth (*pro ipsa sua altitudine*) the Holy Scripture is not received by all in one and the same sense (*non uno sensu universi accipiunt*), but its declarations are subject to interpretation, now in one way, now in another, so that, it would appear, we can find almost as many interpretations as there are men [...] For this reason it is very necessary that, on account of so great intricacies of such varied error, the line used in the exposition of the prophets and apostles be made straight in accordance with the standard of ecclesiastical and catholic interpretation. Likewise in the catholic Church itself especial care must be taken that we hold to that which has been believed everywhere, always, and by everyone (*quod ubique, quod semper, et quod ab omnibus*).[85]

The Vincentian Canon recognised three cardinal values which enable the interpreter to identify *Ecclesiasticae intelligentia*. These are ecumenicity (*universitas*), antiquity (*antiquitas*), and consensus (*consensio*).[86] Yet where is one to look for these three? According to Vincent, the first recourse of the Christian interpreter is 'the authority of a universal council of all the bishops of the Catholic Church (*omnis Ecclesiae Catholicae sacerdotum universalis Concilii auctoritas*)'. The decision of such a body can be taken as the authoritative interpretation of the passage in question. If no conciliar opinion on the issue can be found, then recourse must be had to 'the opinions of the holy Fathers (*sanctorum patrum sententiae*)', those who are approved and in fellowship with the Catholic Church.[87] Nevertheless, Vincent insisted that the role of ecclesiastical interpretation, from either source, is preservation not innovation.[88]

---

[85] Vincent of Lérins, *Commonitorium*, II.2-3 (*PL*, L, 640).
[86] Vincent of Lérins, *Commonitorium*, XXVII.38 (*PL*, L, 674).
[87] Vincent of Lérins, *Commonitorium*, XXIX.41 (*PL*, L, 677).
[88] Vincent of Lérins, *Commonitorium*, XXXIII.43 (*PL*, L, 684-686).

These six developments, then, ensured that the nature and use of Holy Scripture was a live issue throughout the Patristic period. The evidence suggests a conscious attempt to repeatedly restate and defend the apostolic teaching on the subject in the face of new circumstances and pressures. What is equally evident, however, is that at a number of significant points these patristic contributions introduced new elements which would, over time, generate tensions within the conceptual framework of the prevailing approach to the biblical text.

The Nature and Use of Scripture in the Medieval Period

Particular care must be taken when viewing Luther against the backdrop of medieval theological thought. It is important to avoid the extremes of absolute continuity or revolutionary discontinuity.[89] Luther was a medieval thinker who went beyond medieval thought. Nevertheless, we must reckon with the fact that the theology of the schools, as mediated by the late medieval universities, was his most immediate context. He did not, nor could he, study theology purely with reference to the Scriptures and the ancient Fathers of the Church. Even his polemic against scholastic theology did not keep him from quoting the medieval masters when it suited him. More importantly, several features of the medieval hermeneutical debate carried significant consequences for the approach to Scripture which Luther inherited.

A Fundamental Commitment to the Patristic Inheritance

Even a cursory examination of medieval theological literature reveals a profound sense of debt to, and continuity with, the early Church Fathers. Throughout this period, biblical commentary generally took the form of a collection of patristic statements relevant to a particular text, culminating in the *Glossa Ordinaria*. Later, authoritative statements of the Fathers would be arranged topically, producing theological texts such as Peter Lombard's *Sententiarum Libri Quatuor*. A profound commitment to the authority of the Fathers meant that any developments in biblical and theological scholarship in this period took place within the framework set by such works as Augustine's *De Doctrina Christiana*.

This commitment to the patristic inheritance bore directly on the medieval discussion of the nature and use of Scripture. Firstly, and very practically, it allowed a language barrier to develop between the Scriptures and the ordinary believer. Latin remained the official

---

[89] Oberman, *Reformation*, 3.

language of the Church long after it had ceased to be spoken by most of northern Europe.[90] It was also the language in which most Christians made contact with the biblical text. This simple reality carried enormous consequences. Not only was the study of Scripture beyond the ability of the ordinary believer, those who learnt Latin for the purpose had to learn it as a foreign language. This brought its own difficulties, for there were times when the Vulgate did not obey the rules of the Latin grammarians such as Donatus or Priscian. How was the student of Scripture to make sense of a text laced with such 'obscurities'?

A second legacy of the patristic period was a presupposition of the divine inspiration of the Scriptures. Like the Fathers before them, the great theological minds of the medieval period did not hesitate to identify God as the author of the words of Scripture.[91] Thomas Aquinas put it most succinctly in his *Summa Theologiae*: 'God is the author of Holy Scripture (*auctor autem sacrae scripturae Deus est*)'.[92] Apparently he was confident that this was an article of faith which no orthodox thinker would dispute. Henry of Ghent, amongst many others, considered God's authorship of the Scriptures to be the chief explanation of the distinction between the apostolic writings and those of the Fathers: we just don't have the same certainty that God has spoken in the Fathers as he has in the apostles and so we cannot give them an equal weight of authority.[93]

For the most part, these medieval writers and their contemporaries were not satisfied with a vague notion of divine influence upon the human writers. They considered it important to affirm the most intimate involvement of the Holy Spirit with the words of the text themselves.[94] This gave a particular shape to their explanations of the concept of biblical inspiration. Agobard of Lyon provides one of the earliest examples. Speaking of the prophets he insisted 'not only did the Holy Spirit inspire (*inspirauerit*) the meaning of the prediction (*sensum praedicationis*) and the manner or contents of the utterance (*modos uel argumenta dictionum*), but he also fashioned from the

---

[90] Bernard Hamilton, *Religion in the Medieval West*, 59.
[91] F. Kropatscheck, *Das Schriftprinzip der lutherischen Kirche, geschichtliche und dogmatische Untersuchungen: I. Die Vorgeschichte; Das Erbe des Mittelalters*, 424.
[92] Aquinas, *Summa Theologiae*, Ia, q. I, art.10; *Quaestiones Quodlibetales*, VII, q. 6, a. 1. Almost identical words appear in John Wycliffe, *De Fundatione Sectarum*, 16 in Rudolf Buddensieg (ed.), *John Wiclif's Polemical Works in Latin*, I, 80.
[93] Henry of Ghent, *Summae quaestionum ordinarium Theologi*, art. 8, q. 6 (Paris, 1520, fol. LXIX).
[94] Evans, *Earlier Middle Ages*, 168.

outside (*extrinsecus formauerit*) the bodily words themselves (*ipsa corporalia uerba*)'.[95] Later writers tended to employ the patristic language of dictation.[96]

Aquinas made a distinctive contribution on this topic by seeking to relate the idea of the prophet as an instrument to the Aristotelian category of instrumental efficient causality.[97] This allowed a genuine role for both God and the human writer in the production of Holy Scripture. It was of the essence of biblical prophecy, he argued, that it pertains to human cognitive faculties.[98] He was not suggesting that the prophet understood everything to which his prophecy relates.[99] Instead he explained that the Holy Spirit influenced the judgement of the human writer as he chose words from an already existing vocabulary.[100]

A third element of the patristic legacy was the observation that every text of Scripture had multiple levels of meaning. The standard formula of John Cassian became known as the *Quadriga,* and it was so much a part of medieval Christian thinking that it found expression in both the liturgy and iconography of the period.[101] Nevertheless, it reinforced the notion that the ordinary Christian had no clear access to the living meaning of the text. Specialist knowledge was required, not only of the unique grammar of the biblical materials, but also of its connection to deeper, more edifying realities. It was not a large step to argue from this point that such specialist knowledge was to be found in the official teaching of the Church. Alcuin, one of the leading figures in the Carolingian renaissance, even found this reliance upon the

---

[95] Agobard of Lyon, *Contra Obiectiones Fredegisi,* XII (*CCCM,* LII, 291).

[96] Pierre d'Ailly, *Sermo de omnibus sanctis* in Petrus de Alliaco, *Tractatus et sermones* (Brussels: Fratres vitae communis, 1481/83), fol. N 9; Gabriel Biel, *Defensorium Obedientiae Apostolicae,* 8 in Heiko A. Oberman *et al* (eds.), *Defensorium Obedientiae Apostolicae et Alia Documenta,* 114.

[97] Thomas Aquinas, *Summa Theologiae,* IIaIIae. q. 173, art. 4. Kropatscheck, *Schriftprinzip,* 430; Vawter, *Inspiration,* 48, 56.

[98] Aquinas, *Summa Theologiae,* IIaIIae, q. 171, art. 1; contra Bonaventure, *Commentaria in Quatuor Libros Sententiarum Magistri Petri Lombardi,* II, d. 24, art. 2 q. 2 ad obj. 4 (*Opera Omnia,* II, 564).

[99] Aquinas, *Summa Theologiae,* IIaIIae, q. 173, art. 4.

[100] Aquinas, *Summa Theologiae,* IIIa, q. 60, art. 5, ad obj. 1.

[101] Hamilton, *Religion,* p. 66-7. The definitive work on the Quadriga remains Henri de Lubac, *Exégèse Médiévale: les Quatre Sens de l'Écriture.* There were, of course, deviations from this standard, e.g. Angelom of Luxeuil, *Enarrationes in Libros Regum,* praef. (*PL,* CXV, 245-6); John Scotus Erigena, *Commentarius in S. Evangelium Secundum Joannem,* frag. III (*PL,* CXXII, 341-8). Smalley, *Bible,* 41-2.

interpretive keys held by the Church to be anticipated in Scripture itself.[102]

A Renewed Emphasis on the Academic Study of the Scriptures

Biblical study continued to take place at an academic level throughout the entire period from Augustine to Luther.[103] It was fundamental to the educational reforms of the Carolingian renaissance, for Charlemagne's capitulary to Bangulf of Fulda in 787 insisted that all monasteries and bishops' houses become places where the Scriptures were studied. However, this interest in the serious study of the Scriptures continued long after the collapse of Charlemagne's empire. Almost every significant theological mind of the Middle Ages produced commentaries on portions of the Bible. Important centres of biblical study also developed, notably at Laon, Chartres, and the Abbey of St Victor in Paris.

The study of the Bible, of course, was never purely an academic matter. The outstanding biblical scholars of this period were almost always in holy orders, responsible for cultivating a life of devotion in which Holy Scripture was approached not merely as an object of study but as God's means of addressing his people. They followed the programme of Augustine's *De Doctrina Christiana*, supplemented by the *Collationes* of John Cassian, which provided for an integration of academic and devotional approaches to the biblical text.[104] Further, it was the monastic schools which throughout the period provided the context for both the serious study of Scripture and the pursuit of the religious life.

Nevertheless, this dual interest in Scripture as both an object of academic study and a devotional aid would, and did, produce tensions. Amongst some of the religious orders a new hierarchy of religious exercises developed which placed the reading or study of Scripture at the base of a mystic ladder: *lectio* leads to *oratio*, which leads to *meditatio*, which leads to *contemplatio*. According to this programme, the study of Scripture was only a preparation for the primary task of communion with God. In some cases the private use of books was discouraged and religious objects such as crucifixes supplanted the Scriptures as the source of comfort and the medium of divine

---

[102] Alcuin, *Compendium in Canticum Canticorum*, IV.11 (*PL*, C, 652).
[103] Beryl Smalley has, however, identified 'one hundred and twenty-five years of nothing' beginning with the death of Remigius in AD 908. Smalley, *Bible*, 44.
[104] Smalley, *Bible*, 27.

encounter.[105] It was the biblical scholarship centred upon the Abbey of St Victor which refashioned the connection between academic and devotional approaches to Scripture by bringing the methods of spiritual reading (*lectio divina*) into the academic structures which began to thrive in the twelfth century.[106]

All of this carried significant consequences for the use of Holy Scripture. The overlay of biblical study with all the apparatus of patristic and medieval scholarship raised questions about its intelligibility and accessibility. Aquinas argued that precisely because such serious study was so self-evidently necessary if Scripture was to be understood properly, it also became necessary to provide clear, succinct statements of 'the truth of the faith (*veritas fidei*)' for the use of those who were not up to the task:

> The truth of the faith is scattered throughout Holy Scripture under various modes of expression, and in certain places obscurely (*in quibusdam obscure*). So because long study and practice (*longum studium et exercitium*) are needed to draw out (*ad eliciendum*) the truth of the faith from Holy Scripture, and all who need to know the truth of the faith are not able to come and devote themselves to study (*studio vacare*), being busy with many other affairs, it was necessary that something clear be drawn up by way of summary from the sentences of Holy Scripture (*ut ex sententiis sacrae Scripturae aliquid manifestum summarie colligeretur*), which could be set out for the belief of all. Indeed, this is not an addition to Holy Scripture (*non est additum sacrae Scripturae*), rather something taken from Holy Scripture (*ex sacra Scriptura sumptum*).[107]

Academic study of the text, though promoted as a means of furthering knowledge and understanding, ran the risk of generating an academic guild who claimed exclusive possession of the resources which were necessary in order to discern the intention of God as expressed in Holy Scripture. The fact that the members of that guild were drawn from amongst the various functionaries of the Catholic Church reinforced other trends evident throughout the period.

A Developing Ecclesiastical Positivism

The study of the Scriptures in medieval churches, universities, and monasteries took place amidst a continuing debate about authority

---

[105] Louis Gougaud, *Devotional and Ascetic Practices in the Middle Ages*, 75-9; Smalley, *Bible*, 282-83.
[106] Evans, *Earlier Middle Ages*, 29.
[107] Aquinas, *Summa Theologiae*, IIaIIae, q.I, art.9.

within the Church. The public and political dimensions of this debate would have profound ramifications for the development of early modern Europe. Its scholarly dimensions almost inevitably would further influence the shape and direction of biblical study.

While no serious attempt was made to deny the authority of the Scriptures in the medieval period, an articulation of the precise relationship between that authority and the tradition of the Church repeatedly proved controversial. Detailed modern studies have identified two broad positions on this question.[108] 'Tradition I' stressed the coinherence of Scripture and tradition: the tradition of the Church is simply the history of the obedient interpretation of Holy Scripture. If there is disagreement within the tradition, then the matter must be settled by a direct appeal to Scripture. 'Tradition II' invested the ecclesiastical traditions of the Church with the same authority as that of Holy Scripture and in effect endorsed a two-source theory of theological truth. If there is a disagreement within the tradition, under this view, appeal might equally be made to the pope (as the contemporary embodiment of the tradition) or to the Scripture.

The basic contours of this analysis are certainly correct. Nevertheless, it has proven extraordinarily difficult to classify the major thinkers of the period accordingly. Thomas Aquinas upheld the dignity and authority of the Catholic Church, yet he also argued that 'the certitude of faith (*fidei certitudo*) rested upon the authority of Holy Scripture (*quae auctoritati sacrae scripturae innititur*)'.[109] It alone has necessary authority (*ex necessitate argumentando*) and it does not need to be augmented by tradition.[110] Duns Scotus was even more ambiguous. In one place he argued that on the issue of how to formulate the doctrine of the Trinity, Peter Lombard 'has canonical authority (*auctoritatem canonicatam*) on his side, namely that of the Church, which is perhaps greater than that of Scripture (*quae forte maior est quam Scripturae*)'.[111] Yet in another he insisted that 'our theology concerns only those things contained in Scripture (*de his*

---

[108] The following analysis is found in Heiko A. Oberman, *The Harvest of Medieval Theology: Gabriel Biel and Later Medieval Nominalism*, 370-75. See also the critique of Oberman's position in Alister E. McGrath, *The Intellectual Origins of the European Reformation*, 140-48, 152-58.

[109] Aquinas, *Summa Theologiae*, IIaIIae, q. 110 a. 3.

[110] Aquinas, *Summa Theologiae*, Ia, q. 1 a. 8.

[111] Scotus then quotes a famous passage from Augustine's *Contra epistolam Fundamenti*. Johannes Duns Scotus, *Reportatio examinata*, I, d. 5 n. 24. Leo Rosato, 'Ioannis Duns Scoti Doctrina de Scriptura et Traditione', in Charles Balic (ed.), *De Scriptura et Traditione*, 235-236; Brian Tierney, *Origins of Papal Infallibility 1150-1350: A Study on the Concepts of Infallibility, Sovereignty, and Tradition in the Middle Ages*, 142-143.

quae continentur in scriptura) or those things which can be deduced from them (*de his quae possunt elici ex eis*)'.[112] He also claimed that 'Holy Scripture contains all the teaching needed by those travelling through life (*sacra scriptura sufficienter continet doctrinam necessariam viatori*)'.[113] Likewise, William of Occam could say in one place that every Christian (including the Pope) is obliged to hold to the teaching of the universal Church (*quam universalis ecclesia tenet*) rather than a statement of Holy Scripture (*auctoritatem scripturae sacrae*) whenever these two appear to be in conflict.[114] Yet in another he argued that no Christian is obliged to believe 'what is not contained in the Bible (*quod nec in Biblia continetur*) or deduced by clear and necessary consequence from that which is contained there (*nec ex solis contentis in Biblia potest consequentia necessaria et manifesta inferri*)'.[115]

Although medieval thinkers might disagree on this issue, or even express contrary opinions depending on the context of their remarks, one other piece of evidence allows us to conclude that the interpretive tradition itself exercised an increasingly important influence on the study of the Scriptures in the later medieval period. The *Glossa Ordinaria*, a biblical text heavily overlaid with marginal and interlinear comments by the Fathers and doctors of the Church, together with prefatory material to each book, became the standard text used by the late medieval students of the Scriptures, whether in the schools or in the cloister.[116] Under its influence the practice of medieval exegesis increasingly became a matter of glossing the glosses, or commenting on the comments, rather than of direct engagement with the text of Scripture itself. The Fathers and doctors of the Church came to be seen not merely as faithful interpreters of Scripture, but as themselves inspired vehicles of truth.[117]

---

[112] Johannes Duns Scotus, *Ordinatio*, prol. n. 204 (*Opera Omnia*, I, 138).
[113] Johannes Duns Scotus, *Ordinatio*, prol. n. 120 (*Opera Omnia*, I, 85).
[114] William of Occam, *Contra Ioannem*, col. 73. Tierney, 223-24.
[115] William of Occam, *Dialogus super Dignitate Papali et Regia*, 411, quoted in Brian A. Gerrish, 'Biblical Authority and the Continental Reformation', *SJT*, 10 (1957), 339. Compare the comments of Gregory of Rimini in a less polemical context: *Super primum et secundum sententiarum*, prol. q. 1, art. 2 in *Gregorii Ariminensis Oesa Lectura Super Primum et Secundum Sententarium*, 16-23.
[116] Smalley, *Bible*, 46-66; Evans, *Earlier Middle Ages*, 37-47.
[117] Jean Gerson, *Propositiones de Sensu Litterali Sacrae Scripturae et de Causis Errantium*, 2A-3A (*Opera Omnia*, I, cols. 2A- 3A). Heiko A. Oberman, *Forerunners of the Reformation: The Shape of Late Medieval Thought Illustrated by Key Documents*, 289.

Medieval thought on the authority of the Church and its relation to the authority of Holy Scripture thus retained a number of tensions. In the politically volatile fourteenth and fifteenth centuries, these tensions became increasingly evident. Papal conflict with the Conciliarists, Lollards, and Hussites raised questions which had not been settled when Luther took up his university post in 1512.

A Growing Concern for the Plain Historical Meaning

Virtually no medieval writer denied the appropriateness of seeking the spiritual senses of Holy Scripture.[118] Augustine and his contemporaries had been persuasive at this point. However, throughout the medieval period there was considerable debate about how much weight should be given to the literal or historical sense.

Bede had sounded an early warning in his commentary on Genesis. The interpreter who diligently lays out the allegorical senses must recognise the danger he faces: that by allegorising 'he might abandon the explicit faith of history (*apertam historiae fidem allegorizando derelinquat*)'.[119] Bede reminded his readers that the faith of the Church is inseparably tied to the historical particularities surrounding the biblical text. If these historical particularities were to be obscured by excessive use of allegory, then the consequences could be catastrophic. Excessive appeal to hidden meanings of a text ran the risk of clouding its essential meaning.

There is little evidence that Bede's warning had much impact on the practice of exegesis in the early medieval period. However, from around the twelfth century a renewed interest in the historical sense of the biblical text emerged side by side with continued employment of the *Quadriga* and its derivatives. Three factors were at work. The first was a dialogue between Christian and Jewish scholars, such as that which undoubtedly took place between certain teachers at the Abbey of St Victor and the school of Rabbi Solomon ben Isaac (Rashi).[120] An interest in the biblical languages had led the Victorines to seek advice on difficult expressions and significant points of Hebrew grammar and in the process of their inquiries they gained a new respect for the

---

[118] One exception may be William of Auvergne in his *Liber de Fide et Legibus*. See Beryl Smalley, *Studies in Medieval Thought and Learning from Abelard to Wyclif*, 179-181.

[119] Bede, *Commentary on Genesis*, 1.i.1 (*CCSL*, CXVIIIA, 3).

[120] Smalley, *Bible*, 103-5, 110, 149-172.

literal-historical meaning of the text.[121] A second stimulus was the heresy of the Cathari (Albigenses).[122] This Manichaean sect repudiated much of the Old Testament as material irrelevant to the Christian. To counter such charges careful attention was given to the precise historical reference of the text. The third factor at work here was a new refinement in the technical skills of grammar and dialectic.[123] This opened up new possibilities in the exposition of the literal sense, possibilities which removed the need for constant recourse to higher spiritual senses.

In the thirteenth century, Thomas Aquinas produced a defence of multiple spiritual meanings which sought to reassert the Augustinian insistence on the priority of the historical sense. He first established that the multiplicity of meaning arises, not from ambiguity in the words of Scripture, but from the very nature of the things to which the words refer.[124] This enabled him to affirm the historical or literal sense of Scripture as the sole proper basis for theological argument:

> Consequently Holy Scripture sets up no confusion, since all meanings are based on one (*omnes sensus fundentur super unum*), namely the literal sense (*scilicet litteralem*). From this alone can arguments be drawn (*Ex quo solo potest trahi argumentum*) and not from things said by allegory, as St Augustine remarks in his letter to Vincent the Donatist. Nor does this undo the effect of Holy Scripture, for nothing necessary for faith is contained under the spiritual sense that is not openly conveyed through the literal sense elsewhere.[125]

Aquinas was not simply restating the position of Augustine. Whereas Augustine had spoken of 'lifting the veil (*remoto mystico velamento*)' to find the spiritual meanings of the text, Aquinas spoke of all such meanings being 'based on the one literal sense (*omnes sensus fundentur super unum, scilicet litteralem*)'. Aquinas was evidently influenced by the Victorines, who were responsible for a transformation of the controlling metaphor for the relation of literal and spiritual meanings in Scripture. The importance of this development should not be overlooked. Once the literal sense ceased to be regarded as an obstacle to spiritual understanding (a veil), instead

---

[121] This does not mean that the Victorines possessed a thorough knowledge of Hebrew. Evidently their Jewish conversation partners translated many texts into French for them. Smalley, *Bible*, 155.

[122] Gillian R. Evans, *The Language and Logic of the Bible: The Road to Reformation*, 42.

[123] Evans, *Road to Reformation*, 40.

[124] Aquinas, *Summa Theologiae*, Ia, q.I, art.10.

[125] Aquinas, *Summa Theologiae*, Ia, q.I, art.10.

being recognised as integral to that process (the foundation of a building), the way was open for a new and more detailed examination of the text as it stands. Hugh of St Victor boldly suggested that at points the search for allegory had actually prevented a proper understanding of the meaning of Scripture. Some texts might demand an allegorical explanation, but not all do. The exegete must be sensitive to the particular text in front of him:

> All Scripture, once it has been expounded according to its own proper meaning, begins to shine more clearly, and extends easier access to itself in order that it might be understood. Many, not understanding the virtue of Scripture, obscure its elegance and beauty by strange expositions (*expositionibus peregrinis*). When they ought to disclose what is hidden, they obscure even that which is plain. I see similar blame attaching to those who obstinately deny the propriety of seeking a mystical sense and a depth of allegory in Holy Scripture when there is one (*vel qui in sacra Scriptura mysticam intelligentiam et allegoriarum profunditatem, vel inquirendam pertinaciter negant, ubi est*), as to those who superstitiously maintain it, when it is not there (*vel inquirendam superstitiose contendunt, ubi non est*).[126]

Hugh of St. Victor and Thomas Aquinas did not, of course, end the debate. Their approach was influential, but dissenters emerged on both sides. Nicholas of Lyra was prominent in the tradition which gave increased attention to the historical sense.[127] He developed the notion of a 'double literal sense' in relation to the Old Testament (the historical-literal sense and the prophetic-literal or New-Testament-literal sense), which enabled this tradition to reassert the Christian claim to it without resort to allegory.[128] On the other hand, Jacobus Faber Stapulensis, almost two hundred years later, criticised such approaches as a kind of 'Rabbinic exegesis' which failed properly to honour Christ.

> It is impossible for us to believe (*credere*) this literal sense — that which they call the literal sense and which makes David a historian rather than a prophet (*Dauid historicum potius facere quam prophetam*). Instead, let us call that the literal sense which is in accord with the Spirit (*qui cum spiritu concordat*) and is pointed out by the Spirit (*quem spiritus sanctus monstrat*) [...] This true sense is

---

[126] Hugh of St Victor, *In Salomonis Ecclesiasten,* praef. (*PL,* CLXXV, 114-115); cf. *De Scripturis et Scriptoribus Sacris,* v. (*PL,* CLXXV, 13-15).
[127] Smalley, *Bible,* 355.
[128] Steven E. Ozment, *The Age of Reform 1250-1550: An Intellectual and Religious History of Late Medieval and Reformation Europe,* 69.

not what is called the allegorical or tropological sense, but rather that which the Holy Spirit intends as He speaks through the prophet (*quem spiritus sanctus in propheta loquens intendit*). In order to draw out this sense we have given careful attention to how much the Spirit of God has given (*quantum spiritus dei dedit inuigilauimus*).[129]

In line with these convictions, Stapulensis engaged in the sustained use of allegory to establish that the entire Psalter spoke directly of Christ.

Three final things should be said about this fresh concentration on the historical sense of Scripture. Firstly, it provided a means of underlining the unity of the canon of Scripture. Some simply argued for a unity of the whole which meant that nothing in Holy Scripture was superfluous.[130] Others attempted to explain the nature of this unity. One approach was to emphasise that the Old and New Testaments together present a history of salvation (*historia salvationis*). The historical sense itself is fundamental to the unity of Scripture precisely because it chronicles not just the history of the Jews but the history of God's saving purposes.[131] Another approach, also pregnant with possibilities for the future of biblical interpretation, was to locate the unity of Scripture in its relation to the historical figure of Jesus Christ.[132]

A second feature was that this interest in the historical often involved an appeal to authorial intention. Hugh of St Victor saw the discernment of this intention as a first concern of the faithful exegete:

> When we read the divine books, above all let us choose the meaning in the vast multitude of the Fathers (which are drawn from a few words and supported by the soundness of the Catholic faith) which appears certain to have been intended by the author (*quod certum apparuerit, eum sensisse quem legimus*). If this is unknown, [let us choose] that which the context of Scripture certainly does not prevent and [which] accords with sound faith. If it is not possible to study the context of Scripture, then [let us choose] only that which sound faith commands. For it is one thing to recognise the chief thing that the writer intended (*Aliud est enim quod potissimum*

---

[129] Jacques Lefèvre d'Étaples, *Quincuplex Psalterium: Fac-similé de l'édition de 1513*, A.iij.

[130] Hugh of St Victor, *De Scripturis et Scriptoribus Sacris*, 6. (*PL*, CLXXV, 16).

[131] Alexander of Hales, *Summa Theologiae*, I, Tractatus Introductorius, q. 1 cap. 1 ad obj. 1.

[132] John Wycliffe, *De Veritate Sacrae Scripturae*, XXXI in Rudolf Buddensieg (ed.), *John Wyclif's De Veritate Sacrae Scripturae*, III, 242.

scriptor senserit, non dignoscere); it is another to err against the rule of piety. If both are avoided, the enjoyment of reading is complete.[133]

Of course, such a concern did not necessarily exclude the possibility of multiple senses in Scripture. Aquinas was able to say that 'the literal sense is indeed that which the author intends (*vero sensus litteralis est, quem auctor intendit*)', and then complete his sentence with 'and since the author of Holy Scripture is God, who comprehends all things together by his intellect, as Augustine says (*Confessions*, xii), it is not unfitting if according to the literal sense, one word of Holy Scripture should have several senses (*non est inconveniens [...] si etiam secundum litteralem sensum, in una littera sacrae Scripturae plures sint sensus*)'.[134] Nevertheless, the concept of authorial intention was generally intended as a brake on excessively elaborate and fanciful exegesis.[135]

The third development which is important at this point concerns the very word 'historical'. The early Church Fathers and scholars of the early medieval period used the labels 'historical sense (*sensus historicus*)' and 'literal sense (*sensus literalis*)' almost interchangeably. However, around the twelfth century a redefinition informed by Aristotelian theories of signification began to gain widespread acceptance.[136] Hugh of St Victor distinguished the proper and larger uses of the term 'history (*historia*)'. Strictly speaking history was the narration of events: it is 'what I see and tell (*quod est video et narro*)'. Nevertheless, by common usage 'historical sense' was taken to mean 'the primary relation of the words to the things they signify (*qui primo loco ex significatione verborum habetur ad res*)'.[137] Historical narrative (*res gestae*) involved simply one form of signification. Yet careful study of the biblical text itself revealed many others, amongst them 'argument (*argumentum*)' and 'metaphor (*metaphora*)'. Hugh's clarification of the term 'historical sense' was significant, though later writers would prefer a more inclusive term. Aquinas included history, aetiology, and analogy under the one literal sense (*ad unum litteralem sensum pertinent*).[138] William of Nottingham maintained that the literal sense (*sensus litteralis*) was simply 'that which was first intended by the author (*qui primo intenditur ab auctore*)', whether it be strict historical narrative or

---

[133] Hugh of St Victor, *Eruditionis Didascalicae*, vi.11-12. (*PL*, CLXXVI, 808).
[134] Aquinas, *Summa Theologiae*, Ia, q.I, art.10.
[135] Evans, *Road to Reformation*, 44. Smalley, *Medieval Thought*, 285.
[136] Evans, *Earlier Middle Ages*, 68-9.
[137] Hugh of St Victor, *De Scripturis*, iii. (*PL*, CLXXV, 12).
[138] Aquinas, *Summa Theologiae*, Ia, q.I, art.10.

metaphorical explanation.[139] As we have seen, Nicholas of Lyra developed his own unique way of expressing the complex nature of the literal sense, one which protected his basic categories of history and prophecy.

The Rediscovery of Aristotle

The philosophical bequest of antiquity to the medieval West was received indirectly and a key figure in its transmission was Augustine. This explains the fact that, while the work of Aristotle was not completely unknown, the broader framework of thinking in the early medieval period, both in metaphysics and epistemology, remained decidedly Platonic. Augustine had testified to the helpfulness of Platonic philosophy, and in particular of its essential compatibility with the teaching of the Scriptures.[140]

The Platonic-Christian epistemology endorsed by Augustine had profound implications for the practice of theology and biblical interpretation. It emphasised the darkness of the mind (*tenebrae animae meae*) which hindered the natural comprehension of eternal realities, realities which remain hidden beyond sense experience.[141] If the darkened human mind was to achieve a genuine understanding of reality, this would only occur as a result of illumination (*illuminatio*) from above.[142] In practice such a framework tended to devalue the surface meaning of the biblical text by encouraging the search for true meaning beyond 'the mystic veil (*mysticum velamentum*)'.[143]

However, it was Aristotle, not Plato, who came to typify the influence of philosophy on biblical and theological study, particularly in the later medieval period. To be sure, a small number of the works of Aristotle were already known in the early Middle Ages through the translations and commentaries of Porphyry and Boethius, as well as through the writings of certain Arabic philosophers. Indeed, four of the six books of Aristotle's logic (*The Organon*) were the standard texts in medieval courses on the subject.[144] Nevertheless, Aristotle's impact on Western theology is usually dated from the twelfth century, when disturbances in the East and relative peace in the West led to a migration of Eastern scholars and books which made possible the

---

[139] William of Nottingham, *Unum ex Quatuor,* fol. 14. Smalley, *Medieval Thought,* 286.
[140] Augustine, *Confessiones,* VII.9 (*CCSL,* XXVII, 101).
[141] Augustine, *Confessiones,* VII.20 (*CCSL,* XXVII, 109).
[142] Augustine, *De Civitate Dei contra Paganos,* X.2 (*CCSL,* XLVII, 274).
[143] Augustine, *Confessiones,* VI.4 (6) (*CCSL,* XXVII, 77).
[144] Gillian R. Evans, *Philosophy and Theology in the Middle Ages,* 26-7.

recovery of the missing books of Aristotle's logic, namely the *Topics* and the *Sophistici Elenchi*.

The recovery of the lost works of Aristotle generated enormous interest, not least among theologians and biblical scholars. Three points of interaction should be noted. Firstly, the Aristotelian emphasis on knowledge through particulars, when applied to the Scriptures, would suggest that the meaning of Scripture was not hidden behind the text but expressed by it. In this way the renewed interest in the historical sense of Scripture, which we have already noted as a feature of the later medieval period in particular, had important philosophical dimensions.[145] Secondly, the Aristotelian emphasis on causality as an explanation of the nature of things, rather than the Platonic notion of a 'reflection' of the eternal forms, provided the philosophical context for a new focus on authorial intention in the study of Scripture.[146] Finally, study of Aristotle's *Posterior Analytics* generated a search for the first principles of language.[147] The discernment of such principles required, and in turn led to, a more detailed examination of the exact shape of the text itself. Augustine's discussion of words, signs, and signification would take on a new importance, with hope that such things as the logic of equivocation might explain many difficulties of interpretation.[148] In time an attention to metaphor and other figures of speech would lead to a new sophistication in exegesis.

The propriety of engaging in Christian theology from within an Aristotelian framework was questioned at various times during the late Middle Ages. There was lively debate in the thirteenth century, involving a number of attempts to prevent the use of Aristotle's work.[149] In the fifteenth century Lorenzo Valla spoke out against the Aristotelians.[150] Nevertheless, Aristotelian philosophy had provided valuable conceptual resources for the discussion of biblical interpretation. The suggestion that the text of Scripture had an integrity and intelligibility of its own was now philosophically defensible.

The Emergence of the New Learning

While Renaissance humanism did not cause the reformation of theology and church in the sixteenth century it was certainly an

---

[145] Smalley, *Bible*, 293.
[146] Smalley, *Bible*, 293.
[147] Evans, *Earlier Middle Ages*, 73.
[148] Evans, *Road to Reformation*, 115.
[149] Evans, *Philosophy*, 18-21.
[150] Lorenzo Valla, *Dialecticae disputationes contra Aristotelicos* (printed 1499).

important catalyst in a number of areas.[151] Most importantly for our purposes, humanism's characteristic interest in ancient texts and languages, driven by its concern to cultivate eloquence (*eloquentia*), led to the provision of important resources for the practice of biblical interpretation. Valla's *Collatio Novi Testamenti* (1444), Reuchlin's *De Rudimentis Hebraicis* (1506), and Erasmus' *Novum Instrumentum* (1516) all quickly became invaluable tools.

As well as these, humanism provided a critique of scholastic theology which prepared the ground for the more searching, and more specifically theological challenge presented by Luther and others. The main complaint of the humanists centred on the form of medieval theology: an excessive use of philosophical analysis had led to an avalanche of material which was as unintelligible as it was irrelevant. Instead, humanists such as Erasmus insisted that purity and elegance should characterise the explanation of Scripture as befits the nature of the material.

Nevertheless the humanism of the late fifteenth and early sixteenth century remained committed to a spiritual interpretation of the Scriptures. Erasmus illustrates the general consensus admirably. He repeatedly demonstrated his keenness to employ all the new literary, textual and philological techniques in establishing the literal sense of Scripture; nevertheless, he insisted that this was only the first stage in interpretation. He warned that to preach only the literal sense raised the prospect of delivering a Jewish interpretation (*Judaica expositio*), which itself might provide the opportunity for a revived Judaism which could threaten the doctrine of Christ.[152] From his pen too would come one of the strongest attacks on *claritas Scripturae* for centuries.

The medieval period thus witnessed an extraordinarily sustained discussion about the nature and use of Holy Scripture. However, the evidence does not suggest a trajectory which made Reformation approaches to biblical interpretation inevitable. Powerful tensions remained at both a theoretical and practical level. Different emphases generated schools of interpretation which consciously stood over against one another. As Luther took up his post at the University of Wittenberg, much remained undecided.

This then is a brief survey of Christian thinking about the nature and use of Holy Scripture up to the time of Luther. Many of the questions with which he would wrestle had been raised by others before him. Sometimes he would use their suggestions, their terminology and arguments. At other times he forged his own response as his own

---

[151] McGrath, *Intellectual Origins*, 32-68.

[152] Desiderius Erasmus, *Letter to Wolfgang Capito*, 26 February 1517, *Opus epistolarum Erasmi*, II, 491. McGrath, *Intellectual Origins*, 155-56.

exploration of the Scriptures drove him in different directions. Luther scholarship cannot afford to ignore the background to Luther's theological achievement. However, a careful examination of Luther's own words is even more important.

Chapter 2

The Very Words of God?

Luther on Inspiration and the Origin of Holy Scripture

Jaroslav Pelikan, one of the General Editors of the standard edition of Luther's works in English and a student of Luther for over fifty years, has suggested that while 'the theology of Martin Luther was a theology of the word of God [...] he and his immediate followers seemed to manifest a striking lack of specificity, or even interest, in some of the most crucial questions involved in the doctrine of the authority of the word'.[1] As a key piece of evidence pointing in this direction, he presents the fact that neither the Augsburg Confession of 1530 (endorsed by Luther)[2] nor the Schmalkaldic Articles of 1536/7 (drafted by Luther)[3] begin with a statement concerning the nature or authority of Holy Scripture. Perhaps even more significant, according to Pelikan, is the absence of a sustained exposition of the nature and extent of biblical inspiration in Luther's writings. Luther did not write at length on this subject because it was neither a controversial issue in this age of controversy nor was it definitive for his theology as a whole in the way it was for some who came after him. Pelikan concludes that it was not Luther but successive generations of his followers who developed and gave prominence to a doctrine of biblical inspiration which was particularly concerned with the text of Scripture.[4]

This interpretation of the evidence has a considerable pedigree and commands the support of many. Yet even amongst those who would

---

[1] Jaroslav Pelikan, *Reformation of Church and Dogma (1300-1700)*, 183.
[2] Luther's *Glosse auf das vermeinte kaiserliche Edikt* (1531) (*WA* XXX-III, 331-388 = *LW* 34, 67-104) contains a sustained defence of 'our confession (*der unsern bekentnis*)'.
[3] *Die Schmalkaldischen Artikel* (1537) *WA* L, 192-254.
[4] Pelikan, *Reformation*, 181-182.

endorse the general observation there remains significant disagreement about precisely why Luther drew back from an unambiguous affirmation of inspiration attaching to the words of Scripture. In this century alone a variety of possibilities have been presented. Reinhold Seeberg has been very influential in pointing to Luther's 'critical opinions concerning the Scriptures' as an important factor which helps to explain this phenomenon. These, Seeberg argued, helped Luther to frame 'an entirely new conception of the authority and inspiration of the Scriptures' which focuses on their testimony to 'the great facts of salvation and redemption'.[5] Sydney Carter concentrated attention on one part of the evidence which Seeberg had adduced. He argued that Luther's theory of inspiration was 'largely dependent on his view of the Canon of Scripture' and that it is his freedom in the latter area which undermines any suggestion of an inspiration of the actual words of the text. In contrast to Seeberg he concluded that 'in theory, at least, [Luther's] interpretation of inspiration was very broad, indefinite and unsatisfactory'.[6] Recently, similar material has been marshalled to support Miikka Ruokanen's thesis that Luther held to a 'doctrinal content theory of biblical inspiration'.[7] However, according to Ruokanen it is primarily Luther's understanding of the Bible as a theological or doctrinal entity which keeps him from espousing any kind of verbal inspiration.[8]

Gerhard Ebeling has suggested that the real reason for Luther's reluctance to elaborate a doctrine of inspired writings is his preference for talking about the relationship (*Verhältnis*) between the Spirit and the oral word (*das mündliche gesprochene Wort*). According to Ebeling even in those comments in which Luther appears intensely concerned about the actual words in the text — most notably his defence of the words of institution in the Lord's Supper — the real focus is not so much on the words of *the text,* as on the words actually *spoken by Jesus.* Such comments therefore carry with them a contradiction in principle (*grundsätzlich*) of later doctrines of verbal

---

[5] Reinhold Seeberg, *Text-book of the History of Doctrines*, II, 301-302.

[6] C. Sydney Carter, *The Reformers and Holy Scripture: A Historical Investigation,* 25, 28. David Dockery also recognises the problems for Luther's view of inspiration raised by his canonical decisions and yet comes to a different conclusion. David S. Dockery, 'Martin Luther's Christological Hermeneutics', *GTJ* 4.2 (1983), 198.

[7] Miikka Ruokanen, *Doctrina Divinitus Inspirata: Martin Luther's position in the ecumenical problem of biblical inspiration,* 102-112.

[8] Miikka Ruokanen, 'Does Luther have a theory of Biblical Inspiration?', *MTheol*, 4 (1987), 12.

inspination.⁹ Friedrich Beisser, while conceding that we search in vain for a clear doctrine of biblical inspiration in Luther, also points to Luther's emphasis on the speech of God (*das Reden Gottes*). The God Luther knew was the speaking God (*der redende Gott*). Beisser insists it was a wrong turn, by implication made later and by others, which allowed people to equate the Word of God and the Bible.¹⁰

A number of other studies of Luther's thought suggest it was Luther's focus on the priority of Jesus Christ as the Word of God which best explains his assertions and his omissions. They emphasise that for Luther the fundamental authority for Christian faith and life was not the Bible but the Son of God himself. On this basis Philip Watson claimed that it would be inconsistent for Luther to invest the Scriptures with the same kind of authority he denied to the papacy:

> For Luther all authority belongs ultimately to Christ, the Word of God, alone, and even the authority of the Scriptures is secondary and derivative, pertaining to them only inasmuch as they bear witness to Christ and are the vehicle of the Word.¹¹

Warren Quanbeck argued that this new perspective on Scripture involved a deliberate departure from the Occamist tradition in which Luther was trained. Whereas the Occamists related biblical authority to its origin in the inspiration of the Holy Spirit, Luther held that Scripture is authoritative 'because it reveals Jesus Christ'.¹² Willem Kooiman developed the implications of this shift. He maintained that the presuppositions of a doctrine such as the verbal inspiration of Holy Scripture would seem to Luther 'too closely associated with a theoretical view of the Bible' which stands in contradiction to his own perspective on Scripture as 'the holy instrument of the *viva vox*

---

⁹ Gerhard Ebeling, *Evangelische Evangelienauslegung: Eine Untersuchung zu Luthers Hermeneutik*, 368.

¹⁰ Friedrich Beisser, 'Luthers Schriftverständnis', in Peter Manns (ed.), *Martin Luther, Reformator und Vater im Glauben*, 32; cf. Krister Stendahl, 'The Word of God and the Words of Luther', in M. J. Harran (ed.), *Luther and Learning: The Wittenberg University Luther Symposium*, 135-140. A more balanced approach is found in William A. Graham, *Beyond the Written Word: Oral Aspects of Scripture in the History of Religion*, 144-153.

¹¹ Philip S. Watson, *Let God Be God! An Interpretation of the Theology of Martin Luther*, 174; cf. James K. S. Reid, *The Authority of Scripture: A Study of the Reformation and Post-Reformation Understanding of the Bible*, 72.

¹² Warren A. Quanbeck, 'Luther's Early Exegesis', in Roland H. Bainton *et al.* (eds.), *Luther Today*, I, 99.

Christi.¹³ More recently, David Lotz has also expounded this argument that the key to Luther's concept of biblical authority is not the divine origin and external characteristics of Scripture, but his 'christological concentration'.¹⁴

Despite these explanations and others, various insistent voices of dissent continue to be raised. These voices maintain that Luther's perspective on Scripture can be discerned despite the absence of a detailed exposition of biblical inspiration. Luther, they insist, can be seen to operate on the basis of presuppositions approximating to a doctrine of verbal inspiration. Adolf von Harnack, for example, felt obliged to admit that Luther related divine inspiration to the words of the biblical text, but described this as an alien intrusion into Luther's own theology. He believed it should be identified as a remnant of 'the Rabbinic-Catholic idea of the verbal inspiration of Holy Scripture (*die rabbinisch-katholische Vorstellung von der wörtlichen Inspiration der hl. Schrift*)' which 'set up the letter as the Word of God (*den Buchstaben als Wort Gottes aufrichtete*)' and demonstrated that Luther 'lacked power to free himself entirely from the authority of the letter (*Die Kraft, die er nicht besass, sich von der Autorität des Buchstabens völlig zu befreien*)'. What is more, it involved Luther in a 'flagrant contradiction (*ein flagranter Widerspruch*)' whenever he engaged in the criticism of the text.¹⁵ Paul Althaus likewise recognised that 'although Luther criticised the Bible in specific details, he nonetheless followed the tradition of his time and accepted it as an essentially infallible book (*wesentlich unfehlbare Buch*), inspired in its entire content by the Holy Spirit (*das mit seinem gesamten Inhalt vom Heiligen Geist inspirierte*)'. Like Harnack, Althaus saw this as regrettable, making it necessary for theology 'to distinguish within Luther himself between that which reflects the historical situation and tradition of his time, and that which belongs properly to the Reformation (*zwischen dem Zeitgebundenen, Traditionellen und dem Reformatorischen*)'.¹⁶ Karl Barth should also be numbered amongst those who admitted Luther's commitment to verbal inspiration while himself raising questions about such a position. With an acknowledged

---

[13] Willem J. Kooiman, *Luther and the Bible*, 236. A similar conclusion had already been reached by Wilhelm Pauck. Wilhelm Pauck, *The Heritage of the Reformation*, 167-169.

[14] David W. Lotz, 'Sola Scriptura: Luther on Biblical Authority', *Int* 35 (1981), 269-270.

[15] C. G. Adolf von Harnack, *History of Dogma*, VII, 235, 246. Harnack went on to lament the fact that 'the church has not the courage and the power to carry on criticism with Luther against Luther' (248).

[16] Paul Althaus, *The Theology of Martin Luther*, 50, 52.

debt to the earlier work of Paul Schempp,[17] Barth includes both Luther and Calvin in his comment:

> The Reformers took over unquestioningly and unreservedly (*unbedenklich und vorbehaltlos*) the statement on the inspiration, and indeed the verbal inspiration, of the Bible (*Verbalinspiration der Bibel*), as it is explicitly and implicitly contained in those Pauline passages which we have taken as our basis, even including the formula that God is the author of the Bible, and occasionally making use of the idea of dictation through the Biblical writers. How could it be otherwise?[18]

Others have been less disturbed as they have come to the conclusion that Luther presupposed the verbal inspiration of the Scriptures. W. Bodamer claimed overwhelming evidence for the proposition that Luther consistently identified Scripture with the Word of God.[19] Michael Reu, in a much maligned yet heavily documented study first published in 1944, argued that Luther held together both a divine involvement in the production of Scripture which extended to the actual words of the text, and a genuine, conscious participation on the part of the human writers. This enabled Reu to distance Luther from those who equated verbal inspiration with a process of mechanical dictation:

> Both facts were certain to Luther: the divine origin of Scripture and its resultant inerrancy, on the one hand, and, on the other, the active cooperation of the human personality of the authors in their composition. The fact that he appreciated the latter distinguishes his view from the inspiration theories of the later dogmaticians [...] that he did not grow weary of emphasising the former, establishes his agreement with them.[20]

---

[17] Paul Schempp, 'Luthers Stellung zur Heiligen Schrift', in Richard Widemann (ed.), *Theologische Entwürfe*, 10-74.

[18] Karl Barth, *Church Dogmatics*, I/2, 520. Roland Bainton could also be considered here. He maintains that 'the main reformers believed in the verbal inspiration of the Scriptures, though for them the phrase did not carry its modern connotations'. Roland H. Bainton, 'The Bible in the Reformation', in S. L. Greenslade (ed.), *Cambridge History of the Bible: The West from the Reformation to the Present Day,* 12. Bainton goes on to identify those connotations as 'inerrancy in all its details', 'impeccability', and 'uniformity in quality and authority' (12-20).

[19] W. Bodamer, 'Luthers Stellung zur Lehre von der Verbalinspiration', *Theologische Quartalschrift* 33 (1936), 241-266; 34 (1937), 171-200.

[20] Michael Reu, *Luther and the Scriptures,* 114-115.

Much of Reu's argument was endorsed by Brian Gerrish in 1957.[21] He went further though, suggesting that Luther oscillated between two positions on the character of Scripture. On the one hand, Luther could argue that the authority of Scripture is derived from its content, namely its testimony to Christ. On the other, he could insist that the authority of Scripture rests on the fact that 'it is the verbally inspired "Word of God"'.[22] Luther apparently saw no contradiction between these two points of view.

Skevington Wood is another who drew such a conclusion from the evidence of Luther's literary deposit. 'So close is the connection between the actual words of the Bible and the instrumentality of the Spirit', Wood argued, 'that it must be concluded that Luther believed, not only in inspiration, but in verbal inspiration'.[23] However, Wood also suggested a deliberate restraint on Luther's part when it came to providing an analysis of the methods involved in the Spirit's inspiration. His conclusion was that both in what he affirmed and in what he refrained from affirming, Luther's 'only aim was to reflect the attitude of Scripture itself'.[24] Eugene Klug agreed, observing that while 'Luther never hedged or fudged in his childlike trust in the Holy Spirit's inspiration of sacred Scripture', he never tried 'to explain the miracle involved in inspiration'. He simply stood back and bowed.[25]

In the light of such diversity of opinion we might well conclude that there can be no definite answer to Walther Rohnert's question: *'Was lehrt Luther von der Inspiration der Heiligen Schrift?'*[26] Yet must we come to that conclusion? Certainly we must beware the danger of trespassing on Luther's silence. The fact that he penned no detailed explanation of biblical inspiration must be given full weight. Nevertheless, it may be productive to ask whether, in the light of the complex of traditions which Luther inherited, his silence is as absolute as some believe. Against the background of biblical, patristic, and medieval discussion, can Luther's own isolated statements and brief

---

[21] Brian A. Gerrish, 'Biblical Authority', 346. Inexplicably, Gerrish removed his endorsement of Reu from the body of the text, without changing the argument of his own article, when it was republished in 1982. Brian A. Gerrish, 'The Word of God and the Words of Scripture: Luther and Calvin on Biblical Authority', in *The Old Protestantism and the New: Essays on the Reformation Heritage*, 57.

[22] Brian A. Gerrish, 'Biblical Authority', 344.

[23] A. Skevington Wood, *Captive to the Word: Martin Luther, Doctor of Sacred Scripture*, 141.

[24] Wood, *Captive*, 148.

[25] Eugene F. Klug, *From Luther to Chemnitz: On Scripture and the Word*, 23-24.

[26] Walther Rohnert, *Was lehrt Luther von der Inspiration der Heiligen Schrift?*

excurses on the subject take on a new perspective? To what extent does he show an awareness of the primary dimensions of a doctrine of biblical inspiration and its implications? In this chapter and the next we examine again the statements of Luther which bear on this subject. What follows is not an attempt to construct for Luther a doctrine of inspiration — the detailed explanation of the origin and nature of Scripture he would have written had his circumstances permitted — but rather an exploration of what he *did* say and how this correlates with his statements on the authority of Scripture and his practice of biblical exegesis and exposition.

God as the Author of Scripture

As we have seen in the centuries between Paul and Luther, most explanations of biblical inspiration have two interrelated concerns: to defend the uniquely divine origin of this text and to reflect upon the consequent nature of the text so originated. In Pauline terms these approximate to the θεόπνευστος and ὠφέλιμος of Scripture.[27] Our initial question is whether there is any evidence that Luther was committed to a particular way of structuring a response to the first of these concerns.

On 9 May 1518 Luther wrote to his former teacher Jodokus Trutvetter, then Professor of Sacred Theology at the University of Erfurt. Luther's *Disputatio contra scholasticam theologiam*[28] had gained him some notoriety in his old university, but now that much of Europe was abuzz with talk of his *Disputatio pro declaratione virtutis indulgentiarum*[29] he apparently felt obliged to explain himself more personally. In the course of that explanation he remarked:

> But father, although I am your student and most submissive servant, this is what makes me bold: that at the beginning I learned everything from you: that I owe allegiance to the canonical books alone, judging all the others, just as Saint Augustine, indeed Paul and John taught.[30]

---

[27] 2 Tim. 3.16-17.
[28] *Disputatio contra scholasticam theologiam* (1517) *WA* I, 224-228 = *LW* 31, 9-16. Luther himself had sent a copy of the theses prepared for this disputation to his former teachers at Erfurt. Brecht, *Road to Reformation*, 173.
[29] *WA* I, 233-238 = *LW* 31, 25-33.
[30] 'sed si pateris discipuli tui et obsequentissimi famuli tui, id est meam confidentiam, ex te primo omnium didici, solis canonicis libris deberi fidem, caeteris omnibus iudicium, ut B. Augustinus, imo Paulus et Iohannes praecipiunt' *Luther an Jodokus Truttfetter* (9 May 1518) *WABr* I, 171.71-73.

There is no reason to doubt Luther's recollection. There was, after all, nothing exceptional about such a commitment to the unique position of Holy Scripture. Luther could (and did) quote both Augustine and Occam in support of it. It was a principle he embraced as part of his general university education in the years from 1501 to 1505.[31] However it was Luther's application of this principle which generated conflict. Later that same year he would find himself opposed to the papal legate himself, Cardinal Cajetan, when at Augsburg he protested Cajetan's appeal to the 1343 papal bull *Unigenitus* of Clement VI (contained in an appendix of the *Corpus Iuris Canonici* and thus known as *Extravagante*):

> Therefore I do not care whether this statement is contrary to an *Extravagante* or an *Intravagante*. The truth of Scripture comes first. After that is accepted one may determine whether the words of men can be accepted as true.[32]

The point of conflict, it might be argued, centred not so much on his high view of Scripture as on his progressive inclusion of first the writings of the fathers and doctors, then papal decrees, and finally the determinations of General Councils, under the general rubric 'the words of men'.

Luther's ascription of a unique place to Holy Scripture is intrinsically linked to his convictions about its origins. Again, this is nothing exceptional. It is precisely what one would expect from a scholar steeped in the Occamist tradition. However, this is not just the case in Luther's earliest theological writing. He could still make this connection twenty years later, long after his famous comment that he had contradicted 'even my own school of Occamists'.[33] Commenting on Jn. 15:5 in 1538, and exploring the way instruction about everyday matters has been implanted in nature and written on human hearts, he continues 'all books, with the exception of Holy Scripture are derived from that source and spring'.[34] Human literature, sacred and secular,

---

[31] Brecht, *Road to Reformation*, 34-35.

[32] 'Igitur an sit ista propostio contra vel Extravagantem vel Intravagantem, non curo: prior est veritas scripturae, et post hoc, si hominis verba vera esse possunt, videndum.' *Acta F. Martini Luther Augustiniani apud D. Legatum Apostolicum Augustae* (1518) *WA* II, 21.4-6 = *LW* 31, 282.

[33] 'Alioqui, cur et meae sectae resisterem, scilicet Occamiae seu Modernorum, quam penitus imbittitam teneo, si verbis voluissem aut vi compesci?' *Responsio ad condemnationem doctrinalem per Magistros Nostros Lovanienses at Colonienses factam* (1520) *WA* VI, 195.4.

[34] 'Da zu alle bucher, so geschrieben sind ausser der heiligen Schrifft, sind aus dem vorn und quell gefurt.' *Das XIV und XV Kapitel S. Johannis* (1538/9) *WA* XLV, 669.27-29 = *LW* 24, 228.

arises from the structures of the life we live, Luther argued. However, the kingdom of God is a reality which cuts across these everyday structures. Two years later, when a German edition of his works was produced in Wittenberg, Luther would insist on distinguishing them from the Scripture in similar terms. 'Neither councils, fathers, nor we, in spite of the greatest and best success possible, will do as well as the Holy Scriptures, that is, as well as God himself (*als die heilige Schrifft, das ist Gott selbs*) has done'.[35]

The basic dynamic at work in Scripture, according to Luther, is that God is speaking. That is why, he told his students in the midst of lectures on the Book of Judges in 1516, the preacher cannot be effective without the Scriptures:

> If you want to be a leader of war, that is to say a preacher, you will not be bold or very confident without Sacred Scripture, because [in such a case] it is impossible for you to succeed. For the gospel must be heard as if the Lord is present, as if we hear Christ talking. That precious thing which sounds from the mouth of the Lord, has been written for us, preserved for us, recited for us, and will be recited for pastors until the ages end [... this message] is chiefly for us clerics, who all want to be Judah and teach or preach but do not want to touch Simeon the brother of Judah (i. e. to Sacred Scripture) even with the tip of our fingernail. And so it happens that our doctrine and our life are despised simultaneously.[36]

This spiritual interpretation of the agreement between the tribes of Judah and Simeon to work together in their struggle against the Canaanites and Perizzites is instructive for two reasons.[37] Firstly it demonstrates that Luther's characteristic stress on the orality of the

---

[35] 'Denn so gut werdens weder Concilia, Veter, noch wir machen, wens auch auffs höhest und beste geraten kan, als die heilige Schrifft, das ist Gott selbs, gemacht hat.' *Vorrede zum 1. Bande der Wittenberger Ausgabe der deutschen Schriften* (1539) *WA* L, 657.25-27 = *LW* 34, 284.

[36] 'si vis esse dux belli, scilicet predicator, non sis audax aut nimium confidens sine sacra scriptura, quia impossibile est quin vincaris. Nam euangelium audiendum est, quasi dominum presentem, quasi Christum loquentem audiamus: quod enim pretiosum sonabat de ore Domini, et propter nos scriptum est et nobis servatum et propter nos recitatur et propter pastores recitabitur et donec seculum finiatur [...] Maxime autem nobis religiosis, qui omnes esse volumus Iudas, omnes volumus docere et predicare. Sed Symeonem fratrem Iudae sive sacram scripturam nec extremis volumus attingere unguiculis. Inde etiam venit, ut et doctrina simul et vita nostra despiciatur.' *Praelectio in librum Iudicium* (1516) *WA* IV, 534.36-535.4, 535.9-12.

[37] Jdg. 1:3–4.

gospel is present very early in his theological career. This 'rhetoric of the Word' puts a premium on the task of preaching but that is not all it does.[38] As is explicit here, it accents the presentness of Christ and dismisses any suggestion that theology is talk about God which is somehow done in his absence. As the gospel is proclaimed, Luther emphasises, 'we hear Christ talking'. Secondly, and more to the point in this particular context, it reveals that the written dimension of the gospel is not jettisoned in his bid to accent the oral dimension. The gospel might sound (*sonabat*) from the mouth of the Lord and be recited (*recitatur*) to us, but that is not all there is to say: it has also been written (*scriptum est*) and preserved (*servatum*). The writtenness of the text is not an obstacle to the voice of Christ.

The image of God 'speaking' his word to his people, both in the original setting and in the present, features in Luther's writing about Scripture throughout his life. On many occasions he would simply speak in general terms. In 1521 Luther's reply to Latomus included a plea to stick with the words of Scripture and the meaning of those words in Scripture. The way to ensure the truthfulness of dogmatic formulations, he insisted, was to let the Bible itself control the language we use. His basis for this advice was the conviction that the words of the text are the words which have come from the mouth of God:

> The integrity of Scripture must be guarded, and a man ought not to presume that he speaks more safely and clearly with his own mouth than God has spoken with his mouth.[39]

These words spoken by God are not simply abstract and without a context, according to Luther. They are not to be appropriated in an undifferentiated way, as if God's address consisted merely of timeless truths equally and identically applicable to every generation and situation. Certainly Luther seemed to suggest just that in his 1516 lectures on Romans. There, as he expounded the implications of Rom. 3:21-22, he insisted that 'we must accept every word that is spoken [in the prophets] as if the Lord Himself were speaking, no matter by whom it is spoken'.[40] However, in his pamphlet, first preached amidst a series of sermons on Exodus 19 at Wittenberg on 27 August 1525,

---

[38] Graham, *Beyond*, 147-151.

[39] 'scripturae enim sinceritas, custodienda est, nec praesumat homo suo ore eloqui, aut clarius aut securius, quam deus elocutus est ore suo.' *Rationis Latomianae confutatio* (1521) *WA* VIII, 118.4-5 = *LW* 32, 244.

[40] 'Ideo in prophetis vocem absolute Domini appellat, Vt omne verbum vocale, per quemcunque dicatur.' *Divi Pauli apostoli ad Romanos Epistola. Die Glossen* (1516) *WA* LVI, 253.16-17 = *LW* 25, 239-240.

The Very Words of God? 57

Luther encouraged his contemporaries to 'deal cleanly with the Scriptures (*der schrifft feuberlich handeln und faren*)':

> One must deal cleanly with the Scriptures. From the very beginning the word has come to us in various ways. It is not enough simply to look and see whether this is God's word, whether God has said it; rather we must look and see to whom it has been spoken, whether it fits us. That makes all the difference between summer and winter. God said to David, 'Out of you shall come the king', etc. But this does not pertain to me, nor has it been spoken to me. He can indeed speak to me if he chooses to do so. You must keep your eye on the word that applies to you, that is spoken to you and not what applies to another.[41]

Luther himself would find this a difficult distinction to make, as evidenced by his continued use of allegorical interpretation as a device for discerning the text's message for his own time, albeit in a much more attenuated form after around 1515. However, whether to us or to them, Luther had no doubt that it was God who was doing the speaking. That is why he was able to give this advice in one of his last tracts against the Pope, published in 1545: 'He who wants to hear God speak should read Holy Scripture'.[42] It is significant here that he holds hearing and reading together without any sense of tension.[43]

Yet alongside these general references to God speaking his word as Scripture is read, Luther made numerous references of a more specific kind. On occasion he could attribute the speaking to Christ, as we have seen in connection with his lectures on Judges in 1516. In the midst of

---

[41] 'man mus mit der schrifft seuberlich handeln und faren, Das wort ist nu mancherley weise geschehen von anfang, man mus nicht allein ansehen, ob es Gottes wort sey, ob es Gott geredt hab, sondern viel mehr, zu wem es geredt sey, ob es dich treffe oder einen andern, da scheydet sichs denn wie sommer und winter. Gott hat zu David viel geredt, hat yhn heyssen dis und jhenes thuen, Aber es gehet mich nicht an, est ist auch zu mir nicht geredt, Er kan es wol zu mir reden, wil er es haben, Du must auff das wort sehen, das dich betrifft, das zu dir geredt wird undnicht was einen andern antrifft.' *Eyn unterrichtung, wie sich die Christen ynn Mosen sollen schicken* (1525) *WA* XVI, 384.33-385.25 = *LW* 35, 170.

[42] 'Wer Gott wil hören reden, der lese die heilige Schrifft.' *Wider das Papstum zu Rom, vom Teufel gestifft* (1545) *WA* LIV, 263.14-15 = *LW* 41, 332.

[43] Graham is surely right to point out that like all his contemporaries, Luther would have been far more attuned to the sound than to the look of a text. Graham, *Beyond,* 150. Beisser refers to an important lecture given by K. Burdach in 1903 in which the distinctively oral nature of the German language in High Middle Ages was explored in some depth. Friedrich Beisser, *Claritas Scripturae bei Martin Luther,* 83.

controversy in 1520, he protested that those who attacked the Scripture in effect made liars out of 'my Lord Christ and the Holy Spirit'.[44] Much later, as he explained Galatians 2.6 in the Great Commentary of 1535, Luther picked up the same idea: God 'does not want us to admire and adore the apostolate in the persons of Peter and Paul, but the Christ who speaks in them and the Word of God itself that proceeds from their mouth'.[45]

Most frequently it is the Holy Spirit whom Luther represents as speaking Scripture into existence and speaking through Scripture today. In 1521 Luther answered Emser's claim that the Spirit has spoken through the fathers by insisting that 'If the Spirit spoke in the fathers, he spoke even more in his own Scripture'.[46] In the argument which followed he made the patristic claim to the authority of the Spirit contingent upon their proper use of the Scriptures. Five years later, he dismissed the charge that difficulties in the text of Habakkuk demonstrate the Holy Spirit is 'unable to express himself' by arguing that the problem here is not with the text but with those who read it. 'The Holy Spirit is wise and he also makes his prophets wise', Luther protested, and 'a wise man must necessarily be able to speak well'.[47] In 1532 he challenged those who evaluated Christian doctrine on the basis of human reason by reaffirming that Scripture is 'revealed

---

[44] 'wer meynenn hern Christum, durch mich geprediget, unnd den heyligenn geyst zu lugenern machen wil.' *Von dem Papstthum zu Rom wider hochberühmten Romanisten zu Leipzig* (1520) *WA* VI, 323.11-19 = *LW* 39, 103.

[45] 'In Petro et Paulo non vult nos admirari vel adorare Apostolatum, sed Christum in eis loquentem et ipsum verbum Dei, quod de ore ipsorum egreditur.' *In epistolam S. Pauli ad Galatas Commentarius* (1535) *WA* XL-I, 173.21-23 = *LW* 26, 94.

[46] 'Hatt der geyst ynn den vettern geredt, so hatt er vil mehr yn seyner eygen schrifft geredt.' *Auf das überchristlich, übergeistlich und überkunstlich Buch Bocks Emsers zu Leipzig Antwort* (1521) *WA* VII, 638.30-31 = *LW* 39, 164.

[47] 'Nu ists gar unlustig ding, eyn buch lesen, das keine ordnunge helt, da man nicht kan eyns zum andern bringen und an einander hengen, das sichs fein nach einander spünne, wie sichs denn gepürt, wo man recht und wol reden wil. Also hat der heylige geyst mussen die schuld haben, das er nicht wol reden kunde; sondern wie ein trunckenbold odder ein narr redet, so menge ers ynn einander und fure wilde seltzame wort und sprüche. Es ist aber unser schuld, die wyr die sprache nicht verstanden noch der Propheten weyse gewuste haben. Denn das kan yhe nicht anders sein: Der heylige geyst ist weyse und macht die Propheten auch weyse. Ein weyser aber mus wol reden konnen, das feylet nymer mehr.' *Der Prophet Habakuk ausgelegt* (1526) *WA* XIX, 350.15-24 = *LW* 19, 152.

through the Holy Spirit'.[48] This understanding of the relationship between the Holy Spirit and the Scripture explains Luther's practice of introducing quotations from either the Old Testament or the New Testament with the formula 'the Holy Spirit says'.[49] In the end, as he said in 1543, 'we attribute to the Holy Spirit all of Holy Scripture'. However, he does go on to add 'and the external word and sacrament'.[50]

It is the language of speaking which also allows Luther to posit an indissoluble link between the original work of the Spirit in the production of Scripture and the same Spirit's ongoing work of addressing the world, and especially the believer, in Scripture. Luther finds no difficulty in using the present tense of the Holy Spirit's speech. In 1532 he encouraged his readers to devote themselves to the study of Scripture and to marshal biblical texts in support of the articles of faith. Then, he advised, when assaulted by either Satan or heretics they should proclaim 'This is what the Holy Spirit says'.[51] As he expounded Genesis 12 in 1537 he could say the Holy Spirit 'provides instruction',[52] 'commands us',[53] 'impresses comfort on us',[54] and 'points out a hypothetical assertion'.[55] Indeed, a few years earlier (6 November 1527) he had remarked:

---

[48] 'Si possem ista assequi ratione aut sensibus, quid opus esset fide? quid opus esset scriptura divinitus per scriptum sanctum revelata?' *Praelectio in psalmum 45* (1532) *WA* XL-II, 593.24-25 = *LW* 12, 288.

[49] E.g. 'Spiritus sanctus loquitur' *Enarratio Psalmi LI* (1532) *WA* XL-II, 370.18 = *LW* 12, 340 (quoting Psalm 32:5; 'Sanctus spiritus [...] dixit' In *epistolam S. Pauli ad Galatas Commentarius* (1535) *WA* XL-I, 423.22 = *LW* 26, 270 (quoting Gal. 3:12 in 1535).

[50] 'Also gibt man nu dem Heiligen Geist die gantze Heilige Schrifft und das eusserliche wort und sacrament.' *Von den letzten worten Davids* (1543) WA LIV, 35.2-4 = *LW* 15, 275.

[51] 'Ergo vos, qui incumbitis sacris literis, ante omnia constituite, quid credatis in religione Christiana, ut habeatis articulos fidei munitos bonis textibus scripturae sanctae et bene meditatos. Deinde, quando tecum volunt disputare vel Satan vel eius instrumenta, haeretici, tunc obiice eis illos textus et desere eos, dicens: cavillationes et speculaciones tuas audire nolo. Hoc enim dicit spiritus sanctus ...' *Praelectio in psalmum 45* (1532) *WA* XL-II, 592.32-37 = *LW* 12, 287.

[52] '[D]octrinam ostendit Spiritus sanctus' *Genesisvorlesung* (1535-45) WA XLII, 474.6 = *LW* 2, 296.

[53] 'Spiritus sanctus autem iubet praesentia negligi, et intueri in futura' *Genesisvorlesung* (1535-45) WA XLII, 482.19-20 = *LW* 2, 308.

[54] 'Haec consolatio per totam scripturam a spiritu sancto inculcatur' *Genesisvorlesung* (1535-45) WA XLII, 482.28-29 = *LW* 2, 308.

[55] 'Spiritus sanctus autem Hypotheticam (sicut in Scholis vocant) ostendit' *Genesisvorlesung* (1535-45) *WA* XLII, 482.5 = *LW* 2, 307.

Above all, therefore, one must listen to and read the Word, which is the vehicle of the Holy Spirit. When the Word is read, the Holy Spirit is present; and thus it is impossible either to listen to or to read Scripture without profit.[56]

However, it is worth noting that Luther is quite prepared to go beyond the speech of God in this connection and actually use the language of authorship. He was prepared to apply such language to each member of the Godhead. When, in the course of his exposition on Galatians 3:14, Luther reflected on the possibility of his opponents collecting a selection of biblical proof-texts about works, he spoke of Christ as Lord of Scripture and went on to claim 'I have the Author and Lord of Scripture'.[57] In 1542 he spoke of how he believed firmly that 'the Holy Spirit Himself and God, the Creator of all things, is the Author of this book [Genesis]'.[58] Later in the same course of lectures he could say: 'One must always keep in view what I emphasise so often, namely, that the Holy Spirit is the Author of this book'.[59] Related to these affirmations are comments such as 'the Holy Spirit wanted this committed to writing',[60] and even 'the Holy Spirit has written down [these things]'.[61]

---

[56] 'Itaque ante omnia audiendum et legendum verbum, quod vehiculum Spiritus Sancti est. Lecto verbo adest Spiritus Sanctus et sic impossibile est vel audire vel legere Scripturas sine fructu.' *Vorlesung über den 1 Brief des Johannes* (1527) *WA* XX, 790.24-27 = *LW* 30, 321; cf. *In epistolam S. Pauli ad Galatas Commentarius* (1535) *WA* XL-I, 572.16 = *LW* 26, 375.

[57] 'Ego Autorem et Dominum Scripturae habeo' *In epistolam S. Pauli ad Galatas Commentarius* (1535) *WA* XL-I, 458.33-34 = *LW* 26, 295; cf. four lines later: 'Ego cum Autore Scripturae maneo'.

[58] 'Si firmiter crederemus, sicut ego, licet infirmiter credo, spiritum sanctum ipsum et Deum, conditorem omnium rerum, esse authorem huius libri et rerum tam vilium, ut videntur carni: tunc haberemus maximam consolationem.' *Genesisvorlesung* (1535-45) *WA* XLIII, 618.31-33 = *LW* 5, 275.

[59] 'Semper conspectu habendum est, quod toties inculco, Spiritum Sanctum esse authorem huius libri.' *Genesisvorlesung* (1535-45) cf. later in the same lecture series, *WA* XLIII, 671.33-35 = *LW* 5, 352 and *WA* XLIV, 532.20-21 = *LW* 7, 314.

[60] 'Spiritus sanctus id literis voluit mandari' *Genesisvorlesung* (1535-45) *WA* XLII, 474.3-5 = *LW* 2, 296.

[61] 'sie der Heilige Geist beschrieben hatt' *Auslegung des dritten und vierten Kapitels Johannis* (1538-40) *WA* XLVII, 133.4-5 = *LW* 22, 415; cf. 'hae sunt revelationes spiritus sancti' *Genesisvorlesung* (1535-45) *WA* XLII, 482.10 = *LW* 2, 307; 'Saepe monui et semper est inculcandum, quod spiritus sanctus de tantis Patriarchis scribit iocularia et levicula' *Genesisvorlesung* (1535-45) *WA* XLIV, 563.8-9 = *LW* 7, 354.

There is, therefore, overwhelming evidence that Luther accepted the generally held view that the Scriptures have their peculiar origin in the activity of God. God has spoken this text and in this text God continues to speak. We must return to the question of how these two statements are related to each other. However for present purposes it is sufficient to recognise that Luther was not at all uncomfortable with the suggestion that God Himself is the author of Holy Scripture.

The Human Writers as the Authors of Scripture

One might think that such bold statements from Luther call into question any significant commitment to genuine human authorship. After all, Luther repeatedly emphasised a distinction between Holy Scripture and 'the words of men'. He could, at points, even go so far as to say that every piece of writing except Scripture is a purely human product.[62] Notwithstanding such comments, almost inevitable in the polemical contexts in which they are found, there is ample evidence that Luther did indeed take the human authorship of the Scriptures seriously.[63]

In the first place, just as Luther could attribute an individual text to God, he could also mention its human author without any reference to its divine dimension. Once again this can be demonstrated in material from every period of his life. In his early lectures on Psalms, for all the accent on spiritual meanings intended by God, he could still unambiguously talk of David confessing his own innocence.[64] In the 1517 lectures on Hebrews, he could describe the author writing 'as one learned in the Scriptures'.[65] In the same series he would speak of Paul

---

[62] 'Da zu alle bucher, so geschrieben sind ausser der heiligen Schrifft, sind aus dem Vorn und quell gefurt, Darumb mus man Christi lere und Wort dahin nicht zihen, als habe er etwas anders, mehr oder bessers wollen leren und ordnen.' *Das XIV und XV Kapitel S. Johannis* (1537-8) *WA* XLV, 669.27-29 = *LW* 24, 228.

[63] This is the conclusion of, amongst others, Lewis W. Spitz, 'Luther's Sola Scriptura', *CTM* 31 (1960), 744; Klug, *Luther*, 21; Julius Köstlin, *The Theology of Luther in its Historical Development and Inner Harmony*, 252.

[64] 'Hoc sufficit, Quod David in dorso huius Psalmi ipsam suam innocentiam confitetur et ex ipsa hystoria eruditus prophetat de Innocentia Christi. Loquitur in persona nature assumpte, non aperte, Sed in figura. Seu Sic loquitur Dauid figuratiue de Christo quasi de se sumpta occasione ex casu suo.' *Dictata Super Psalterium* (1513-15) *WA* LV-I, 46.16-48.15.

[65] 'Cur autem hac observatione loquitur, ut dicat: "in diebus carnis suae", cum sufficere videretur "in diebus suis"? Respondetur: Hoc fecit ut eruditus in Scripturis, siquidem Christus, sicut duplicis est naturae persona, temporalis et aeternae, ita Scriptura tribuit ei duplices dies, tempora et secula. Nam

following the Septuagint translation at one point.[66] One part of his 1519 dispute with Eck was apparently supported by the argument that, in the text then under discussion, Paul makes no mention of Peter.[67]

The first section of Luther's 1522 treatise, *Von Menschenlehre zu meiden,* demonstrates that this awareness of genuine human authorship continued past the point of breach with Rome and the Empire:

> Moses says in Deuteronomy 4, 'You shall not add anything to the word which I speak to you, nor take anything from it'. Now some will say that Moses here speaks only of his own word, for many books of the prophets as well as the entire New Testament have been added beyond the books of Moses. I reply: Nevertheless nothing new has been added, for the same thing that is found in the books of Moses is found also in the others. These other books, while using different words and narratives, do nothing more than illustrate how the word of Moses has been kept or not kept. Throughout them all there is one and the same teaching and thought. And here we can challenge them to show us one word in all the books outside those of Moses that is not already found in the books of Moses. For this much is beyond question, that all the Scriptures point to Christ alone.[68]

Micheae dicitur cap. 5.: "Egressus eius ab initio, a diebus aeternitatis", ubi iterum "dies" collective dicit, scilicet ipsam aeternam claritatem. Quam vocat pluraliter "dies aeternitatis" ad differentiam dierum temporalitatis, a qua coepit "egredi in Bethlehem dominator in Israel". Sic Esaias 26. manifeste distinguens secula dicit: "Sperastis in Domino in seculis aeternis", id est sperastis in eum, qui est Dominus, in seculis aeternis. Hinc ista vox in psalmis: "in seculum" et "in seculum seculi". Et ad Titum 1.: "Quam promisit Deus ante tempora secularia et mundana." Ita ergo hic Paulus "dies carnis Christi" vocat tempus vitae huius praesentis ad differentiam dierum divinitatis eius.' *Commentariolus in epistolam divi Pauli Apostoli ad Hebreos* (1517) *WA* LVII-III, 173.4-18 = *LW* 29, 174-175.

[66] 'Superest illud: 'Aures autem perfecisti mihi', quonam modo consonet huic: 'Corpus aptasti mihi.' In Haebreo verbum est aequivocum, quod 'aptare, parare, ordinare', item 'fodere' et 'aperire', item 'emere' quoque significat. Ideo LXX primam secuti significationem dixerunt 'corpus' pro 'auribus'. Sic enim in Haebreo, 'corpus' autem non habetur. Quare eorum sensum Apostolus hic sequitur intelligens aptatum corpus Christi id esse, quod pro corporibus pecudum propter peccata sit oblatum, ut sequitur in textu. Haebreum vero aliud sonat.' *Commentariolus in epistolam divi Pauli Apostoli ad Hebreos* (1517) *WA* LVII-III, 220.15-221.1 = *LW* 29, 223.

[67] *Disputatio I. Eccii et M. Luther Lipsiae habita* (1519) *WA* II, 263.20-30 (the text concerned is 1 Cor. 3:4ff.).

[68] 'Moses Deuteronomio, das ist, ym funfften buch am vierden Capitel spricht: Ihr sollt nichts tzu thun tzu dem wortt, das ich euch sage, und auch nichts davon thun.' Wirt aber yemand sagen, das Moses rede von seynem wort

Luther's choice of expression here is all the more notable given the general argument of the treatise. In a treatise warning about the dangers of human doctrine, Luther dares to speak of the words of Moses without a reference to the Holy Spirit.[69] The preface to his 1525 commentary on Deuteronomy described it as 'the Deuteronomy of Moses' and describes Moses as 'the foremost and chief among the authors of all the sacred books'.[70]

In a piece of the *Tischreden* from Spring 1533 Luther responded to a question about the Book of Job. Luther suggested that the author of this enigmatic Old Testament book 'wished to paint a picture of patience'. He then took further a discussion of the human dimensions of the book:

> It's possible that Solomon himself wrote this book for the style is not very different from his. At the time of Solomon the story which he undertook to write was old and well known. It was as if I today were to take up the stories of Joseph or Rebekah. The Hebrew poet, whoever he was, saw and wrote about those temptations, just as Vergil described Aeneas, led him through all the seas and resting places, and made him a statesman and soldier. Whoever wrote Job, it appears that he was a great theologian.[71]

---

allein, Denn uber Moses bücher sind auch vil Propheten bücher und das gantz new testament dazu than. Antwort: eß ist aber nichts newes datzu than, ßondern eben dasselb, das yn Moses büchern steht, das steht yn den andern. Denn die andern bücher thun nichts mehr denn tzeygen die exempel, wye Moses wort gehalten odder nicht gehalten sey, Und wirtt woll mit anderley worten und geschichten beschriben. Eß ist aber alles die selbige eynige lere und meynung. Und hie ist zu trotzen wider sie, Das sie yn allen büchern außer Moses bücher eyn wortt tzeygen, das nicht tzuvor yn Moses buch erfunden werd. Denn das ist ungetzweyfflet, das die gantze schrifft auff Christum allein ist gericht.' *Von Menschenlehre zu meiden* (1522) *WA* X-II, 73.3-16 = *LW* 35, 132.

[69] Note, however, that Luther insists 'we do not condemn the doctrines of men just because they are the doctrines of men but because [...] they are contrary to the Scriptures (Menschen lere taddelln wyr nicht darumb, das menschen gesagt haben, ßondern das es lügen und gottis lesterung sind widder die schrifft)' *Von Menschenlehre zu meiden* (1522) *WA* X-II, 92.4-6 = *LW* 35, 153.

[70] 'Non quod dignum existimem tanto, viro, quicquid mea tenuitas in praestantissimo et principe omnium sacrorum librorum autore tentauit.' *Deuteronomion Mosi cum annotationibus* (1525) *WA* XIV, 497.11-14 = *LW* 9, 3.

[71] 'Voluit pingere exemplum patientiae. Possibile est, das es wol Salomo selb gemacht hab; phrasis non multum est dissimilis. Fuit vetus et celebris historia tempore Salomonis, quam suscepit scribendam, ac si ego nunc accipiam historiam Ioseph vel Rebeccam. Hebreus poeta, quisquis fuit, vidit tentationes

This record of Luther's dinner conversation, from the generally reliable Veit Dietrich, is instructive at a number of points.[72] Firstly, it reveals that Luther felt free to recognise differences of style amongst the biblical writings and to attribute those differences to the human writers of each book. He quite clearly had moved beyond any suggestion of an ahistorical, one-dimensional text which demanded uniform treatment throughout. Secondly, it reveals a characteristic of Luther's approach to unresolved issues to do with the text: he is both concerned to identify the nature of the issue (in this case the anonymous nature of the Book of Job) as well as to proffer a suggestion which nevertheless always remains tentative. Thirdly, this comment reveals that Luther's approach to Scripture cannot be completely isolated from his broader theological concerns. Here it appears he is prepared to evaluate the work of the biblical writer in terms of a fundamental principle of the *theologia crucis:* 'Not understanding, reading, or speculation, but living, no, dying and being damned make a theologian'.[73]

The 1535 Galatians commentary alone provides sufficient evidence that this perspective survived despite Luther's insistence that God is the author of Holy Scripture. Luther begins by outlining 'the issue with which Paul deals in this epistle', arguing that 'Paul wants to establish the doctrine of faith, grace, the forgiveness of sins or Christian righteousness'.[74] When he turns to the exposition of Galatians itself, Luther refers to Paul's 'composition of the epistle' and 'his discussion of righteousness'.[75] Paul is the subject of many of the verbs associated

---

illa et scripsit, sicut Vergilius Aeneam describit und furet yhn per omnia maria et hospitia, macht yhn politicum et militarem. Apparet fuisse magnum theologum, quisquis Hiobem scripsit.' *Tischreden* #475 (1533) *WATr* I, 207.2-9 = *LW* 54, 79-80.

[72] On the reliability of the Table Talk and its various contributors, see Theodore Tappert's comment in *LW* 54, xv-xxiii.

[73] 'Vivendo, immo moriendo et damnando fit theologus, non intelligendo, legendo aut speculando.' *Operationes in Psalmos* (1519-21) *WA* V, 163.28-29.

[74] 'Primum omnium dicendum est de argumento, hoc est, de qua re agat Paulus in hac Epistola. Est autem hoc argumentum: Paulus vult stabilire doctrinam illam fidei, Gratiae, Remissionis peccatorum seu Iustitiae Christianae.' *In epistolam S Pauli ad Galatas Commentarius* (1535) *WA* XL-I, 40.15-18, = *LW* 26,4.

[75] 'Nunc argumento tradito et ostensa summa huius Epistolae ad Galatas praemittemus, antequam ad rem ipsam veniamus, quae occasio fuerit Paulo scribendae huius Epistolae [...] Dixi supra Paulum in hac Epistola occasionem tractandi de Christiana iusticia hinc sumpsisse' *In epistolam S. Pauli ad Galatas Commentarius* (1535) *WA* XL-I, 52.11-13, 54.15-16 = *LW* 26,13, 14.

The Very Words of God? 65

with the content of the letter.[76] When Luther takes issue with an interpretation of Jerome and Erasmus, he accuses them of 'doing Paul an injustice'.[77] Others who use Galatians 5:6 to teach the necessity of both faith and love in justification are said to 'suppress the true and genuine meaning of Paul'.[78] As we have seen, Luther is convinced that 'the Word of God proceeds from the mouths' of the apostles Peter and Paul.[79]

It is not surprising, then, that in Luther's last great exegetical work, the 1535-1545 lectures on Genesis, we find alongside his repeated emphasis on the Holy Spirit as 'the Author of this book' a plethora of references to the literary work of Moses.[80] He opened the lectures with a discussion of how we are to understand the account of creation in Genesis 1. In this context he referred to Augustine's view that the universe was created instantaneously and that the six days of Genesis are 'days of knowledge among the angels'. Luther considered such a resort to allegory as unnecessary and concludes:

> Therefore so far as this opinion of Augustine is concerned, we assert that Moses spoke in the literal sense, not allegorically or figuratively, i.e., that the world, with all its creatures, was created within six days,

---

[76] Note the following instances just in the first chapter of the 1535 Galatians commentary: *WA* XL-I, 53.19 = *LW* 26,14; *WA* XL-I, 56.14 = *LW* 26, 15; *WA* XL-I, 65.10 = *LW* 26,21; *WA* XL-I, 80.17 = *LW* 26,30; *WA* XL-I, 83.14 = *LW* 26,32; *WA* XL-I, 84.26 = *LW* 26, 33; *WA* XL-I, 94.14 = *LW* 26, 39; *WA* XL-I, 98.14-15 = *LW* 26, 42; *WA* XL-I, 107.19 = *LW* 26, 48; *WA* XL-I, 110.28 = *LW* 26, 51; *WA* XL-I, 111.28 = *LW* 26, 52; *WA* XL-I, 119.18 = *LW* 26, 56; *WA* XL-I, 127.21 = *LW* 26, 62; *WA* XL-I, 135.13, 15 = *LW* 26, 68; *WA* XL-I, 146.18, 146.28 = *LW* 26, 76.

[77] 'Quare iniuriam faciunt Paulo Hieronymus et Erasmus qui particulam: "secundum faciem" exponunt.' *In epistolam S. Pauli ad Galatas Commentarius* (1535) *WA* XL-I, 195.11-12 = *LW* 26, 108.

[78] 'Clara enim et aperta sunt verba Pauli: "Fides per charitatem OPERATUR". Quare manifestum, furtum est, quod illi vero et germano sensu Pauli sublato pro "operari" intelligunt iustificari et per "opera" iusticiam, cum etiam in morali Philosophia fateri cogantur opera non esse iusticiam, sed a iustitia fieri opera.' *In epistolam S. Pauli ad Galatas Commentarius* (1535) *WA* XL-II, 35.27-31 = *LW* 27, 29.

[79] 'In Petro et Paulo non vult nos admirari vel adorare Apostolatum, sed Christum in eis loquentem et ipsum verbum Dei, quod de ore ipsorum egreditur.' *In epistolam S. Pauli ad Galatas Commentarius* (1535) *WA* XL-I, 173.21 = *LW* 26, 94.

[80] An observation made some time ago in J. H. Johansen, 'Martin Luther on Scripture and Authority and the Church, Ministry and Sacraments', *SJT* 15 (1962), 355.

as the words read. If we do not comprehend the reason for this, let us remain pupils and leave the job of teacher to the Holy Spirit.[81]

Luther can refer to Moses' literary intention and the Holy Spirit's teaching role in the same context and without even a hint of tension or difficulty. To acknowledge the Holy Spirit's use of precisely this text (the words as they read) to teach us does not, it appeared to Luther, eliminate Moses' conscious involvement in selecting the mode of discourse. Indeed, within the space of a few lines he can dismiss the opinions of philosophers about creation saying 'Let us turn to Moses as the better teacher'.[82] It is Moses who recounts the story of Abraham and the birth of Ishmael,[83] Moses who chooses not to record the details of Abraham's habit of fasting,[84] Moses who related that Isaac buried his father Abraham with reverence,[85] and Moses who records that Jacob offered sacrifices to the God of his father.[86]

As we have already noted in passing, Luther's references to genuine human authorship of the biblical texts include a recognition that the human writers made decisions about vocabulary, expression, and style. When Luther introduced his sermons on 1 Peter in 1522, he felt free both to compare and contrast the work of Peter and that of Paul: 'Therefore, what is preached about Christ is all one Gospel, although every writer has his own distinctive literary style'.[87] In 1535 Luther

---

[81] 'Quod igitur ad hanc Augustini sententiam attinet, statuimus Mosen proprie locutum, non allegorice aut figurate, hoc est, mundum cum omnibus Creaturis intra sex dies, ut verba sonant, creatum esse. Quodsi causam non adsequimur, maneamus discipuli et relinquamus magisterium Spiritui sancto.' *Genesisvorlesung* (1535-45) *WA* XLII, 5.15-18 = *LW* 1, 5.

[82] 'Quare omissis istis non necessariis accedamus ad Mosen tanquam meliorem Doctorem.' *Genesisvorlesung* (1535-45) *WA* XLII, 5.30-31 = *LW* 1, 6.

[83] 'Hactenus recitavit Moses historiam Abrahae usque ad nativitatem Ismaelis.' *Genesisvorlesung* (1535-45) *WA* XLII, 601.30-31 = *LW* 3, 75.

[84] 'Abrahae non fuisset difficile certis diebus ieiunare, id quod sine dubio fecit, sed de ieiunio eius nihil scribit Moses, voluit enim veras virtutes eius scribere, non talia opera, quae hypocritae imitari possunt et solent.' *Genesisvorlesung* (1535-45) *WA* XLIII, 20.3-6 = *LW* 3, 203.

[85] 'Item Moses narravit supra sepeliisse eum cum reverentia patrem suum Abraham, quod argumento est, non fuisse eum alienum ab Ecclesia, quae fuit in domo Isaac.' *Genesisvorlesung* (1535-45) *WA* XLIII, 372.15-17 = *LW* 4, 327.

[86] 'Cum enim scribit Moses Iacob sacrificasse sacrificia Deo patris sui Isaac.' *Genesisvorlesung* (1535-45) *WA* XLIV, 634.38-39 = *LW* 8, 75.

[87] 'Drumb ist es alles ein Evangelion, was man predigt von Christo, wie wol eyner eyn andere weyß furet und mit andern worten davon redet denn der ander.' *Epistel Sanct Petri gepredigt und ausgelegt* (1522-3) *WA* XII, 260.1-3 = *LW* 30, 3.

could refer to the evangelist Matthew's expression,[88] in 1539 to John's delight in a particular way of speaking,[89] and in 1544 to the way Moses had 'set up a crux for the grammarians' by his choice of vocabulary in Genesis 42:33.[90] On occasion Luther could also posit a relationship between the character of the writer and his work. For instance, his description of Joel in 1532 as 'a kindly and gentle man' is proffered as an explanation of why 'he does not denounce and rebuke as do the other prophets, but pleads and laments'.[91]

Dual Authorship

We must recognise the incidental nature of most of these comments. Luther does not develop them into a detailed and coherent doctrine of Scripture in the way this was done by some of his successors and any attempt to do so on his behalf runs the risk of distorting the evidence we have examined. Nevertheless, it is evident that when Luther reflected upon the origin of Scripture, he felt free to affirm both its divine authorship (most often attributed to the Holy Spirit) and a genuine human authorship of the individual books.[92] Not only that, he was able to move between these affirmations with apparent ease. Yet we may well ask whether Luther attributed the Scriptures to God and their human authors with equal priority. Put another way, are these completely coordinate and interchangeable propositions as far as Luther is concerned? In addition to the hints he gives in the material we have already quoted, the very last paragraph of his treatise against the doctrines of men suggests that Luther was not unaware of such questions:

> We censure the doctrines of men not because men have spoken them, but because they are lies and blasphemies against the

---

[88] 'Sicut Euangelista Matthaeus capite ultimo hanc phrasin quoque retinet, cum scribit, Christum resurrexisse vespera Sabbatorum, quae in unam Sabbatorum illucescebat.' *Genesisvorlesung* (1535-45) *WA* XLII, 5.9-11 = *LW* 1, 5.

[89] 'Ac Iohannes praecipue hac loquendi forma delectatus est.' *Genesisvorlesung* (1535-45) *WA* XLIII, 88.8-9 = *LW* 3, 297.

[90] 'Porro hoc in loco Moses crucem fixit Grammaticis in vocabulo.' *Genesisvorlesung* (1535-45) *WA* XLIV, 510.28-29 = *LW* 7, 285.

[91] 'Es ist aber ein gütiger und sanffter man gewest, schilt und strafft nicht so wie die andern Propheten, ßondern flehet und klagt.' *Vorrhede auff den Propheten Joel* (1532) *WADB* XI-II, 212.5-6 = *LW* 35, 318.

[92] Dockery, 'Hermeneutics', 197.

Scriptures. And the Scriptures, *although they too are written by men, are neither of men nor from men but from God'.*[93]

Luther's comment here returns us to one of the focal concerns of the doctrine of biblical inspiration throughout the Christian era: an affirmation of the uniqueness of the Scriptures. In the face of what he perceived to be competing authorities, there was something which could and must be said about the Scriptures which distinguishes them from all other literature. It is clear that Luther refused to dissolve one of these propositions into the other. Both were allowed to stand. For Luther, the Scriptures have been 'written by men' *and* they are 'from God'. However, these propositions always stand in a relationship which ensures that priority must be given to their divine origin. It is this commitment which accounts for the emphatic nature of many of Luther's comments regarding the divine authorship of the Scriptures while most of those concerning their human authorship remain without such emphasis. It also provides an important part of the context for Luther's use of the expression 'the Word of God'.

The Word of God

Luther's affirmation of the divine and human dimensions of the origins of Holy Scripture raises the question of whether he would describe the text itself as the Word of God. Here once again it would be almost irresponsible to carry on an investigation without an acknowledgment of the modern scholarly debate over the issue.[94] On the one hand, a recognition that Luther distinguished the Bible from the Word of God is almost axiomatic in some Luther studies. At times the distinction is emphasised to the point of separation, though not without a measure of special pleading. Hence Philip Watson argued:

> When Luther speaks of the Word of God, therefore, he means, on the one hand, the Law as interpreted by Christ, and on the other, the Gospel as constituted by Christ, who is himself the Word [...] it is understandable that Luther can speak at times as if he simply equated the written words of the Bible, or the spoken words that convey the biblical message, with the Word of God itself. Yet that is never quite

---

[93] 'Menschen lere taddelln wyr nicht darumb, das menschen gesagt haben, ßondern das es lügen und gottis lesterung sind widder die schrift, *wie wol sie auch durch menschen geschrieben ist*, doch nicht von oder auß menschen ßondern auß gott.' *Von Menschenlehre zu meiden* (1522) WA X-II, 92.4-7 = LW 35, 153 (emphasis mine).

[94] A very helpful survey of the debate in the second half of the twentieth century has been put together by Eugene Klug. Eugene F. Klug, 'Word and Scripture in Luther Studies since World War II', *Trinity Journal* 5 ns (1984), 20–27.

his meaning. For him, the Word is always fundamentally Christ, even when he does not explicitly say so.[95]

James Reid built upon Watson, observing that those expressions of Luther which seem to equate Scripture and the Word of God, though frequent, are isolated. The decisive consideration, he argues, is the credence Luther gives to certain critical conclusions regarding Scripture. These are 'irreconcilable with a view that equates Scripture with the Word of God'. This causes him to conclude that Luther held no such identification, a conclusion which Reid is convinced frees Luther from embarrassment.[96] Most forthright of all, though, is the Finnish scholar Miikka Ruokanen, who is prepared to argue that Luther would not refer to any text of the Bible, nor to any proclamation of the Scriptures, as the Word of God.[97]

Others have maintained this distinction, while affirming that Luther considered the Scriptures could contain the Word of God, or become the Word of God. Gerhard Ebeling has been most influential here. His explorations in Luther's *Dictata super Psalterium* led him to conclude that 'the Word of God is hidden in Scripture'.[98] In a similar vein, Heiko Oberman interprets Luther's theological quest, not in terms of the authority of the Bible, but in terms of how this authority could be properly expressed, or 'how the Word of God could be ascertained among the wealth of scriptural testimony'.[99] On this view, Luther can be distinguished from his successors by his conviction that the Scriptures are a point of access to the Word of God, not the Word of God itself.

On the other hand, there are those who are convinced that Luther used, and intended to use, the expression 'Word of God' with reference to the Scriptures. For some, however, such a conclusion must always carry the qualification that Luther only meant this in a derivative sense.

---

[95] Watson, *Let God be God*, 151-152; cf. Bernhard Lohse, 'Conscience and Authority in Luther', in Heiko A. Oberman (ed.), *Luther and the Dawn of the Modern Era: Papers for the Fourth International Congress for Luther Research*, 179.
[96] Reid, *Authority*, 66-68.
[97] Ruokanen, 'Biblical Inspiration?', 9.
[98] Gerhard Ebeling, 'The Beginnings of Luther's Hermeneutics II', *LQ* 7 (1993), 320.
[99] Oberman, *Luther*, 223. Note also Alister McGrath's comment: 'The general consensus of the magisterial Reformation was that Scripture was the container of the Word of God. This Word, although uniquely given at a definite point in the past, could be recovered and appropriated by every generation through the guidance of the Holy Spirit'. Alister E. McGrath, *Reformation Thought: An Introduction*, 151.

Regin Prenter's *Spiritus Creator* has been highly influential at this point. Prenter insisted that 'for Luther, the Word in its most real sense (*im eigentlichsten Sinne*) is nothing other than Christ himself'. Scripture and the Gospel proclamation, which he describes as 'the twin forms of the Word (*die Doppelgestalt des Wortes*)', certainly remain important. Nevertheless, each is only able to operate as an 'organ of revelation' by virtue of the relationship between Word and Spirit. If the external word (*äußere Wort*) is separated from the living Christ as God's gift to us, it represents only a series of dead letters (*tote Buchstaben*).[100]

Still others, while acknowledging that Luther uses the expression 'Word of God' in a variety of ways, conclude that Luther was prepared to use it of Scripture without qualification. Eugene Klug insisted that while Luther distinguished between the proclaimed Word and the inscripturated Word, 'he never set them into sharp opposition'.[101] Richard Muller has argued more recently that it is only a one-sided presentation of the relation of the incarnate Word and the inscripturated Word which supports the conclusion that the latter is derivative in Luther's thought. Not only does Luther see the Word as a witness to God's revelation in Christ, Muller contends, but he also holds to Christ as the fulfilment of God's revelatory Word.[102]

Any examination of the evidence in Luther's writings is complicated by the sheer bulk of relevant material. The concept and its associated terminology was widely used by him throughout his lifetime in lectures, sermons, treatises, letters, and table talk. On occasion he could use the expression in the most unexpected of contexts, as when he referred to 'every word which proceeds from the mouth of a leader of the church or from the mouth of a good and holy man' as the Word of Christ in 1515, or when he asked 'What else is the entire creation than the Word of God uttered by God, or extended to the outside?' in 1535.[103]

---

[100] Regin Prenter, *Spiritus Creator*, 116-117, 124; cf. Thomas F. Torrance, 'The Eschatology of Faith: Martin Luther', in *Kingdom and Church: A Study in the Theology of the Reformation*, 40; Jaroslav Pelikan, *Luther the Expositor: Introduction to the Reformer's Exegetical Writings*, 67-68.

[101] Klug, *Luther*, 36.

[102] Richard A. Muller, *Post-Reformation Reformed Dogmatics — Volume 2 Holy Scripture: The Cognitive Foundation of Theology*, 55-56.

[103] 'et omne verbum, quod ex ore prelati Ecclesie procedit Vel boni et sancti viri, Christi verbum est.' *Divi Pauli apostoli ad Romanos Epistola* (1515-16) *WA* LVI, 251.25-26 = *LW* 25, 238; Nam quid est aliud tota creatura quam verbum Dei a Deo prolatum, seu productum foras.' *Genesisvorlesung* (1535-45) *WA* XLII, 17.25-26 = *LW* 1, 22.

The Very Words of God?

Of course, Luther himself recognised that the expression 'Word of God' had more than one referent, and commented on this on a number of occasions. His explanation of Psalm 45:1 in the *Dictata* gave rise to this excursus on the subject:

> Thus we must know that the Word of God is spoken and revealed in a threefold manner. First, by God the Father in the saints in glory and in Himself. Second, in the saints in this life in the spirit. Third, through the external word and tongue addressed to human ears. And thus it is as if it were poured into a third vessel. This is symbolised by the fact that in ancient times God spoke in the prophets and fathers, and thus, by human mediation, there was created the veil of the letter and a middle wall. Afterwards the Word was spoken in the Son. This is still in concealment but is the second Word, nevertheless. Finally the Father in heaven Himself will speak to us in Himself, when He will disclose His Word to us without any intermediary, so that we may hear and see and be blessed.[104]

Here Luther emphasised the fact that God uses human intermediaries to bring his Word to us. The Word comes always in a veil or in concealment, whether from God to his human agents or from those agents to us. Nevertheless, Luther's explanation also emphasises that through each of these stages, or to use his terminology, 'in its threefold manner', the one Word of God is spoken. Further, we await the day when there will no longer be any need for human mediation of the Word of God.

The prominence of the expression 'Word of God' in Luther's theology, and the flexible way in which he seemed to use it, obviously raised questions in the minds of some of his students. A conversation over dinner in 1540 centred on the difference between two forms of the

---

[104] 'Sciendum itaque, quod verbum dei triplici modo dicitur et revelatur. Primo a deo patre in sanctis in gloria et in seipso. Secundo in sanctis in hac vita in spiritu. Tercio per verbum externum et linguam ad aures hominum. Et sic est velut in tercium vas transfusum. Et hoc est figuratum per hoc, quod olim deus locutus est in prophetis et patribus, et sic mediante homine factum est velum litere et paries medius. Postea locutus est in filio: hoc adhuc est in velamento, sed tamen secundum. Tandem pater ipse in coelo loquetur nobis in seipso, cum nobis verbum suum ipse sine ullo medio revelabit, ut audiamus et videamus et beati simus.' *Dictata super Psalterium* (1513-15) *WA* III, 262.6-15 = *LW* 10, 220. In a sermon on Mt. 23:34 preached around the same time, on 26 December 1514, Luther meditated on the threefoldness of the human word and a parallel threeness of prophet, wise man and scribe. Interestingly, in this context he speaks of the prophets being inspired and receiving revelation from the Spirit, referring explicitly to 2 Pet. 1. *Sermo de propria sapientia et voluntate* (1514) *WA* I, 30.1-26.

Word, in this instance the incarnate Word (Christ) and the proclaimed Word (preaching):

> Then the inquirer asked, 'Doctor, isn't there a difference between the Word that became flesh and the Word that is proclaimed by Christ or by a minister?'
>
> 'By all means!' he replied. 'The former is the incarnate Word who was true God from the beginning, and the latter is the Word that's proclaimed. The former Word is in substance God; the latter Word is in its effect the power of God, but isn't God in substance, for it has a man's nature, whether it's spoken by Christ or by a minister. But nevertheless it brings about everything it says, for through this instrument God does and makes all things for us and offers us all his treasures.'[105]

Here it is evident that Luther could recognise a distinction between these two forms of the Word. Yet he does this without denying that they are both the Word. The Word that is God's effective instrument in creation and redemption is no less the Word than that which is 'in substance God'. However, only one form of the Word of God is actually God. It is this simple distinction which lies behind comments such as those in the Galatians commentary: 'Christ is Lord over Scripture and over all works'.[106]

In line with the teaching of the New Testament, Luther considered Jesus Christ to be the Word of God. That much is clear in the comments we have just examined, where Luther could speak of the Word which was spoken in the Son, or of the *Verbum incarnatum* who is *substantialiter Deus*. As one might expect, though, this idea is particularly prominent in his sermons on John 1, where he preferred the expression the 'Word in God'. Luther struggles in his explanation, aware that any analogy with human words is fraught with the danger of misunderstanding:

> Any attempt to fathom and comprehend such statements with human reason and understanding will avail nothing, for none of this has its

---

[105] 'Tum ille: Domine Doctor, sed interestne inter verbum illud, quod caro factum est, et verbum a Christo prolatum vel a ministro? — Maxime! inquit. Illud est verbum incarnatum, quod fuit a principio verus Deus, hoc verbum prolatum; illud verbum est substantialiter Deus, hoc verbum effective, est potentia Dei et virtus, non substantialiter Deus, nam est habitus hominis sive Christi sive ministri. Sed efficit tamen omnia, quae dicit. Nam per hoc instrumentum Deus nobiscum agit et facit omnia et offert nobis omnes suos thesauros.' *Tischreden* #5177 (August 1540) *WATr* IV, 695.16-696.2 = *LW* 54, 395 (note that the English edition omits the last two sentences of this record).

[106] 'Christum autem Dominus est Scripturae et omnium operum.' *In epistolam S. Pauli ad Galatas Commentarius* (1535) *WA* XL-I, 458.20-21 = *LW* 26, 295.

source in the reason: that there was a Word in God before the world's creation, and that this Word was God; that, as John says further on, this same Word, the Only-begotten of the Father, full of grace and truth, rested in the Father's bosom or heart and became flesh; and that no one else had ever seen or known God, because the Word, who is God's only-begotten Son, rested in the bosom of the Father and revealed Him to us. Nothing but faith can comprehend this [...] Therefore this analogy of our word is very inadequate and vague. But although our word cannot be compared to His Word, it affords us a faint idea. Indeed, it impels us to ponder the matter and to obtain a better insight into its meaning, comparing the thoughts and speculations of the human heart with those of God and thus perceiving how God's Son is a Word.[107]

Luther also used the term 'Word' with reference to Jesus in his opening lectures on Genesis, as he drew intertestamentary parallels between Genesis 1 and John 1:

This is what Moses has now taught us concerning the first day, but we shall see that Moses also retains this expression in the creation of the remaining things: 'God said: "Let there be a firmament"', etc. This very repetition should be most welcome to us because, as I said above, it provides an important witness for our faith that the Son, in His divine nature, is true God and that in the unity of the Godhead there is a certain plurality of Persons, because one Person is that of the speaker, and another is the Word, or the λόγος.[108]

---

[107] 'Es thuts nichts, das man solche reden mit der Menschlichen vernunfft und verstande messen und fassen wil, denn es fleust nicht aus der vernunfft, das für der welt schöpffung in Gott ein wort sey, und dasselbige Wort Gott sey. Item, wie er hernacher saget, das dasselbige wort, der eingeborne Son Gottes, voller gnaden und warheit, sey in des Vaters Schos oder Hertz und sey fleisch worden, und das Gott sonst niemand gesehen noch erkant habe, denn das wort ist der eingeborne Son Gottes, der in des Vaters Schos est, der es uns verkündigt hat. Da gehört nu Glaube zu [...] Darümb ist diese Gleichnis von unserm wort genomen seer tunckel und finster, aber gleichwol gibt unser wort, wiewol es nicht mit jenem wort zuvergleichen ist, einen kleinen bericht, ja ursache, der sachen nachzudencken und deste leichter zu fassen, auch die gedancken und speculation des Menschlichen Hertzens gegen diesem Göttlichem Gespreche und wort zuhalten und zu lernen, wie Gottes Son ein wort sey.' *Auslegung des ersten und zweiten Kapitels Johannis* (1537-38) *WA* XLVI, 543.6-13, 544.21-26 = *LW* 22, 8, 9-10.

[108] 'Haec nunc de primo die Mose nos edocuit, videmus autem, quod Moses hanc phrasin etiam in aliarum rerum conditione retinet: "Dixit Deus: Fiat firmamentum" etc. Haec ipsa repetitio nobis debet gratissima esse, quod, ut supra dixi, magnum affert testimonium fidei nostrae, quod Filius in divinus sit

Another prominent use of the expression 'Word of God' in Luther's writings is connected with the proclamation of the gospel. Luther was strongly influenced by the simple observation that God *speaks* his Word. The writing of that Word is something that happens later in order that it might be preserved; nevertheless it remains fundamental to its very character that the Word is spoken. Proclamation is therefore imperative. In the Old Testament this was nowhere clearer, according to Luther, than in the prophetic material. So in his 1526 lecture on Mal. 2:7 he argued:

> This is a passage against those who hold the spoken Word in contempt. The lips are the public reservoirs of the church. In them alone is kept the Word of God. You see, unless the Word is preached publicly, it slips away. The more it is preached, the more firmly it is retained. Reading it is not as profitable as hearing it, for the living voice teaches, exhorts, defends, and resists the spirit of error. Satan does not care a hoot for the written Word of God, but He flees at the speaking of the Word. You see, this penetrates hearts and leads back those who stray.[109]

A number of important observations can be made. The first is that Luther is not actually discussing the nature or even the authority of the written Word in relation to the spoken Word at this point. Rather, he is emphasising the ability of the spoken Word to arrest the attention of the listener more powerfully than the written word can grip the reader.[110] There is something about the living voice which highlights

---

verus Deus, et quod in unitate divinitatis sit quaedam personarum pluralitas, quia alia persona est Dicentis, *et al*ia Verbum seu λόγος.' *Genesisvorlesung* (1535-45) *WA* XLII, 16.18-23 = *LW* 1, 20.

[109] 'Locus est contra contemptores verbi vocalis. Labia sunt receptacula publica ecclesiae, in quibus solis reservatur verbum dei. Nisi enim publice praedicetur, dilabitur et quo magis praedicatur, eo fortius retinetur. Lectio non proficit tantum, quantum auditio. Viva vox docet, hortatur, defendit, resistit, spiritus erroris. Et satan nihil moratur verbum dei scriptum, ad eloquium verbi vero fugit. Hoc enim penetrat corda et reducit errantes.' *Praelectiones in Malachiam* (1526) *WA* XIII, 686.6-12 = *LW* 18, 401.

[110] Six years later, in a sermon on Matthew 7.15 Luther elaborated on this point: 'There are many people nowadays who say: "Oh, I have read and learned it all, and I know it very well. I do not need [to listen]". They may even come out and say: "What do we need with any more clergy or preachers? I can read it just as well at home". Then they go their way and don't read it at home either. Or even if they do read it, it is not as fruitful or powerful as it is through a public preacher whom God has ordained to say and preach this.[Es sind yhr viel ißt, die da sagen: O ich habs schon gelesen und gelernet, kan es wol, hat kein not mit mir, Ja durffen auch wol er aus fahren und sagen: was durffen wir mehr pfaffen oder prediger? kan ichs doch wol da heim lesen,

the personal nature of the Word, drawing the hearer into a relationship with the speaker. The Word of God always carries the form of a word spoken to us. That is why preaching the Word is not only appropriate but necessary.[111] If a church has the written Word but does not proclaim it, that church will lose even what it has. Secondly, it is telling that for all this insistence on the effectiveness of the spoken Word, Luther does not deny that the written Word remains the Word of God. Indeed, the proclaimed Word is essentially no different in content to the written Word.

It is particularly in relation to the New Testament that Luther emphasises the oral nature of the Word of God. He was deeply suspicious of those who considered the New Testament a replacement for the Old, as well as those who approached the New Testament as a fresh code of divine law. Instead, he insisted that the paradigm for New Testament life and ministry is the proclamation of the gospel by Jesus himself. In 1521 he wrote:

> But what a fine lot of tender and pious children we are! In order that we might not have to study in the Scriptures and learn Christ there, we simply regard the entire Old Testament as of no account, as done for and no longer valid. Yet it alone bears the name of Holy Scripture. And the gospel should really not be something written, but a spoken word which brought forth the Scriptures, as Christ and the apostles have done. This is why Christ himself did not write anything but only spoke. He called his teaching not Scripture but gospel, meaning good news or a proclamation that is spread not by pen but by word of mouth. So we go on and make the gospel into a

---

sehen also dahin, lesen es da heim auch nicht, oder wo sie es lesen, so ists doch nicht so fruchtbar noch krefftig, als es ist durch den offentlichen prediger, den Gott dazu geordnet hat, das er dirs sol sagen und predigen.]' *Predigt am 8 Sonntag nach Trinitatis* (21 July 1532) *WA* XXXVI, 220.23-29.

[111] This emphasis can be seen at various points in Luther's writings, e. g. 'It is the nature of the Word to be heard [Natura enim verbi est audiri]' *Dictata super Psalterium* (1513-15) *WA* IV, 9.18-19 = *LW* 11, 160; 'In the church it is not enough to write and read books, but it is essential to speak and hear. For on this account Christ wrote nothing, but spoke everything; the apostles wrote a little, but spoke more [...] This is why we desire that there shall be more good speakers than good writers in the church [in Ecclesia non satis esse libros scribi et legi sed necessarium esse dici et audiri. Ideo enim Christus nihil scripsit, sed omnia dixit, Apostoli pauca scripserunt, sed plurima dixerunt (...) Unde magis conandum, ut multi sint concionatores quam boni scriptores in Ecclesia.]' *Operationes in Psalmos* (1519-21) *WA* V, 537.10-12, 537.21-22; 'The church is not a pen-house but a mouth-house [Darumb ist die kirch eyn mundhawß, nit eyn fedderhawß]' *Adventspostille* (1522) *WA* X-1/2, 48.5. cf. Graham, *Beyond*, 149.

law book, a teaching of commandments, changing Christ into a Moses, the One who would help us into simply an instructor.[112]

Luther's distinction between the Old Testament (Holy Scripture in the proper sense) and the New Testament (properly the proclamation of Christ) will occupy our attention in a later chapter of this study. What is significant at this juncture is the way in which this perception of the basic character of the New Testament influences Luther's use of the expressions 'Word', or 'Word of God' in connection with the proclamation of the gospel. A year earlier, in his treatise on genuine Christian liberty, Luther had argued that 'one thing, and one thing only is necessary for the Christian life, righteousness and freedom. That one thing is the most holy Word of God, the gospel of Christ.'[113]

Nevertheless, Luther refused to isolate the proclaimed Word from the written Word. His 1531 sermon on Jn. 6:45–46 is a case in point. Luther's paraphrase of verse 45, 'When I hear the mouth of Christ the Lord speak, I hear the Father', leads to a long excursus on the hearing of the Word of God. In the midst of it he declares: 'Christ wants to exhort us to adhere and cling to the external, oral Word'.[114] Yet even here, within two pages of this remark, Luther once again shows the intimate relationship between what is proclaimed and what has been written:

> You are preserved by the words which you hear; they also illumine you, teach you, draw you, and bring you to Christ. First of all, you hear the Father speaking through the Son. You hear the Word or the

---

[112] 'Aber sihe tzu, wie feyn tzart frume kinder wyr sind; auff das wyr nit durfften ynn der schrifft studirn und Christum alda lernen, halten wyr das gantz allte testament vor nichts, als das nu auß sey und nichts mehr gelte, ßo es doch alleyn den namen hatt, das es heylige schrifft heyst, Und Euangeli eygentlich nitt schrifft, ßondern mundlich wort seyn solt, das die schrifft erfur truge, wie Christus und die Apostel than haben; Darumb auch Christus selbs nichts geschrieben, ßondern nur geredt hatt, und seyn lere nit schrifft, sonder Euangeli, das ist eyn gutt botschafft odder vorkundigung genennet hatt, das nitt mit der feddern, ßondern mit dem mund soll getrieben werden. Alßo faren wyr tzu und machen auß dem Euangeli eyn gesetz buch, eyn gepott lare, auß Christo eynen Mosen, auß helffer nur eynen lerer.' *Eyn kleyn unterricht, was man ynn den Euangelius suchen und gewartten soll — Kirchenpostille* (1522) *WA* X-I/1, 17.4-14 = *LW* 35, 123.

[113] 'Una re eaque sola opus est ad vitam, iustitiam et libertatem Christianam. Ea est sacrosanctum verbum dei, Euangelium Christi.' *Tractatus de Libertate Christiana* (1520) *WA* VII, 50.33-35 = *LW* 31, 345.

[114] 'wen ich Christum höre reden, so höre ich den vater' *Die Predigten über Joh. 6-8, Die Eilffte Predigt* (4 February 1531) *WA* XXXIII, 143.15-17, 'Das meinet nun der herr Christus, das wir bei dem eusserlichen und mundlichen wort bleiben und dabey fest halten sollen' *WA* XXXIII, 145.15-18 = *LW* 23, 95.

voice. But this does not mean that you have already been drawn, for reason says that Christ is only human and that His speech is only human speech. But then, when you delight in occupying yourself with the Word, when you read it, hear it preached, and love it, the time will come when you will confess that God Himself uttered these words, and you will exclaim: 'This is truly the Word of God!' Thus faith is added.[115]

Luther is suggesting that the Word of God may be read or heard, or indeed both.[116]

The evidence for Luther's identification of Holy Scripture itself as the Word of God falls into three groups. First, there are quite a number of explicit statements to this effect in Luther's writings. Some of these, to be sure, appear in polemical contexts. For example, Luther makes the equation in his 1520 treatise *De captivitate Babylonica ecclesiae praeludium,* as he provides reasons for his rejection of the Roman doctrine of transubstantiation:

> But there are good grounds for my view, and this above all — no violence is to be done to the words of God, whether by man or angel. They are to be retained in their simplest meaning as far as possible. Unless the context manifestly compels it, they are not to be understood apart from their grammatical and proper sense, lest we give our adversaries occasion to make a mockery of all the Scriptures [...] Even so here, when the Evangelists plainly write that Christ took bread and blessed it, and when the Book of Acts and the

---

[115] 'so du hörest, da wirst du erhalten, da wirst du auch erleucht, geleret, gezogen und zu Christo gebracht. Denn erstlich hörest du den Vater in dem Son reden, du hörest die stimme oder das Wort, damit bist du noch nicht gezogen, denn die Vernunfft spricht, es sey Christus nur ein Mensch und seine rede nur menschen wort. Aber darnach, wenn du gerne mit dem wort umbgehest, liesest, hörest es predigen und liebest dasselbige, so wirds ein mal und balde dazu komen, das du sagest: Gott hats selber geredet, und sprechest: warlich das ist Gottes wort. Also kömet der Glaube dazu' vater' *Die Predigten über Joh. 6-8, Die Eilffte Predigt* (4 February 1531) *WA* XXXIII, 147.26-148.1 = *LW* 23, 97.

[116] Cf. 'Above all, therefore, one must listen to and read the Word, which is the vehicle of the Holy Spirit. When the Word is read, the Holy Spirit is present; and thus it is impossible either to listen to or to read Scripture without profit. [Itaque ante omnia audiendum et legendum verbum, quod vehiculum Spiritus Sancti est. Lecto verbo adest Spiritus Sanctus et sic impossibile est vel audire vel legere Scripturas sine fructu.]' *Vorlesung über den 1. Brief des Johannes* (1527) *WA* XX, 790.24-27 = *LW* 30, 321.

Apostle Paul in turn call it bread, we have to think of real bread and real wine just as we do of a real cup.[117]

Two years later, after controversy with Albrecht of Mainz, Luther was even more explicit. He was prepared to insist, 'We have no other word than Scripture. That is why all the wicked should be reproved with it'.[118] He obviously did not think this was a new idea, or one that separated him from the accepted teaching of the church. This much is clear from a later section of the same treatise:

> Furthermore, I ask whether or not St. Paul's word and order are derived from God's word and order? I think that the pope himself, with all his devils, even though he suppresses every word of God, cannot deny that St. Paul's word is God's word and that his order is the order of the Holy Spirit.[119]

Similar statements can also be found in the midst of the controversy over the words of institution with Zwingli and others. In his *Vom Abendmahl Christi Bekenntnis*, Luther responded to the suggestion that he was obstinately clinging to 'five poor, miserable words', namely the phrase τοῦτό ἐστιν τὸ σῶμά μου in Matthew 26:26:

> With such arguments, however, they reveal against their own intention what kind of spirit they have and how dearly they value God's words, since they abuse these precious words as 'five poor, miserable words', that is, they do not believe that they are God's words. For if they believed that these were God's words, they would not call them 'poor, miserable words', but would prize a single tittle

---

[117] 'Est autem meae sententiae ratio magna, imprimis illa, quod verbis divinis non est ulla facienda vis, neque per hominem neque per angelum, sed quantum fieri potest in simplicissima significatione servanda sunt, et nisis manifesta circumstantia cogat, extra grammaticam et propriam accipienda non sunt, ne detur adversariis occasio universam scripturam eludendi [...] Ita et hic, cum Euangelistae clare scribant, Christum accepisse panem ac benedixisse, et actuum liber et Paulus Apostolus panem deinceps appellent, verum oportet intelligi panem verumque vinum, sicut verum calicem' *De captivitate Babylonica ecclesiae praeludium* (1520) *WA* VI, 509.8-12, 509.15-18 = *LW* 36, 30-31.

[118] 'Nu haben wyr keyn wort denn die schrifft, darumb soll man damit straffen alle gottloßen' *Wider den falsch genannten geistlichen Stand des Papsts und der Bischöfe* (1522) *WA* X-II, 108.25-26 = *LW* 39, 250.

[119] 'Weytter frag ich, ob Sanct Paulus wortt und ordenung auß gottis wort und ordenung seyen oder nit? Ich acht, das der Bapst selb mit allen teuffelln, wie wol er alle gottis wortt unterdruckt, dennoch nit leucken müge odder thar, Das S. Paulus wortt gottis wortt und seyn ordnung des heyligen geystis ordenung sey.' *Wider den falsch genannten geistlichen Stand des Papsts und der Bischöfe* (1522) *WA* X-II, 139.14-18 = *LW* 39, 277.

The Very Words of God? 79

and letter more highly than the whole world, and would fear and tremble before them as before God himself. For he who despises a single word of God certainly prizes none at all.[120]

Two considerations in particular prevent us from agreeing with Ebeling that Luther has in mind here the words spoken by Christ rather than words of the text. Firstly, Luther's reference to 'a single tittle and letter (*eine tutel und buchstabe*)' indicates the written word rather than the spoken word. Secondly, throughout this section of Luther's treatise he refers to 'this text (*dieser text*)', again making clear that the written New Testament is under examination here. In the final analysis, of course, Luther considered the words spoken by Christ to be identical, and in a real sense inseparable, from the words of the text.

There is one other polemical context which provokes such statements from Luther. In his 1537 examination of 'the three symbols' (the Apostles' Creed, Athanasian Creed, and the Te Deum), Luther attacked the Jewish and Turkish attempts to undermine the doctrine of the Trinity by appeal to the Christian Scriptures themselves. After declaring that 'the Scriptures are God's testimony of himself (*die schrifft Gottes zeugnis von jm selbs ist*)', Luther continued:

> If they now rap on the Scriptures saying that there is one God, so let us rap thereon in turn, since the Scriptures indicate just as strongly that in this one God there are more than one. Our scriptural texts are as valid as theirs, because there is not a superfluous letter in the Scriptures. But we will not submit to their attempts to interpret our Scriptures, because they have neither the right nor the might to do it. They are God's Scriptures and God's Word, which no man is supposed to or can interpret.[121]

---

[120] 'Aber mit solcher rede zeugen sie widder sich selbs, was sie fur einen geist haben, und wie theur sie Gotts wort achten, das sie die selbigen theuren wort schelten als arme, elende funff wort, Das ist, sie gleuben nicht, das Gotts wort sind. Denn wo sie gleubten, das Gotts wort weren, wurden sie es nicht elende, arme wort heissen, sondern auch einen tutel und buchstaben grösser ahcten denn die gantze welt und dafur zittern und furchten als fur Gott selbs, Denn wer ein eintzel Gotts wort veracht, der achtet freylich auch keines nicht gros.' *Vom Abendmahl Christi. Bekenntnis WA* XXVI, 449.34-450.24 = *LW* 37, 308.

[121] 'Wenn sie nu pochen auff die schrifft, das ein einiger Got sey, So pochen wir widerumb, das die schrifft auch eben so starck anzeigt, das jnn dem einigen Gott viel sind. Und gilt unser schrifft so viel als jre, sintemal kein buchstabe jnn der schrifft vergeblich ist. Das sie aber unser schrifft wollen deuten, das gestehen wir nicht, und sie habens auch nicht macht noch recht. Denn es ist Gottes schrifft und Gottes wort, die kein mensch deuten sol noch kan.' *Die drei Symbola oder Bekenntnis des Glaubens Christi* (1538) *WA* L, 282.11-17 = *LW* 34, 227-228.

One might expect a degree of hyperbole when Luther was engaged in fierce debate with the Romans, the Swiss, or the Turks. However, Luther is no less bold in contexts which are ostensively non-polemical. In fact, some of his most direct statements are found in the normal course of his pastoral and academic work. In his 1522 sermons on 1 Peter he gave this advice to the congregation at Wittenberg:

> Therefore if people refuse to believe, you should keep silence; for you have no obligation to force them to regard Scripture as God's Book or Word. It is sufficient for you to base your proof on Scripture. This you must do when they take it upon themselves to say: 'You preach that one should not hold to the teaching of men, even though Peter and Paul, yes, even Christ, were men too'. If you hear people who are so completely blinded and hardened that they deny that this is God's Word or are in doubt about it, just keep silence, do not say a word to them, and let them go their way. Just say: 'I will give you enough proof from Scripture. If you want to believe it, this is good; if not, I will give you nothing else'. Then you may say: 'Ah, in this way God's Word must needs be brought into disgrace!' Leave this to God.[122]

This advice is given, not in the midst of controversy, but as Luther explains and applies 1 Pet. 3:15: 'Always be prepared to make a defence to anyone who calls you to account for the hope that is in you'.

When Luther wrote to the Councilmen of Germany urging them to set up and maintain Christian schools, he argued that the study of the languages should be an essential part of the education they provide:

> Since it becomes Christians then to make good use of the Holy Scriptures as their one and only book and it is a sin and a shame not to know our own book or to understand the speech and words of our God, it is a still greater sin and loss that we do not study languages, especially in these days when God is offering and giving us men and

---

[122] 'Darumb wenn die leut nicht glewben wollen, so soltu stillschweygen, denn du bist nicht schuldig, das du sie dazu zwingest, das sie die schrifft fur Gottis buch oder wort halten. Ist gnug, das du deynen grund darauff gibst. Als wenn sie es so furnemen und sagen: 'Du prdigt, man solle nicht menschen lere hallten, so doch Petrus und Paulus, jha Christus auch menschen sind gewest', Wenn du solche leut hörist, die so gar verblendt und verstockt sind, das sie leucknen, das diss Gottis wortt sey, oder daran zweyffeln, so schweyg nur still, rede keyn wortt mit yhn, und lass sie faren, sprich nur also: 'Ich will dyr grund gnug auss der schrifft geben, willtu es glawben, so ists gutt, willtu nicht, so will ich dyr nicht mehr geben.' So sagistu: 'Ey so muss denn Gottis wortt mit schanden bestehen!' Das befilh du Gott.' *Epistel Sanct Petri gepredigt und ausgelegt* (1522) *WA* XII, 362.17-27 = *LW* 30, 107.

books and every facility and inducement to this study, and desires his Bible to be an open book.[123]

Here again a judgement as to the nature of Holy Scripture lies behind Luther's advice. No effort should be spared in teaching the ancient languages if we grant that the words written in Hebrew and Greek (Luther did not mention Aramaic) are to be considered the Word of God.

The later writings of Luther are a rich source of explicit identification of Scripture and the Word of God. The spread of material is such, combined with a continuity of theme and vocabulary between the relevant statements here and those to be found in the earlier material, that these statements cannot be dismissed as simply the work of those who prepared Luther's later sermons and lectures for publication. In the early pages of the 1532 commentary on the Sermon on the Mount, Luther made this observation:

> But now since it is so common that everyone has it written in a book and can read it every day, no one thinks of it as anything special or precious. Yes, we grow sated and neglect it, as if it had been spoken by some shoemaker rather than the High Majesty of heaven. Therefore it is in punishment for our ingratitude and neglect that we get so little out of it and never feel or taste what a treasure, power, and might there is in the words of Christ. But whoever has the grace to recognise it as the Word of God rather than the word of man, will also think of it more highly and dearly, and will never grow sick and tired of it.[124]

---

[123] 'Weyl denn nu den Christen gepürt, die heyligen schrifft zu uben alls yhr eygen eyniges buch, und eyn sunde und schande ist, das wyr unser eygen buch nicht wissen noch unsers Gottis sprach und wort nicht kennen, so ists noch viel mehr sunde und schaden, das wyr nicht sprachen leren, sonderlich so uns ist Gott dar beut und gibt leute und bücher und allerley, was dazu dienet, und uns gleich dazu reitzt und seyn buch gern wollt offen haben.' *An die Ratherren aller Städte deutsches Lands* (1524) *WA* XV, 41.16-22 = *LW* 45, 364.

[124] 'Itzt aber, nu es so gemein ist, das es jderman jm buch geschrieben hat und teglich lesen kan, achtets niemand fur was sonderlichs und kostlichs, Ja wir werdens dazu uberdruss und schlahens inn wind, als hette es nicht die hohe maiestet von himel, sondern jrgent ein schuster gered. Darumb widderferet uns auch zur straffe unsers undancks und verachtung, das wir wenig gnug davon haben und nimer fulen noch schmecken, was fur ein schatz, krafft und gewalt jnn Christus worten ist. Wer aber die gnade hat, das ers recht ansehe als Gottes und nicht menschen wort, der wirds auch wol hoher und teurer achten und nymer mehr müde noch uberdrus werden.' *Wochenpredigten über Matth. 5-7* (1532) *WA* XXXII, 305.22-30 = *LW* 21, 10.

The first of Luther's sermons on 1 Cor. 15, from the same year, repeats this theme and makes the same identification:

> And today every place is also teeming with such spirits, confused by the devil, who regard Scripture a dead letter and boast of nothing but the Spirit, although these people retain neither Word nor Spirit. But here you notice how Paul adduces Scripture as his strongest proof, for there is no other enduring way of preserving our doctrine and our faith than the physical or written Word, poured into letters and preached orally by him or others; for here we find it stated clearly: 'Scripture! Scripture!' But Scripture is not all spirit, about which they drivel, saying that the Spirit alone must do it and that Scripture is a dead letter which cannot impart life. But the fact of the matter is that, although the letter by itself does not impart life, yet it must be present, and it must be heard or received. And the Holy Spirit must work through this in the heart, and the heart must be preserved in the faith through and in the Word against the devil and every trial. Otherwise, where this is surrendered, Christ and the Spirit will soon be lost. Therefore do not boast so much of the Spirit if you do not have the revealed external Word.[125]

Here again we find an intimate connection maintained between the written and oral forms of the Word. It is by means of engagement with these that the Spirit brings the believer to the incarnate Word, Christ. Five years later, in his first sermon in the series on John's Gospel, Luther speaks twice of 'Holy Scripture, which is God's Word'.[126] This is all the more remarkable since the context is a discussion of Christ as

---

[125] 'wie es ist allenthalden schwermet von solchen geistern, durch den Teuffel zurüttet, so die Schrifft also ansehen als einen todten buchstaben und eitel geist rhümen, Und doch wedder Wort noch geist behalten, Aber hie hörestu, wie S. Paulus die Schrifft fur sein sterdest zeugnis füret und zeigt, das kein bestand ist unser lere und glauben zu erhalten denn das leiblich odder schrifftliche wort, jnn buchstaben gefasset und durch jn odder andere mündlich gepredigt, Denn es stehet hie klar: Schrifft, Schrifft. Schrifft aber ist nicht eitel geist, davon sie geissern, der Geist musse es allein thun, die Schrifft sey ein todter buchstabe und konne nicht das leben geben. Es heisst aber also: Ob wol der buchstabe an sich selbs nicht das leben gibt, doch mus es dabey sein und gehöret odder empfangen werden und der Heilig geist durch dasselbige jm hertzen wircken und das hertz, sich durch das wort und jnn dem wort jm glauben erhalten widder Teuffel und alle anfechtung, Odder wo er das lesset faren, bald Christum und den Geist gar verlieren mus, Darumb rhüme nur nicht viel vom Geist, wenn du nicht das offenberliche eusserliche wort hast' *Predigt am 11 Sonntag nach Trinitatis, nachmittags* (11 August 1532) *WA* XXXVI, 500.25-501.10 = *LW* 28, 76-77.

[126] '[D]ie Schrifft, so Gottes wort ist' *Auslegung des ersten und zweiten Kapitels Johannis* (1537) *WA* XLVI, 542.6, 548.32-33 =*LW* 22, 6, 14.

the Word of God. Finally, in 1541 he described Scripture as 'the Word of God written and lettered and formed in letters just as Christ is the eternal Word of God cloaked in human flesh'. He goes on to say, 'And just as Christ was embraced and handled by the world, so is the written Word of God too'.[127]

These explicit statements by Luther are only part of the evidence. A second group of comments are those in which Luther uses the expressions 'Word of God' and 'Holy Scripture' as if they were parallel or interchangeable terms. These too can be found throughout his teaching and writing career. A representative sample with suffice for our purposes here. In the *Dictata,* Luther insists that the Church is 'captive to Scripture, teaching nothing but the Word of God'.[128] In the series of lectures on Romans that followed, Luther spoke in one breath about the way Holy Scripture can be understood as a snare and then in another about the need for care when it comes to handling the Word of God, 'because it immediately catches those of proud mind and traps them and makes them stumble'.[129] It was not only in these early lectures that he could speak like this. In the defence of his theology in the face of attacks by Augustinus Alveld in 1520 Luther admitted he was 'more cutting and passionate when defending Scripture than some

---

[127] 'Die heilige Schrifft ist Gottes wort, geschrieben und (das ich so rede) gebuchstabet und in buchstaben gebildet, Gleich wie Christus ist das ewige Gottes wort, in die menscheit verhullet, Und gleich wie Christus in der Welt gehalten und gehandelt ist, so gehets dem schrifftlichn Gottes wort auch.' *Sprüche aus dem Alten Testament* (1541) *WA* XLVIII, 31.4-8; cf. Luther's inscription from the same year in a copy of the Bible, presented to the princes of the House of Ols and now housed in the Luther-Room in the City Museum of Worms Andreasstift, includes a quotation of John 5:39 and then this comment: 'This means that since we consider the Holy Scriptures to be the word of a salutary God, which can save us eternally, so ought we also to read and study their contents so that we will find testimony about Christ there. [Das ist weil wir selbst halten, daß die Heilige Schrift sei Gottes heilsames Wort, welches uns ewiglich kann selig machen, So sollen wir also drinnen lesen und studieren, daß wir Christum drinnen finden bezeuget]'

[128] 'Similiter significat, quod Ecclesia ubera, quibus lacte pascit infirmos, non habet discincta sicut Heretici, qui sua docent, sed captiva in auctoritatem Scripture, non docens nisi verbum dei.' *Dictata super Psalterium* (1513-15) *WA* III, 261.13-16 = *LW* 10, 219.

[129] 'Est Ipsa diuina Scriptura subdole intellecta et tradita [...] verbum Dei, Quod superbos mente statim illaqueatet capit et Schandalisat' *Divi Pauli apostoli ad Romanos Epistola. Die Glossen* (1516) *WA* LVI, 432.12-13, 433.2-3 = *LW* 25, 424-425.

can stand' and then proceeded to vow 'I shall defend Christ's Word with a joyful heart and renewed courage'.[130]

This interchange of terms is evident also in Luther's great debate with Erasmus in 1525. Luther insists that he will have no part of Scripture called obscure, citing in support 2 Pet. 1:19, and in particular the description of the Word of God as 'a lamp shining in a dark place'. 'If part of this lamp does not shine', Luther explains, 'it will be a part of the dark place rather than of the lamp itself'.[131] That Luther is not distinguishing between the Scripture and the Word of God here is evident by his use of two parallel constructions:

> I say with respect to *the whole of Scripture*, I will not have *any part of it* called obscure [...] Christ has not so enlightened us as deliberately to leave *some part of his Word* obscure.[132]

The same pattern is a regular feature of the later lectures as well. Commenting on Ps. 45:6 in 1532 Luther insisted:

> The Word is so irreproachable that not a single iota can err in the Law or the divine promises. For that reason we must yield to no sect, not even in one tittle of Scripture, no matter how much they clamour and accuse us of violating love when we hold so strictly to the Word.[133]

Attention to the details of the text is here equated with rigidly adhering to the Word of God. So too, in the Galatians commentary of 1535 Luther is adamant that all who teach should be subject to Holy Scripture which he goes on to explain means that no other doctrine should be taught or heard in the church 'than the pure Word of

---

[130] 'das ich aber scharffer und hitziger byn uber die schrifft zuerhalten, wen etlich leyden mugen [...] aber Christus wort wil ich mit frolichem hertzen und frischem mut vorantworten' *Von dem Papstthum zu Rom wider den hochberühmten Romanisten zu Leipzig* (1520) *WA* VI, 323.13-14, 323.19-20 = *LW* 39, 103.

[131] 'Quod si pars huius lampadis non lucet, potius pars caliginosi loci quam ipsius lampadis erit' *De servo arbitrio* (1525) *WA* XVIII, 656.17-18 = *LW* 33, 95.

[132] 'Deinde contra te de tota scriptura dico, nullam eius partem volo obscuram dici [...] Non sic illuminavit nos Christus, ut aliquam partem obscuram voluerit relictam nobis in suo verbo' *De servo arbitrio* (1525) *WA* XVIII, 656.15-16, 656.18-20 = *LW* 33, 94, 95.

[133] 'Verbum enim sic est irreprehensibile, ut ne iota quidem viciosum sit in lege et promissionibus divinis. Quare nulli sectae cedendum est, ne in uno quidem apice scripturae, quantumcunque clament et calumnientur nos caritatem dissolvere, dum verba sic stricte retinemus.' *Praelectio in psalmum 45* (1533) *WA* XL-II, 531.30-34 = *LW* 12, 242.

God'.[134] Finally, the lecture on Gn. 19:23–25, given in 1539, first rejects any suggestion that we have liberty 'to evade Holy Scripture' and then adds 'let us not change the Word of God'.[135]

The third component of the evidence is a collection of statements by Luther in which the expressions 'Word of God' and 'Holy Scripture' are linked by a conjunction. In each case the context demonstrates that Luther is speaking about one thing, not two. In his fourth response to the papal bull *Exsurge Domine,* his 1521 treatise *Grund und Ursach aller Artikel,* Luther closed his defence of the fourteenth article with such an expression:

> Do not make your own ideas into articles of faith as that abomination at Rome does. For then your faith may become a nightmare. Hold to Scripture and the Word of God. There you will find truth and security — assurance and a faith that is complete, pure, sufficient, and abiding.[136]

The expression 'Word of God', in this context, explains 'Scripture' rather than adds to it.[137] This is also the case in the *Kirchenpostille,* as Luther draws his homily on the Gospel for the Epiphany (Mt. 2:1–12) to a close:

> Would to God that my exposition and that of all doctors might perish and each Christian himself hold to the bare Scriptures and God's pure word! You can tell by my verbosity how immeasurably different God's words are in comparison with any human word, how

---

[134] 'Angelum e coelo, doctores in terra et quicquid est Magistorum, hoc totum rapit et subiicit sacrae scripturae [...] Neque alia doctrina in Ecclesia tradi et audiri debet quam purum verbum Dei' *In epistolam S. Pauli ad Galatas Commentarius* (1535) *WA* XL-I, 120.19-20, 120.23-24 = *LW* 26, 58. In the 1531 lectures this paragraph ends with an explanation in German *'Das ist der text'* (120.8).

[135] 'Sed quis hos iussit eos hoc audere in Dei libro, si enim ad hunc modum liceret eludere scripturam sanctam, nullus fidei articulus maneret integer. Igitur magistrum fieri spiritus sancti, et docere eum, quid aut quomodo scribat: incredulorum Iudaeorum et impiorum Papistarum est, Nos autem simus et maneamus discipuli, nec mutemus verbum Dei, sed mutemur ipsi per verbum' *Genesisvorlesung* (1535-45) *WA* XLIII, 87.37-40 = *LW* 3, 297.

[136] 'mach nit Artickell des glawbensz ausz deynen gedanckenn, wye der grewel zu Rom thut, das nit villeicht ausz deynem glawben eyn trawm werde. Halt dich an die schrifft und gottis wort, da ist die warheyt, da wirstu sicher sein, da ist trew und glawb, gantz, lautter, gnugsam und bestendig.' *Grund und Ursach aller Artikel D. Martin Luthers* (1521) *WA* VII, 455.21-24 = *LW* 32, 98.

[137] Parallel to this is Luther's use of the expression 'believers and Christians (*pii et christiani*)' in *Tischreden* #2938b (January 1533) *WATr* III, 106.9.

no one is able to fathom sufficiently a single word of God and expound it with all his words [...] And so, my dear Christians, get to it, get to it, and let my exposition and that of all the doctors be no more than a scaffold, an aid for the construction of the true building, so that we may ourselves grasp and taste the pure and simple word of God and abide by it. [138]

It is particularly noticeable here that the adjectives used to describe both the Scripture and God's word at one point are both used of the Word of God at another. This reinforces the argument from the context that Luther has in mind one thing here rather than two.

This is not just a feature of the early period of Luther's teaching and writing but can be found in the later lectures as well. The 1527 series on Isaiah provides an interesting case. In the course of explaining Is. 29:14 Luther speaks of those who have 'no wisdom, no faith and understanding, no discernment of Scripture and the Word'.[139] Here it may seem that Luther is speaking of a distinction or difference between Scripture and the Word. However two considerations make this unlikely. The first is the purely grammatical consideration that Luther says *discrimen scripturae et verbi,* not *discrimen inter scripturam et verbum.* The genitives *scripturae* and *verbi* are properly read as objective genitives. This is confirmed by the context. Within the space of a number of lines Luther illustrates the kind of people he has in mind:

> Such are the Jews and especially the papists, who in their security and traditions have boasted only of their church against the whole Scripture and the doctrine of faith and love, and very, very few shine with outward mortification, with which they tire the body for a little while as is their pleasure. However, there has been nothing in them of the Word, of faith, of conscience, and of love.[140]

---

[138] 'O das gott wollt, meyn und aller lerer außlegung untergiengen, unnd eyn iglicher Christenn selbs die blosse schrifft und lautter gottis wortt fur sich nehme! Du sihest yhe auß dissem meynen geschwetz, wie unmeßlich ungleych gottis wortt sind gegen aller menschen wortt, wie gar keyn mensch mag eyn eyniges gottis wort gnugsam erreychen und vorkleren mit allen seynen wortten [...] Darumb hyneyn, hyneyn, lieben Christen, und last meyn und aller lerer außlegen nur eyn gerust seyn zum rechten baw, das wyr das blosse, lautter gottis wort selbs fassen, schmecken unnd da bleyben.' *Kirchenpostille* (1522) *WA* X-I/1, 728.9-13, 728.18-21 = *LW* 52, 286.

[139] 'Sic hic vides, quia nullam habent sapienciam, fidem neque Intelligenciam, discrimen scripturae et verbi.' *Vorlesung über Iesaias* (1527) *WA* XXXI-II, 178.21-23 = *LW* 16, 246.

[140] 'quales sunt Iudei et imprimis Papistae, qui solum suam ecclesiam sua securitate et tradicionibus contra totam scripturam et fidei et charitatis

The Very Words of God? 87

The parallel constructions make clear that Luther is using the two terms to refer to the same thing. Luther is speaking of that discrimination which comes from 'Scripture and the Word of God'.

The Genesis lectures provide a number of examples of this phenomenon. For instance, Luther's exposition of Gn. 1:14 dismissed Plato's suggestion that the stars and heavenly bodies are endowed with life and reason:

> But this opinion must be entirely rejected, and our intellect must adjust itself to the Word of God and to Holy Scripture, which plainly teaches that God created all these things in order to prepare a house and an inn, as it were, for the future man, and that He governs and preserves these creatures by the power of His Word, by which He also created them [...] Other ideas, which are advanced without the support of Scripture, must be rejected.[141]

Once again the context makes clear that Luther uses the second term to further define the first, rather than to add to it. This is also the case when Luther arrives at Gn. 2:21, where he says 'Therefore let us learn that true wisdom is in Holy Scripture and in the Word of God'. He then continues, 'This gives information not only about the matter of the entire creation, not only about its form, but also about the efficient and final cause'.[142] In this context, then, Luther does not consider Scripture and the Word of God to be two things but one. Other examples could be cited from the sermons on John's Gospel from 1537 and 1538.[143]

Alongside these three strands of evidence there are a number of statements in Luther's writings which, given the variety of meanings

---

racionem gloriati sunt et vix paucissimi externis mortificacionibus splendent, quibus paulisper fatigant corpus pro libidine. Nihil autem verbi, fidei, conscienciae, charitatis in illis fuit.' *Vorlesung über Iesaias* (1527) *WA* XXXI-II, 178.27-31 = *LW* 16, 246.

[141] 'Sed haec sententia plane est explodenda et accommodandus intellectus noster ad verbum Dei et ad scripturam sanctam, quae clare docet Deum ista omnia condidisse, ut futuro homini pararet ceu domum et hospicium ac gubernari et conservari ista virtute verbi, quo sunt condita [...] Alia, quae sine autoritate scripturae afferuntur, repudianda sunt.' *Genesisvorlesung* (1535-45) *WA* XLII, 35.22-29 = *LW* 1, 47.

[142] 'Ergo discamus veram sapientiam esse in scriptura sancta et in verbo Dei. Id enim non solum de materia, non solum de forma totius creaturae sed etiam de efficienti et finali causa' *Genesisvorlesung* (1535-45) *WA* XLII, 94.3-6 = *LW* 1, 125.

[143] 'Davon die schrifft und Gottes wort nichts leret ...' *Das XIV und XV Capitel S. Johannis* (1537-38) *WA* XLV, 494.12-13 = *LW* 24, 37; 'Du habest nicht allein die Schrifft und Gottes wort ...' *Das XIV und XV Capitel S. Johannis* (1537-38) *WA* XLV, 728.22-23 = *LW* 24, 293.

attached to the expression 'Word of God', remain ambiguous.[144] Further, there are two passages in particular which have sometimes been taken as proof that Luther believed the Word of God is something to be extracted from Scripture and therefore ought not to be identified with Scripture itself. Both are from 1522. The first is found in *Von Menschenlehre zu meiden:*

> This conflict between the Scriptures and the doctrines of men we cannot reconcile. Therefore because these two forms of doctrine contradict one another we allow even young children to judge here whether we are to give up the Scriptures, in which the one Word of God is taught from the beginning of the world, or whether we are to give up the doctrines of men, which were newly devised yesterday and which change daily.[145]

An examination of the context raises questions about the way this passage is sometimes used. It reveals that the critical distinction at this point is that between Scripture and human doctrine. Luther insisted that this distinction does not simply rest upon their origin but extends to their content as well. That is why he was able to speak of an irreconcilable conflict (*zwytracht*) between Scripture and human doctrine. Whereas Scripture addresses us with God's ancient determination to act for our deliverance and the proclamation of this determination and its fulfilment in the gospel itself liberates our consciences, human teaching constantly invents new ways to capture our consciences all over again. Given this context, which itself explains Luther's use of the adjective *eynerley* to qualify the expression *gottis wort*, the passage cannot be used to support the kind of separation between Scripture and the Word of God suggested by Watson, Reid, and especially Ruokanen.

The second piece of evidence which appears to confuse the picture is a very brief but oft-quoted line from the homily Luther prepared on the Epistle for the Second Sunday in Advent (Rom. 15:4): 'It holds God's Word (*sie fasset gottis wortt*)'. No less a figure than Karl Barth quotes this line as 'a statement of the indirectness of the identity of

---

[144] Amongst these are *WA* XLII, 295.1-16 = *LW* 2, 47 from *Genesisvorlesung* (1535-45) and *WA* XIX, 589.22-32 = *LW* 14, 251 from *Vier tröstliche Psalmen an die Königin zu Ungarn* (1526).

[145] 'Diße zwytracht unter der schrifft unnd menschenn lere konnen wyr nicht eynes machen. Darumb lassen wyr hie richter seyn auch die iungen kinder, die weyll diße zwo lere widdernander sind, ob man solle die schrifft (darynn eynerley gottis wort von anfang der welt her geleret ist) oder die menschen lere (die gistern new erfunden und teglich sich endern) faren lassen' *Von Menschenlehre zu meiden und Antwort auf Sprüche* (1522) *WA* X-II, 91.25-29 = *LW* 35, 153.

revelation and the Bible'.[146] Scripture *contains* God's Word rather than *is* God's Word. However, the context reveals a somewhat different emphasis:

> Where is God's word in all the books apart from the Holy Scripture? What are we doing then, when we read other books and let this one lie. Even though they may torment and kill us, no book may comfort us except the Holy Scripture. That alone has the title which Paul gives it here, that it is a book of comfort which can preserve the soul in all its distress, so that it does not despair, but contains hope. Then it takes hold of God's Word, through that it learns his gracious will, for it holds fast to it, and it continues to stay by one in life and death. But whoever does not know the will of God must have doubts, for he does not know how he stands with God.[147]

While Luther's syntax is a little difficult here, the context suggests that he has the believing soul in mind as the subject of the famous quotation, rather than the Scriptures. It is the believer who is enabled to continue in life and death by a tight grasp of God's Word. Taking hold of God's Word is identical with, not additional to, holding on to the book of comfort in every distress. Read in its own context then, and in the context of Luther's other statements both before and after the production of the *Kirchenpostille*, this passage does not support Barth's suggestion of 'the indirectness of the identity of revelation and the Bible'.

One of the primary concerns of any doctrine of biblical inspiration is the origin of Holy Scripture. The burden of the above evidence is that Luther was vitally interested in this question. Throughout his teaching career, in polemical and non-polemical settings, he affirmed both the divine and human dimensions to the authorship of Scripture. It is also clear that Luther was able to describe the finished product as the Word of God. Yet such a description stood side by side with Luther's affirmations of Christ as the Word of God, and those of the preaching

---

[146] 'das ist die Indirektheit der Identität von Offenbarung und Bibel' Barth, *Kirchliche Dogmatik*, I/2, 544 (*Church Dogmatics*, I/2, 492).

[147] 'Wo ist aber gottis wortt ynn allen buchernn außer der heyligen schrifft? was machenn wyr denn, das wyr andere bucher leßen und lassen diz ligen? Martern und todten mugen sie uns wol, aber trosten mag keyn buch, denn die heyligen schrifft, den titel hatt sie alleyn, den hie S. Paulus yhr gibt, das sie eyn trostbuch ist, wilchs die seelen erhalten kan yn allem trubsall, das sie nicht vorzage, ßondern hoffnung behallte; denn sie fasset gottis wortt, dabey lernet sie seynen gnedigen willen, daran hanget sie denn fest, und bleybt bestehen ynn leben und sterben. Wer aber gottis willen nicht weyß, der muß zweyffellen, denn er weyß nicht, wie er mit gott dran ist.' *Adventspostille* (1522) *WA* X-I/2, 75.1-10.

of Christ, the apostles, and their faithful successors as the Word of God. He would even on occasion speak of the threefold nature of the Word, carefully inserting the caveat that only one form of the Word is actually God himself. Thus while Luther could unreservedly identify Scripture with the Word, he would not unreservedly identify the Word with Scripture. In the final analysis, Luther recognised that no one form of the Word can be totally separated from the others.[148] He remained convinced our only access to Christ the Living Word is through Scripture the written Word and the only guarantee of preaching as the proclaimed Word is its fidelity to Scripture.

---

[148] Robert Goesar goes even further, suggesting that Luther's entire theology is held together by 'a rich and complex understanding of the Word of God'. Robert Goeser, 'Luther: Word of God, Language, and Art', *CurTM* 18.1 (1991), 11.

Chapter 3

Divine Words?

Luther on Inspiration and the Nature of Holy Scripture

The question of just how Luther understood the process behind his affirmation of the divine and human authorship of the Scriptures brings us once again to the simple historical fact that he did not leave us a detailed exposition of his thought on the matter. While he was fond of quoting 2 Tim. 3:16–17, whenever he went beyond mere quotation his emphasis was usually on the profitability ($\omega\phi\epsilon\lambda\iota\mu o\varsigma$) of the text rather than its inspiration.[1] Nevertheless there has been sustained scholarly interest in Luther's view of biblical inspiration, developed most recently by Miikka Ruokanen.[2] Ruokanen, it would seem, is not satisfied with Skevington Wood's assessment that Luther 'refused to be tied down to any doctrinaire account of the Spirit's inspiration'.[3]

A Theory of Inspiration?

Ruokanen begins his study by distinguishing three almost standard positions on this issue. The first, which he attributes to Lutheran Orthodoxy and modern Lutheran Fundamentalists, argues that Luther held a 'direct instrumental theory of inspiration', endorsing verbal

---

[1] E. g. *Operationes in Psalmos* (1518-21) *WA* V, 66.17-20 = *LW* 14, 338; *De servo arbitrio* (1525) *WA* XVIII, 607.6-7 = *LW* 33, 27; *Vorlesung über das Hohelied* (1530-31) *WA* XXXI-II, 588.31-589.24 = *LW* 15, 194 and *WA* XXXI-II, 684.23-29 = *LW* 15, 230; *Genesisvorlesung* (1535-45) *WA* XLII, 494.29-33 = *LW* 2, 325; *WA* XLII, 598.17-21 = *LW* 3, 70; *WA* XLIII, 46.16-19 = *LW* 3, 239; *WA* XLIII, 336.1-4 = *LW* 4, 279; and *WA* XLIV, 615.8-15 = *LW* 8, 49.
[2] Miikka Ruokanen, *Doctrina Divinitus Inspirata*; and his later article, 'Biblical Inspiration?'
[3] Wood, *Captive*, 148.

inspiration and corollaries such as inerrancy and sufficiency.[4] The second position is that which has been advanced by 'the Neo-Protestants of the Ritschlian school', arguing that Luther did not regard the Scriptures as the Word of God, but reserved this term for that which addresses us in and through the oral proclamation of the Scriptures. Precisely because the Scriptures were only potentially the Word of God for Luther, he 'had no need for a theory of biblical inspiration'.[5] Ruokanen claims that another group of Luther scholars have created a third position between these two. They have argued that Luther was primarily concerned with the uniquely inspired witnesses of Christ, generating what might be termed an 'integrated community theory of biblical inspiration'.[6]

Ruokanen's own examination of Luther's writings confirms the line of interpretation implied by those in this third, middle group, though with some modification. He concludes that it is possible to speak of Luther's commitment to biblical inspiration, but this must be understood as a statement about the doctrinal content of Scripture, not its verbal form:

> Here we are at the heart of Luther's own peculiar theory of biblical inspiration: not the text of the Scriptures, but its content, its christological message which is inalterable and the same throughout the Bible, is what Luther called inspired.[7]

However, to what extent is it still legitimate to describe this as *biblical* inspiration? Is the text of Scripture really necessary? Ruokanen goes on to answer such questions:

> It is essential to notice that *doctrina divinitus inspirata* is for Luther not an idea of Christ but a substantial content which is inseparable

---

[4] This, according to Ruokanen, is the position of Johann Quenstedt, David Hollaz, and Abraham Calov (though not Johann Gerhard) in the seventeenth century and Walther Rohnert, Franz Pieper, Hermann Sasse, and John Warwick Montgomery in the late nineteenth and twentieth centuries. Ruokanen, *Doctrina Divinitus*, 9-10.

[5] Ruokanen cites Albrecht Ritschl, Wilhelm Herrmann, Karl Holl, Reinhold Seeberg, Paul Althaus, Friedrich Beisser, Heinrich Bornkamm, Rudolf Hermann, and Gerhard Ebeling as the key exponents of this position. Ruokanen, *Doctrina Divinitus*, 11-15.

[6] Ruokanen understands this to be the position of Otto Scheel, Paul Schempp, and Wilhelm Maurer. Ruokanen, *Doctrina Divinitus*, 15-16.

[7] Ruokanen, *Doctrina Divinitus*, 91.

from the clear texts of the Bible. The doctrine and the text belong together.[8]

Ruokanen's study is stimulating and well-documented. However, it is also open to a number of methodological criticisms. He has been too ready to construct a detailed theory for Luther despite the absence of any sustained exposition of such a theory in Luther's own writings. This problem is compounded by the categories Ruokanen uses to analyse the possibilities. He does not shrink from concluding that Luther's particular 'doctrinal content theory' was in fact a combination of 'the direct instrumental theory' and 'the integrated content theory'.[9] Yet what evidence is there that Luther recognised these two elements in his inheritance and consciously brought them together in this way? Further, at a number of points Ruokanen's interpretation of the evidence is somewhat forced, as when he highlights Luther's misquote of 2 Tim. 3:16 in the course of his *scholia* on Isaiah 51, published in 1534,[10] or suggests the dominance of *doctrina pura* over *scriptura* with reference to a comment on Gal. 5:10–11 in 1535.[11] In other places he goes well beyond the evidence he has adduced. So he claims 'Luther reserves the concept of inspiration exclusively for the description of the ecstatic mode of prophetic inspiration and the christological content of the inspired message received'.[12] We are told that it is 'completely impossible to combine Luther's concept of inspiration with his view of the generation of the Gospels in the New Testament'.[13] Most telling of all perhaps is this comment: 'Luther,

---

[8] Ruokanen, *Doctrina Divinitus*, 111. Ruokanen had earlier discussed the notion of a 'clear text' (102-110).

[9] Ruokanen, *Doctrina Divinitus*, 112.

[10] 'Omnis doctrina divinitus inspirata ad docendum utilis ...' *Vorlesung über Iesaia – Scholia* (1532-34) *WA* XXV, 321.13. Ruokanen, *Doctrina Divinitus*, 90. It should be noted that this sentence does not appear in the Lauterbach manuscript of Luther's lectures, which is the basis of the text in *LW* 17, 205.

[11] 'Sed doctrina nostra, Dei gratia, pura est, omnes articulos fidei solidos et fundatos in sacris literis habemus.' *In epistolam S. Pauli ad Galatas Commentarius* (1535) *WA* XL-II, 52.22-23 = *LW* 27, 42. Ruokanen, *Doctrina Divinitus*, 91.

[12] Ruokanen, *Doctrina Divinitus*, 90. I remain unconvinced by Ruokanen's conclusion that Luther valued most highly 'a direct ecstatic encounter between God and a prophetic person' (66). Many of the passages he adduces have little to do with the production of the Scriptures when read in their context. In fact, a number have more to do with the awakening of faith in an individual than with the inspiration of a messenger and/or his message. e.g. *Genesisvorlesung* (1535-45) *WA* XLII, 560.41-561.11 = *LW* 3, 17-18 and *WA* XLIV, 813.31-38 = *LW* 8, 318.

[13] Ruokanen, *Doctrina Divinitus*, 96.

however, could not call any text of the Bible or any proclamation referring to the Scriptures the Word of God. The *res,* not the *verba,* of the Bible is inspired'.[14] Finally, it appears that Ruokanen's study is strongly influenced by late twentieth century ecumenical interests.[15]

What then of the evidence? Luther may not have left a treatise outlining a theory of biblical inspiration, but his writings are littered with relevant comments.[16] The early Psalm lectures place the production of Scripture within the larger framework of divine revelation. So, as Luther came to the title of Psalm 4, he reflected upon the significance of what he called 'the particle of the dative case'. 'This', he said, 'gives expression to the motion of the Holy Spirit, who produced the psalm and revealed it for David or to David'. In this way he was able to draw a parallel between the title of this psalm and the prophetic expression 'the Word of the Lord came to Hosea, Isaiah, etc.'.[17] In each case God has taken the initiative by addressing his servant with a word that has a wider reference. Almost twenty years later, in the process of explaining another psalm, Luther advised his readers to challenge those who appeal to reason in order to support their accusation that belief in the Trinity constitutes a breach of the first commandment. His suggested retort once again related Scripture to the idea of revelation:

> If I do not understand how the Persons are differentiated, it is enough for me that the Holy Scriptures say this and call Father, Son, and Holy Spirit by name. If I could grasp this with my reason or senses,

---

[14] Ruokanen, 'Biblical Inspiration?', 9.

[15] Note the subtitle of his larger work, *Martin Luther's Position in the Ecumenical Problem of Biblical Inspiration,* and the conclusion of his article: 'Luther's concept of inspiration is basically in full accordance with the deepest intentions of Catholic theology' (Ruokanen, 'Biblical Inspiration?', 13.

[16] A compilation of the evidence from Luther's writings is complicated by the fact that Luther used the vocabulary of inspiration to describe the activity of the Holy Spirit in creation and redemption, as well as in connection with revelation and inscripturation. Ruokanen, *Doctrina Divinitus,* 49-57.

[17] 'Sed notandum, quod in omnibus titulis preponitur huic nomini David articulus Dativi casus, quod Iudei dicunt tamen esse genitivi in superscriptionibus et titulis. Quod mihi non placet. Sed volo, quod sit dativi casus sicut alias semper, ita etiam in titulis psalmorum. Et tunc significat psalmum non esse ipsius David proprie, sed ipsi David sive ad David: per quod exprimitur motus spiritus sancti, qui fecit psalmum et revelavit Davidi seu ad David: quomodo in prophetis legimus: "factum est verbum domini ad Osee, Isaiam, etc."' *Dictata super Psalterium* (1513-15) *WA* III, 41.3-10 = *LW* 10, 44.

Divine Words?

what need would there be for faith? Of what use is Scripture revealed by God through the Holy Spirit?[18]

It is in this context that Luther made his famous comments about the task of theology. These in fact arise from his perspective on Scripture as the revelation of God through the Spirit:

> For this reason this should be the first concern of a theologian: that he be a good textualist, as it is called, and that he hold fast to the first principle of not disputing or philosophising about sacred things [...] in theology one must simply hear, believe, and hold firmly in his heart: 'God is faithful, no matter how absurd what He says in His Word may appear to our reason'.[19]

In many of Luther's comments on inspiration it is clear that the prophetic pattern of the Old Testament is most influential. The preface to his *scholia* in the *Dictata super Psalterium* included a brief reflection on 2 Sa. 23:1–4:

> However, I implore you by God, whence comes such great presumption and unique boasting beyond all prophets, and the same often repeated, that the Lord spoke by him, that by His tongue came the latter's speech, 'to whom it was appointed concerning the Christ of the God of Jacob, the excellent psalmist of Israel'? Other prophets used the expression 'The word of the Lord came to me'. This one, however, does not say, 'The word of the Lord came to me', but he says, in a new manner of speaking, 'His word was spoken by me'. With this expression he indicates some extremely intimate and friendly kind of inspiration. Other prophets confess that they spoke, but this one declares in a unique way it was not he who spoke but the Spirit who spoke through him. Although the Spirit spoke by all the prophets, as we sing, it is not stated thus regarding any of them.[20]

---

[18] 'Quomodo autem different personae, si non intelligo, sufficit mihi scriptura sancta, quae dicit ac nominat patrem, filium et spiritum sanctum, Matth. Ultimo. Si possem ista assequi ratione aut sensibus, quid opus esset fide? Quid opus esset scriptura divinitus per spiritum sanctum revelata?' *Praelectio in psalmum 45* (1532) *WA* XL-II, 593.22-25 = *LW* 12, 288.

[19] 'Quare prima haec Theologi cura sit, ut sit bonus textualis, ut appellant, et teneat hoc principium primum, in sacris rebus non esse disputandum aut Philosophandum [...] Sed in Theologia tantum est audiendum et credendum et statuendum in corde: Deus est verax, quantumcumque rationi videantur absurda, quae Deus in verbo suo dicit.' *Praelectio in psalmum 45* (1532) *WA* XL-II, 593.30-32, 34-36 = *LW* 12, 288.

[20] 'Obsecro autem per Deum, vnde tanta presumptio et singularis pre omnibus prophetis Iactantia, et eadem sepius repetita, Quod Dominus 'per eum sit locutus, per linguam eius sermo illius, cui constitutum est de Christo Dei

Luther considered David to be a prophet, but one who experienced 'some extremely intimate and friendly kind of inspiration'. Though in the final analysis what was said of David could be said of all the prophets, Luther highlighted this statement of David in order to underline the importance and dignity of the Psalter. Like all the prophets, David 'wants his tongue to be an instrument of the Holy Spirit'.[21] Much later, when Luther devoted one of his final treatises to 2 Samuel 23, he would put it slightly differently: 'Therefore these words of David are also those of the Holy Spirit'.[22] The principal difference between the two expositions is that in this latter one Luther saw no need to deny to David what he wanted to ascribe also (*auch*) to the Holy Spirit. This shift is perfectly in line with Luther's increased recognition of the importance of the original historical setting of each part of Scripture, a recognition which James Preus has suggested begins to emerge within the *Dictata* itself.[23]

This connection between prophecy and the inspiration of the Spirit was developed by Luther in the *Kirchenpostille* of 1522. The Gospel for St. Stephen's Day, a section of the apocalyptic discourse in Matthew 23, provided Luther with an opportunity to explain the variety of ways in which divine truth is revealed. As he did so, the priority he gave to Old Testament prophecy as solely the product of divine inspiration became clear:

> The present Gospel also describes such obstinate, murderous wilfulness in the first place in this way, that God tries various things with Jerusalem. He sends her various preachers whom he enumerates

---

Iacob, Qui egregius psaltes Israel'? Aliorum prophetarum ista vox est: 'factum est verbum Domini ad me'; hic autem nouo loquendi genere Non ait; factum est verbum Domini ad me, Sed: verbum eius 'per me locutum est', nescio, quid intimioris familiarissimeque inspirationis in isto verbo significat. Alii prophete sese locutos esse fatentur, hic autem non se, Sed per se locutum esse spiritum singulari modo pronunciat. Quamuis enim per omnes prophetas locutus sit, vt canimus, tamen de nullo ita dicitur.' *Dictata super Psalterium* (1513-15) *WA* LV-II, 26.25-27.10 = *LW* 10, 9-10.

[21] 'De tali ergo velocitate, que hodie est in Christo, propheta vult, quod lingua sua sit organum spiritus sancti: qui nunc velociter scribit, quia spiritum dat litera deposita.' *Dictata super Psalterium* (1513-15) *WA* III, 262.30-32 = *LW* 10, 221.

[22] 'Darumb sind diese wort Davids auch des Heiligen geistes' *Von den letzten Worten Davids* (1543) *WA* LIV, 35.37 = *LW* 15, 276.

[23] James S. Preus, 'Old Testament Promissio and Luther's New Hermeneutic', *HTR* 60 (1967), 145-161. Preus's work has not gone unchallenged. Note in particular: J. J. Pilch, 'Luther's Hermeneutical Shift', *HTR* 63 (1970), 445-448; Darrell R. Reinke, 'From Allegory to Metaphor: More Notes on Luther's Hermeneutical Shift', *HTR* 66 (1973), 386-395.

under the three names of prophets, wise men, and scribes. Prophets preach solely by inspiration of the Holy Spirit, and they have not derived their preaching from books or through men; Moses and Amos were such prophets. These are the highest and the best; they are wise and can make others wise; they can set forth sacred writings and interpret them [...] Wise men derive their message not only from God, but also from books and human beings. They are the disciples and followers of the prophets, yet they preach and teach with their own mouths and speak their own words. Such a one was Aaron: he spoke everything Moses commanded him to say [...] The scribes or those learned in the law teach by means of writings and books when they are unable to teach by talking because they are at another place. The apostles belong in this category, too, as do the evangelists and their followers, e.g., the holy fathers. However they do not write and set forth their own self-conceit, but the word of God which they have learned from the wise men and from Holy Scripture.[24]

Luther's concern here was not primarily the degree of authority pertaining to the literary deposits of the prophets, wise men, and scribes. Rather, he was concerned with the precise means by which their message, and the Scriptures which they produce and which embody this message, came to be. The distinction between the Old Testament prophets on the one hand and the apostles and evangelists on the other, he argued, exists at this level. The former make little or no reference to previous writings ('Thus says the Lord'); whilst the latter consciously place their message in the context of the Old Testament Scriptures ('This was to fulfil what was written ...'). The

---

[24] 'Solchen halstarcken, mordischen eygensynn zeygt diz Euangelium auch, zum ersten damit, das gott allerley mit yhr vorsucht. Sendet zu yhr allerley prediger, die er mit dreyen namen erzelet; propheten, weyßen, schreyber. Propheten sind, die auß bloßer eyngebung des heyligen geysts predigenn, die es nitt auß der schrifft odder durch menschen geschopfft haben, als Moses und Amos waren. Unnd das sind die hohisten unnd besten, die sind weyße und kunden andere weyße machen, schrifft setzen und außlegen [...] Die weyßen sind, die es nit bloß auß gott, ßondern durch schrifft und menschen haben, und sind die iunger und solger der propheten, doch die mit dem mund und lebendigen wortt selbs predigen unnd leren. Eyn solcher war Aaron, der da redet allis, was yhn Moses hieß [...] Die schreyber odder schrifftgelertenn sind, die mit schrifften unnd buchern leren, wo sie gegenwertig mundlich nit leren kundnen. Als die Apostell auch geweßen sind, zuuor die Euangelisten und yhr folger, als die heyligen vetter, doch das sie nit yhr dunckel, ßondern gottis wortt schreyben und handelln, wilchs sie von den weyßen und auß der schrifft erlernet haben.' *Kirchenpostille* (1522) *WA* X-I/1, 272.18-273.3, 273.6-10, 273.12-17 = *LW* 52, 89-90; cf. the earlier sermon on Mt. 23:34, preached on 26 December 1514. *WA* I, 30.1-21.

similarity between the apostles, evangelists, and the 'holy fathers' exists at this level as well. Writers in each of these groups consciously and regularly refer to those writings which preceded them. This is why Luther was able to describe the Old Testament prophets as the highest and the best. The direct, unmediated, 'Thus says the Lord' quality of their message highlights its divine origin.

Nevertheless, Luther was also able to use the prophetic model to understand the phenomenon of the New Testament. Later in the *Kirchenpostille*, in the homily prepared on the Gospel for the Sunday after Christmas (Lk. 2:33–40), Luther spoke of Simeon in this way:

> Now we find Simeon in the same temple; Luke says of Simeon that he is a personification of all prophets filled with the Holy Spirit. They spoke and wrote as they were inspired by the Holy Spirit, and they waited for the coming of Christ as did Simeon, and they never ceased to do this until Christ had come, as St. Peter says in Acts 4 that all prophets have spoken of the time of Christ.[25]

As the Holy Spirit was intimately involved in the speaking and writing of the prophets, so too he is involved in the production of the apostolic writings. In the midst of comments on Gal. 5:2, Luther pointed to Paul's zealous and angry language, observing that 'the Holy Spirit wrests such passionate words out of him'.[26] When it came to questions of authority, Luther almost did away with his distinction between the apostles and the Old Testament prophets. The theses Luther prepared for the licentiate examination of Jacob Schenck and Philip Motz on 10 October 1536 began with the uncompromising declaration that after Christ there is no authority which is equal to that of the apostles and prophets.[27] Luther went on to justify the inclusion of the apostles at this point by reference to the unique promise of the Holy Spirit which

---

[25] 'Nu ist ynn demselben tempell Simeon, der ist ein person aller propheten, die vol heyligiß geysts waren, wie Lucas vom Simeon sagt, unnd haben auß dem heyligen geyst geredt und geschrieben und gewartten auff den tzukunfftigen Christum, wie dißer Simeon, haben auch nitt auffgehoret, noch ende, biß das Christus ist kommen, wie S. Peter sagt Act. 4., das alle propheten auff Christus tzeytt geredt haben.' *Kirchenpostille* (1522) *WA* X-I/1, 384.11-16 = *LW* 52, 105.

[26] 'Paulus vehementer commotus loquitur ex magno Zelo et fervore Spiritus mera fulmina contra Legem et Circumcisionem, Illaque tam ardentia verba ei irato propter magnam indignitatem rei extorquet Spiritus sanctus' *In epistolam S. Pauli ad GalatasCommentarius* (1535) *WA* XL-II, 9.26-28 = *LW* 27, 9.

[27] 'Nulla autoritas post Christum est Apostolis et Prophetis aequanda.' *Die Disputation die potestate concilii* (1536) *WA* XXXIX-I, 184.4-6.

had been given to them.[28] Again, a year later, as he preached on Jn. 1:3, Luther told the Wittenberg congregation that 'we cling to the Scriptures of the prophets and apostles, who spoke as they were moved by the Holy Spirit'.[29] This extension of the language of 2 Pet. 1:21 to cover the apostolic writings makes sense once it is realised that an analogous operation of the Spirit is involved in both.

It is evident then, that the prophetic model was important for Luther when he considered biblical inspiration in regard to either the Old Testament or the New. However, Luther rarely provided any detail on the processes involved. We have already noted his general reference to being 'moved by the Holy Spirit' and his inclusion of references to earlier writings within the scope of the Spirit's activity. Another important piece of evidence here is the brief discussion of revelation and inspiration in the course of his series on the minor prophets in 1524. As he lectured on Joel 2:28, Luther distinguished between 'hidden inspiration (*occulta inspiratio*)' and 'manifest vision (*manifesta visio*)'.[30] While the first of these is closely related to salvation, in that it involves the awakening of faith and love in the heart of the believer, the second is a particular pouring out of the Spirit upon the apostles and prophets in order that they might make public the hidden work of God in creation and redemption. It is accompanied by obvious signs which authenticate any claim that a particular message comes from the Spirit.[31] As he distinguished prophecy from dreams and visions, Luther went further:

---

[28] 'Apostoli certam (non in specie solum, sed individuo quoque) promissionem Spiritus sancti habuerunt.' *Die Disputation die potestate concilii* (1536) *WA* XXXIX-I, 184.10-12.

[29] 'wir halten uns an der Propheten und Aposteln Schrifft, die da vom heiligen Geist getrieben geredet haben' *Auslegung des ersten und zweiten Kapitels Johannis* (1537-8) *WA* XLVI, 556.13-15 = *LW* 22, 23.

[30] *Praelectiones in prophetas minores* (1524) *WA* XIII, 80.2. Two things should be noted. (1) Ruokanen misquotes Luther here when he draws a parallel between *occulta inspiratio* and *manifesta inspiratio*. In neither of the forms of Luther's comment on this verse included in the Weimar edition does he use the second expression. The 'b' text has *manifesta visione seu revelatione et occulta inspiratione. WA* XIII, 109.2-3. Ruokanen, *Doctrina Divinitus,* 58-59. (2) These lectures were given around the time that Erasmus published his *De libero arbitrio.* The distinction Luther makes here may in fact be an early form of the distinction between the external and internal clarity of the Word, which he makes in his reply, *De servo arbitrio.*

[31] 'Et ergo maxime oportebat hoc renum plane diversum ab illo priori manifestis signis institui et confirmari et aperta spiritus revelatione seu effusione, siquidem occulta spiritus revelatio et in synagoga erat.' *Praelectiones in prophetas minores* (1524) *WA* XIII, 109.12-15 = *LW* 18, 106.

> Here he sets down three kinds of divine illumination: first, prophecy. This occurs when the mystery of Christ or the grace shown to the world through Christ is preached in clear detail, as when Jeremiah says: 'I will put My law within them'. Also, when Paul or the other apostles are manifestly interpreting Scripture, this interpretation is prophecy.[32]

The apostolic citation and interpretation of the Old Testament (the meaning of *scriptura* in this context) was now included under the heading 'prophecy'.

Such prophecy entailed messages spoken or written at God's command. Thus, in the treatise on the doctrines of men, Luther openly stated that 'the words of the apostles were committed to them by God'.[33] However Luther developed the idea in more detail with reference to Moses in his lecture on Dt 1:3:

> But note this: 'He spoke to the Children of Israel all that the Lord had commanded him to say to them'. He speaks nothing unless it has been commanded him by the Lord, for to the point of tedium he repeats and impresses this in this book, in order to teach that among the people of God nothing is to be declared except what is assuredly the Word of God. Yet it is not enough to be certain that it is the Word of God, but through the commandment of God each should be forced to speak the Word of God, as he says: 'Everything the Lord commanded him'. He does not say: 'Which the Lord put into his mind'; for thus godless men would vainly flatter themselves about the inspiration of the Holy Spirit, while they fancy themselves to be infallible in their statutes and counsels. What is said here — 'Moses began to explain the Law' — also pertains to the fact that he speaks nothing but what is divinely commanded.[34]

---

[32] 'Tria hic genera divinae illustrationis ponit: primo prophetiam, quae est, ubi clare et rotunde dicitur mysterium Christi sive gratia per Christum mundo exhibita, ut quando Hieremias ait: dabo legem meam in visceribus eorum. Et quando Paulus aut alii apostoli evidenter scripturam interpretantur, haec interpretatio est prophetia.' *Praelectiones in prophetas minores* (1524) *WA* XIII, 110.27-111.3 = *LW* 18, 108.

[33] 'Der Apostel rede ist yhn von gott befolhen.' *Von Menschenlehre zu meiden* (1522) *WA* X-II, 91.14-15 = *LW* 35, 152.

[34] 'Observa autem id "locutus est ad filios Israel omnia, quae praecepit ei dominus ad illos". Nihil nisi mandatum sibi a domino loquitur, hoc enim usque ad tedium in isto libro repetit et inculcat, ut doceat Nihil esse in populo dei dicendum, nisi quod certum sit esse verbum dei, imo nec hoc satis est certum esse de verbo dei, sed praecepto dei cogi oportet quemlibet ad dicendum verbum dei, ut hic dicit: omnia, quae praecepit illi dominus, non ait, quae suggessit illi dominus, ut frustra sibi impii homines de afflatu spiritus

Divine Words?

Clearly Luther did not consider that divine inspiration necessarily bypasses the consciousness of the divine messenger. Indeed in this particular example he actually held that such consciousness is required. The proclamation of the message is itself an act of obedience. So too is the production of the biblical text, even though Luther was willing to hypothesise about Moses' use of more ancient sources.[35] In the final analysis, as he said with reference to some seemingly insignificant details in Genesis 12, 'the Holy Spirit wanted this to be committed to writing'.[36] Luther would suggest to the Councilmen of Germany that God's directions to the Levites concerning the Book of the Law and other writings fit right here: 'Thence have come the Holy Scriptures of the Old Testament, which would never have been collected or preserved had God not required such care to be bestowed on them'.[37] The production, collection, and preservation of the Scriptures is related to God's purpose and activity.

Only at a very few points, however, does Luther use the language commonly associated with a view of inspiration as dictation. The most celebrated case is found in the *Dictata super Psalterium*, where in the *scholia* to Psalm 45 Luther wrote:

> When one has put another's word and the sense of the words into the heart, this is not yet writing, but only the stylus poised over the tablet, which is then reduced to living letters, when God gives the increase and grants it to be efficacious and wise. This is something He can do very swiftly. Therefore, as he who waters and plants is nothing, but God who gives the increase, so he who has the stylus or is the stylus or puts it to the tablet is nothing, but He who writes,

---

sancti placeant, dum in suis statutis et consiliis sese non errare divinant. Nam quod hic dicitur 'coepit Moses explanare legem ipsum quoque eo pertinet, ut non nisi divinitus mandatum loquatur.' *Annotationes M. Lutheri in Deuteronomion Mosi* (1525) *WA* XIV, 547.17-548.13 = *LW* 9, 15.

[35] 'When somebody asked about Moses and how he could write about the creation and other things that happened so long before his time, [Luther] said, "I think many things had been written before Moses and that Moses took these things and added to them what God commanded him". [Cum quidam quaereret de Mose, quomodo potuerit scribere de creatione et aliis rebus tanto ante se factis, dicebat: Ego puto multa scripta esse ante Mosen, das es Moses darnach hat genommen und dazu gemacht, was yhm Gott befolhen hatt.' *Tischreden* #291 (Summer 1532) *WATr* I, 121.13-28 = *LW* 54, 40-41.

[36] 'Spiritus sanctus id literis voluit mandari' *Genesisvorlesung* (1535-45) *WA* XLII, 474.4 = *LW* 2, 296.

[37] 'Daher ist komen die heylige schrifft des Alten Testaments, wilche sonst nymer mehr were zu samen bracht odder blieben, wo Gott nicht hette sollchen fleys drauss heyssen haben.' *An die Ratherren aller Stadte deutsches Lands* (1524) *WA* XV, 50.1-3 = *LW* 45, 373.

namely the writer writing swiftly, the Holy Spirit. Therefore, O prophet, it is for you to utter and be the pen. You can openly proclaim out of the fullness of your heart and spirit, but you cannot openly pour out the Spirit Himself, nor can you infuse Him and so make others feel the feeling you have.[38]

The comment, with its allusions to 1 Cor. 3:7 and certain statements of Gregory the Great, emphasised the instrumental nature of human authorship. However, several observations suggest caution is required when appealing to this text. Firstly, the language of writer and pen which Luther used here is actually the language of the text itself (מהיר לשוני עט סופר). It is not simply imported into the discussion from Luther's understanding of the processes of inspiration. Secondly, this is an extremely early comment by Luther, probably from the first half of 1514, and its key ideas are not as prominent in his later writings. Indeed, in his 1532 lecture on the same verse his emphasis is on the word 'swiftly (*velociter*)' rather than 'pen (*calamus*)'. On that latter occasion he spent most time on the contrast between the joyful spirit and heart of the psalmist and Moses who was 'slow of speech'.[39]

---

[38] 'Quando enim quis alteri verbum in cor miserit et sensum verborum, nondum ests scriptura, sed solum stilus positus in tabulam, qui tunc ducitur in literas vivas, quando deus incrementum dat et afficere et sapere concedit: quod quidem potest velocissime facere. Igitur sicut qui rigat et plantat nihil est, sed qui incrementum dat deus: ita qui stilum habet vel est vel ponit eum ad tabulam, nihil est, sed qui scribit, scriba scilicet velociter scribens, spiritus sanctus. Quare ructare et calamum esse tuum est, o propheta: foris pronunciare potes ex abundantia cordis et spiritus, sed non potes ipsum spiritum effundere foris, neque ipsum infundere ac sic sentificare, sicut tu sentis.' *Dictata super Psalterium* (1513-15) *WA* III, 256.12-20 = *LW* 10, 212.

[39] 'In fact, he glances out of the corner of his eye at Moses when he speaks of his tongue as the pen of the fast-writing scribe. Moses' tongue was the pen of a slow-moving writer, as he himself confesses that he was "slow of speech". For that reason his brother was pressed to take his place in speaking. Moses performed the miracles, whereas Aaron spoke. This, however, was a prototype signifying that the kingdom of the Law should not be delightful. He plays on this and says: "Moses was not eloquent; he had a heavy tongue and heavy hands. Therefore he was unable to sing well, but was a slow and stumbling writer. I, however, have a joyful spirit and a joyful heart. I do not teach the tyranny of the Law and of sin, but sweet promises and the glad message of peace and certainty of conscience." Thus you see that all these things are allegorical. So throughout the psalm an antithesis is set up with Moses, or between the Law and the Gospel. If you recognize this, the psalm will be quite clear. [Respicit enim oblique ad Mosen, quod linguam suam vocat calamum velocis scribae. Nam Mose lingua fuit calamus scribae impediti, Sicut confitetur quoque se "blaesum" esse, quare frater eius coactus est vicem eius implere in dicendo, Moses autem miracula faciebat, Aaron loquebatur. Fuit

Thirdly, the context suggests that what Luther had in mind in the earlier lecture was the way in which, through the text, the Spirit arouses faith and obedience in the heart of the believer, rather than the way the text itself came into existence.

Much of this also applies to Luther's reflections on 2 Cor. 3:2 in the midst of his 1540 lectures on John 4. However, he does appear to take the language a little further.

> Listen to St. Paul [...] 'I do not mean to say', he declares, 'that I wrote the letter with my own hand. The letter was actually written by a deacon, and the true author is Jesus Christ'. It is not ink that He uses in His pen, that is, in His ministry. He comes with the Holy Spirit and His gifts, as we read in 1 Corinthians 12. The ink is the proclamation which He writes through the apostles; and the Holy Spirit transmits this message through us.[40]

The point of this comment is the reality of the Spirit's application of Christ's truth to the heart of the believer. Yet the first and indispensable stage in this is the inscripturation of the apostolic proclamation of Christ. One and the same message is both 'the ink' and that which is transmitted by the Spirit.

Inspiration, Incarnation, Accommodation, and the Cross

The model of the prophets was not the only paradigm employed by Luther to explain the origin of the Scriptures. The use of the term 'Word of God' in connection with Scripture suggested an analogy with the incarnation of Christ. Luther did not hesitate to exploit such an

---

autem haec figura, quod regnum legis non sit iucundum. Ad id alludit et dicit: Moses non fuit eloquens, sed habuit gravem linguam et manus graves, ergo non potuit bene canere, sed fuit tardus et impeditus scriba. Ego autem habeo laetum spiritum et cor nec doceo tyrannidem legis et peccati, sed suaves promissiones et laetas istas doctrinas pacis et securitatis conscientiae. Vides ita omnia esse allegorica, quare per totum Psalmum est facienda antithesis Mosi seu legis cum Euangelio, tunc erit Psalmus clarior.]' *Praelectio in psalmum 45* (1532) *WA* XL-II, 483.21-31 = *LW* 12, 205.

[40] 'Sihe, was S. Paulus thut, der spricht [...] nicht, spricht ehr, das wir der ertzschreiber weren, sondern durch einen Diaconum. Den Jhesus Christus ist der warhafftige schreiber, in seiner feddern, das ist: in seinem predigtampt, bringet ehr nicht tindten, sondern den heiligen Geist und seine gabe, wie den in der ersten Epistel zun Corinthern am 12. Capittel gesaget wirdt. Das ist die tindte, die Predigt, das schreibet er durch die Apostel, und der heilige Geist hatts durch uns geschrieben.' *Die funf und viertzigste Predigt, am Sonnabendt nach dem tage Timothej* (23 August 1539) *WA* XLVII, 183.20, 183.23-29 = *LW* 22, 472.

analogy and boldly explore its implications.[41] Nevertheless, this did not lead him to abandon the prophetic model, which we have seen in use throughout his teaching career. Instead, the evidence suggests he saw these two approaches to the origin of Holy Scripture as intimately connected and complementing one another.[42]

At one level, the analogy between incarnation and inscripturation served to highlight the fact that Scripture, like Christ himself, is the self-revelation of God. This appears to be how it was used when it first surfaces in Luther's writings, in the rather convoluted explanation of Ps. 45:1 in the *Dictata*. Luther here endorsed Augustine's interpretation, which related the psalmist's utterance first to the person of God, who produced the Only-Begotten 'from his heart', and then to the fact that 'by comparison God explains his Word not in sounds but in writing for the purpose of denoting permanence, because writing remains while the spoken word passes away'.[43] The connection is suggested by the expression 'Word' and led Luther into the discussion of the threefold manner in which the Word of God is spoken and revealed which we examined earlier. In that discussion, Luther moved with apparent ease between the various uses of the term 'Word', precisely because he was confident that the Word, in whatever form it is found, always functions as God's self-expression.[44] This was not a momentary and idle thought as far as Luther was concerned. In 1537 he declared 'The Scriptures are God's testimony of himself'.[45]

Luther considered this principle to have the most profound of implications. If God is truly known when this Word is heard and believed, precisely because this Word is God's own self-expression,

---

[41] Wood, *Captive*, 139; Klug, *Luther*, 29-32; Rogers and McKim, *Authority*, 78-79; W. Robert Godfrey, 'Biblical Authority in the Sixteenth and Seventeenth Centuries: A Question of Transition', in D. A. Carson and John D. Woodbridge (eds.), *Scripture and Truth*, 228; Ruokanen, *Doctrina Divinitus*, 102, 120.

[42] Willem Kooiman goes further than the evidence when he argues that Luther's 'view of the Bible had closer bonds with his doctrine of the incarnation than with any theory of inspiration'. Kooiman, *Luther*, 237.

[43] 'Et sic solus, quia non aliunde sicut vir ex muliere, sed ex corde produxit unigenitum, ut pulchre Augustinus exponit [...] Deus suum verbum non sonis, sed scriptis explicat, ad significandam permanentiam: quia scriptum manet, prolatum transit.' *Dictata super Psalterium* (1513-15) *WA* III, 261.19-21, 261.33-35 = *LW* 10, 219-220.

[44] Gerhard Ebeling speaks of Luther's 'striking concentration on the word as *the* way of God's self-disclosure and on faith as *the* mode of man's response'. Ebeling, 'The New Hermeneutics', 37.

[45] 'die schrifft Gottes zeugnis von ym selbs ist' *Die drei Symbola oder Bekenntnis des Glaubens Christi* (1537/38) *WA* L, 281.7 = *LW* 34, 227.

Divine Words?

then to tamper with this Word is to tamper with God. So, in the 1517 Hebrews lectures he could say 'one falls away from the living God when one falls away from His Word, which is alive and gives life to all things, yes, is God himself'.[46] This line of thought was developed six years later, as he lectured on Deuteronomy:

> After a man has begun to mistrust God, whom he previously considered propitious, he makes God an object of his hatred. For when His Word is changed, He Himself is changed; for He Himself is in His Word.[47]

Luther has not confused God and the proclaimed or inscripturated Word here. There is no conflict between these statements and his insistence that only one form of the Word is *substantialiter Deus*. Rather, Luther's point is that we have no access to the God who has spoken his Word other than this Word itself.[48] To disbelieve or change the Word is to say that God is not in reality what he has presented himself to be. Thus to fall away from the Word is to fall away from the God who has spoken and to change the Word is to change the God who has spoken.

At another level Luther could use the analogy between incarnation and inscripturation to highlight the dual nature of Scripture. The clearest statement of this is his comment from 1541:

> The Holy Scripture is the Word of God, written and (as I might say) lettered and formed in letters, just as Christ is the eternal Word of God cloaked in human flesh. And just as Christ was embraced and handled by the world, so is the written Word of God too. It is a worm and no book, when compared with other books.[49]

---

[46] 'A Deo enim vivo disceditur, dum a verbo eius disceditur, quod est vivum et omnia vivificans, imo Deus ipse' *Die Vorlesung über den Hebraerbrief* (1517-18) *WA* LVII-III, 148.12-14 = *LW* 29, 153.

[47] 'Postquam homo diffidere coeperit deo, quem prius propitium habuit, odibilem sibi reddit. Nam quando mutatur eius verbum, ipse mutatur, est enim ipse in verbo suo' *Deuteronomion Mosi cum annotationibus* (1525) *WA* XIV, 557.1-3 = *LW* 9, 22. The lectures were delivered in 1523 and published in 1525.

[48] 'He cannot be known or thought of except through his Word. [ipse autem nisi per verbum suum nec teneri nec cogitari potest.]' *Deuteronomion Mosi cum annotationibus* (1525) *WA* XIV, 648.26-27 = *LW* 9, 131.

[49] 'Die heilige Schrifft ist Gottes wort, geschrieben und (das ich so rede) gebuchstabet und in buchstaben gebildet, Gleich wie Christus ist das ewige Gottes wort, in die menscheit verhullet, Und gleich wie Christus in der Welt gehalten und gehandelt ist, so gehets dem schrifftlichn Gottes wort auch. Es ist ein wurm und kein Buch, gegen ander Bucher gerechnet.' *Spüche aus dem Alten Testament* (1541) *WA* XLVIII, 31.4-8.

This parallel between the eternal Word of God and the written Word of God could be tightly drawn, even to the point of a rejection of both by the world. However, Luther was acutely aware of the limitations of the analogy. He did not develop it in terms of the inseparability of the two 'natures' or even a *communicatio idiomatum*.[50] The Word which is written or proclaimed is to be honoured highly and taken seriously, for God's Word will always accomplish what he has intended it to do. Nevertheless, it is vital to remember that only one form of the Word is substantially God (*substantialiter Deus*).[51] Luther spelt this out most clearly in *De servo arbitrio,* as he sought to explain to Erasmus the difference between the incomprehensibility of the subject of Scripture (God) and the clarity of Scripture which speaks of that subject: 'God and the Scripture of God are two things, no less than the Creator and the creature of God are two things'.[52]

Luther could also use this analogy to stress God's condescension in Scripture. Here, of course, he was echoing the language of Chrysostom, Augustine, and Gregory the Great. The *Kirchenpostille* of 1522 provides an excellent example in Luther's explanation of Mt. 23:37:

> The words are to be interpreted most simply without sophistication and as having to do with the divine will, in accordance with the usage of Scripture which speaks of God, for the sake of the simplest people, as if he were a human being [...] These passages are all written in accordance with our understanding and ability and not in accordance with the essential state of the divine nature. Therefore these words are not to be transformed into lofty speculation or recondite descriptions of the divine nature; rather, they are to be left for the simplest people, to be spoken and interpreted in keeping with our understanding; for according to our understanding God acts as

---

[50] Wood provides no evidence from Luther for his assertion to the contrary. Wood, *Captive,* 176.

[51] 'Illud est verbum incarnatum, quod fuit a principio verus Deus, hoc verbum prolatum; illud verbum est substantialiter Deus, hoc verbum effective, est potentia Dei et virtus, non substantialiter Deus, nam est habitus hominis sive Christi sive ministri.' *Tischreden* #5177 (August 1540) *WATr* IV, 695.19-21 = *LW* 54, 395.

[52] 'Duae res sunt Deus et Scriptura Dei, non minus quam duae res sunt, Creator et creatura Dei' *De servo arbitrio* (1525) *WA* XVIII, 606.11-12 = *LW* 33, 25; cf. *WA* XVIII, 685.25-27 = *LW* 33, 140: 'Diatribe, however, deceives herself in her ignorance by not making any distinction between God preached and God hidden, that is, between the Word of God and God himself. [Illudit autem sese Diatribe ignorantia sua, dum nihil distinguit inter Deum praedicatum et absconditum, hoc est, inter verbum Dei et Deum ipsum].'

the words sound. This is a beautiful and comforting manner of speaking of God who is neither terrifying nor far removed.[53]

God addresses us, Luther observed, with anthropomorphisms and phenomenological language. In this way it is God who has overcome the epistemological gap between himself and us.[54] Luther insisted that there was no other way by which we could know or speak of God, except by this divine condescension.

Luther developed this aspect of the origin of Scripture in his last series of lectures, those on Genesis. Here he used the expression 'the coverings of God (*involucra Dei*)' to indicate the means by which God in his glory is made known to humanity in its sinfulness:

> God also does not manifest Himself except through His works and the Word, because the meaning of these is understood in some measure. Whatever else belongs essentially to the Divinity cannot be grasped and understood, such as being outside time, before the world, etc. Perhaps God appeared to Adam without a covering, but after the fall into sin He appeared in a gentle breeze as though enveloped in a covering. Similarly he was enveloped later on in the tabernacle by the mercy seat and in the desert by a cloud and fire. Moses, therefore, also calls these objects 'faces of God', through which God manifested Himself. Cain, too, calls the place at which he had previously sacrificed 'the face of God'. This nature of ours has become so misshapen by sin, so depraved and utterly corrupted, that it cannot recognise God or comprehend His nature without a covering. It is for this reason that those coverings are necessary.[55]

---

[53] 'Das die wortt nur auffs aller schlechts und eynfeltigst vorstanden werden von dem gottlichen willen, nach gewonheytt der schrifft, die da von gott redet alß von eynem menschen umb der eynfelltigen willen [...] Wilche spruch sind alle gesagt nach unßerm fulen und dunckel, nit nach dem weßentlichen stand gottlicher natur. Darumb sind sie nit yn die hohe speculation tzu furen von den hymlichen redten gottlicher natur, ßondern solln fur die eynfeltigen hienyden gelassen werden und nach unßerm fulen sie vorstehen und gesagt seyn lassen; denn wyr fulen nit anders, er thu alßo, wie die wort lautten. Und ist eyn feyn trostlich weyße tzu reden von gott, der nit schrecklich und hoch ist.' *Kirchenpostille* (1522) *WA* X-I/1, 279.12-14, 279.22-280.6 = *LW* 52, 95.

[54] The assumption by Rogers and McKim that this *accommodatio* necessarily involves the presence of error takes us beyond the statements of Luther and raises serious questions about the nature of genuine humanity, especially in the light of the incarnation. Rogers and McKim, *Authority,* 77-79, 87-88.

[55] 'Ideo Deus quoque se non manifestat nisi in operibus et verbo, quia haec aliquo modo capiuntur; reliqua, quae propria divinitatis sunt, capi aut intelligi non possunt, ut sunt: esse extra tempus ante mundum, etc. Forte Adae apparuit nudus, sed post peccatum in sibilo apparuit, quo ceu involucro fuit involutus.

Luther recognised that the alienation from God which is the result of the fall into sin has serious epistemological consequences. Unaided, we are now unable to understand God and his purposes. All talk about God must deal with God as he presents himself to us, rather than speculate about how God may be in himself:

> Whoever desires to be saved and to be safe when he deals with such great matters, let him simply hold to the form, the signs, and the coverings of the Godhead, such as His Word and His works. For in His Word and in His works He shows Himself to us.[56]

Luther was convinced that God's condescension is genuine. The *involucra Dei* are neither deceptive nor illusory. The real God is really encountered in the manner in which he reveals himself.

> When God reveals Himself to us, it is necessary for Him to do so through some such veil or wrapper and to say: 'Look! Under this wrapper you will be sure to take hold of Me'. When we embrace this wrapper, adoring, praying, and sacrificing to God there, we are said to be praying to God and sacrificing to Him properly.[57]

He was also convinced that the divine motive behind this manner of revelation is benevolence:

> It is for this reason that God lowers Himself to the level of our weak comprehension and presents Himself to us in images, in coverings, as it were, in simplicity adapted to a child, that in some measure it may be possible for Him to be known by us.[58]

Sic postea involutus fuit in tabernaculo propiciatorio, in deserto nube et igni. Quare Moses ista etiam vocat Dei 'facies', per quae se Deus manifestavit. Et Cain vocat faciem Dei locum, in quo immolaverat antea. Haec enim natura sic est peccato deformata, imo corrupta et perdita, ut non possit Deum nudum cognoscere seu comprehendere, qualis sit. Ideo involucra ista necessaria sunt.' *Genesisvorlesung* (1535-45) *WA* XLII, 9.32-10.2 = *LW* 1, 11.

[56] 'Nam qui vult tutus esse et sine periculo in tantis rebus versari, is simpliciter se intra species, signa et involucra ista divinitatis contineat, qualia sunt verbum eius et opera eius. Nam in verbo et operibus se nobis ostendit.' *Genesisvorlesung* (1535-45) *WA* XLII, 11.22-25 = *LW* 1, 13.

[57] 'Necesse enim est, ut Deus, cum se nobis revelat, id faciat per velamen et involucrum quoddam et dicat: Ecce sub hoc involucro me certo apprehendes. Id involucrum cum amplectimur, cum ibi adoramus, invocamus, sacrificamus, Deum invocasse, Deo sacrificasse recte dicimur.' *Genesisvorlesung* (1535-45) *WA* XLII, 12.21-25 = *LW* 1, 15.

[58] 'Ideo ipse Deus se demittit ad captum infirmitatis nostrae, et sub similitudinibus ceu involucris puerili simplicitate se nobis offert, ut aliquo modo a nobis cognosci possit.' *Genesisvorlesung* (1535-45) *WA* XLII, 294.3-5 = *LW* 2, 45.

However, we can go further. A number of scholars have pointed to an even more profoundly theological dimension to this *condescensio* or *accommodatio* of God. Luther's understanding of Scripture, they argue, does not stand in isolation from the rest of his theology but rather is best seen in the context of his most central theological convictions, particularly the *theologia crucis*. Ruokanen is one amongst many who identify this as the real driving force behind Luther's approach to Scripture:

> For Luther the question of communication between God and man is not a philosophical but a theological problem. Therefore it is fundamentally based on the principle of incarnation, on the condescension of the Triune God into humanity and matter. This can be understood only in terms of the theology of the cross.[59]

According to the theology of the cross, the glory of God and the fallenness of humanity necessitates revelation that is veiled or hidden. The glory of God comes to us under the form of its contrary: his victory, dominion, and life is displayed under the form of the defeat, humiliation, and death on the cross. It is here that the real theologian recognises the *posteriora Dei*.[60]

While it is possible to read too much into Luther at this point and to expect a theological integration and systematic precision that is inappropriate and anachronistic, the theology of the cross is indeed the proper context for at least two comments by Luther on Holy Scripture, both of which have been misunderstood and misused in much of the modern literature. In 1516, as he commented on Rom. 12:2, Luther remarked:

> And thus just as the wisdom of God is hidden under the appearance of stupidity, and truth under the form of lying — for so the Word of God, as often it comes, comes in a form contrary to our own thinking, which seems in its own opinion to have the truth, so it judges that the Word which is contrary to it is a lie, and so much so

---

[59] Ruokanen, *Doctrina Divinitus*, 120; cf. Kooiman, *Luther*, 17.

[60] '19. That person does not deserve to be called a theologian who looks upon the invisible things of God as though they were clearly perceptible in those things which have actually happened. 20. He deserves to be called a theologian, however, who comprehends the visible and manifest things of God seen through suffering and the cross. 21. A theologian of glory calls evil good and good evil. A theologian of the cross calls the thing what it actually is. [19. Non ille digne Theologus dicitur, qui invisibilia Dei per ea, facta sunt, intellecta conspicit, 20. Sed qui visibilia et posteriora Dei per passiones et crucem conspecta intelligit. 21. Theologus gloriae dicit malum bonum et bonum malum, Theologus crucis dicit id quod res est.]' *Disputatio Heidelbergae habita* (1518) *WA* I, 354.17-22 = *LW* 31, 40.

that Christ called His Word our adversary in Matthew 5: 'Make friends with your accuser', and Hosea 5: 'For I will be like a lion to Ephraim, and like a young lion to the house of Judah', that is I will be contrary — so also the will of God, although it is truly and naturally 'good and acceptable and perfect', yet it is so hidden under the disguise of the evil, the displeasing, and the hopeless, that to our will and good intention, so to speak, it seems to be nothing but a most evil and hopeless thing and in no way the will of God, but rather the will of the devil, unless man abandons his own will and good intentions and submits himself in complete denial of his own righteousness, goodness and truth.[61]

The notion of 'revelation under the form of its contrary', one of the critical elements of the *theologia crucis,* is here applied to the Word of God, which in this context is clearly Holy Scripture and in particular the instructions which follow Rom. 12:1–2 and which fill out what is the good and acceptable and perfect will of God. Luther's point is that the Word which comes to us is so able to challenge us and our preconceived notions of wisdom, glory, and truth, to insist on a response to God's mercy which might conflict with our own perspective on piety and righteousness, that without the work of God it would be possible to dismiss its teaching as foolishness and lies. In a fallen world, this dissonance is what we are to expect.

The second text is from Luther's sermon on Exodus 2, preached on 20 November 1524. His allegorical interpretation of the chapter included his reflections on the significance of Moses being preserved in a basket of reeds (*Rohrkasten*): that which may have looked weak and pitiable to an observer actually furthered the redemptive purposes of God. As Luther began to apply this principle to the Word of God itself, he commented in passing that even the apostle Paul found it

---

[61] 'Sicut Itaque Dei Sapientia abscondita est Sub spetie stultitie et veritas sub forma mendacii — Ita enim verbum Dei, quoties venit, venit in spetie contraria menti nostre, que sibi vera sapere videtur; ideo verbum contrarium sibi mendacium Iudicat adeo, vt Christus Verbum suum appellauerit aduersarium nostrum, Matt. 5.: 'Esto consentiens aduersario tuo'; Et Osee 5.: 'Ego quasi Leena Ephraim, et quasi catulus leonis domui Iuda' i. e. contrarius — Ita et voluntas Dei, cum sit vere et naturaliter 'bona, beneplacens, perfecta', Sed ita abscondita sub spetie mali, displicentis ac desperati, vt nostre voluntati et bone, vt dicitur, intentioni non nisi pessima, desperatissima et nullo modo Dei, Sed diaboli voluntas videatur, Nisi homo relicta sua voluntate et intentione bona submittat se in omnem abnegationem Iustitie, ,bonitatis, veritatis a se preconcepte.' *Divi Pauli apostoli ad Romanos Epistola* (1516) *WA* LVI, 446.31-447.9 = *LW* 25, 438-439.

necessary to remind the Corinthians that the words he brought to them were not simply the wisdom of men. Luther continued:

> Holy Scripture presents itself as something weak, being without beauty and adornment. We forget that we are supposed to believe the divine word while it appears to be nothing and unattractive. But faith comes from *the divine Word and is given through divine power alone and not external decoration.* It is through the inward inspiration of the Holy Spirit that we can have confidence in the disfigured Word of God. That is why it is shocking and horrifying when you see *that everything Holy Scripture asks and requires appears unceremonial*, as when it teaches that we should not be covetous, that we should put to death the flesh and the old Adam. The pretty harlot Reason, on the other hand, teaches how one might get hold of money and treasure, wisdom, goodwill and honour.[62]

The contours of the *theologia crucis* are evident. Two evaluations of Holy Scripture are possible. To the human eye it is weak and ineffectual, even repulsive. The pattern of life it commends is uninviting. Yet to the one who sees beyond appearances, to the one in whom the Spirit of God is working, this disfigured word is a powerful, living word.

The theology of the cross, tied as it is to the life and work of the incarnate Word, provides us with a perspective on God's condescension that in turn prevents us from falling into a misunderstanding which makes Luther's own exegetical method problematical. Luther is decidedly not calling on his congregation and

---

[62] 'Die heilige Schrifft lautet als ein uberdrüssig ding, ist ungezieret und ungeschmuckt, das einer nicht gedechte, das Menschen dem Göttlichen Wort gleuben solten, dieweil es gar nichts scheinet noch geschmuckt ist. Aber der Glaube kömet aus dem Göttlichen Wort *und wird der Göttlichen krafft alleine gegeben und nicht dem eusserlichen Schmuck,* Sondern der inwendigen Eingebung des heiligen Geistes, das man dem ungestalten Wort Gottes trawet. Darnach so ists noch grewlicher und scheuslicher, wenn du sihest, *das alles unförmlich scheinet, was die heilige Schrifft gebent und erfoddert,* Als wenn sie leret, Man sol nicht geitzig sein, das fleisch und den alten Adam tödten, dawider die vernunfft, die schöne Metze, leret, wie man Gelt und gut, weisheit, gunst und ehre uberkome.' *Predigten über das 2. Buch Mose* (1524) *WA* XVI, 82.21-31 (emphasis original). Kooiman's reorganisation of this comment (omitting the second half of the paragraph and inserting several lines from the previous one, beginning with the dubious translation [due to the translator J. Schmidt?] of 'the Bible is merely' for *sie scheinet als*) gives a completely different impression, which he uses to support his rejection of the 'legalistic manipulation of a once-and-for-all inspired book'. Kooiman, *Luther*, 237.

readers to look *behind* the text or *beyond* the text, but to look *at* the text with a mind and heart shaped by the Holy Spirit. Indeed, the cross itself provides the pattern: the believer does not look behind the cross or beyond the cross to see the redemptive power of God, but recognises that power at work there on the cross.[63]

The Extent of Inspiration

Much of the scholarly debate, as we discovered at the very beginning of the last chapter, really concerns Luther's understanding of the extent of biblical inspiration. Is the inspiration of the Holy Spirit properly connected with the human authors, the historical or doctrinal content of the biblical text, the text itself in a general way, or the actual words of the text themselves? It is clear from our investigation so far that Luther assumed an intimate relationship between God and the prophetic or apostolic writers. It is also clear that he considered the text they produced to be inspired. Our task at this point is to explore just how far Luther thought this inspiration extended.

There can be little doubt that Luther regarded the content of Scripture, especially its doctrinal content, to be the result of God's inspiration.[64] In 1525 he was willing to argue against Erasmus the divine origin of certain Christian assertions:

> Nothing is better known or more common among Christians than assertion. Take away assertions and you take away Christianity. Why, the Holy Spirit is given to Christians from heaven in order that he might glorify Christ and in them confess him even unto death — and is this not assertion, to die for what you confess and assert?[65]

Just a few lines earlier he had reminded Erasmus that he was speaking about 'the assertion of those things which have been divinely transmitted to us in the sacred writings'.[66] Ten years later, in the

---

[63] Ian D. K. Siggins, 'Luther on the Word of God and Scripture', *Tyndale Papers* (1960), 7.

[64] Ruokanen is thus correct in what he affirms, but, as we shall see, mistaken in what he denies. Ruokanen, *Doctrina Divinitus,* 89.

[65] 'Nihil apud Christianos notius et coelebratius, quam assertio. Tolle assertiones, et Christianismum tulisti. Quin spiritus sanctus de coelo illis datur, ut clarificet Christum et confiteatur usque ad mortem, nisi hoc non est asserere, ob confessionem et assertionem mori.' *De servo arbitrio* (1525) *WA* XVIII, 603.28-31 = *LW* 33, 21. The translation I have preferred here is that of Packer and Johnston. *The Bondage of the Will*, 67.

[66] 'Deinde loquor de rebus illis asserendis, quae nobis traditae sunt divinitus in sacris literis' *De servo arbitrio* (1525) *WA* XVIII, 603.15 = *LW* 33, 20. Peter F.

Galatians commentary, Luther suggested that it was necessary for Paul to boast of his vocation and the knowledge of the gospel revealed to him by Christ because only then would his readers be completely persuaded that 'Paul's doctrine is the Word of God'.[67] It is this commitment to the divine character of the doctrine taught in Scripture which explains Luther's refusal to retract his own books, though sorely pressed by church and empire. His books were, after all, much more than simply anthologies of biblical texts. Luther certainly insisted upon the personal and existential elements of biblical teaching, as we have seen, but he remained convinced throughout his life that there is a definite and inviolable shape to that teaching, a shape given to it by God himself.

However, Luther would not have been satisfied with an affirmation of the inspiration of the doctrinal content of Scripture which stopped there. On occasion his focus was more clearly on the text of Scripture. For instance, his 1521 treatise on monastic vows included a quotation of 1 Tim. 4:1–3 and then continued 'On the authority of this text alone (since it is a word of the Holy Spirit, who is our God blessed forever, Amen) I am bold enough to absolve all monks from their vows, and I pronounce with confidence that their vows are unacceptable and worthless.'[68] Sometimes the text of Scripture was almost hypostasised in Luther's speeches and his writing. The most famous instance is his defence before the Emperor and the authorities of the Roman church at Worms: 'I have been conquered by the Scriptures adduced by me and my conscience is captive to the Word of God'.[69] A similar sentiment was expressed in writing to the Christians in Strasbourg in 1524. On that occasion, speaking of why he felt unable to agree with Karlstadt, Hoen and Kolb, Luther explained: 'I am a captive and cannot free myself. The text is too powerfully present, and will not allow itself to

---

Jensen, 'Luther for Today — With Special Reference to Scripture', *Tyndale Papers* 28 (1983), 4.

[67] 'Requireabat igitur necessitas ministerii Pauli et omnium Ecclesiarum, ut necessaria ac sancta superbia iactaret suam vocationem et revelationem Evangelii sibi a Christo factum, Ut certae redderentur conscientiae, Pauli doctrinam esse Dei verbum.' *In epistolam S. Pauli ad Galatas Commentarius* (1535) *WA* XL-I, 147.25-29 = *LW* 26, 76-77.

[68] 'Ego plane huius solius verbi autoritate, cum sit verbum spiritus sancti, qui est deus noster benedictus, Amen, ausim universos monachos a suis votis absolvere et cum fiducia pronunciare, vota eorum esse coram deo reproba et nulla.' *De votis monasticas Martini Lutheri iudicium* (1521) *WA* VIII, 597.1-4 = *LW* 44, 282.

[69] 'victus sum scripturis a me adductis et capta conscientia in verbis dei' *Verhandlungen mit D. Martin Luther auf dem Reichstage zu Worms* (1521) *WA* VII, 838.6-7 = *LW* 32, 112.

be torn from its meaning by mere verbiage'.[70] Clearly more is in evidence here than simply a commitment to the doctrinal substructure of Scripture.

More specifically, Luther spoke of the biblical languages as the instruments of the Holy Spirit. The conclusion to his treatise on the adoration of the sacrament urged the Bohemian Christians to take these languages seriously for precisely this reason. He argued:

> For it has been my experience that the languages are extraordinarily helpful for a clear understanding of the divine Scriptures. This also was the feeling and opinion of St. Augustine; he held that there should be some people in the church who could use Greek and Hebrew before they deal with the Word, because it was in these two languages that the Holy Spirit wrote the Old and New Testaments.[71]

The same advice, supported by the same perspective on Scripture, was delivered to the Councilmen of Germany the following year:

> In proportion then as we love the gospel, let us hold firmly to the languages. For it was not without purpose that God caused his Scriptures to be set down in these two languages alone — the Old Testament in Hebrew, the New in Greek.[72]

This evidence of Luther's concern for the languages in which Scripture was originally written prevents us from attributing to him a view of inspiration which bypasses the text itself. Latin, and indeed German, might convey the content of the text, but Luther stresses the biblical languages because he believes the form of the text is also the result of a decision by God. As Luther warned in the same treatise, 'let us be sure of this: we will not long preserve the gospel without the

---

[70] 'Aber ich byn gefangen, kan nicht eraus, der text ist zu gewalltig da und will sich mit worten nicht laffen aus dem synn reyssen.' *Ein Brief an die Christen zu Straßburg wider den Schwärmergeist* (17 December 1524) *WA* XV, 394.19-20 = *LW* 40, 68.

[71] 'Denn ich erfare, wie die sprachen uber die maß helfffen zum lauttern verstandt gotlicher schrift. Das hatt auch S. Augustinus gefulet und gemeynet, das ynn der kirchen seyn sollen, die auch Kriechisch unnd Ebreisch kunden, zuvor die das wort handeln sollen, denn der heylig geyst hatt ynn dißen zwo sprachen das allt und neu testament geschrieben.' *Von Anbeten des Sakraments des heiligen Leichnams Christi* (1523) *WA* XI, 455.33-456.3 = *LW* 36, 304.

[72] 'So lieb nu alls uns das Euangelion ist, so hart last uns uber den sprachen hallten. Denn Gott hat seyne schrifft nicht umb sonst alleyn ynn die zwo sprachen schreiben lassen, das alte testament ynn die Ebreische, das new ynn die Kriechische.' *An die Rathherren aller Städte deutsches Lands* (1524) *WA* XV, 37.17-20 = *LW* 45, 359.

languages. The languages are the sheath in which this sword of the Spirit is contained'.[73]

Luther was also interested in the component parts of the languages. On a number of occasions he related particular grammatical constructions to the wider issue of divine authorship and inspiration. His debate with Zwingli over the presence of Christ in the Supper provided one such occasion. As the argument turned to Zwingli's rendering of ἡ σὰρξ οὐκ ὠφελεῖ οὐδέν in Jn. 6:63, Luther wrote:

> Now this spirit must acknowledge that in this passage, 'The flesh is of no avail', there is no pronoun but an article. Yet he makes a pronoun out of it not only in the translation, where he says *das* is equivalent to *eben das*, 'precisely this', but also in his interpretation that in this passage 'the same flesh' is referred to as that which Christ had previously spoken 'My flesh is food indeed'. Here, then, he demonstrates that he falsifies the Word of God and treats the common people shamelessly. For an article never refers to an antecedent or to particular objects, as a pronoun does, but merely indicates things in general, which could be equally well understood if the article were omitted, though the style would not be so nice and elegant.[74]

Luther was treading a fine line at this point. While he accused Zwingli of tampering with the grammar of the passage and thus 'falsifying the Word of God', earlier in the discussion of Jn. 6:63 he had to defend himself against Zwingli's charge that he, Luther, had improperly translated the text by omitting the article altogether. Luther argued that 'no one can lay down a definite rule when it is to be omitted or inserted, but its use or omission must be learned from the common

---

[73] 'Und last uns das gesagt seyn, Das wyr das Euangelion nicht wol werden erhallten on die sprachen. Die sprachen sind die scheyden, darynn dis messer des geysts stickt.' *An die Rathherren aller Städte deutschs Lands* (1524) *WA* XV, 38.7-9 = *LW* 45, 360.

[74] 'Weil nu dieser geist bekennen mus das hie kein Pronomen sondern ein artickel stehet (Das fleisch ist kein nutze) und er dochein pronomen draus macht nicht allein mit dem Dolmetschen da er spricht (Das) vermuge so viel als (Eben das) sondern auch mit der auslegüng [da er sagt] das an dem ort dasselbige fleisch solle heissen davon Christo droben geredt hat (Mein fleisch ist die rechte speise) so bezeuget er hie mit selbs das er Gotts wort verfelsschet und bubisch mit den einfeltigen umbgehet Denn ein artickel nymer mehr von vorigem odder sonderlichem dinge redet wie ein pronomen sondern frey dahin ynn gemein davon redet das mans gleich so wol verstehen kan wo man on artickel davon redet obs gleich nicht so wol und sein lautet.' *Vom Abendmahl Christi. Bekenntnis* (1528) *WA* XXVI, 363.11-364.4 = *LW* 37, 243.

usage of a language'.[75] The consistency of his argument against Zwingli seems to be put under further strain by his own statement in the Galatians commentary, admittedly seven years later than *Vom Abendmahl Christi Bekenntnis,* that 'it is forgivable if the Holy Spirit, speaking through Paul, sins a little against the rules of grammar'.[76]

However, we ought not to be too hasty to charge Luther with an irreconcilable inconsistency at this point. For Luther, grammar is almost self-evidently a servant of meaning. It is a human convention in ordering a language which facilitates the recognition of meaning. In this way it is not, Luther could maintain, an end in itself. Of course the grammar of a text should not be overthrown, but the goal of understanding the meaning remains paramount. If that goal is achieved in a way which does not conform to the expectations generated by a human convention, then that is perfectly acceptable. Luther put it this way in a piece of *Tischreden* from 1540: 'It's not enough to know the grammar. One must observe the sense, for a knowledge of the matters treated brings with it an understanding of the words'.[77]

Luther was willing to comment on the style employed by the Holy Spirit in Scripture as well. Particular patterns of expression, recognisable from human discourse, were to be found here. For instance, in his commentary on Ps. 45:11 Luther remarked that at this point 'the Holy Spirit employs very elevated language'.[78] Not only did Luther feel competent to identify the style employed at any given point, he could also exclude certain stylistic parallels, as he did in his comment on the use of the plural by God in Gn. 1:26:

> It is utterly ridiculous when Jews say that God is following the custom of princes, who, to indicate respect, speak of themselves in the plural number. The Holy Spirit is not imitating this court

---

[75] 'Und kan niemand gewisse mas noch regel stellen wenn sie auszulassen odder da bey zu setzen find sondern man mus auff den gemeisten brauch der sprachen solchs stellen und lassen. *Von Abendmahl Christi. Bekenntnis* (1528) *WA* XXVI, 357.15-17 = *LW* 37, 240.

[76] 'Condonandum est autem Spirituisancto in Paulo loquenti, si peccet aliquando in grammaticam.' *In epistolam S. Pauli ad Galatas Commentarius* (1535) *WA* XL-I, 171.25-26 = *LW* 26, 92; cf. *WA* XL-I, 244.12-13 = *LW* 26, 139: 'But the Holy Spirit does not observe this strict rule of grammar. [Verum Spiritussanctus non servat illum rigorem grammatices.]'

[77] 'Non satis est nosse grammatica, sed observare sensum, nam cognitio rerum affert cognitionem verborum.' *Tischreden* #5002 (May-June 1540) *WATr* IV, 608.6-8 = *LW* 54, 375; cf. *Genesisvorlesung* (1535-45) *WA* XLII, 599.7-8 = *LW* 3, 70-71.

[78] 'Utitur autem spiritus sanctus amplissimis verbis' *Praelectio in psalmum 45* (1533) *WA* XL-II, 582.17-18 = *LW* 12, 279.

mannerism (to give it this name); nor does the Holy Scripture sanction this manner of speech.[79]

Finally, there is also plenty of evidence that Luther believed the inspiration of the Scriptures extended to the words themselves. At one level this is clear by the way in which Luther argued about particular words in biblical texts. Well-known examples are the debate with Prierias over the meaning of the Greek word μετάνοια in 1518 and the dispute with Zwingli and several other Swiss Reformers over the words of institution, τοῦτό ἐστιν τὸ σῶμά μου, in the late 1520s.[80] Luther's arguments in both cases presuppose that the words themselves are authoritative. So too does his use of the language of Mt. 5:18 concerning the binding authority of even the smallest part of the Law until it is fulfilled. Luther's 1522 homily on the Gospel for the Sunday after Christmas (Lk. 2:33–40) provides an example:

> Let this be enough of our rambling for this time. It has shown us how not a single tittle in Scripture is written for nothing, and how the dear fathers of old with their faith have provided us with examples and how they, with their works always pointed out what we are to believe, namely, Christ and his gospel. Hence nothing concerning them is read in vain: rather everything concerning them strengthens and improves our faith.[81]

However, we are able to go beyond inferences from Luther's arguments. As we have already observed, both in polemical contexts and non-polemical ones, Luther explicitly claimed that the words of

---

[79] 'Hoc autem extreme ridiculum est, quod Iudaei dicunt Deum sequi principum consuetudinem, qui reverentiae causa de se in plurali numero loquuntur. Sed hanc cancellariam (ut sic dicam) Spiritus sanctus non imitatur nec agnoscit scriptura sancta hunc loquendi modum.' *Genesisvorlesung* (1535-45) *WA* XLII, 43.35-38 = *LW* 1, 58.

[80] *Ad dialogum Silvestri Prieratis de potestate papae responsio* (1518) *WA* I, 648.27-31; *Vom Abendmahl Christi. Bekenntnis* (1528) *WA* XXVI, 448.26-470.17 = *LW* 37, 307-327. Examples from his non-polemical writings would include *Dictata super Psalterium* (1513-15) *WA* III, 63.24-36 = *LW* 11, 240 and *Divi Pauli apostoli ad Romanos Epistola* (1516) *WA* LVI, 254.19-255.19 = *LW* 25, 241-242.

[81] 'Das sey ditz mal gnug spacirt, auff das man sehe, wie gar keyn tuttel ynn der schrifft sey vorgebens geschrieben. Und wie die lieben alten vetter mit yhrem glawben uns habenn exempell furtragen; Aber mit yhren wercken altzeyt furgebildet das, daran wyr glewben sollen, nemlich Christum und seyn Euangelium; alßo das nichts vorgebens von yhn geleßen wirtt, ßondern all yhr ding unßern glawben sterck und bessere.' *Kirchenpostille* (1522) *WA* X-I/1, 430.21-431.1 = *LW* 52, 136; cf. *Predigt am Pfingstmontage* (9/6/1522) *WA* X-III, 162.25-163.3.

the text are the words of God. It is not surprising, then, to find that in his early lectures on Romans he spoke of Jewish sinfulness in this way:

> They removed the letters and words from Scripture, which is not only a holy but a holy of holies, by perverting them and distorting them into a false meaning and thus casting and forming a spiritual idol from them.[82]

Luther does not simply attack what he sees as Jewish neglect of the teaching of Scripture, for he is more specifically concerned with their tampering with the letters and words of Scripture, a tampering which enables them to fashion an alternative to the living God out of the place where God himself is meant to be found. Six years later Luther's concern for the words of Scripture was still apparent. In a context in which Luther was stressing the properly oral nature of the gospel, he could still speak of how both the Old Testament and the New 'have been put on paper word for word'.[83]

This concern for the actual words of Scripture is one Luther was convinced he shared with the Apostle Paul,[84] but most importantly with the Holy Spirit. Commenting on the expression 'Create in me a clean heart, O God' (Ps. 51:10), he explained: 'It is not in our power to acquire such a heart, but it comes by divine creation. This is why the Spirit wanted to use the term "create" here'.[85] The Spirit was so intimately involved in the production of the Scriptures that his influence extended to the choice of particular words. Luther himself drew this conclusion in a lecture on Ps. 127. After discussing the order with which subjects are handled in this psalm and remarking on the

---

[82] 'Literam et verba non solum sacre, sed sacratissime Scripture auferentes et in falsum sensum detorquentes et sic Idolum spirituale ex ipsa conflantes et sculpentes.' *Divi Pauli apostoli ad Romanos Epistola* (1516) *WA* LVI, 207.24-26 = *LW* 25, 192.

[83] 'Denn wie wol beydes dem buchstaben nach ist auff papyr geschrieben, so soll doch das Euangelion odder das new Testament eygentlich nicht geschrieben, sondern ynn die lebendige stym gefasset werden, die da erschalle und uberal gehört werde ynn der wellt.' *Epistle Sanct Petri gepredigt und ausgelegt* (1523) *WA* XII, 275.8-11 = *LW* 30, 19.

[84] 'You see here with what diligence Paul read the Scriptures and how carefully he weighed and considered the individual words of this passage: "In you shall all the nations be blessed." [Atque hic vides quanta diligentia Paulus legerit Scripturas Et quam studiosissimus fuerit pensitator et ponderator singulorum verborum istius loci: "In semine tuo benedicentur omnes gentes terrae".]' *In epistolam S. Pauli ad Galatas Commentarius* (1535) *WA* XL-I, 450.15-16 = *LW* 26, 289.

[85] 'Neque autem est in potestate nostra, tale cor assumere, sed est creationis divinae, ideo vocabulo Creandi spiritus hic uti voluit' *Enarratio Psalmi LI* (1538) *WA* XL-II, 424.33 = *LW* 12, 379.

difficulty of conveying the sense of the Hebrew in 'mortal Latin', Luther continued: 'For not only the words but also the order of the words which the Holy Spirit and Scripture use is divine'.[86]

It may indeed be anachronistic to speak of Luther holding to a doctrine of verbal inspiration, although the evidence we have examined suggests that Luther presupposed, and even articulated, most of the basic concerns of that later theological construct. Further, many of the alternatives suggested in modern studies of Luther on this subject do not adequately deal with his bold affirmations of the Holy Spirit's involvement in this text right down to the choice and order of the words. Nevertheless, there remains nothing mechanical about Luther's view either. He could just as boldly affirm the conscious and deliberate activity of the human writers of both testaments.

Inspiration and the Authority of Scripture

How did such perspectives on the origin and nature of Holy Scripture affect Luther's view of its authority? In contrast to the conclusions of some modern interpreters of Luther, the evidence already cited reveals that he did on occasion relate the authority of the Scriptures to their origin in God himself.[87] Luther could and did speak of the Scriptures proceeding from the mouth of God and carrying the authority of God. On one level, such statements simply reiterate a basic conviction of the patristic and medieval periods. As we saw in chapter one, the inheritance into which Luther entered entailed a commitment to the divine inspiration of the Bible and its consequently unique authority, despite the fact that in some quarters the theological tradition had emerged as a second source of authority which tended to circumscribe that of Scripture itself. Further, and particularly in the period prior to the indulgence controversy, Luther appeared to have no consciousness of departing from the accepted teaching of the church on this subject.

---

[86] 'Non solum enim vocabula, sed et phrasis est divina, qua Spiritus sanctus et scriptura utitur.' *In Quindecim Psalmos Graduum* (1532–3) *WA* XL-III, 254.23-24.

[87] David Lotz suggests it is 'inadequate and misleading' to conclude that 'Luther's position on biblical authority was based on, or derived from, a doctrine of Scripture's plenary inspiration and inerrancy'. He prefers to conclude that 'Luther has articulated a subtly nuanced, highly dialectical, intrinsically complex approach to Scripture. He sharply distinguishes between written Word and spoken Word, asserts Scripture's servant status relative to Christ and the gospel, and locates the church's "total life and substance" in the gospel rather than in canonical Scripture as such'. Lotz, 'Sola Scriptura', 267, 269. Lotz's conclusion inflates one part of the evidence we have adduced above at the expense of others.

His letter to Trutvetter in 1517 made this much clear.[88] He was not so much formulating a new principle of theological method, as calling errant practitioners back to a principle he believed they would readily endorse. His grief and anger that this was not in fact the case generated much of the heat found in his writings of 1517 to 1521.

Examples of an explicit relation of the authority of Scripture and its origin from God himself are not, in fact, difficult to find in Luther's writings. In the treatise against Latomus from 1521 Luther argued that 'human words are not sacred' and then went on to insist that 'the integrity of Scripture must be guarded'. He made the reason for such a distinction abundantly clear: 'a man ought not to presume that he speaks more safely and clearly with his mouth than God spoke with his mouth'.[89] In a sermon two years later he confronted the difficulty his hearers might experience in understanding how God could have created the world in six days. His advice once again made this same point: 'Do the Holy Spirit the honour of admitting that he is more learned than you. You ought to treat what has been written as if God himself said it'.[90] Genesis 1 is to be believed because God is its author. Almost twenty years later, when the heat of the indulgence controversy was only a memory, Luther would still be teaching that we must sit at the feet of the prophets and apostles, listening to them rather than demanding that they listen to us, precisely because their words have come from God.[91]

---

[88] 'But if, father, I am your student and your most submissive servant, this is what makes me bold: that at the beginning I learned everything from you: that I owe allegiance to the canonical books alone, judging all the others, as Saint Augustine, and indeed Paul and John taught. [sed si pateris discipuli tui et obsequentissimi famuli tui, id est meam confidentiam, ex te primo omnium didici, solis canonicis libris deberi fidem, caeteris omnibus iudicium, ut B. Augustinus, imo Paulus et Iohannes praecipiunt.]' *Brief an Jodokus Trutfetter in Erfurt* (9 May 1518) *WABr* I, 171.71-73.

[89] 'At humanum non est sacrum [...] Scripturae enim sinceritas custodienda est, nec praesumat homo suo ore eloqui, aut clarius aut securius, quam deus elocutus est ore suo.' *Rationis Latomianae confutatio* (1521) *WA* VIII, 117.19, 118.4-5 = *LW* 32, 243, 244.

[90] '[S]o thue dem heyligen geist die eer, das er gelerter gewesen sey dann du. Drumb soltu mit der geschrifft also handeln, das du gedenckst, wie es Gott selbs rede.' *Ein Sermon und Eingang in das erste Buch Mosi* (15 March 1523) *WA* XII, 440.16-18.

[91] 'Als die wir müssen die Propheten und Apostel lassen auff dem Pult sitzen und wir hie nieden zu iren Füssen hören, was sie sagen und nich sagen, was sie hören müssen.*Vorrede zum 1. Bande der Wittenberger Ausgabe der deutschen Schriften* (1539) *WA* L, 657.28-30 = *LW* 34, 284. cf. *Wochenpredigten über Joh. 6-8* (1530-32) *WA* XXXIII, 363.4-32 = *LW* 23, 229.

Luther's identification of Scripture with the Word of God carried with it a claim to final authority.[92] This is what Luther insisted in the midst of the eucharistic controversies of the late 1520s. If the words of Scripture are indeed the very words of God, then the believer should value them most highly and 'tremble before them as before God himself'.[93] In 1530 he argued 'the word is the Word of God originally and authoritatively, not passively and ministered by the church. Therefore the church is under the word and command of God, not above it'.[94]

It is important to understand Luther properly at this point. There can be no suggestion that the Bible became for him a 'hollow pontifical document',[95] or a 'paper pope'.[96] Three elements of Luther's treatment of the origin and nature of the text prevent such an interpretation of his position. Firstly, Luther believed that God not only spoke these words, but speaks them still. We have already noted the way in which he regularly used the present tense of God's address of the believer in and through Scripture. The Bible is not, therefore, to be seen as the law book of an absent lord. 'The gospel must be heard as if the Lord is present', Luther insisted, 'as if we hear Christ talking'.[97] Secondly, he held that this text and the work of the Spirit are interconnected. He was certainly wary of those who appealed to the Spirit apart from the Word,[98] but he was just as adamant that the Word could not be properly apprehended without the Spirit. The Word is 'the vehicle of the Holy Spirit', and 'when the Word is read, the Holy Spirit is

---

[92] 'When the Word of God comes, it comes with an authority which must be absolute and final.' D. Broughton Knox, 'Authority and the Word of God', *RTR*, 9 (1950), 14.

[93] 'Denn wo sie gleubten das gotts wort weren wurden sie es nicht elende arme wort heissen sondern auch einen tutel und buchstaben grosser achten denn die gantze wellt und dafur zittern und furchten als for gott selbs.' *Vom Abendmahl Christi. Bekenntnis* (1528) *WA* XXVI, 450.3-6 = *LW* 37, 308.

[94] 'Ergo verbum ist verbum Dei originaliter et autoritative, non Ecclesiae nisi passive et ministerialiter. Ergo Ecclesia est sub verbo et mandato Dei et non supra.' *De potestate leges ferendi in ecclesia* (1530) *WA* XXX-II, 682.1-3.

[95] Oberman, *Luther*, 174.

[96] Barth, *Church Dogmatics*, I/2, 525.

[97] 'Nam euangelium audiendum est, quasi dominum presentem, quasi Christum loquentem audiamus' *Praelectio in librum Iudicum* (1516) *WA* IV, 535.1-2.

[98] *Wochenpredigten über Joh. 6-8* (1530-32) *WA* XXXIII, 277.21-31 = *LW* 23, 175; *Vorlesung über die Briefe an Titus und Philemon* (1527) *WA* XXV, 64.36-37 = *LW* 29, 83; *Genesisvorlesung* (1535-45) *WA* XLIII, 505.12-13 = *LW* 5, 111.

present'.[99] Thirdly, Luther always maintained an intimate relationship between the written Word and the incarnate Word, Jesus Christ. In this way the words of Scripture were always properly the Word of Christ.[100]

Luther's conviction that the inscripturated Word carried the authority of God himself led him to relativise all other authorities. Catharinus may well have concluded that Luther's rejection of the authority of the church had led him to reject the authority of Scripture,[101] yet Luther himself regularly argued that reverence for the authority of Scripture led him to reject the authority of the Roman church. Even before the final break, Luther made this quite clear. In the preface to his early commentary on Galatians he remarked:

> Furthermore, most noble sirs, to speak seriously to you, I have this respect for the Roman pontiff and his decrees that there is no one superior to him; and I except no one but this vicar's Prince, Jesus Christ, our Lord and Lord of all. I give His Word such preference over the words of His vicar that I have no hesitation at all in passing judgement according to it on all the words and deeds of His vicar.[102]

The importance of rightly ordering the authority of the church and the authority of the Word is a recurring theme in Luther's writings. It is clearly spelt out in his early treatise on the mass from 1521:

> It is not God's Word just because the church speaks it; rather, the church comes into being because God's Word is spoken. The church does not constitute the Word, but is constituted by the Word.[103]

---

[99] 'Itaque ante omnia audiendum et legendum verbum, quod vehiculum Spiritus Sancti est. Lecto verbo adest Spiritus Sanctus et sic impossibile est vel audire vel legere Scripturas sine fructu.' *Vorlesung über den 1. Brief des Johannes* (1527) *WA* XX, 790.24-27 = *LW* 30, 321; *Auslegung des dritten und vierten Kapitels Johannis* (1538-40) *WA* XLVII, 184.17-18; *Enarratio psalmi XC* (1534) *WA* XL-III, 543.29-30 = *LW* 13, 111.

[100] Muller, *Dogmatics,* 244; cf. Lotz, 'Sola Scriptura', 273.

[101] Ambrosius Catharinus, *Apologia pro veritate catholicae et apostolicae fidei ac doctrinae adversus impia et valde pestifera Martini Lutheri dogmata* (*CC,* XXVII, 286). Inge Lønning, *Kanon im Kanon: zum dogmatischen Grundlagenproblem des neutestamentlichen Kanons,* 273.

[102] 'Porro, optimi viri, ut vobis serio dicam, ego Rhomano Pontifici eiusque decretis eum honorem habeo, quo nullus est superior, nec excipio nisi principem huius Vicarii, Iesum Christum, dominum nostrum et omnium. Huius verbum ita praefero Vicarii verbis, ut nihil dubitem secundum ipsum iudicare de omnibus et dictis et factis Vicarii.' *In epistolam Pauli ad Galatas Commentarius* (1519) *WA* II, 446.38-447.3 = *LW* 27, 155.

[103] 'Non enim verbum dei est, quia ecclesia dicit, sed quia verbum dicitur, ideo ecclesia est. Ipsa non facit verbum, sed fit verbo.' *De Abroganda Missa*

There is ample evidence to suggest that Luther was able to relate the authority of Scripture to its origin in divine inspiration and to the basic character of the written text as the Word of God. How then are we to understand the 'critical statements of Luther about Scripture' which are often presented as evidence that Luther held a view of Holy Scripture which is thoroughly irreconcilable with the concerns and structures of the later doctrine of verbal inspiration? Although there had been earlier attempts to document these, Reinhold Seeberg's *Lehrbuch der Dogmengeschichte* has been most influential here.[104] Seeberg's list of eleven examples of criticism of the biblical text by Luther enabled him to conclude that Luther produced 'an entirely new conception of the authority and inspiration of the Scriptures'.[105] However, more recently a growing band of scholars have raised serious questions about Seeberg's influential list. Lewis Spitz is one amongst many who have concluded that Seeberg's quotations from Luther's writings 'do not prove what Seeberg and others try to prove with them'.[106] So what are we to make of these statements by Luther?

Too often appeal is made to Luther's critical opinions regarding Scripture with little or no effort to distinguish the exact nature of the opinion Luther is giving at each point. However, such discrimination is vital if we are properly to weigh the evidence. Five different types of comment can be identified.

Luther's Questions about the Authorship and Date of Particular Biblical Books

As we have seen, Luther repeatedly referred to Genesis as the work of Moses. However, two separate records in the *Tischreden* suggest that he did not feel bound to believe that the entire Pentateuch had been written by Moses in the first instance. In 1532 Luther suggested 'it doesn't matter if they say the Pentateuch was not written by Moses; it is of Moses'.[107] Eight years later he went further:

Privata Martini Lutheri Sententia (1521) *WA* VIII, 419.33-35 = *LW* 36, 144-145. Note Luther's comment from his reply to Catharinus: 'The church's entire life and substance reside in the Word of God [tota vita et substantia ecclesiae est in verbo Dei].' *Ad librum eximii magistri nostri Mag. Ambrosii Catharini, defensoris Silv. Prieratis acerrimi, responsio* (1521) *WA* VII, 721.12-13.

[104] Seeberg, *History*, II, 300-301.
[105] Seeberg, *History*, II, 301.
[106] Spitz, 'Luther's Sola Scriptura', 743. cf. Gerrish, 'Biblical Authority', 345; Godfrey, 'Biblical Authority', 229.
[107] 'Et nihil nocet, si qui dicunt Pentateuchum non esse scriptum a Mose; est tamen Mosi.' *Tischreden* #2844a (1532-3) *WATr* III, 23.1-2.

In my opinion, however, Genesis was not by Moses, for there were books before his time and books are cited — for example, the Book of the Wars of the Lord and the Book of Jashar. I believe that Adam wrote for several generations, after him Noah and the rest, to describe what happened to them. For the Jews were writers in very ancient times.[108]

Similar sentiments lie behind his comment on Ecclesiastes. In his 1534 preface to the book he remarked: 'Now this book was certainly not written or set down by King Solomon with his own hand. Instead scholars put together what others had heard from Solomon's lips'.[109] Likewise the prefaces to a number of the prophetic books of the Old Testament describe them as non-chronological compilations of the prophet's preaching by others.[110] When it came to the New Testament Luther saw a similar practice at work in at least one place: he observed that much of the epistle of Jude was derived from 2 Peter.[111] In each of these comments Luther made provision for the use of earlier materials in the composition and arrangement of biblical books. This would seem perfectly consistent with his comments about the human and divine authorship of the Scriptures.

Luther's Statements about the Canonical Status of Particular Biblical Books

This second group of comments by Luther does not constitute simply a repetition or continuation of the patristic debates about τὰ ὁμολογούμενα and τὰ ἀντιλεγόμενα. A radical application of his Christological understanding of the Bible's message led to Luther's

---

[108] 'Es ist aber meins bedunckens nicht Moisis, denn man hat vor auch bucher gehabt und citirt bucher: In libro bellorum Domini, et iustorum Domini. Ego credo quod Adam scripsit aliquot generationes, denn Noah et reliqui, wie es inen gegangen ist. Iudaei enim sunt antiquissimi scriptores' *Tischreden* #4964 (May-June 1540) *WATr* IV, 594.7-13 = *LW* 54, 373.

[109] 'Es ist aber das buch freylich nicht durch den könig Salomo selbst mit eygener hand geschrieben odder gestellet, sondern aus seynem munde durch andere gehöret.' *Vorrede auf den Prediger Salomonis* (1524) *WADB* X-II, 104.4-7 = *LW* 35, 263. The oft-quoted table talk from 1532 (#2777*WATr* II, 653.9-13) is actually about Ecclesiasticus rather than Ecclesiastes.

[110] *Vorrede auf den Propheten Iesaja* (1545) *WADB* XI-I, 21.38-23.5 = *LW* 35, 277; *Vorrede über den Propheten Jeremia* (1545) *WADB* XI-I, 193.14-17 = *LW* 35, 280-281; *Vorrede über den Propheten Hosea* (1532) *WADB* XI-II, 182.14-16 = *LW* 35, 317; *Tischreden* #1839 (September-October 1532) *WATr* II, 234.15-18.

[111] *Vorrede auf die Episteln S. Jacobi und Judas* (1522) *WADB* VII, 386.22-24 = *LW* 35, 397.

willingness to ask questions about canonicity based on theological content rather than just convictions about human authorship. Other questions generally gave way to the overriding canonical criterion: 'that which promotes Christ (*was Christum treibet*)'. As Luther put it in his preface to James and Jude in 1522, 'all the genuine sacred books agree in this, that all of them preach and promote Christ. And that is the true test by which to judge all books, when we see whether or not they promote Christ'.[112] Here the centre of Holy Scripture was determining its own outer limits. It is this principle which allows Luther to question the Book of Revelation because 'Christ is neither taught nor known in it'[113] and the Epistle of James because 'in all this long teaching it does not once mention the Passion, the resurrection, or the Spirit of Christ. He names Christ several times; however he teaches nothing about him, but only speaks of general faith in God'.[114] To be sure, Luther's canonical decisions were sometimes attached to evaluations of the usefulness and authority of the particular book under discussion, however it remains important to distinguish these two types of comment. At least in his own mind, Luther's canonical judgements did not jeopardise the nature and authority of those books he endorsed as canonical.

Luther's Exploration of the Problems of Biblical Chronology

Luther recognised the difficulty of producing a precise chronology from the biblical record of events. As he observed in 1535, 'the histories in the Scriptures are often concise and confused, so that they cannot be easily harmonised'.[115] The classic Old Testament example

---

[112] 'Und daryn stymmen alle rechtschaffene heylige bucher ober eyns, das sie alle sampt Christum predigen und treyben, Auch ist das der rechte prufesteyn alle bucher zu taddelln, wenn man sihet, ob sie Christum treyben, odder nit' *Vorrede auf die Episteln S. Jacobi und Judas* (1522) *WADB* VII, 384.25-27 = *LW* 35, 396.

[113] 'das Christus, drynnen widder geleret noch erkandt wirt' *Vorrede auf die Offenbarung S. Johannis* (1522) *WADB* VII, 404.27 = *LW* 35, 398.

[114] 'das sie will Christen leutt leren, unnd gedenckt nicht eyn mal ynn solcher langer lere, des leydens, der aufferstehung, des geysts Christi, er nennet Christum ettlich mal, aber er leret nichts von yhm, sondern sagt von gemeynem glawben an Gott.' *Vorrede auf die Episteln S. Jacobi und Judas* (1522) *WADB* VII, 384.19-22 = *LW* 35, 396.

[115] 'Sunt autem historiae in scripturis saepe concisae et confusae, ut conciliari facile non possint' *In epistolam S. Pauli ad Galatas Commentarius WA* XL-I, 126.3-4 = *LW* 26, 62 (NB the form in the lectures from which the commentary was taken: 'Historiae in scripturis frequenter concisae et confusae, das schwerlich zu samen' *WA* XL-I, 126.3-4).

was the chronology of the kings of Judah, and in particular such details as the age of Ahaziah when he began to reign.[116] Was Ahaziah twenty-two years old, as stated in 2 Ki. 8:26, or forty-two years old, as stated in 2 Ch. 22:2? If he was forty-two years old when he became king, how are we to account for the fact that his father Jehoram appears to have been forty years old when he died? How could Ahaziah be born two years prior to the birth of his own father? Luther dealt with this as one of two hesitations (*scrupuli*) he had about his own reconstruction of world history, the *Supputatio annorum mundi* of 1541. In fact he considered two ways of solving the problem. He dismissed the first, that Jehoram might have adopted a man older than himself in order to guarantee the succession, pointing out that the text makes reference to Ahaziah's mother, Athaliah the wife of Jehoram, and that all the mothers mentioned in Scripture are natural mothers.[117] Instead Luther followed a suggestion of Jerome and Lyra: 'twenty years of Jehoram's reign were passed over in silence in 2 Kings because of his evil life, in that he reigned wickedly and oppressively'. However, in order that the historical total might remain correct, those twenty years were marked in the age of his son Ahaziah.[118] It must be admitted that Luther had more than just the integrity of both biblical books in mind when he reconciled the chronological differences in this way. His larger chronological scheme, tied to the seventy weeks of the prophecy of Daniel as it was, made these extra twenty years necessary: 'I would more gladly follow this opinion because, if you add on these twenty years or fit them into the chronology of the world, then the resurrection of Christ will fall beautifully into the end of the fourth millennium'.[119] James Barr rightly observes that Luther's judgement here was the reverse of critical.[120]

Another obvious example, for Luther as much as any other interpreter, was the order of events in the four Gospels. He had no embarrassment about pointing out the differences he encountered. 'All four evangelists', he admitted in a sermon from 1525, 'have not paid such great attention that they put the history in an order and tell it in

---

[116] James Barr, 'Luther and Biblical Chronology', *BJRL* 72 (1990), 55-56.
[117] *Supputatio annorum mundi* (1541) *WA* LIII, 180.2-4.
[118] 'Viginti autem taceri in Historia, propter eius malitiam, qua impie et tyrannice regnavit, Sed eosdem annos signari in aetate filij Ahasiae, ne fieret error in Historia.' *Supputatio annorum mundi* (1541) *WA* LIII, 180.2-4. Note Luther's explicit concern to avoid any attribution of error to this canonical book.
[119] 'Hanc sententiam libentius sequerer, quia si hos .20. annos adieceris vel interserueris annis mundi, cadet resurrectio Christi pulchre in finem quarti mellenarij.' *Supputatio annorum mundi* (1541) *WA* LIII, 180.n.I.
[120] Barr, 'Chronology', 56.

the same way'.[121] However, this did not prevent Luther from advancing his own hypothetical chronology when faced with specific instances. That is precisely what he did in his discussion of the order of the temptations of Jesus (despite admitting that their order cannot be determined with any certainty),[122] the timing of the cleansing of the temple (despite describing this as one of those 'questions which will remain questions'),[123] and the thorny issue of the denials of Peter.[124] Luther understood that, in attempting to reconstruct the chronology of the Gospel events, the interpreter was operating on the basis of concerns which were different from those of the biblical writers.

Perhaps the most notorious of the chronological difficulties with which Luther wrestled was the apparent conflict between Gn. 11 – 12 and Acts 7 on the date of Abraham's journey from Haran. This problem actually consists of a series of questions: the birth order of Terah's children, Terah's age when he died, and the age of Abraham when he left his home in response to God's call. In Genesis Abraham heads the list of Terah's children and might be assumed to be the firstborn. He is therefore born when Terah is seventy years old, leaves for Canaan when Terah is one hundred and forty-five years old, and presumably hears news of his father's death sixty years later. In Stephen's speech in Acts 7, however, Abraham leaves for Canaan after the death of his father. Luther dealt with the problem in two different contexts. The first was as one of the *scrupuli* in his *Supputatio annorum mundi*. He left his readers free to decide between the two presentations but added that 'it will be difficult to correct Moses'.[125] The critical element, he suggested, was the intention of the biblical author in each case. In contrast to Moses, it was possible to view Stephen's account not so much as a 'formal assertion' but as 'a story told according to the conventions of everyday speech', which is often confused and unclear.[126] Luther was convinced that Stephen was not trying to give an accurate historical account when he referred to Abraham's departure from his homeland. Thus he finds no difficulty in

---

[121] 'Die Euangelisten all vier haben nit groß achtung gehabt, das sie die geschicht in ain ordnung bringen und nach ainander erzelen.' *Predigt am Ostertag* (16/4/1525) *WA* XVII-I, 179.15-16.

[122] *Fastenpostille* (1525) *WA* XVII-II, 196.5-31.

[123] 'Aber es sind fragen und bleiben fragen' *Auslegung des ersten und zweiten Kapitels Johannis* (1537-8) *WA* XLVI, 726.20 = *LW* 22, 218-219.

[124] *Wochenpredigten über Joh. 16-20* (1528-9) *WA* XXVIII, 268.29-273.31.

[125] 'Sed difficile erit Mosen corrigere.' *Supputatio annorum Mundi* (1545) *WA* LIII, 178.12.

[126] 'Ad narrationem Stephani dici potest, Non fuisse assertionem propriam, sed e vulgo sumptam narrationem, quae solet esse confusa et obscura.' *Supputatio annorum Mundi* (1545) *WA* LIII, 179.6-7.

recognising that 'it is a clear error that he says the Lord appeared in Mesopotamia, before he dwelt in Haran'.[127] Acts 7 presents us with a faithful recounting of Stephen's more general recollection.

The second context in which Luther discussed these passages was his course of lectures on Genesis. Here again Luther tackled the question of whether the mention of Abraham at the head of the list of Terah's children requires us to recognise him as Terah's firstborn, as well as just what happened to the 'missing' sixty years:

> It is senseless to imitate the foolhardy geniuses who immediately shout that an obvious error has been committed whenever such a difficulty arises and who unabashedly dare emend books that are not their own. As yet I have no real answer for this question, even though I have carefully computed the years of the world. Therefore with due and humble admission of my lack of knowledge (for it is the Holy Spirit alone who knows and understands all things) I offer the conjecture that in the case of Abraham God wanted these sixty years to be lost because of a definite plan, that no one might venture to foretell anything definite about the end of the world on the basis of an accurate calculation of the years of the world.[128]

It is worth noting here, not only that Luther distanced himself from any suggestion of error in the biblical text, in contrast to his own bold comment in the *Supputatio,* but that he admitted to having no final answer to the difficulty despite having completed his chronology of the world. Later in the same course of lectures he took up more specifically the apparent conflict between Gn. 12 and Acts 7:

> But this statement conflicts with the passage, Acts 7:2, and Stephen's authority must not be disparaged. He repeats these very words and states that these words were spoken to Abraham in Mesopotamia. Hence Moses and Stephen contradict each other. How shall we harmonize them? Each of the two is a trustworthy witness, and yet they do not agree with each other.

---

[127] 'Iste enim error perspicuus est, quod dicit Dominum apparuisse in Mesopotamia, antequam habitaret in Haran' *Supputatio annorum Mundi* (1545) *WA* LIII, 179.12-13.

[128] 'Absurdum autem est imitari audacia ingenia, quae cum talis difficultas incidit, statim clamant manifestum errorem commissum, et alienos libros sine pudore emendare audent. Ego quid ad hanc questionem recte respondeam, nondum habeo, cum tamen diligenter subduxerim annos mundi. Itaque cum debita et humili confessione ignorantiae (solus enim spiritus sanctus est, qui omnia scit et intelligit) sic coniicio, Deum certo suo consilio, in Abraha hos LX annos voluisse intercidere, ne ex annorum mundi certa ratione, quisquam de fine mundi certi aliquid praedicere praesumeret.' *Genesisvorlesung* (1535-45) *WA* XLII, 431.40-432.5 = *LW* 2, 239.

Divine Words?

The customary answer is that Abraham was called twice, once in Ur of the Chaldeans, perhaps by the patriarch Shem, and later on in Haran, but that Moses is satisfied with relating the later call in Haran. Thus these witnesses do not disagree; for Moses relates the later, Stephen the earlier call.

Nevertheless, it seems to me that the accurate account of what happened is given by Moses and not by Stephen, who certainly derived his knowledge of this story from Moses alone. But when we relate something incidentally, it often happens that we do not pay such close attention to all details as do those who are engaged in leaving behind a written account of an event for their descendants. And so Moses is the historian, but Stephen is little concerned about the details; for the account appears in Moses, and Stephen merely aims at having his hearers realize that the father of this people had neither Law nor temple and yet was acceptable to God and pleased Him.[129]

In the final resort then, Luther believes that authorial intent provides the best explanation of the difference in chronology.

---

[129] 'Sed cum hac sententia pugnat locus, Actorum 7., nec Stephani auctoritas elevanda est, haec ipsa verba repetentis, et clare dicentis, in Mesopotamia ad Abraham dicta haec verba esse. Pugnant igitur Moses et Stephanus. Hos quomodo conciliabimus? Uterque enim fide dignus est testis, et tamen inter se non conveniunt. Responderi solet. Bis vocatum Abrahamum: Semel in UR Chaldaeorum, fortasse per Patriarcham Sem, et postea in Haran. Mosen autem contentum esse recitatione posterioris vocationis in Haran. Ita non pugnabunt hi testes. Nam Mose posteriorem, Stephanus priorem recitat. Mihi Tamen si videtur, accuratam rei gestae narrationem a Mose texi, non a Stephano, qui profecto huius Historiae cognitionem tantum ex Mose hausit. Saepe autem fit, cum obiter recitamus aliquid, ut circumstantias omnes non ita observemus diligenter, Sicut qui in eo sunt, ut historiam rei gestae relinquant posteris scriptam. Mose igitur Historicus est: Stephanus cum historia apud Mosen sit, de circumstantiis parum sollicitus, hoc tantum agit, ut intelligant auditores, Patrem huius populi, neque legem, nec templum habuisse, et tamen Deo gratum fuisse ac placuisse.' *Genesisvorlesung* (1535-45) *WA* XLII, 459.37-460.14 = *LW* 2, 277-278.

Luther's Evaluation of Particular Biblical Books[130]

This fourth category contains some of the best known comments of Luther which raise questions about any consistent position on the nature and authority of Scripture. Not every comment is as straightforward as it appears when quoted out of context and in a list of other isolated quotations. For instance, in a homily on Rom. 12:6 in the 1525 *Fastenpostille,* Luther admitted that even the Old Testament prophets often erred when they applied their mind to the future of kings and worldly princes. However, the context in that homily is his description of the continuing gift of prophecy as an explanation of Scripture rather than as a prediction of the future, one which he illustrates by distinguishing two types of prophetic activity in Old Testament times:

> But to explain Scripture is the noblest, highest, and greatest gift of prophecy. For all the prophets of the Old Testament have chiefly deserved the name because they prophesied concerning Christ (as Peter says, Acts 4 and 1 Peter 1). Furthermore, because they guided the people in their day into real faith by the explanation and understanding of God's Word rather than because they occasionally proclaimed something concerning kings and worldly princes, which they did only seldom and in which they often erred. But the other form of prophecy they exercised daily and were not deceived. For faith does not err in those whose prophesying is like theirs.[131]

Later Luther would argue that it was not necessary to hold that the Old Testament prophets were continuously under the influence of the Holy Spirit.[132]

---

[130] I have omitted those comments in which Luther remarks on the foolishness or sinfulness of a biblical character (e. g. *In epistolam S. Pauli ad Galatas Commentarius* (1535) *WA* XL-I, 195.22-196.12 = *LW* 26, 108; *Genesisvorlesung* (1535-45) *WA* XLIII, 43.4-13 = *LW* 3, 234). Such judgements have sometimes been misread as an evaluation of the text itself.

[131] 'Aber die schrifft aus zu legen, das ist die edliste höhiste and groste gabe der weyssagung. Denn auch alle propheten des allten testaments damit den namen haben allermeyst, das sie propheten heyssen, das sie von Christo geweyssagt haben (wie Petrus sagt Act. 4. und 1. Pe. 1.). Dazu das sie das volck zu yhrer zeyt durch auslegung und verstand göttlichs wortts ym glauben recht fureten, viel mehr denn darumb, das sie zu weilen von den konigen und weltlichen leufften ettwas verkundigeten, wilchs sie auch selden ubeten und offt auch feyleten. Aber ihenes ubeten sie teglich und seyleten nicht. Denn der glaub feylet nicht, dem yhr weyssagen ehnlich war.' *Fastenpostille* (1525) *WA* XVII-II, 39.26-35.

[132] 'Spiritus sanctus non semper tangit corda prophetarum.' *Genesisvorlesung* (1535-45) *WA* XLIV, 575.25-26 = *LW* 7, 370.

Divine Words? 131

The most direct remarks in this category concern certain books of the New Testament. The conclusion of Luther's preface to the New Testament, from 1522, contains a comparison and evaluation of the various books, a section which he removed from the preface included in the 1534 edition of the German Bible:

> From all this you can now judge all the books and decide among them which are the best. John's Gospel and St. Paul's epistles, especially that to the Romans, and St Peter's first epistle are the true kernel and marrow of all the books [...] Now John writes very little about the works of Christ, but very much about his preaching, while the other evangelists write much about his works and little about his preaching. Therefore John's Gospel is the one, fine, true, and chief gospel, and is far, far to be preferred over the other three and placed high above them. So, too, the epistles of St. Paul and St. Peter far surpass the other three gospels, Matthew, Mark, and Luke.[133]

Such a willingness to construct a hierarchy of books within the canon does indeed appear to raise questions about Luther's affirmation of a divine inspiration and authority pertaining to them all. Certainly this was the way it would be used by others in the future. However, caution needs to be exercised at this point. We must be wary of reading into Luther's comments the use made of them in later centuries. There is no evidence that Luther himself ever doubted the inspiration or authority of the synoptic gospels. He preached regularly on synoptic texts and allowed a collection of his sermons to be published as a commentary on the Sermon on the Mount in 1532.[134] Luther's judgement that they were not to be considered amongst *die Hauptbücher* is an assessment of an entirely different order. It arises from his description of the New Testament as 'a book in which are written the gospel and the promises

---

[133] 'Aus disem allen kanstu nu recht urteylen unter allen buchern, und unterscheyd nehmen, wilchs die besten sind, Denn nemlich ist Johannis Euangelion unnd Sanct Paulus Epistelln, sonderlich die zu den Romern, und sanct Peters erste Epistel der rechte kern und marck unter allen buchern [...] Weyl nu Johannes gar wenig werck von Christo, aber gar viel seyner predigt schreybt, widderumb die andern drey Euangelisten viel seyner werck, wenig seyner wort beschreyben. Ist Johannis Euangelion das eynige zartte recht hewbt Euangelion und den andern dreyen weyt fur zu zihen und hoher zu heben, Also auch Sanct Paulus und Petrus Epistelln, weyt uber die drey Euangelia Matthei, Marci und Luce furgehen.' *Das Newe Testament Deutzsch. Vorrede* (1522) *WADB* VI, 10.9-13, 10.23-28 = *LW* 35, 361-362.

[134] *Das fünfte, sechste und siebente Kapitel Matthaei gepredigt und ausgelegt* (1532) *WA* XXXII, 299-544 = *LW* 21, 1-294. Jaroslav Pelikan has observed that 'it would be possible to piece together practically an entire commentary on St. Matthew out of Luther's sermons'. *LW* 21, xvii.

of God' while this gospel is further defined as 'nothing but the preaching about Christ, Son of God and of David, true God and man, who by his death and resurrection has overcome for us the sin, death, and hell of all men who believe in him'.[135] Luther's assessment of each book concerns the degree of focus upon the proclamation of Christ crucified and risen. Precisely because Christ is valued as the centre of God's saving purposes, those books which concentrate on the proclamation of Christ are valued as the core of God's revelation. Karl Holl's assessment of this decision as in Luther's case 'an act of piety (*eine religiöse Tat*)' rather than one of biblical criticism, accords with the evidence.[136]

Yet while this may be an appropriate response to Luther's elevation of John and Paul above the synoptic Gospels, the questions remain, and indeed intensify, when we come to Luther's comments about Hebrews, Jude, Revelation, and especially James. As a simple matter of historical fact, Luther placed these four books as an unnumbered addendum to the rest of the New Testament. His preface to Hebrews made explicit the reasons for this: 'Up to this point we have had [to do with] the true and certain chief books of the New Testament. The four which follow have from ancient times had a different reputation'.[137] Once again we are faced with the question of canonicity and, as this comment makes clear, Luther does not see himself as an innovator at this point. The debate about the canonical standing of these books goes back to the early church, and Erasmus himself had expressed similar reservations in his *Annotationes* to the 1516 Greek New Testament. Even Luther's opponent Cajetan accepted there was some doubt about them.[138] However, often more than mere canonical decisions are being made in the prefaces to these books. Luther's reasons for doubting them include an evaluation of their content. Further, in each case the evaluation of content appears to be the determining factor in the

---

[135] 'Also ist das newe Testament ein Buch, darinnen das Euangelium und Gottes verheissung, da neben auch Geschichte, beide dere, die daran gleuben und nicht gleuben, geschrieben sind [...] So ist nu das Euangelium nichts anders, denn eine predigt von Christo, Gottes und Dauids Son, warem Gott und Mensch, der fur uns mit seinem sterben und aufferstehen, aller menschen Sünde, Tod und Helle uberwunden hat, die an jn gleuben.' *Das Neue Testament. Vorrede* (1546) *WADB* VI, 3.19-22, 7.23-26 = *LW* 35, 358, 360.

[136] Karl Holl, 'Luthers Bedeutung für den Fortschritt der Auslegungskunst', in *Gesammelte Aufsätze zur Kirchengeschichte I (Luther)*, 561.

[137] 'Bis her haben wyr die rechten gewissen hewbt bucher des newen testaments gehabt, Dise vier nach solgende aber, haben vor zeytten eyn ander ansehen gehabt.' *Vorrede auf die Epistel an die Hebräer* (1522) *WADB* VII, 344.2-4 = *LW* 35, 394.

[138] Michael Reu, *Luther's German Bible*, 175-176.

canonical decision rather than that decision being the precondition for his freedom to make an evaluation of the book's content. Nevertheless, there is no evidence that the composition of these prefaces led Luther to modify his statements about the origin and nature of Holy Scripture. Many of his boldest claims on behalf of the text of Scripture come from long after 1522. As a matter of fact, the evidence points in the opposite direction. There is ample evidence that Luther modified his earlier judgement on these books in the course of his teaching career. The straightforward judgement that the teaching of Heb. 6 and 10 'is contrary to all the gospels and to St. Paul's epistles' in the 1522 preface, became '[it] seems, as it stands, to be contrary to all the gospels and to St. Paul's epistles' after 1530.[139] Luther wrote an entirely new preface to the Book of Revelation in 1530 muting even further the qualified comments he had made in the earlier one.[140]

Particular attention must be given to Luther's comments on the epistle of James. Of no other book was his criticism as violent or as sustained. True, in his 1516 lectures on Romans he did make an attempt to reconcile the teaching of James with his emerging understanding of justification by faith as taught by Paul.[141] However, in the general preface to the September Testament, Luther compared this book to his *Hauptbücher* and remarked, 'Therefore St. James' epistle is really an epistle of straw, compared to these others, for it has nothing of the nature of the gospel about it'.[142] While it is helpful to be reminded that this famous description involves a comparative assessment rather than an absolute one — it is an epistle of straw *compared to all the others* — the negative evaluation remains.[143] Further, in the more specific preface to the epistles of James and Jude he lists his reasons for rejecting James as non-apostolic and therefore extra-canonical:

---

[139] 'widder alle Euangeli und Epistel Sanct Pauli ist' *Vorrede auf die Epistel an die Hebräer* (1522) *WADB* VII, 344.15-16; 'wie es lautet, scheinet, wider alle Euangelia und Epistel S. Pauli sein' *Vorrede auf die Epistel an die Hebräer* (1546) 345.15-16 = *LW* 35, 394.

[140] *Vorrede auff die offenbarung S. Johannis* (1546) *WADB* VII, 406-420 = *LW* 35, 399-411.

[141] *Divi Pauli apostoli ad Romanos Epistola* (1516) *WA* LVI, 248.5-249.11 = *LW* 25, 234-235.

[142] 'Darumb ist sanct Jacobs Epistel eyn rechte stroern Epistel gegen sie, denn sie doch keyn Euangelisch art an yhr hat' *Das New Testament Deutzsch. Vorrede* (1522) *WADB* VI, 10.33-34 = *LW* 35, 362.

[143] Luther's more positive comments about this epistle are all couched in terms of concession and do not change his conclusions. *Vorrede auf die Episteln S. Jacobi und Jude* (1546) *WADB* VII, 385.3-5 = *LW* 35, 395.

> In the first place it is flatly against St. Paul and all the rest of Scripture in ascribing justification to works [...] This fault, therefore, proves that this epistle is not the work of any apostle.
>
> In the second place its purpose is to teach Christians, but in all this long teaching it does not once mention the Passion, the resurrection, or the Spirit of Christ. He names Christ several times; however he teaches nothing about him, but only speaks of general faith in God [...] Whatever does not teach Christ is not apostolic, even though St. Peter or St. Paul does the teaching. Again, whatever preaches Christ would be apostolic, even if Judas, Annas, Pilate, and Herod were doing it [...]
>
> In a word, he wanted to guard against those who relied on faith without works, but was unequal to the task *in spirit, thought, and words. He mangles the Scriptures and thereby opposes Paul and all Scripture.* He tries to accomplish by harping on the law what the apostles accomplish by stimulating people to love. Therefore, I will not have him in my Bible to be numbered among the true chief books, though I would not thereby prevent anyone from including or extolling him as he pleases, for there are otherwise many good sayings in him. *One man is no man in worldly things; how, then, should this single man alone avail against Paul and all the rest of Scripture?*[144]

Luther's judgement was harsh and based on the threat he perceived to the doctrine of justification by faith. While it is true that later editions

---

[144] 'Auffs erst, das sie stracks widder Sanct Paulon unnd alle ander schrifft, den wercken die rechtfertigung gibt [...] Darumb diser mangel schleust, das sie keyns Apostel sey. Auffs ander, das sie will Christen leutt leren, unnd gedenckt nicht eyn mal ynn solcher langer lere, des leydens, der aufferstehung, des geysts Christi, er nennet Christum ettlich mal, aber er leret nichts von yhm, sondern sagt von gemeynem glawben an Gott [...] Was Christum nicht leret, das ist nicht Apostolisch, wens gleich Petrus odder Paulus leret, Widerumb, was Christum predigt, das ist Apostolisch, wens gleych Judas, Annas, Pilatus und Herodes thett [...] Summa, Er hatt wollen denen weren, die auff den glawben, on werck sich verliessen, und ist der sach mit geyst, verstand, und wortten zu schwach gewesen, und zureysset die schrifft, und widerstehet damit Paulo und aller schrifft, wils mit gesetz treyben außrichten, das die Apostel mit reytzen zur lieb außrichten. Darumb will ich yhn nicht haben ynn meyner Bibel ynn der zal der rechten hewbtbucher, will aber damit niemant weren, das er yhn setz und hebe, wie es yhn gelustet, denn es viel guter spruch sonst drynnen sind, Eyn man ist keyn man ynn welltlichen sachen, wie solt denn dißer eyntzeler, nur alleyn, widder Paulum unnd alle andere schrifft gellten?' *Vorrede auf die Episteln S. Jacobi und Judas* (1522) *WADB* VII, 384.9-10, 384.18, 384.19-22, 384.29-32, 386.13-21 = *LW* 35, 396-397.

of this preface were modified by Luther (e. g. he removed those portions italicised in the quotations above), his judgement remained overwhelmingly negative.

Luther's criticism of James was not confined to this preface. In a lecture on Gn. 22:12 in 1539 he commented:

> Next the question is usually considered at this point whether Abraham was justified on the basis of his works, as James argues in his letter. Because the text says: 'Now I see that you are righteous', he wants to conclude from this that previously Abraham was not righteous. But the answer, which the words themselves point out, is easy. For it is one thing, even grammatically speaking, to be righteous and another thing to know that one is righteous.
>
> Abraham was righteous by faith before God acknowledged him as such. Therefore James concludes falsely that now at last he was justified after that obedience; for faith and righteousness are known by works as by the fruits. But it does not follow, as James raves: 'Hence the fruits justify', just as it does not follow: 'I know a tree by its fruit; therefore the tree becomes good as a result of its fruit'.[145]

Once again the difficulty for Luther was a perceived contradiction of the doctrine of justification by faith, and his language is every bit as strong as it was in 1522.

However, it appears that for all the strong language Luther had not quite given up hope of rehabilitating this errant epistle. At table in 1532 he offered to give his doctor's beret to anyone who could reconcile Paul and James and promised that when it was done he would allow himself to be called a fool.[146] Later still, the record of

---

[145] 'Deinde quaestio hic agitari solet, an Abraham sit iustificatus ex operibus? Sicut disputat Iacobus in sua Epistola. Quia enim dicitur: "Nunc video te iustum", vult inde colligere, quod prius non fuerit iustus. Sed facilis est responsio, quam ipsa verba ostendunt. Aliud enim est esse iustum, etiam Grammatice loquendo: aliud cognoscere iustum. Abraham fuit iustus fide, antequam cognoscitur a Deo talis. Igitur male concludit Iacobus, quod nunc demum iustificatus sit post istam obedientiam, per opera enim, tanquam per fructus cognoscitur fides et iustitia. Non autem sequitur, ut Iacobus delirat: "Igitur fructus iustificant." Sicut non sequitur: ego agnosco arborem ex fructu. Igitur arbor ex fructibus fit bona.' *Genesisvorlesung* (1535-45) *WA* XLIII, 231.31-41 = *LW* 4, 133-134.

[146] 'Multi valde sudant, ut concordent Iacobum cum Paulo, velut etiam Philippus in Apologia, sed non serio. Pugnantia sunt: fides iustificat, fides non iustificat. Wer die zusamen reymen kan, dem wil ich mein pirreth auffsetzen und wil mich yhn einen narren lassen schelten.' *Tischreden* #3292a (1532) *WATr* III, 253.25-29.

Heinrich Schmedenstede's licentiate examination on 7 July 1542 shows that Luther continued to wrestle with James:

> Thesis 21: James says that Abraham was justified by works. Therefore, justification is not by faith.
>
> Master Heinrich responds: James is speaking of works as the effect of justification, not as the cause.
>
> Dr. Martin Luther: That epistle of James gives us much trouble, for the papists embrace it alone and leave out all the rest. Up to this point I have been accustomed just to deal with and interpret it according to the sense of the rest of the Scriptures. For you will judge that none of it must be set forth contrary to manifest Holy Scripture. Accordingly, if they will not admit my interpretations, then I shall make rubble also of it. I almost feel like throwing Jimmy into the stove, as the priest in Kalenberg did.[147]

It is doubtful whether this evidence can be dismissed as irrelevant to a discussion of Luther's view of biblical inspiration simply by arguing that it concerns a book he considered extra or at best deutero-canonical. Nor will an appeal to the open-endedness of the canon in the early sixteenth century fully account for Luther's comments about James. Yet in spite of all that he said about this book, he continued to wrestle with it throughout his life and sought to interpret it 'according to the sense of the rest of the Scriptures'. Luther was not prepared simply to ignore James.[148]

It must be frankly admitted that Luther's harsh statements about this epistle appear to represent a genuine tension point in his approach to Holy Scripture. However, two observations can be made which, although they do not remove the difficulty, explain in part the strength of his language. The first is that the statements of Luther on this epistle

---

[147] 'XIX. Contra 21. Iacobus ait, Abraham ex factis iustificatum esse. Ergo non ex fide. Magister Heinricus respondit: Iacobus loquitur de factis ut de effectu iustificationis, non ut de causa. D. M. L. Illa epistola Iacobi nobis multum facescit negotii. Eam enim solam amplectuntur reliquis aomnibus omissis papistae. Ego hactenus solitus sum iam operare et interpretari secundum sententiam reliquae scripturae. Nam nihil ex ea contra manifestam scripturam sanctam statuendum esse iudicabitis. Si igitur non admittent meas interpretationes, tum faciam quoque ex ea vastationem. Ich wil schier den Jeckel in den offen werffen wie der pfaff vom Kalenberg.' *Die Promotionsdisputation von Heinrich Schmedenstede* (1542) *WA* XXXIX-II, 199.15-25 = *LW* 34, 317; cf. *Tischreden* #5443 (1542) *WATr* V, 157.17-31 = *LW* 54, 424-425; *Tischreden* #5854 (n.d.) *WATr* V, 382.14-18; *Tischreden* #5974 (n.d.) *WATr* V, 414.1-8.

[148] This remains true despite his refusal to preach on Jas. 1:22 in 1531. *Predigt am Sonntag Bocem Jocunditatis* (1531) *WA* XXXIV-I, 391.8-9.

show both his desire and his continued difficulty in reconciling the teaching of James and that of the Pauline epistles. He was evidently unsatisfied with the attempts of others to do so, as shown by his response to Heinrich Schmedenstede quoted above. This created the most enduring exegetical frustration of Luther's career and yet he himself never gave up. At stake was not some peripheral doctrine but that which he considered the very heart of a properly ordered life before the God who has redeemed us in Christ. Luther said of the doctrine of justification by faith: 'the Church stands because this article stands, when it falls the Church falls'.[149] The desire to preserve the doctrine of justification by faith from any compromise is the principal cause of his frustration with the epistle of James. This frustration was intensified by another factor, namely the use of James by Luther's adversaries. There is evidence to suggest that the increasingly irritating Karlstadt was appealing to James in support of his programme of accelerated reform even prior to the publication of the September Testament of 1522.[150] Moreover, Luther explicitly referred to the use of James made by the papists in the licentiate examination of July 1542. When taken together these two factors, the perceived threat to justification by faith and the use of James by his opponents, were bound to provoke the volatile Luther into statements which even his friends found difficult.[151]

Yet for all the untidiness of Luther's treatment of this epistle, it must be just as frankly admitted that it is his interpreters, and not Luther himself, who have seen his view on James as a threat to the coherence of his approach to Holy Scripture.[152] Luther never related the two and continued to draw attention to what he held to be his uncompromising submission to the authority of the biblical text. Nor is

---

[149] 'quia isto articulo stante stat Ecclesia, ruente ruit Ecclesia.' *In XV Psalmos graduum* (1532) *WA* XL-III, 352.3; cf. 'Articulus iustificationis est magister et princeps, dominus, rector et iudex super omnia genera doctrinarum, qui conservat et gubernat omnem doctrinam ecclesiasticam et erigit conscientiam nostram coram Deo.' *Die Promotionsdisputation von Palladius und Tilemann* (1 June 1537) *WA* XXXIX-I, 205.2-5.

[150] See the references cited in *WADB* VI, 537, n. 10, 6-34.

[151] The intensity of Luther's language may also be related to his conviction that his theological struggles were in fact struggles with 'the sneering devil [der spöttische teufel]'. *Daß diese Wort Christi "Das ist mein leib" noch fest stehen* (1527) *WA* XXIII, 97.9 = *LW* 37, 34; cf. Oberman, *Luther,* 109.

[152] It is doubtful that Luther would have concurred with Brecht that by his comments on James he 'formally surrendered a part of the biblical basis on which he built his case against the pope, canon law, and traditional theology'. Martin Brecht, *Martin Luther: Shaping and Defining the Reformation 1521-1532,* 52.

there evidence that his enemies charged him with compromising the authority of Scripture by his comments on James. Once again caution is needed lest we impose upon Luther a dispassionate and precise coherence of thought which is out of keeping with his own situation. It is possible to draw too many connections.

Luther's Treatment of Prima Facie Error in the Biblical Texts

Many of the chronological difficulties we have already mentioned could easily fit into this category. In addition attention is often drawn to Luther's handling of the problem found in Mt. 27:9. There Matthew quotes words which almost certainly come from Zc. 11:12–13 and then attributes them to the prophet Jeremiah. Luther was almost dismissive of the question in his commentary on Zechariah from 1527:

> This chapter raises the question why Matthew ascribes the text of the thirty shekels of silver to Jeremiah when, after all, it is found here in Zechariah. This question, to be sure, and others like it do not bother me greatly, because they do not serve any great purpose. Moreover, Matthew does quite enough when he quotes certain Scripture passages even though he may not hit upon the exactly correct name, especially since at other places he quotes passages without using the words exactly as they are in Scripture. If one can bear with this practice of his, and if the sense is not endangered when he does not quote the exact word, what harm is there if he does not put down the exact name, especially since the words are more important than the name? Furthermore, it is the custom of all the apostles to do this: to present the sense of Scripture without such a quarrelsome zeal for the exactness and completeness of the text; and about this custom one might question these apostles much more sharply than one might question Matthew here about the name of Jeremiah. But whoever likes idle strife, let him go on questioning; he will find that he is doing more questioning than answering.[153]

---

[153] 'Aus diesem Capitel kompt die frage, warumb Mattheus den text von den dreyssig sylberlingen dem Propheten Jeremias zu schreibe, so er doch hie ynn Sacharia stehet? Zwar solche und der gleichen fragen bekommern mich nicht hoch, weil sie wenig zur sachen dienen, Und Mattheus gleich gnug thut, das er gewisse schrifft furet, ob er gleich nicht so eben den namen trifft, Syntemal er auch an andern orten spruche furet und doch nicht so eben die wort setzt, wie sie ynn der schrifft stehen. Kan man nu das selbige leiden, und geschicht on alle fahr des synnes, das er nicht so eben die wort furet, was solts denn hindern, ob er den namen nicht so eben setzt? Sintemal mehr an den worten den am namen ligt. Und ist auch aller Apostel weise, das sie also thun und der schrifft meynung einfuren on solchen zencksschen genawen oleys und fulle

Divine Words?

Undoubtedly, Luther saw this question as a distraction from the intended meaning of the passage. He made no attempt to resolve it and certainly did not explore the passages in Jeremiah which might have provided an alternative source for the ideas of Mt. 27.[154] Instead he spoke of 'a quarrelsome zeal for the exactness and completeness of the text' which is completely out of step with the practice of the apostles. He insisted on keeping this particular problem in perspective. After all, Luther reminded his readers, the apostles have much more worrying habits when it comes to quoting the Old Testament. The reader of Matthew's Gospel should be content that 'the sense' of the quotation is not endangered by the reference to Jeremiah. In all of this Luther seems oblivious to the possibility that such a cavalier attitude could compromise his strong statements about a biblical inspiration that extended to 'the words and the order of the words'. He could continue to make such statements long after he had written on Zc. 11.

Luther's responses to the difficulties which he encountered as he expounded the Scriptures do not require the qualification of his more explicit statements about the authority of the inspired text. On the contrary, on those occasions in which he found himself unable to resolve a particular difficulty, his commitment to biblical inspiration actually determined the response. 'We must honour the Holy Spirit', he said when faced with the incomprehensibility of the details of Gn. 1 in 1537, 'by believing his words and accepting them as divine truth'.[155] Later that year, faced with the question of the Passover in Jn. 2, he advised 'If one account in Holy Scripture is at variance with another and it is impossible to solve the difficulty, just dismiss it from your mind'.[156] Luther never tired of confessing that 'the Holy Spirit is more learned than I'.[157]

---

des texts, Darumb sie viel herter zu fragen weren denn Mattheus hie umb den namen Jeremia. Wer aber mussig gezencke liebet, der frage ymer hin, Er wird mehr finden, das er fragt denn das er antwortet.' *Der Prophet Sacharja ausgelegt* (1527) *WA* XXIII, 642.23-36 = *LW* 20, 321-322.

[154] Je. 18, 19, and 32 have been proposed in more recent explorations of the issue.

[155] 'sondern dem heiligen Geist die ehre geben, das, was er redet, die Göttliche warheit sey, und seinen worten gleuben' *Auslegung des ersten und zweiten Kaptiels des Johannesevangeliums* (1537-8) *WA* XLVI, 545.18-20 = *LW* 22, 10.

[156] 'Wenn ein streit in der heiligen Schrifft fürfellet, und man kan jn nicht vergleichen, so las mans faren, dis hie streitet nicht' *Auslegung des ersten und zweiten Kaptiels des Johannesevangeliums* (1537-8) *WA* XLVI, 727.12-13 = *LW* 22, 218-219.

[157] 'Ich will aber dem Spiritui Sancto die her geben und sagen, wie ichs auch weis, das er gelerter ist den ich.' *Tischreden* #1610 (May 1532) *WATr* II,

This perspective explains why Luther was able to dismiss the astronomical conclusions of Copernicus when they were raised at his table on 4 June 1539. Anton Lauterbach recorded Luther's words:

> So it goes now. Whoever wants to be clever must agree with nothing that others esteem. He must do something of his own. This is what that fellow does who wishes to turn the whole of astronomy upside down. Even in these things that are thrown into disorder I believe the Holy Scriptures, for Joshua commanded the sun to stand still and not the earth.[158]

Luther would not allow anything outside of the Scriptures to overturn what he considered to be the plain teaching of the Scriptures. No matter how clever the world might seem, Luther kept insisting, 'I intend to stand by the Word of God'.[159]

Far more numerous than the oft-quoted 'critical opinions' of Luther, are his affirmations of the inerrancy of Holy Scripture. Of course such comments are totally unremarkable against the background of Luther's theological inheritance. Yet since his 'critical opinions' have been given such prominence in recent scholarship, it is important to emphasise the simple fact that Luther's insistence on the truthfulness of Scripture can be found throughout his teaching and writing career. It is in evidence before, during, and after his wrestling with the difficulties we have examined. Further, such statements are found in both the polemical and the non-polemical material. In 1518 Luther's reply to Sylvester Prierias was built upon three axioms, one of which was Augustine's judgement that none of the canonical writers have erred.[160] Ten years later, in a lecture on 1 Tim. 1:11, he spoke of how

---

151.13-14; 'so thue dem heiligen geist die ehre, das er gelerter sey denn du.' *Über das 1. Buch Mose. Predigten* (1527) *WA* XXIV, 20.10.

[158] 'Aber es gehet jtzunder also: Wer do wil klug sein, der sol ihme nichts lassen gefallen, das andere achten; er mus ihme etwas eigen machen, sicut ille facit, qui totam astrologiam invertere vult. Etiam illa confusa tamen ego credo sacrae scripturae, nam Iosua iussit solem stare, non terram.' *Tischreden* #4638 (4 June 1539) *WATr* IV, 412.35-413.3 = *LW* 54, 359. This is the only statement of Luther concerning Copernicus (who is not named). It should be noted that it could only have been made on the basis of verbal reports of his theory. *De revolutionibus orbium coelestium* was not published until four years later. Martin Brecht, *Martin Luther: The Preservation of the Church 1532-1546*, 118.

[159] 'Bey dem Wort Gottes wil ich bleiben' *Sommerpostille* (1525) *WA* XXII, 277.30.

[160] 'Ego solis eis libris, qui Canonici appellantur, hunc honorem deferre didici, ut nullum scriptorem eorum errasse firmissime credam.' *Ad dialogum Silvestri Prieratis de potestate papae responsio* (1518) *WA* I, 647.22-24.

Divine Words?

great a thing it is to know that you have 'the very sure and infallible Word of God'.[161] That same year (1528), in his *Von Abendmahl Christi Bekenntnis*, Luther insisted: 'If the fanatics have been discovered in a single detail to be manifestly false, we would be sufficiently warned by God not to believe them, but to cling to his words. For the Holy Spirit neither lies nor errs nor doubts'.[162] Luther's boldest comment in this regard comes from the Galatians commentary of 1535: 'it is impossible that Scripture should contradict itself. It only appears so to senseless and obstinate hypocrites'.[163] His reflection upon the Law of Moses, as he expounded Ps. 110:2 that same year, included the same sentiment about God's Word: 'His Word is such perfect truth and righteousness that it needs no patching or repair; in its course it makes a perfectly straight line, without any bends in any direction'.[164] It is therefore not surprising that it is the infallibility of the Word of God, in contrast to the fallibility of the words and writings of men, which leads Luther to describe it as 'the touchstone (*Streichstein oder Probirstein*)' by which everything else should be tested.[165]

Inspiration and the Interpretation of Scripture

Such commitments concerning the origin and nature of the biblical text were bound to have implications for the interpretive task. Indeed, on a number of occasions Luther explicitly related the practice of interpretation and the inspiration of the Spirit. At the most basic level,

---

[161] 'Est magna res scire se certissimum et infallibile habere verbum dei, non potest edici hoc donum.' *Vorlesung über den 1. Timotheusbrief* (1528) *WA* XXVI, 19.31-33 = *LW* 28, 239; cf. *Der 112. Psalm Davids gepredigt* (1526) *WA* XIX, 300.19-21 = *LW* 13, 393; *Der 111. Psalm ausgelegt* (1530) *WA* XXXI-I, 423.23-26 = *LW* 13, 383; *Praelectio in psalmum 45* (1532) *WA* XL-II, 531.30-34 = *LW* 12, 242.

[162] 'Wenn die schwermer mit einem stück öffentlich falsch erfunden würden, so weren wir damit gnugsam von Gott gewarnet yhn nicht zu gleuben und bey den worten Gotts zu bleiben, denn der heilige geist leuget noch feylet noch zweivelt nicht.' *Von Abendmahl Christi. Bekenntnis* (1528) *WA* XXVI, 418.17-20 = *LW* 37, 278-279.

[163] 'Quanquam impossibile sit Scripturam pugnare nisi apud insensatos et induratos Hypocritas' *In epistolam S. Pauli ad Galatas Commentarius* (1535) *WA* XL-I, 458.35-36 = *LW* 26, 295.

[164] 'Und sein wort ist solche warheit und gerechtigkeit, die da keines flickens noch besserns darff, gehet sein stracks hindurch und machet eine gerade linien on alle beuge und krümme.' *Predigt über den 110 Psalm* (10 May 1535) *WA* XLI, 127.9-12 = *LW* 13, 268.

[165] '*Auslegung des ersten und zweiten Kapitels Johannis* (1537-8) *WA* XLVI, 766.24-769.22 = *LW* 22, 254.

a serious engagement with the text itself was demanded by the fact that the Holy Spirit caused it to be produced. Lecturing on Heb. 11:7 in 1518 he insisted: 'The words of Holy Scripture should not be treated carelessly. For since they are the words of the Spirit, they are necessarily full of weight and majesty'.[166] This implication was still being drawn by Luther in 1536, when he explained: 'The student of sacred things will not consider anything too small to be useful, at least for directing life and conduct, since the Holy Spirit wanted it to be committed to writing'.[167] While preaching on 21 December 1538 Luther came across what he considered an unimportant story (*eine Gerienge Historia*) in Jn. 3:23. Nevertheless, he refused simply to ignore it, insisting 'since it was recorded by the Holy Spirit, we dare not casually pass over this text'.[168]

Luther was convinced that the same Holy Spirit who produced the biblical text is necessarily involved in the act of interpreting it. Here he stood firmly within the exegetical tradition stretching back through the fathers to the *prima facie* teaching of Scripture itself. Thus it is not surprising to find such a connection drawn even in his early lectures. When expounding Rom. 7:6 he complained about the proud mishandling of the Scriptures by the Jews and others. In contrast he maintained that 'only the Spirit understands the Scriptures correctly and in accord with God'.[169] Three years later he gave this encouragement to those who studied the Psalter with him: 'So listen now with the Spirit to the prophet who speaks by the Spirit'.[170] The importance of this dependence upon the Spirit of God when interpreting Holy Scripture evidently remained Luther's settled conviction. When Erasmus complained that some parts are difficult to understand, Luther argued that the work of the Spirit is integral to what he called the 'internal

---

[166] 'Non sunt oscitanter Scripturae sanctae verba tractanda. Cum enim sint verba spiritus, necesse est, ut sint plena ponderis et maiestatis.' *Commentariolus in epistolam divi Pauli Apostoli ad Hebreos* (1517) *WA* LVII-III, 233.22-23 = *LW* 29, 236; cf. *Praelectio in psalmum 45* (1532) *WA* XL-II, 472.31-34 = *LW* 12, 197.

[167] 'Sed sacrarum rerum studiosus nihil putabit tam esse exiguum, siquidem Spiritus sanctus id literis voluit mandari, quod non prosit, saltem ad vitam et mores regendos.' *Genesisvorlesung* (1535-45) *WA* XLII, 474.-3-5 = *LW* 2, 296.

[168] 'Jedoch weil sie der Heilige Geist beschrieben hatt, so mussen wir diesen Text nicht uberhin lauffen.' *Auslegung des dritten und vierten Kapitels Johannis* (1538-40) *WA* XLVII, 133.4-5 = *LW* 22, 415; cf. *Deutsche Auslegung des 67 Psalmes* (1521) *WA* VIII, 17.1-4 = *LW* 13, 16-17.

[169] 'Spiritus enim solus intelligit Scripturas recte et secundum Deum.' *Diui Pauli apostoli ad Romanos Epistola* (1516) *WA* LVI, 336.10 = *LW* 25, 324.

[170] ' Item in spiritu loquentem audi in spiritu.' *Operationes in Psalmos* (1519-21) *WA* V, 42.28 = *LW* 14, 305.

clarity (*interna claritas*)' of Scripture: 'the Spirit is required for the understanding of Scripture, both as a whole and in any part of it'.[171]

As we noted earlier, it is the inspiration of the biblical text itself, an inspiration we have established Luther believed extended to the words themselves, which explains his emphasis on the biblical languages. The classic statement of this emphasis was produced in February 1524.[172] This early date, prior to the debate with Erasmus and at the very beginning of the eucharistic debates with the Swiss, makes it highly unlikely that this emphasis should be interpreted as a retreat from the exegetical optimism of the early reformation, brought about by the failure of their common appeal to the Scriptures actually to settle theological questions.[173] There is abundant evidence that Luther consistently pointed out the errors and controversies which arose from faulty translation and the neglect of the biblical languages.[174] In this he was hardly distinguishable from Valla or Erasmus. Yet Luther had another, more basic reason for insisting on a knowledge of Greek and Hebrew amongst those who took it upon themselves to interpret the Scriptures:

> In proportion then as we value the gospel, let us zealously hold to the languages. For it was not without purpose that God caused his Scriptures to be set down in these two languages alone — the Old

---

[171] 'Spiritus enim requiritur ad totam scripturam et ad quamlibet eius partem intelligendam.' *De servo arbitrio* (1525) *WA* XVIII, 609.11-12 = *LW* 33, 28. Wood may well be correct when he attributes one early and isolated reference to the inspiration of church leaders rather than merely their letters to Luther's early conviction that the Spirit-led church remained the guardian of correct biblical interpretation. However, the context of that comment reveals that Luther was attacking the unbelief and quest for novelty which leads some to be dissatisfied 'with what Scripture expressly contains and what the practice of the church clearly deals with [que expressa continet Scriptura et manifesta agit practica Ecclesia]'. *Dictata super Psalterium* (1513-15) *WA* III, 578.14-579.7 = *LW* 11, 63-64. Wood, *Captive*, 139.

[172] *An die Ratherren aller Städte deutschen Lands, daß sie christliche Schlulen aufrichten und halten sollen* (1524) *WA* XV, 27-53. Though note Luther's slightly earlier mention of the importance of the biblical languages from April 1523: *Von Anbeten des Sakraments des heiligen Leichnams Christi* (1523) *WA* XI, 455.33-456.3 = *LW* 36, 304.

[173] McGrath, *Intellectual Origins*, 138; McGrath, *Reformation Thought*, 151-152. There is little warrant for suggesting Luther ever advocated an unqualified right of private judgement in matters of biblical interpretation. Note his own widespread use of the patristic testimony, especially that of Augustine, in this connection.

[174] E.g. *Resolutiones disputationum de indulgentiarum virtute* (1518) *WA* I, 525.15-30 = *LW* 31, 83-84.

Testament in Hebrew, the New in Greek. Now if God did not despise them but chose them above all others for his word, then we too ought to honour them above all others.[175]

Luther was convinced that a knowledge of the languages would undoubtedly prevent the interpreter from falling into error.[176] However, it is the Spirit's intimate involvement in the Scripture, extending to form as well as content, which Luther emphasised here.

Likewise, Luther explicitly tied the inspiration of the Scriptures by the Holy Spirit to the importance of authorial intention in the practice of biblical interpretation. This is evident in his advice to those who would study theology, included in his preface to the 1539 edition of his German writings:

> Secondly, you should meditate, that is, not only in your heart, but also externally, by actually repeating and comparing oral speech and literal words of the book, reading and rereading them with diligent attention and reflection, so that you may see what the Holy Spirit means by them.[177]

The interpreter is to be concerned with correctly conveying the meaning intended by the Holy Spirit, which, of course, is not necessarily different from that of the human writer. What is important to note here is that Luther expected the Spirit's meaning would be discerned by paying careful attention to the actual words of the text. As we have seen, Luther's exposition of a biblical passage could even include appeal to the Holy Spirit's choice of a particular word or expression.

What is explicit at these points is implicit at a number of others. For example, Luther's willingness to explore ways of harmonising biblical

---

[175] 'So lieb nu alls das Euangelion ist, so hart last uns uber den sprachen hallten. Denn Gott hat seyne schrifft nicht umb sonst alleyn ynn die zwo sprachen schreiben lassen, das allte testament ynn die Ebreische, das new ynn die Kriechische. Welche nu Gott nicht veracht, sondern zu seynem wort erwelet hat fur allen andern, sollen auch wyr die selben fur allen andern ehren.' *An die Ratherren aller Städte deutsches Lands* (1524) *WA* xv, 37.17-22 = *LW* 45, 359.

[176] 'Denn es gar ferlich ist von Gottis sachen anders reden odder mit andern worten, denn Gott selbs braucht.' *An die Ratherren aller Städte deutsches Lands* (1524) *WA* xv, 43.12-13 = *LW* 45, 366.

[177] 'Zum andern soltu meditirn, das ist: Nicht allein im hertzen, sondern auch eusserlich die mündliche rede und buchstabische wort im Buch jmer treiben und reiben, lesen und widerlesen, mit vleissigem auffmercken und nachbencken, was der heilige Geist damit meinet.' *Vorrede zum 1. Bande der Wittenberger Ausgabe* (1539) *WA* L, 659.22-25 =*LW* 34, 286. The preceding paragraph makes it clear that 'the book' he has in mind is Holy Scripture.

parallels, even though he admits he cannot solve all the problems, presupposes the inspiration of each account.[178] His commitment to the principle 'Scripture is its own interpreter (*Scriptura sui ipsius interpres*)' likewise follows from the conviction that Scripture is the gift of a benevolent God who has superintended its production down to the very words themselves. 'I do not wish to boast that I am more learned than all', he wrote in 1520, 'but that Scripture alone should reign. Nor do I want to interpret it by my spirit or that of any human being, but rather to understand it on its own terms and by its spirit'.[179] Luther even relates his rejection of an easy appeal to the multiple spiritual senses of Scripture to the fact that this book is the work of the Holy Spirit. In response to Emser in 1521 he explained: 'the Holy Spirit is the simplest writer and speaker in heaven and on earth. This is why his words can have no more than the one simplest meaning which we call the written one, or the literal meaning of the tongue'.[180]

Martin Luther may not have left a treatise devoted to the origin and nature of Holy Scripture yet it is clear that he was far from uninterested in the subject. In incidental comments and in several sustained discussions in the wider context of other questions, Luther made known the convictions which underlay his affirmations of Scripture's authority and his own interpretive method. According to Luther, Holy Scripture is the Word of God, at once God's self-expression and a human communication, accommodated to our finitude and fallenness without compromise to its own truth and divinity. Precisely because God's Spirit has been involved to the level of 'the words and the order of the words', Luther will insist that his opponents bow to the plain meaning of the words. For this same reason, his biblical exposition will take the form of a serious engagement with the words as they stand and a call to trust the God who has so spoken.

---

[178] *Fastenpostille* (1525) *WA* XVII-II, 196.5-31; *Auslegung des ersten und zweiten Kapitels Johannis* (1537-8) *WA* XLVI, 726.20 = *LW* 22, 218-219; *Wochenpredigten über Joh. 16-20* (1528-9) *WA* XXVIII, 268.29-273.31.

[179] 'Nolo omnium doctior iactari, sed solam scripturam regnare, nec eam meo spiritu aut ullorum hominum interpretari, sed per seipsam et suo spiritu intelligi volo. *Assertio omnium articulorum M. Lutheri per bullam Leonis X* (1520) *WA* VII, 98.40-99.2; cf. 97.20-26; 'Das ist dann fein, wenn sich die schrifft selbs außlegt, darumb glaubt nit und haltet frey für finster was nit beweret wirdt mit klaren sprüchen der Biblien.' *Ain Sermon von sant Jacob dem meereren und hailigen zwolffpotten* (25 July 1522) *WA* X-III, 238.10-12.

[180] 'Der heylig geyst ist der aller eynfeltigst schreyber und rether, der ynn hymell und erden ist, drumb auch seyne wortt nit mehr denn eynen einfeltigsten synn haben kunden, wilchen wir den schrifftlichen odder buchstabischen tzungen synn nennen.' *Auf das überchristlich, übergeistlich und überkünstlich Buch Bocks Emsers* (1521) *WA* VII, 650.21-24 = *LW* 39, 178.

In this way Luther's commitment to a biblical inspiration which extended to the very words of the text forms an important conceptual bridge between his statements of Scripture's authority and the way he expounded it at his desk, in the lecture hall, or in the pulpit. It is not the entire bridge, for there is more to be said than merely that this text is the Word of God, inspired by the Spirit in the most profound and extensive sense. Yet Luther's confidence in the benevolence of God towards those in Christ means that his convictions concerning the involvement of God with this text go a long way towards explaining his boldness both in asserting its authority and explaining its meaning.

Chapter 4

A Focused Text?

Luther on the Unity of Holy Scripture

Luther's affirmation of the uniquely inspired character of the biblical text generated a number of important assumptions which influenced his general approach to Holy Scripture. Amongst these was his conviction that these books constitute a coherent unit, both by virtue of their common primary authorship in and through the Holy Spirit and by virtue of their unique role in the benevolent self-disclosure of the one living God. In so far as this perspective is entailed in the confession that 'all Scripture is inspired by God', Luther once again stood within the theological and exegetical tradition which he inherited. However, the emphasis on a spiritual interpretation and application of individual passages — an emphasis which had dominated Christian exegesis since the time of Origen — had frequently tended to undermine the unity of Scripture in practice.[1] Aquinas, the Victorines, and others such as Nicholas of Lyra had all insisted on the priority of the historical sense, but rarely did even they attempt to place the individual passages and books which made up the Bible in the wider framework of a unity which stretched from Genesis to Revelation. Rarely did anyone attempt to articulate the theological dimensions of the unity of Scripture. It is against this background that Luther's commitment to Scripture as a whole becomes significant. The shift from a fragmented, even atomistic conception of the Scriptures to

---

[1] We have to go back to Irenaeus for someone with as profound a grasp of the unity of Scripture as Luther. Irenaeus, *Adversus Haereses,* IV (PG VII, 974-1118); John Lawson, *The Biblical Theology of St. Irenaeus*; Bengt Hägglund, *History of Theology*, 43-51.

'the Bible as a whole' was indeed critical for his contribution to the history of biblical interpretation.[2]

Though it was not at all extraordinary when Luther spoke in general and collective terms about the teaching of Scripture, the frequency of such language in his writings marks this out as a specific concern. Throughout his life he would continue to refer to what 'all the Scriptures (*tota scriptura, die gantze schrift*)' teach,[3] attest,[4] point to,[5] command,[6] or say.[7] He understood authority to attach, not merely to individual passages, but to the entire Scripture.[8] He believed it was possible to articulate the message of the whole,[9] predicate clarity of the whole,[10] and insist that Christ fulfils the whole.[11] Though Luther was clearly aware of the diversity within Scripture, as we have seen, he nevertheless considered that from another perspective the biblical writers spoke with a single voice. As he lectured on Genesis at the end of 1538 he spoke of 'the constant and unanimous judgement of Scripture' and early the next year he argued that 'Holy Scripture is in excellent agreement with itself and is uniformly consistent

---

[2] Evans, Road to Reformation, 158; cf. Hermann Sasse, 'Luther and the Word of God', in Heino O. Kadai (ed.), *Accents in Luther's Theology: Essays in Commemoration of the 450th Anniversary of the Reformation*, 63.

[3] *Enarratio Psalmi LI* (1532) WA XL-II, 385.27-28 = LW 12, 351.

[4] *In epistolam S. Pauli ad Galatas Commentarius* (1535) WA XL-I, 604.31 = LW 26, 397; WA XL-II, 17.26 = LW 27, 15.

[5] *Die sieben Bußpsalmen* (1525) WA XVIII, 501.7 = LW 14, 168; *Wochenpredigten über Joh. 6-8* (1530-32) WA XXXIII, 19.24-25 = LW 23, 16; WA XXXIII, 448.31 = LW 23, 281; *Von Ordnung Gottesdiensts in der Gemeine* (1523) WA XII, 36.5-6 = LW 53, 14.

[6] *Wochenpredigten über Joh. 6-8* (1530-32) WA XXXIII, 21.4-5 = LW 23, 17.

[7] *Auslegung des 118 Psalms* (1529-30) WA XXXI-I, 175.10 = LW 14, 99.

[8] *Commentariolus in epistolam divi Pauli Apostoli ad Hebreos* (1517) WA LVII-III, 181.13-14 = LW 29, 181; *In epistolam Pauli ad Galatas commentarius* (1519) WA II, 484.29-30 = LW 27, 212.

[9] *Kirchenpostille* (1522) WA X-1/1, 80.4-7 = LW 52, 21-23; cf. *Die andere Epistel S. Petri und eine S. Judas gepredigt und ausgelegt* (1523-4) WA XIV, 29.19-20 = LW 30, 165; *In epistolam S. Pauli ad Galatas Commentarius* (1535) WA XL-I, 634.29-31 = LW 26, 418; *Wider das Papsttum zu Rom, vom Teufel gestiftet* (1545) WA LIV, 247.25-28 = LW 41, 313-314.

[10] *De servo arbitrio* (1525) WA XVIII, 656.15-16 = LW 33, 94.

[11] *Dictata super Psalterium* (1513-16) WA III, 46.17-20 = LW 10, 52; *Eyn kleyn unterricht, was man ynn den Euangelijs suchen und gewartten soll. Kirchenpostille* (1522) WA X-1/1, 15.1-5 = LW 35, 122; *Adventspostille* (1522) WA X-II, 73.15-16 = LW 35, 132; *Wochenpredigten über Joh. 6-8* (1530-32) WA XXXIII, 19.24-25 = LW 23, 16; *In epistolam S. Pauli ad Galatas Commentarius* (1535) WA XL-II, 17.26-27 = LW 27, 15; *Vorrede auff die Epistel S. Jacobi und Jude* (1546) WADB VII, 385.25-32 = LW 35, 396.

everywhere'.[12] In a preface to the Wittenberg edition of his German writings, Luther again affirmed the coherence and unity of biblical texts: 'Firstly, you should know that the Holy Scriptures constitute a single book which turns the wisdom of all other books into foolishness, because not one teaches about eternal life except this one alone'.[13]

Such comments almost inevitably raise again the question of how Luther's canonical judgements influenced his doctrine of Scripture. There seems to be some tension between this affirmation of Scripture's unity and, for instance, his marginalisation of the Epistle of James.[14] Was the unity Luther saw in Scripture an artificial construct, one which could only be affirmed after certain troublesome portions had been removed? The evidence we have already examined does not support such a conclusion. While it was true that James, Hebrews, Jude and Revelation were placed at the end of the New Testament and remained unnumbered even in the later editions of *die Deutsche Bibel*, Luther never felt able to remove them completely from his canon. In the case of James, notwithstanding Luther's undeniably strong attacks upon the epistle, it is clear that he continued to struggle with its teaching throughout his life and hoped to discover how it could be harmonised with the teaching of his beloved apostle Paul. Indeed, in some measure it was precisely his presupposition of the unity of Scripture which caused him to persevere with James. Scripture could not be in conflict with itself and so either James and Paul were really agreed and the problem was to do with Luther's own understanding, or else the writing of one or the other was not genuinely Scripture.[15]

Often the unity of Holy Scripture remains an implicit presupposition of Luther's theological work. At other times he reflected at some length on how this unity should be understood and what followed for proper interpretative method. This chapter examines the various threads Luther identified in the fabric of Scripture which enabled him to argue 'Scripture says' with confidence.

---

[12] 'perpetua scripturae et consentiens sententia' *Genesisvorlesung* (1535-45) WA XLIII, 25.49 = LW 3, 210; 'Videmus scripturam sanctam pulchre sibi constare ac consentire ubique perpetuo tenore' WA XLIII, 51.33-34 = LW 3, 247.

[13] 'Erstlich soltu wissen, das die heilige Schrifft ein solch Buch ist, das aller ander Bücher weisheit zur narrheit macht, weil keins vom ewigen leben Leret on bis allein.' *Vorrede zum 1. Bande der Wittenberger Ausgabe* (1539) WA L, 659.5-7 = LW 34, 285.

[14] Wood, *Captive*, 158.

[15] *In epistolam S. Pauli ad Galatas Commentarius* (1535) WA XL-I, 458.35-36 = LW 26, 295.

Unity in Terms of Origin

Luther endorsed the judgement of 2 Tim. 3:16: 'All Scripture is inspired by God'. Here was perhaps the most basic affirmation of Scripture's unity, one which located that unity in the Holy Spirit as primary author. However, this dimension, though present, is not prominent in Luther's writing. He recognised this common primary authorship, as we have seen, but rarely developed it as a defence of Scripture's unity.

One of the earliest references to this dimension of the unity of Scripture is found in Luther's Romans lectures from 1515:

> Thus in the prophets the term 'voice' applies without exception to the 'voice of the Lord', so that we must accept every word which is spoken as if the Lord Himself were speaking, no matter by whom it is spoken, and we must believe it, yield to it, and humbly subject our reason to it.[16]

The context is Luther's discussion of the nature of that faith through which righteousness comes according to Rom. 3:22. Saving faith, he explained, is not simply a matter of believing in Christ, but also 'in all things which pertain to Christ (*ea que ipsius sunt*)'. This led him to insist upon the indivisibility of Christian truth. In support of this notion he quoted the words of Jesus in Mt. 4:4: 'Man shall not live by bread alone but by every word that proceeds from the mouth of God'. His explanation of this verse included one of his strongest statements on the unity of Scripture:

> But why does Christ say 'every word'? Because if you fail to believe even one word, you no longer are living in the Word of God. For the whole Christ is in every word and wholly in each individual word. When he is denied, therefore, in one word, he is totally denied, for he is in every word.[17]

Even at this early stage, when Luther was still prepared to accept 'the priest and the prelate' as the mouth of God on the basis of Mal. 2:7, he was convinced that there is a profound unity to Holy Scripture, a unity

---

[16] 'Ideo in prophetis Vocem absolute Domini appellat, Vt omne verbum vocale, per quemcunque dicatur, Velut Domino ipso dicente, suscipiamus, credamus, cedamus et humiliter subiiciamus nostrum sensum.' *Epistola beati Pauli apostoli ad Romanos incipit* (1515-16) WA LVI, 253.16-19 = LW 25, 239-240.

[17] 'Sed cur dicit: "omni Verbo"? quia scil. Si vnum verbum non credideris, iam non viuis in verbo Dei. Quia in omni Verbo totus est Christus et in singulis totus. Ergo in vno negatus totus negatus est, qui in omnibus.' *Epistola beati Pauli apostoli ad Romanos incipit* (1515-16) WA LVI, 252.10-13 = LW 25, 238.

which is best preserved by accepting 'every word which is spoken as if the Lord himself were speaking'.

After lecturing on Romans Luther turned to Galatians and then to Hebrews. Commenting on Heb. 10:5 in 1518, he again affirmed a unity of Scripture which is related to its origin in the work of the Holy Spirit. 'Throughout Scripture', he argued, 'the Spirit has only one aim: that we hear the voice of God, that is, that we believe'.[18] The affinities with his comments on Rom. 3 are obvious, yet Luther did go further here. He maintained that there is an overarching divine intention which explains Scripture as we have it. This 'aim' of the Spirit is common to all Scripture and in some sense unites all Scripture.

In later life Luther continued to maintain the unity of Holy Scripture and the relationship of this fact to the same Spirit's involvement in the production of each part. In 1543 Luther's treatise *Von den letzten Worten Davids,* intended as a defence of his Christological understanding of the Old Testament and based on 2 Sa. 23:1–7, included the affirmation, supported by 2 Pet. 1.21 and a collection of sayings from the Gospels, that 'we attribute to the Holy Spirit all of Scripture and the external Word and the sacraments, which touch and move our external ears and other senses'.[19] It was later in the same treatise that he maintained a consistency between the Old Testament and the New which requires the doctrine of the Trinity and which is based on the Holy Spirit's authorship of both testaments: 'If this is the Lord of whom Moses writes, how can it be Christ of whom St. Paul writes? But they must both be correct; for the Holy Spirit does not contradict Himself.'[20] Such sentiments correspond with a statement about the articles of faith which Luther made in 1544 in the midst of what would be his final treatise on the Lord's Supper:

---

[18] 'Inde per totam Scripturam id agit unice spiritus, ut vocem Dei audiamus id est credamus.' *Commentariolus in epistolam divi Pauli Apostoli ad Hebreos* (1517) WA LVII-III, 221.8-9 = LW 29, 223.

[19] 'Also gibt man nu dem Heiligen Geist die gantze Heilige Schrifft und das eusserliche wort und Sacrament, so unser eusserliche ohren und synne ruren oder bewegen.' *Von den letzten Worten Davids* (1543) WA LIV, 35.2-4 = LW 15, 275.

[20] 'Ists der HERR, wie Mose schreibet, wie kans Christus sein, wie Paulus schreibt? Nu mussen sie beide recht schreiben, Denn der Heilige geist ist nicht wider sich selbs.' *Von den letzten Worten Davids* (1543) WA LIV, 66.40-42 = LW 15, 313. Luther was discussing an apparent discrepancy between Moses' record that the Israelites tested the Lord (Ex. 17:2; Nu. 14:22; cf. Nu. 21:7) and Paul's exhortation not to 'put Christ to the test, as some of them did and were destroyed by serpents' (1 Cor. 10:9).

For this reason we say that everything is to be believed completely and without exception, or nothing is to be believed. The Holy Spirit does not allow himself to be divided or cut up so that he should let one point be taught and believed as trustworthy and another as false.[21]

Given the Holy Spirit's consistently truthful character, Luther was convinced the Spirit's inspiration of the biblical texts guaranteed their own consistency or unity. Scripture could not contradict itself because the Spirit does not contradict himself and he stands behind each text as the primary author. Nevertheless, it was a unity of content, rather than a unity of origin which most often occupied Luther's attention when he thought of the Bible as a whole.

Unity in Terms of Content

Luther was a biblical theologian in more than one sense. He was convinced that the task of theology was the exposition and application of the Scriptures. His own work, whether in his lectures on various books of the Bible, his polemical treatises which are full of biblical exposition, or his sermons, all remained thoroughly consistent with such a conviction. So too was his work in reshaping the theological curriculum in the university at Wittenberg. However, he was also a biblical theologian in the sense of one who explores the internal connections of Holy Scripture and its own theological substructure. Such an exploration proved profoundly significant for both his understanding of Scripture's authority and the appropriate method of biblical interpretation.

Christ as the Centre of Scripture

Undoubtedly the most consistent and easily recognisable feature of Luther's interpretive method is his recognition that Christ is the central subject of Holy Scripture.[22] However, as we have seen, a Christological approach to the Old Testament was nothing new. It was the common

---

[21] 'Darumb heissts, rund und rein gantz und alles gegleubt, oder nichts gegleubt, Der heilige Geist lesst sich nicht trennen noch teilen, das er ein stück solt warhafftig und das ander falsch leren oder gleuben lassen.' *Kurtz bekentnis D, Mart. Luthers, vom heiligen Sacrament* (1544) WA LIV, 158.28-30 = LW 38, 308; cf. *Daß diese Worte Christi (Das ist mein Leib etc.) noch fest stehen wider die Schwarmgeister* (1527) WA XXIII, 83.31-85.12 = LW 37, 26.

[22] Althaus, *Theology*, 74; Preus, 'Promissio', 146; Marc Lienhard, *Luther: Witness to Jesus Christ: Stages and Themes of the Reformer's Christology*, 25, 39-40, 43; Dockery, 'Hermeneutics', 189-203; Oberman, *Luther*, 171-173.

A Focused Text? 153

property of the exegetical tradition. The Psalms in particular had been a focus of attention in this regard, especially in the two centuries prior to Luther.[23] Luther's own contribution lies not so much in the Christological approach itself, as in the intensity with which he applied this principle to the whole of Scripture and the way in which he articulated it throughout his life.[24]

Luther's commitment to Christ as the centre of Scripture is apparent from the very first page of the first series of lectures he delivered. Three 'prefaces' to these lectures have survived. The first introduced the printed psalm texts which Luther provided for his students in 1513. His approach was clear from the title: 'THE PREFACE OF JESUS CHRIST, the Son of God and our Lord, to the Psalter of DAVID'.[25] After a collection of texts from the Old and New Testaments, this preface explained the principle upon which Luther's exposition would proceed:

> Every prophecy and every prophet must be understood as referring to Christ the Lord, except where it is clear from plain words that someone else is spoken of. For thus He Himself says: 'Search the Scriptures: for it is they that bear witness to Me'.[26]

The preface makes it clear that Luther did not consider this approach something which he was imposing upon Scripture from without. He was convinced that he was following the clear and explicit teaching of the Bible. Indeed, it was Jesus himself who had provided his followers with this interpretive principle. Further, as a follower of Christ, one redeemed under the new covenant, he could not do otherwise than approach any Old Testament text from the perspective of its fulfilment

---

[23] Significant contributions had been made by Nicholas of Lyra (1270-1340), Paul of Burgos (1351-1435), Jacobus Pérez (d. 1480), and Faber Stapulensis (1455-1536). Oberman, *Forerunners*, 286-287. Alister McGrath has drawn attention to the work of Wendelein Steinbach (1454-1519) as further evidence that Luther's Christological concentration was by no means novel. Steinbach was lecturing on Galatians at Tübingen at the same time that Luther was delivering his first series of lectures on the Psalms at Wittenberg. Alister E. McGrath, *Luther's Theology of the Cross: Martin Luther's Theological Breakthrough*, 78-80; Helmut Feld, *Die Anfänge der Modernen Biblischen Hermeneutik in der Spätmittelalterlichen Theologie*, 70.

[24] Ebeling, *Evangelienauslegung*, 280.

[25] 'PRAEFATIO IHESV CHRISTI filii dei et domini nostri in Psalterium DAVID' *Dictata super Psalterium* (1513-16) WA LV-I, 6.1-3 = LW 10, 6.

[26] 'Omnis prophetia et omnis propheta de Christo domino debet intelligi nisi ubi manifestis uerbis appareat de alio loqui. Sic enim ipse dicit. Scrutamini scripturas: ille enim sunt quae testimonium perhibent de me.' *Dictata super Psalterium* (1513-16) WA LV-I, 6.25-8.2 = LW 10, 6.

in Christ. Glossing his own preface he added 'If the Old Testament can be interpreted by human wisdom without the New Testament, I should say that the New Testament has been given to no purpose'.[27]

The second preface is that preserved on the reverse of the title page of the manuscript which contains the glosses of these lectures and may have been prepared when there was talk of publishing them in 1516.[28] Here again Luther spoke of the importance of understanding the Psalter in the light of Christ. He rebuked those 'who have a carnal understanding of the Psalms, like the Jews, who always apply the Psalms to ancient history apart from Christ'. Luther expected something more from a Christian interpreter, for 'Christ has opened the mind of those who are His so that they might understand the Scriptures'.[29]

The third preface is that attached to the *Scholia*.[30] The Christological focus of the psalms is by no means as explicit here, though Luther stresses from the beginning that these lectures are 'a study of this illustrious prophet, David'.[31] This is significant because Luther's insistence upon the prophetic character of the entire Old Testament provided the essential background to his thoroughgoing Christological exegesis. For Luther it was not David's royal or military achievements which were most important, but rather David's self-description as one appointed to speak about 'the Christ of the God of Jacob'.[32]

The influence of the *Quintuplex Psalterium* of Faber Stapulensis is everywhere apparent in these prefaces penned by Luther.[33] Stapulensis

---

[27] 'Si vetus testamentum per humanum sensum potest exponi sine nouo testamento, dicam Quod nouum testamentum gratis datum fit.' *Dictata super Psalterium* (1513-16) WA LV-I, 6.26-27 = LW 10, 6 n.2.

[28] LW 10, x; *Luther an Spalatin* (9 September 1516) WABr I, 56.5-6 = LW 48, 18-19.

[29] 'Alii qui carnalem Intelligentiam habent in Psalmis Sicut Iudei applicantes semper Psalmos ad veteres hystorias extra Christum. Sed Christus "aperuit suis mentem, vt intelligerent Scripturas".' *Dictata super Psalterium* (1513-16) WA LV-I, 2.9-12 = LW 10, 3.

[30] In the Dresdner manuscript this preface followed the lectures on Psalm 1.

[31] 'spiritu ad honorem prophete huius Inclyti Dauid incipiendi' *Dictata super Psalterium* (1513-16) WA LV-II, 25.3-4 = LW 10, 8.

[32] '[D]e Christo Dei Iacob' *Dictata super Psalterium* (1513-16) WA LV-II, 26.19 = LW 10, 9. It is Luther's rendering of 2 Samuel 23:1 which provided the support for this approach: 'the man to whom it was appointed concerning the Christ of the God of Jacob, the excellent psalmist of Israel said: "The Spirit of the Lord has spoken by me" (Es sprach der Man der versichert ist, von dem Messia des Gottes Jacob, Lieblich mit Psalmen Israel [...] Der Geist des HERRR hat durch mich geredt)'. WA LIV, 31.24-33.14 = LW 15, 271-273.

[33] Luther's 1513 Annotationes on this work are found in WA IV, 466-526.

had set out his approach in his own introduction: 'I have tried to write a short exposition of the Psalms with the assistance of Christ, who is the key to the understanding of David and about whom David spoke, commissioned by the Holy Spirit, in the book of Psalms'. He too had referred to 2 Sa. 23 in support of the prophetic stance of the Psalter. He too had distanced himself from a purely historical reading of the Psalms insisting that even here David wrote as a prophet.[34]

The lectures which followed Luther's introduction are themselves a rich source of comments on the essentially Christological nature of all Holy Scripture. They reveal that while he had certainly not yet abandoned the *Quadriga*, this traditional four-fold system of biblical interpretation was being subjected to great strain by his rigorous application of Christological principle.[35] Instead of the reference to Christ flowing out of the literal sense, all other senses are explored as extensions of the reference to Christ. For instance, as he explained Ps. 4:1 Luther remarked:

> Since Christ is the Head of all saints, the Fountain of all, the Source of all rivers, of whom all partake, and 'from His fullness all have received', it follows that 'in the roll' (that is, in the chief sense) 'of the book', that is of the entire Scripture and especially of the Psalms, 'it is written concerning him'. And as all His saints flow from Him like rivers, so Scripture, being similarly constituted and thus representing Him with His saints, speaks of Him in the sense of the first source. Then it distributes the same sense to the rivers (that is, individual explanations), speaking the same words concerning the saints by way of participation. For if they participate with Him in grace and inherit all things from Him, then also the words of Scripture which speak of Christ participate with Him in a similar way and inherit the same words of praise and description from Him and with Him and in Him, 'who is blessed'. In this way all four senses of Scripture flow together into one very large stream.[36]

---

[34] Jacques Lefèvre d'Étaples, *Quincuplex Psalterium*, Aij.

[35] Luther could still endorse the Quadriga, though with reservations and a warning against 'tearing the Scriptures to pieces', as late as his comment on Gal. 4:24, published in 1519. *In epistolam Pauli ad Galatas commentarius* (1519) WA II, 550.20-551.15 = LW 27, 311-312.

[36] 'Quoniam Christus est Caput omnium sanctorum, fons omnium, origo omnium riuulorum, ex quo participant omnes, "et de plenitudine eius omnes accipiunt", hinc est, Quod "in capite" (i.e. principali sensu) "libri", i. e. totius Scripture et precipue psalmorum "de eo Scriptum est". Ac Sicut omnes sui sancti fluunt ex ipso velut riuuli, Ita Scriptura conformiter sese habens et ita representans ipsum cum suis sanctis, primo fontali sensu de ipso loquitur. Deinde eundem sensum deriuat in riuulos (i.e. particulares expositions)

This remained Luther's understanding throughout these lectures. The starting point of the interpretive exercise must be a recognition of the text's prophetic sense, that is, its reference to Christ.[37] Luther was still prepared to concede other legitimate levels of meaning within the text, but he insisted that if an interpreter did not begin with the prophetic sense he could not expect to understand the other senses properly. This was the problem he discerned with past approaches to Ps. 119 as he began his own exposition of it in 1515:

> I have not yet seen this psalm expounded by anyone in a prophetic sense, nor is there anyone who has kept the sequence and order of exposition in it without doing violence to and twisting the verses and words. I think this comes about because they did not seek first the prophetic, that is, the literal sense, which is the foundation of the rest, the master and light, the author and fountain and origin.[38]

There were, of course, other developments as Luther lectured his way through the Psalter. He seems, albeit rather tentatively, to find an increasing place for the original historical context of the psalms. James Preus has noted the prominence of the 'faithful synagogue' as a speaker in the later *Dictata*.[39] However in Ps. 101, the psalm immediately prior to that in which Preus identifies Luther's 'hermeneutical shift', Luther was still able to criticise Nicholas of Lyra for referring the psalm to David. Commenting on verse five he says:

> Here at last it is clearly evident that this psalm is only speaking in the person of Him who is God, or rather of the church, which has the spirit of her Bridegroom. For it is He alone who searches the kidneys and hearts. Hence David could not say, 'I did not eat with an insatiable heart', or, as the Hebrew says, 'the proud in eye and lofty

---

participatiue de sanctis loquens eadem verba. Si enim in gratia cum eo participant et hereditant omnia ex ipso, igitur et verba Scripture de Christo loquentia similiter cum eo participant et hereditant easdem laudes et descriptiones ex ipso et cum ipso et in ipso, "qui est benedictus". Et hoc modo omnes quatuor sensus Scripture in vnum confluunt amplissimum flumen.' *Dictata super Psalterium* (1513-16) WA LV-II, 62.15-63.11 = LW 10, 52; cf. WA III, 368.18-24 = LW 10, 311.

[37] Gerhard Ebeling, 'The Beginnings of Luther's Hermeneutics III', *LQ* 7 (1993), 459.

[38] 'Istum psalmum nondum vidi ab aliquo expositum in sensu prophetico, nec ullus est, qui seriem et ordinem expositionis in eo tenerit sine violentia et contorsione versuum et verborum. Quod inde puto venire, quia propheticum, id est literalem, primo non quesierunt: qui est fundamentum ceterorum, magister et lux et author et fons atque origo.' *Dictata super Psalterium* (1513-16) WA IV, 305.3-8 = LW 11, 414.

[39] Preus, 'Promissio', 148-153.

in heart, with him I could not be'. For who would always reveal to David what sort of people they were in their heart? Therefore Lyra badly twists this psalm in referring it to David.[40]

Similar comments can be found as Luther begins to expound Ps. 112.[41] However, the tentative nature of Luther's interest in the Old Testament history itself ensures that it almost always gives way to his primary concern with the relation of each psalm to Christ. As late as his exposition of Ps. 143 he could say 'in Christ all words are one Word, and outside of Christ they are many and vain'.[42]

Others have observed Luther's increasing interest in the tropological sense throughout the *Dictata*.[43] Reference is usually made to two comments in particular. The first is a comment on Ps. 77:1: 'we have often said that the tropological sense is the primary sense of Scripture'.[44] The second is a slightly earlier comment, one which has been the subject of controversy both because of irregularities in the manuscript known as the Dresdner Psalter and because of its critical significance for understanding Luther's emerging doctrine of justification.[45] It now appears that the comment concerned belongs with the beginning of his exposition of Ps. 72:

---

[40] 'Patet tandem hic clare hunc psalmum non nisi in persona eius dici, qui sit dues, vel Ecclesie potius, que habet spiritum sponsi sui. Nam solus ipse est, qui scrutatur renes et corda. Quare David non potuit dicere: "Cum corde insatiabili non edebam:, vel ut hebr. Habet: "Superbum oculo et altum corde, cum hoc esse non potero". Quis enim David semper revelaret, quales essent in corde suo? Igitur male Lyra detorquet hunc psalmum ad David.' *Dictata super Psalterium* (1513-16) WA IV, 137.23-28 = LW 11, 290.

[41] *Dictata super Psalterium* (1513-16) WA IV, 249.23-250.5 = LW 11, 384.

[42] 'Quia in Christo omnia verba sunt unum verbum, et extra Christum sunt plurima et vana' *Dictata super Psalterium* (1513-16) WA IV, 439.20-21. Pilch, 'Luther's Hermeneutical Shift', 445-448; Reinke, 'Allegory', 386-395.

[43] Emanuel Hirsch, 'Initium theologiae Lutheri', in *Lutherstudien*. II, 30-34; Erich Vogelsang, *Die Anfänge von Luthers Christologie nach der ersten Psalmenvorlesung*, 48ff.; Holl, 'Luthers Bedeutung', 546; Ebeling, 'Hermeneutics III', 460-464; McGrath, *Theology of the Cross*, 121-122; Karl-Heinz zur Mühlen, 'Der Begriff sensus in der Exegese der Reformationszeit', 11-12.

[44] 'Cum autem frequenter dixerimus Tropologiam esse primarium sensum Scripture' *Dictata super Psalterium* (1513-16) WA III, 531.33-34 = LW 11, 12; cf. WA III, 335.21-22; WA III, 432.22-25 = LW 10, 372-373; WA III, 440.31-33 = LW 10, 384.

[45] J. Wendorf, 'Der Durchbruch der neuen Erkenntnis Luthers im Lichte der handschriftlichen Überlieferung', *Historische Vierteljahrschrift*, 27 (1932), 134-142; Heinrich Bornkamm, 'Iustitia Dei beim jungen Luther', in Bernhard

Therefore, whoever wants to understand the apostle and other Scriptures wisely must understand everything tropologically: truth, wisdom, strength, salvation, righteousness, namely, that by which he makes us strong, safe, righteous, wise, etc. So it is with all the works of God and the ways of God: every one of them is Christ literally, and faith in him morally.[46]

How are we to understand this interest in the tropological sense, especially in the light of Luther's principle that 'every prophecy and every prophet must be understood as referring to Christ the Lord, except where it is clear from plain words that someone else is spoken of'?[47] The important thing to note in the comment from Ps. 72 is the last sentence. There Luther drew a close connection between the literal reference to Christ in each text and the tropological sense. Precisely because the literal sense of a text is its relation to Christ, each text demands the application of faith in him. The Christ about whom the Scriptures speak is Christ *for us*, and thus no understanding of the biblical text is complete without a recognition that we are called to trust him and receive from him.[48] This is not quite the existentialist interpretation which Ebeling finds in Luther. More is at stake than simply 'a person's self-understanding of existence'.[49] For Luther, the application of the Christ-centred text to the believer is necessitated, not primarily by the nature of human existence itself, but by the nature of Christ and what He has done.

Luther never abandoned his commitment to this principle that Christ is the centre of Holy Scripture. References to it abound throughout his

---

Lohse (ed.), *Der Durchbruch der reformatorischen Erkenntnis bei Luther*, 292-299; McGrath, *Theology of the Cross*, 120-123.

[46] 'Unde qui Apostolum et alias scripturas vult sapide intelligere, oportet ista omnia tropologice intelligere: Veritas, sapientia, virtus, salus, iustitia, scilicet qua nos facit fortes, salvos, iustos, sapientes, &c. Sic opera dei, vie dei: que omnia Christus est literaliter. Et fides eius moraliter hec omnia.' *Dictata super Psalterium* (1513-16) WA III, 458.8-11 = LW 10, 402.

[47] 'Omnis prophetia et omnis propheta de Christo domino debet intelligi nisi ubi manifestis uerbis appareat de alio loqui.' *Dictata super Psalterium* (1513-16) WA LV-I, 6.25-8.1 = LW 10, 6.

[48] 'The reality of faith demands to be applied to the life of the believer. Christ calls forth faith. There is no Christology without soteriology.' Lienhard, *Luther*, 41; cf. Victor C. Pfitzner, 'Luther as Interpreter of John's Gospel: With Special Reference to his Sermons on the Gospel of John', *LTJ* 18 (1984) 71; McGrath, *Theology of the Cross*, 122.

[49] Ebeling, 'Hermeneutics III', 463. It is interesting to note that the passage quoted by Ebeling, from Luther's comment on Ps. 85:13, is in context a reference to Christ's second coming. *Dictata super Psalterium* (1513-16) WA IV, 19.33-36 = LW 11, 174.

exegetical writings. One particularly graphic way of explaining what he meant was first used in his *Kirchenpostille*, one of the products of Luther's 'exile' in the Wartburg from 1521 to 1522. In the introduction Luther reflected on the purpose of the New Testament books:

> Now the gospels and epistles of the apostles were written for this very purpose. They want themselves to be our guides, to direct us to the writings of the prophets and of Moses in the Old Testament so that we might there read and see for ourselves how Christ is wrapped in swaddling cloths and laid in the manger, that is, how he is comprehended in the writings of the prophets. It is there that people like us should read and study, drill ourselves, and see what Christ is, for what purpose he has been given, how he was promised, and how all Scripture tends toward him. For he himself says in John 5, 'If you believed Moses, you would also believe me, for he wrote of me'. Again, 'Search and look up the Scriptures, for it is they that bear witness to me'.[50]

Luther equated the Old Testament with the swaddling cloths and manger in which the infant Christ was first presented to the nations. This language was not intended to imply that the Old Testament was irrelevant or of little value. Nor did it reflect a clear distinction between Scripture and the Word of God.[51] The point of Luther's imagery is that the relevance and value of the Old Testament for the Christian lies precisely in its proclamation of Christ. This is the context in which he used the same image in the preface to his translation of the Pentateuch in 1523 (which, with minor modification, became his Preface to the Old Testament from 1534):

---

[50] 'Syntemal die Euangeli und Epistel der Apostel darumb geschrieben sind, das sie selb solche tzeyger seyn wollen und uns weyßen ynn die schrifft der propheten und Mosi des allten testaments, das wyr alda selbs leßen und sehen sollen, wie Christus ynn die windel thucher gewicklet und yn die krippen gelegt sey, das ist, wie er ynn der schrifft der propheten vorfassett sey. Da sollt unßer studirn und leßen sich uben und sehen, was Christus sey, wo zu er geben sey, wie er vorsprochen sey, und wie sich alle schrifft auff yhn ziehe, als er selb sagt Johan. 5: Wenn yhr Mosi glewbetet, ßo glewbetet yhr auch myr, denn von myr hatt er geschrieben. Item: forschet und suchet die schrifft, denn die selbige ists, die von myr gezeugniß gibt.' *Eyn kleyn unterricht, was man ynn den Euangelijs suchen und gewartten soll. Kirchenpostille* (1522) WA X-I/1, 15.1-10 = LW 35, 122; cf. *Kirchenpostille* (1522) WA X-I/1, 80.3-82.22 = LW 52, 21-23; WA X-I/1, 576.4-17 = LW 52, 171-172; WA X-I/1, 625.12-626.23 = LW 52, 205-206.

[51] Contra William H. Lazareth, 'Luther's "Sola Scriptura": Traditions of the Gospel for Norming Christian Righteousness', in R. J. Neuhaus (ed.), *Biblical Interpretation in Crisis: The Ratzinger Conference on Bible and Church*, 61.

There are some who have little regard for the Old Testament. They think of it as a book that was given to the Jewish people only and is now out of date, containing only stories of past times. They think they have enough in the New Testament and assert that only a spiritual sense is to be sought in the Old Testament. Origen, Jerome, and many other distinguished people held this view. But Christ says in John 5, 'Search the Scriptures, for it is they that bear witness to me' [...] Therefore dismiss your own opinions and feelings, and think of the Scriptures as the loftiest and noblest of holy things, as the richest of mines which can never be sufficiently explored, in order that you may find that divine wisdom which God here lays before you in such simple guise as to quench all pride. Here you will find the swaddling cloths and the manger in which Christ lies, and to which the angel points the shepherds. Simple and lowly are these swaddling cloths, but dear is the treasure, Christ, who lies in them.[52]

If the birth narratives of the Gospels could be adapted as an image of Christ in the Scriptures, so too could the crucifixion narratives. In the same year that Luther penned the Preface to the Pentateuch, he preached on Lk. 2. In that context he remarked: 'Christ has been wrapped up utterly in Scripture, just as the body in a piece of cloth'.[53] The emphasis is undoubtedly the same: the substance of the entire Old Testament, its central subject and point of unity, is Christ himself. To expound the Old Testament without reference to him would be to distort its message. Luther developed this idea in a sermon on the passion narrative in Matthew's Gospel, part of the *Fastenpostille* of 1545:

---

[52] 'Das alte testament halten ettlich geringe, als das dem Judischen volck alleyne gegeben und nu fort aus sey, und nur von vergangenen geschichten schreybe, meynen, sie haben gnug am newen testament, und geben fur eytel geystliche synn ym alten testament zu suchen wie auch, Origenes, Hieron. Und viel hoher leutt mehr gehalten haben, Aber Christus spricht Johannis. 5. forschet ynn der schrifft, denn die selbige gibt zeugnis von myr [...] Darumb laß deyn dunckel und fulen faren, und halte von diser schrifft, als von dem aller hohisten edlisten heyltum, als von der aller reichisten fund gruben, die nymer mehr gnug aus gegrund werden mag, auff das du die gottliche weyscheyt finden mugest, wilche Gott hie so alber und schlecht furlegt, das er allen hohmut dempffe, Hie wirstu die windeln und die krippen finden, da Christus ynnen ligt, dahyn auch der engel die hirtten weysset, Schlechte und geringe windel sind es, aber theur ist der schatz Christus, der drynnen ligt.' *Das Alte Testament. Luthers Vorrede.* (1523) WADB VIII, 10.1-7, 12.1-8 = LW 35, 235, 236.

[53] 'Christus ist in der Schrift eingewickelt durch und durch, gleych wie der leyb ynn den tuchlen'. *Sermon am I. Sonntag nach Epiphania* (11 January 1523) WA XII, 418.24.

> For Holy Scripture is the garment which our Lord Christ has put on and in which He lets Himself be seen and found. This garment is woven throughout and so wrought together into one that cannot be cut or parted. But the soldiers take it from Christ crucified, i.e. heretics and schismatics. It is their particular mischief to want to have the coat entire, persuading everyone that all Scripture agrees with them and is of their opinion.[54]

Luther explained his conviction that the unity of Scripture can be seen in its testimony to Christ in other ways as well. In a piece of the *Tischreden* dated January 1532, Konrad Cordatus records Luther's use of terminology taken from the field of geometry. Luther is reported to have told his students: 'Christ is the central point of the circle around which everything else in the Bible revolves'.[55] In 1539 he picked up the same language as he expounded Jn. 3:14:

> In this way the Lord shows us the proper method of interpreting Moses and all the prophets and helps us to understand that Moses, in all his stories and illustrations, points and belongs to Christ. His purpose is to show that Christ is the point and centre of a circle, with all eyes inside the circle focused on Him. Whoever turns his eyes on Him finds his proper place in the circle of which Christ is the centre. All the stories of Holy Scripture, if viewed aright, point to Christ.[56]

The emphasis on the Old Testament in these quotations from Luther's exegetical writings is striking. The strongest statements of Nicholas of Lyra, and others who had been heavily influenced by Rabbinic

---

[54] 'Denn die heylige Schrifft ist das kleyd, das unser Herr Christus angezogen hat und sich drinn sehen und finden lest, Solches kleyd ist durchauß gewürcket und in einander dermassen gefasset, das mans nicht schneyden noch teylen kan. Es nemen sich aber die Kriegßknechte drumb an, die Christum creutzigen, das ist: die Ketzer und Rotten. Die haben sonderlich dise unart, das die den rock wöllen gantz haben und yederman uberreden, die gantz schrifft stymme mit jnen und sey jr meynung.' *Hauspostille* (1545) WA LII, 802.1-8.

[55] 'Christus est punctus mathematicus sacrae scripturae, Caesar punctus physicus legum.' *Tishchreden* #2383 (1-9 January 1532) WATr II, 439.25-26.

[56] 'Aber der Herr weiset uns damit den rechten grieff, Mosen und alle propheten auszulegen, und gibt zu verstehen, das Moses mit allen seinen geschiechten und Bildern auff in deute und auff Christum gehöre und ihnen meine, nemlich, das Christus sej der punct im Circkel, da der gantze Circkel ausgezogn ist, und auff in sehet, und wer sich nach ime richtet, gehort auch drein. Den er ist das mittel punctlein im Circkel, und alle Historien in der heiligen schriefft, so sie recht angesehen werden, gehen auff Christum.' *Auslegung des 3. und 4. Kapitels Johannes* (1538-40) WA XLVII, 66.18-24 = LW 22, 339.

exegesis, made it particularly important for Luther to stress that the Old Testament finds its own internal unity as well as its unity with the New Testament in the proclamation of Christ. However, he did not tire of making the more obvious point that the focus of the New Testament is also Christ. His Preface to the Old Testament, from 1522, described the New Testament as 'a public preaching and proclamation of Christ set forth through the sayings of the Old Testament and fulfilled through Christ'.[57] The next year, as he introduced a sermonic commentary on 1 Peter, Luther explained that 'the word "Gospel" signifies nothing else than a sermon or report concerning the grace and mercy of God merited and acquired through the Lord Jesus Christ with his death'.[58] His comment on Gal. 2:17, from 1535, included the acknowledgement that, 'Holy Scripture, especially the New Testament, always promotes faith in Christ and magnificently proclaims him'.[59] Further, as we have seen in an earlier chapter, it is this perspective on the New Testament which is cited by Luther in support of his canonical judgements concerning a small number of New Testament books.[60]

As one might expect, Luther did not treat this insight as an exegetical nicety to be hidden away in the lectures to his students at the University. The same insistence on the centrality of Christ in the Scriptures is found in his polemical literature. In *De servo arbitrio* he asked Erasmus: 'Take Christ out of the Scriptures and what will you find left in them?'[61] In his last great treatise against the Papacy, *Wider das Papsttum zu Rom, vom Teufel gestiftet*, Luther once more testified to the one message of Scripture. The immediate occasion was an exposition of Mt. 16, and especially the confession of Peter at Caesarea-Philippi:

> In these few words of Peter, which he confesses with all the other disciples (for they are all represented in Peter's reply), is included

---

[57] 'Und was ist das newe Testament anders, denn ein öffentliche predigt und verkündigung von Christo, durch die Sprüche im alten Testament gesetzt, und durch Christum erfüllet.' *Vorrede auff das Alte Testament* (1545) WADB VIII, 11.19-21 = LW 35, 236.

[58] 'Euangelion aber heysset nichts anders, denn ein predig und geschrey von der genad und barmhertzikeytt Gottis, durch den herrren Christum mit seynem todt verdienet und erworben' *Epistel Sanct Petri gepredigt und ausgelegt* (1523) WA XII, 259.8-10 = LW 30, 3.

[59] 'Scriptura, praesertim novi Testamenti, ubique inculcat fidem in Christum et magnifice eam preadicat.' *In epistolam S. Pauli ad Galatas Commentarius* (1535) WA XL-I, 254.17-18 = LW 26, 146.

[60] *Vorrede auff die Epistel S. Jacobi und Jüde* (1546) WADB VII, 385.22-32 = LW 35, 396.

[61] 'Tolle Christum e scripturis, quid amplius in illis invenies?' *De servo arbitrio* (1525) WA XVIII, 606.29 = LW 33, 26.

A Focused Text? 163

the whole of the gospel, indeed, all of Holy Scripture. For what else does Scripture intend from beginning to end, except that the Messiah, the Son of God, should come and through his sacrifice, 'like that of a lamb without blemish', bear and take away the sin of the world and thus deliver from eternal death to eternal salvation? Holy Scripture was written for the sake of the Messiah and Son of God, and for His sake everything that happened took place.[62]

Whatever other patterns of unity or diversity Luther found within the pages of Holy Scripture, he was convinced of a profound unanimity at its core. There was indeed much more that might be said, but this one thing remained central: 'everything must be understood in relation to Christ'.[63]

A Common Predicament and Solution

According to Luther, Scripture by its very nature as the self-expression of the triune God promotes (*treiben*) Christ. However, this does not mean that he believed every question was to be answered purely in terms of Christology. Luther recognised other dimensions to the unity of Scripture as well. In a number of his earlier works in particular he pointed out that there is a common understanding of the human predicament and its remedy throughout the Scriptures. In 1519, as he lectured on Psalm 1, he explained why the Psalmist did not identify the godly and the ungodly by name:

> And this was most necessary so that the Word of God, because it is eternal, should apply to all men of all times. For although in the course of time customs, people, places, and usages may vary,

---

[62] 'Denn in diesen wenigen Worten Petri, die er sampt den andern Jüngern bekennet, (denn sie stehen alle für einen Man in dieser Antwort Petri) ist begriffen das gantz Euangelium, ja die gantze heilige Schrifft. Denn was wil die Schrifft von anfang zum ende aus anders, denn das Messias Gottes Son komen solt, und durch sein opffer, als eins unschüldigen Lemblin Gottes, der welt Sünd tragen und weg nemen, und also vom ewigen Tod erlösen zur ewigen seligkeit? Umb des Messia und Gottes Sons willen, ist die heilige Schrifft geschrieben, und umb seinen willen alles geschehen, was geschehen ist.' *Wider das Papsttum zu Rom, vom Teufel gestiftet* (1545) WA LIV, 247.25-33 = LW 41, 313-314 (Note that the last two lines are omitted in the standard English translation).

[63] 'tota de Christo sit intelligenda' *Epistola beati Pauli apostoli ad Romanos incipit* (1515-16) WA LVI, 5.10; cf. 'In the entire Scripture there is nothing other than Christ either in clear words and or in involved words (Sic in tota scriptura nihil aliud est quam Christus vel apertis verbis vel eingewickelten worten).' *Predigt am Stephanstage* (1523) WA XI, 223.1-2.

godliness and ungodliness remain the same throughout all the ages. Thus we see the prophets opposed the false prophets, apostles against the pseudo-apostles, church fathers against heretics, all using the same Scriptures; yet neither the prophets nor the apostles nor the doctors nor their adversaries are named, but only the terms 'godly' and 'ungodly' appear.[64]

The basic character of 'godliness' and 'ungodliness' remain constant throughout the Scriptures and indeed throughout human history. Luther was convinced that this simple fact provided a sure foundation for the application of the Scriptures to the contemporary situation.

In 1521 Luther made the same point in response to Latomus, only this time approaching it from a different angle. Again recognising the temporal, geographical, and cultural distance between the situation of the biblical text and that of his own readers, Luther went on to say:

> This same Spirit who was in Isaiah in the midst of his time and tribulation was also in Job, in Abraham, in Adam, and is still in all the members of the whole Body of Christ from the beginning to the end of the world, and is with each and every one in his particular time and tribulation. Unless, perhaps, Paul ought not to have said in 2 Cor. 4, 'We too believe, and so we speak', because he did not experience the same rapture and at the same time as David. Times change, as do things, bodies, and tribulations, but the same Spirit, the same meaning, the same food and drink abide in all and through all.[65]

It is this basic similarity, amidst the genuine and continuing differences between the situation of the biblical writer and that of the

---

[64] 'Et hoc fieri fuit summe necessarium, ut verbum dei, cum sit aeternum, omnibus omnium hominum saeculis conveniret. Nam etsi varient per tempora mores, personae, loca ritus, eadem tamen vel pietas vel impietas transit per omnia saecula. Sic videmus prophetas adversus falsos prophetas, Apostolos contra pseudapostolos, doctores contra haereticos eisdem scripturis usos, cum tamen nec prophetarum nec apostolorum nec doctorum aut suorum adversariorum nomen, sed piorum et impiorum in illis invenirent' *Operationes in Psalmnos* (1519-21) WA v, 29.27-33 = LW 14, 290-291.

[65] 'Idem iste spiritus, quem hic Isaias habet suo seculo et sua tribulatione, fuit in Iob, fuit in Abraham, in Adam, et est adhuc in omnibus membris totius corporis Christi ab initio mundi in finem, in suo cuiusque seculo et sua cuiusque tribulatione. Nisi forte Paulus ii. Corint. Iii. Non debuit dicere: "Et nos credidimus, propter quod et loquimur", quia non habuit eandem extasin et eodem tempore cum David. Variant secula, res et corpora et tribulations, sed idem spiritus, idem sensus, eadem esca, idem potus omnium per omnia manet.' *Rationis Latomianae confutatio* (1521) WA VIII, 69.19-26 = LW 32, 176.

contemporary reader, which reinforced for Luther the centrality of Christ and his work in the Scriptures. A common predicament pointed to a common solution. In this way Luther was able to use this understanding to argue that justification by faith in Christ was taught in the Old Testament as well as the New Testament. There were, after all, good reasons why the Apostle had appealed to the Old Testament in places like Rom. 4 and Gal. 3. Luther's contributions to two of the later disputations in the University demonstrate his line of reasoning. The theses for *Die Disputation über Daniel 4.24*,[66] held on 16 October 1535 begin in this bold way:

> Theme: Whether Daniel attributed justification to works when he said, 'Redeem your sins by showing mercy'.
>
> 1. All the faith of believers in ancient times was faith in the Christ to come, just as it is written: 'Christ yesterday and today'.
>
> 2. They believed in God, but the God who had promised the Christ, and they waited for him.
>
> 3. Everything spoken about sins and good works presupposed faith, Hebrews 11.
>
> 4. Because it is not possible to understand sin without the knowledge of God, the one who does not believe in the avenging God does not understand sin.
>
> 5. Likewise it is not possible to understand good works without the knowledge of God, therefore the one who does not believe in the approving and recompensing God does not do good.[67]

In the course of twenty-one theses Luther set out to prove that Daniel's advice to King Nebuchadnezzar does not teach anything contrary to the doctrine of justification by faith in Christ alone. He began, however, by pointing out that certain things have remained constant in both the Old Testament and the New. The object of saving faith is Christ in both testaments. In both, an understanding of sin cannot be separated from the knowledge of the God who promised (and in due course sent) Christ. Genuine good works have their place as a product of faith in the Christ promised (and now sent) by God, whether in the

---

[66] Actually, Dn. 4:27.

[67] 'Utrum Daniel operibus tribuat iustificationem, dicens: Redime peccata tua Eleemosynis. 1. Omnium Fidelium antiquorum fides fuit fides in Christum futurum, Sicut scriptum est: Christus heri et hodie. 2. Credebant in Deum, sed eum, qui Christum promiserat, et hunc exspectabant. 3. Omnia dicta de peccatis vel bonis operibus praesupponunt fidem, Ebrae. 11. 4. Quia peccatum non potest intelligi sine notitia Dei. Neque enim peccatum novit, qui Deum vindicem non credit. 5. Nec opus bonum intelligi potest sine notitia Dei. Neque enim bonum faciet, qui Deum probantem et remunerantem non credit.' *Die Disputation über Daniel 4.24* (1535) WA XXXIX-I, 64.1-8.

Old Testament or the New. On the basis of Heb. 13:8 and Heb. 11 Luther argued that the universal human dilemma, together with its one and only solution in Christ, transcends the historical particularities of exilic Israel. The Old Testament teaches nothing other than what is found in the New Testament.

A similar line of argument can be found in Luther's comment during Johann Macchabaus' doctoral disputation on 3 February 1542. Drawing the line from Old Testament faith to faith in his own time, Luther interjected:

> God said 'I will be today and tomorrow'. The Jews believed in the Christ to come; we, to be sure, believe in the Christ present. Therefore they believed in the one Christ with us.[68]

Luther recognised the unity of Scripture as part of a wider unity grounded in the saving purpose of God in Christ. He identified very significant points of continuity between the situation of the believer in his own time and the situation described in the Scriptures. It is chiefly this continuity which explains why the historical gap between the first and sixteenth centuries seems to fade from view in many of Luther's expositions.[69] Yet Luther would never have regarded his commitment to contemporary application as in any way a violation of the integrity of the biblical text and its intended reference. The gospel has been given to be proclaimed, not just in the first century world but throughout the ages. Lessing's philosophical objections to all attempts at deriving lessons for our own time from the words and events of the past are only anachronistically applied to Luther. He was convinced that the gospel speaks to us and into our own experience of life under the shadow of the cross. Yet, as we have seen, Luther was not entirely cavalier in his movement from the biblical setting to his contemporary situation. He did seek to promote a responsible application of the teaching of Scripture, one that pays careful attention to 'the word that applies to you'.[70]

---

[68] 'Deus inquit: Ego ero hodie et cras. Iudaei credebant in futurum Christum, nos vero credimus in exhibitum Christum. Ergo in unum Christum crediderunt nobiscum.' *Die Promotionsdisputation von Johannes Macchabäus Scotus* (1542) WA XXXIX-II, 162.18-20.

[69] E.g. Timothy Maschke, 'Contemporaneity: A Hermeneutical Perspective in Martin Luther's Work', in *Ad Fontes Lutheri: Toward the Recovery of the Real Luther,* 165–182.

[70] 'Du must auff das wort sehen, das dich betrifft, das zu dyr geredt wird.' *Eyn Unterrichtung wie sich die Christen ynn Mosen sollen schicken* (1525) *WA* XVI, 385.12 = *LW* 35, 170.

Letter and Spirit

We noted in an earlier chapter the diverse use of 2 Cor. 3:6 amongst the patristic exegetes. Origen and others had used the distinction between 'killing letter and life-giving spirit (*litera occidens et spiritus vivificans*)' to justify a distinction between the literal (historical) sense of Scripture and the various spiritual (allegorical) senses. Although Augustine later questioned this use of Paul's words, preferring to understand them as another way of talking about the distinction between law and grace, it was the understanding first associated with Origen which dominated Western exegesis in the centuries leading up to the Reformation.[71]

Luther's early knowledge of the distinction between letter and spirit appears to have come to him from at least three sources: his nominalist training at Erfurt, his brief encounters with German mysticism, and the resources he used as he prepared his first exegetical lectures, in particular Augustine's exposition of the Psalter. Whatever the precise combination of these influences, Luther's first lectures on the Psalms are marked by the rigour with which he applies this distinction. It first appears in the Preface to the Glosses: 'In the Holy Scriptures it is best to distinguish between the Spirit and the letter; for it is this that makes a true theologian'.[72] This statement occurs in the context of a discussion of the four-fold sense of Scripture. Luther outlined the traditional procedure and then set about modifying it by relating each sense to either 'the killing letter' or 'the life-giving spirit'.[73] In this way he was able to suggest eight possible meanings of the expression 'Mount Zion'! Nevertheless, Luther's innovation should not be allowed to obscure one simple fact: Luther began his lectures on the psalms with an understanding of the letter and the spirit which was related to the quest for the spiritual meaning of each text.[74]

---

[71] Gerhard Ebeling, 'The Beginnings of Luther's Hermeneutics I', *LQ* 7 (1993), 136-139.

[72] 'In Scripturis Sanctis optimum est Spiritum a litera discernere, hoc enim facit vero theologum.' *Dictata super Psalterium* (1513-15) WA LV-I, 4.25 = LW 10, 4.

[73] *Dictata super Psalterium* (1513-15) WA LV-I, 4.6-18 = LW 10, 4.

[74] 'But here it is better taken in the second meaning, "secrets", because in this psalm almost all the words must be understood in a spiritual sense, not in a literal one. And thus they are of the spirit and not of the letter. (Sed melius hic capitur in significato secundo pro "occultis", quia in isto Psalmo fere omnia verba non literaliter, Sed spiritualiter sunt intelligenda. Et sic sunt de spiritu et non litera.)' *Dictata super Psalterium* (1513-15) WA LV-II, 105.1-3 = LW 10, 91.

Luther saw this two-fold perspective on the text as something applicable to all Scripture, not just the psalms, and used the distinction to reinforce his commitment to the unity of Scripture in its testimony to Christ. This is explicit in his comment on Ps. 16:5:

> Thus the cup is altogether the Holy Scripture, or the book of Scripture, especially of the Old Testament. In Scripture there is a twofold sense, namely, the veil and clarity, the letter and the spirit, the figure and truth, the shadow and the form. In Ps. 75 there is a reference to a cup 'full of mixture', and yet it is 'pure wine'. For truly, if this is understood spiritually, it is pure wine. Otherwise the cup has the dregs of the letter mixed in with it. Therefore this cup has two parts: The one is the letter, the other is the spirit. Thus he says now, 'The Lord is the portion of My cup', that is, for me Scripture is understood as speaking about Christ. Then he says below, "I will bless the Lord who has given Me understanding". But for the ungodly the "portion of the cup" is snow, ice, brimstone, that is, the letter, etc. This is what it is for them in the soul, just as it is pure wine in the soul for the righteous. But now, because Scripture approves of mercy and judgement (spiritually understood, so that it becomes the same as the Gospel), it thus also has two parts in the spirit.[75]

The distinction between letter and spirit served the interests of Luther's Christological interpretation of all Scripture. It enabled him to justify his insistence that the reference to Christ was part of the text itself. As far as Luther was concerned, to remain content with the literal interpretation of a passage was to remain imprisoned by 'the letter which kills'. Only by recognising the spirit which was concealed in the letter, only by seeing even in the Old Testament Law a testimony to Christ, would Christian readers find themselves connected to the text.

---

[75] 'Igitur Calix est omnino Sacra scriptura seu liber Scripturae, Maxime veteris legis. Consequenter et liber naturae. In qua est uplex sensus, scil. velamen et claritas, litera et spiritus, figura et vertas, vmbra et species. Vunde Psal. 74. dicitur: 'plenus mixto' et tamen 'vini meri'. Quia vere, si Intelligatur Spiritualiter, est merum vinum: Alias in se est mixtus fece literae. Igitur habet duas partes iste Calix: Vna est litera, altera spiritus. Sic dicit Nunc: 'Dominus pars calicis mei', i.e. de Christo est mihi Intellecta Scriptura. Vnde infra: 'benedicam Dominum, qui tribuit mihi intellectum.' Sed Impiis 'pars calicis' est nix, glacies, sulphur, i.e. litera etc. est illis in anima talia, Sicut illis Iustis est vinum merum in Anima. Sed Nunc, Quia Scriptura commendat misericordiam et Iudicium (spiritualiter intellecta, vt fiat idem cum Euangelio), Ideo sic in spiritu quoque habet duas partes. *Dictata super Psalterium* (1513-15) WA LV-II, 123.19-124.7 = LW 10, 109-110; cf. WA III, 518.33-35 = LW 10, 464.

A Focused Text? 169

Hence the critical task lying before the Christian interpreter, as he saw it, was always to make the move from the letter to the spirit.[76]

The distinction between letter and spirit undoubtedly played a key role in Luther's first exposition of the Psalter. Yet in his later exegesis it is nowhere near as prominent. Clearly he did not abandon the terminology completely, for it can still be found in his lectures on Romans, his 1518 sermons on the Ten Commandments, his *Operationes in Psalmos* from 1519 and 1520, and his treatise against Emser and Murner in 1521.[77] Nevertheless, his abandonment of the *Quadriga* in the years immediately following the first series on Psalms entailed a shift in terminology. This may well have been accelerated by further reading in Augustine.[78] Actually, there is a small body of evidence which suggests that even during the delivery of the *Dictata* themselves Luther's understanding of the letter/spirit distinction was developing in a more Augustinian direction.[79] A hint of the change to come is found in Luther's comment on Ps. 45:1:

> Again, 'to utter' can also signify by another mystery that it declares the spirit from the letter. The spirit is concealed in the letter, which is a word that is not good, because it is the law of wrath. But the spirit is a good word, because it is a word of grace. Therefore to draw this out of the letter is to utter the spirit itself.[80]

---

[76] Luther recognised a danger that the spiritus vivificans of one generation could become the litera occidens of the next. This led him to speak about the theologian's continuing engagement with Scripture as a series of steps. *Dictata super Psalterium* (1513-16) WA IV, 318.40-319.16 = LW 11, 433-434; cf. WA IV, 365.5-14 = LW 11, 497.

[77] *Epistola beati Pauli apostoli ad Romanos incipit* (1515-16) WA LVI, 208.23 = LW 25, 192; *Decem praecepta Wittenbergensi praedicata populo* (1518) WA I, 507.33-508.5; *Operationes in Psalmos* (1519-21) WA V, 65.21-22 = LW 14, 337; *Auff das ubirchristlich, ubirgeystlich und ubirkunstlich Buch Bocks Emsers zu Leypczick Antwortt* (1521) WA VII, 651.9-652.37 = LW 39, 179-181.

[78] There remains some uncertainty about the date of Luther's acquaintance with Augustine's *De Spiritu et Littera*. Karl Bauer, *Die Wittenberger Universitätstheologie und die Anfänge der deutschen Reformation,* 34; Fritz Hahn, 'Luthers Auslegungsgrundsätze und ihre theologischen Voraussetzungen', *ZST* 12 (1934/5), 174; Ebeling, 'Hermeneutics I', 154 nn. 44-45.

[79] Mark Ellingsen, 'Luther as Narrative Exegete', *JR* 63 (1983), 398-406; Ebeling, 'Hermeneutics I', 140.

[80] 'Item eructare potest etiam alio mysterio significare, quod ex litera spiritum pronunciet: Spiritus enim latet in litera, que est verbum non bonum, quia lex ire. Sed spiritus est verbum bonum, quia verbum gratiae. Et ideo illud educere

As these lectures continued, Luther began to identify the letter with the Law and the spirit with grace or the Gospel. No doubt this identification was made easier by Luther's emerging theology of the cross. In such a context his comment on Ps. 102:2 is suggestive: 'It has often been said that the face of the Lord signifies the spirit itself in contradistinction to the letter, which is the back'.[81] Luther's commitment to the letter/spirit distinction as a guide to correct interpretation gradually came to be replaced by an appreciation of the hiddenness of God, the revelation which takes place under the form of its contrary, and the Law which is the presupposition and arena of grace.[82] Luther came to see that the employment of such terminology was more theologically productive than the letter/spirit distinction while it still maintained the unity of Holy Scripture. The later lectures in this series mark a period of transition in which Luther is not entirely consistent. He could paraphrase Ps. 119:17 as 'Give grace instead of the Law, the spirit instead of the letter', but also as 'O give the life of spiritual understanding to all Israelites, remove the death of the letter'.[83]

However, perhaps Luther had other reasons as well for relinquishing the primacy of the letter/spirit distinction when it came to the interpretation of Scripture. A clue to one of these can be found in the Schmalkald Articles of 1536/7:

> In these matters, which concern the spoken, external Word, we must hold firmly to the conviction that God gives no one his Spirit or grace except through or with the external Word which comes before. Thus we shall be protected from the Enthusiasts, that is, from the spirits who boast that they possess the Spirit without and before the Word and who therefore judge, interpret, and twist the Scriptures or spoken Word according to their pleasure. Müntzer did this, and there are still many who do it today. They want to be shrewd judges

---

de litera est ipsum eructare.' *Dictata super Psalterium* (1513-16) WA III, 256.27-30 = LW 10, 212-213.

[81] 'Sepe dictum est, quid facies domini significet, scilicet ipsum spiritum distinctum contra literam, que est dorsum.' *Dictata super Psalterium* (1513-16) WA IV, 150.5-7 = LW 11, 299.

[82] Gerhard Ebeling, *Luther: An Introduction to his Thought*, 110.

[83] 'Retribue gratiam pro lege, spiritum pro litera [...] O vitam spiritualis intelligentie retribue omnibus Israelitis, aufer mortem litere.' *Dictata super Psalterium* (1513-16) WA IV, 312.37, 313.25-26 = LW 11, 424, 425; cf. WA IV, 314.20-23 = LW 11, 427.

A Focused Text? 171

between the spirit and the letter without knowing what they say or teach.[84]

The abuse of the distinction between the letter and the spirit, by the practitioners of the *Quadriga* on the one side and by Müntzer and the Enthusiasts on the other, may have made it more difficult for Luther to use it extensively in his later work. He would not tolerate any evasion of the text itself.

Law and Gospel

By 1520 Luther was teaching that the critical distinction in Holy Scripture is not that between the letter and the spirit but that between the Law and the Gospel. Preparation for this shift in his thinking can be detected, as we have seen, even in the *Dictata*. Luther moved closer as he delivered lectures on Romans between 1515 and 1516. There can be no doubt of the influence of Augustine here. Luther had not only read Augustine's treatment on the subject but refers to it on the very first page of the *scholia*.[85] His exposition of Rom. 10:15 included an extended treatment of the contrast between Law and Gospel:

> For the Law shows us nothing but our sin, makes us guilty, and thus produces an anguished conscience; but the Gospel supplies a longed for remedy to people in anguish of this kind. Therefore the Law is evil, and the Gospel good; the Law announces wrath, but the Gospel peace [...] Therefore we have these two sets of contrary terms: Law — sin. The Law shows up sin and makes man guilty and sick; indeed proves him worthy of being damned. Gospel — grace. The Gospel offers grace and remits sin and cures the sickness unto salvation.[86]

---

[84] 'Und jnn diesen stücken, so das mündlich, eusserlich wort betreffen, ist fest darauff zu bleiben, das Gott niemand seinen Geist oder gnade gibt on durch oder mit dem vorgehend eusserlichem wort, Damit wir uns bewaren fur den Enthusiasten, das ist geistern, so sich rhümen, on und vor dem wort den geist zu haben, und darnach die Schrifft oder mündlich wort richten, deuten und dehnen jres gefallens, wie der Müntzer thet, und noch viel thun heutigs tages, die zwisschen dem Geist und Buchstaben scharfe richter sein wollen und wissen nicht, was sie sagen oder setzen.' *Die Schmalkaldischen Artikel, Von der Beight.* (1536-7) WA L, 245.1-12 = Russell, *Theological Testament,* 145.

[85] *Epistola beati Pauli apostoli ad Romanos incipit* (1515-16) WA LVI, 157.7 = LW 25, 135.

[86] 'Nam lex non nisi peccatum ostendit et reos facit ac sic conscientiam angustat, Euangelium autem angustatis eiusmodi optatum nunciat remedium. Ideo lex mala, Euangelium bona, lex iram, Euangelium pacem nunciat [...] Igitur duo et duo contraria: Lex — peccatum, Quod ostendit et reum facit ac egrum, immo damnatum probat. Euangelium — gratiam, Quam offert et peccatum

However, it was not until his *Von der Freiheit eines Christenmenschen* was published in September 1520 that it was clear he had recognised this as a common principle throughout the Scriptures:

> It is to be understood that the entire Holy Scripture is divided into two words: the commandments or Law of God and his promise or pledge.[87]

Luther's exegetical work in the Wartburg, which included some of his classic treatments of the centrality of Christ in Scripture, also gave him the opportunity to explore the Law/Gospel dynamic and to reflect on its import for the Scripture as a whole. In his 1521 sermon on the Gospel for the Third Sunday in Advent, he claimed that 'virtually every Scripture and an understanding of the whole of theology depends upon a right understanding of Law and Gospel'.[88] This would be the basis of his later claim that it is the person who can properly distinguish these two in the text of Scripture who should be recognised as a good theologian.[89] However a fuller treatment of this came later in the *Kirchenpostille*, again in the course of a message on the Gospel for the Third Sunday in Advent (Mt. 11:2–10):

> There is no book in the Bible which does not contain both. Everywhere God has placed law and promise side by side. Through the law he teaches us what must be done; through the promise, how we can do it. That we refer to the New Testament as Gospel, more than we do the remainder of the Bible, is because it was written after Christ's coming and therefore after the divine promise had been fulfilled and publicly proclaimed through preaching, which before that time had been hidden in Scripture. Pay careful attention to this distinction no matter which book you may be reading, whether in the

---

remittit ac morbo medetur ad salutem.' *Epistola beati Pauli apostoli ad Romanos incipit* (1515-16) WA LVI, 424.8-11, 426.5-9 = LW 25, 416, 417-418.

[87] 'Und ist zu wissen, das die gantze heylige schrifft wirt yn zweyerley wort geteyllet, wilche seyn Gebot oder gesetz gottis und vorheyschen oder zusagunge.' *Von der Freiheit eines Christenmenschen* (1520) WA VII, 23.29-30 = LW 31, 348. We have used the German edition of this work, following Brecht's judgement that its freshness of style suggests it was written before the Latin edition. Brecht, *Road to Reformation*, 405.

[88] 'Quando autem pene universa scriptura totiusque Theologiae cognitio pendet in recta cognitione legis et Euangelii' *Enarrationes epistolarum et euangeliorum, quas postillas vocant* (1521) WA VII, 502.34-35.

[89] 'Qui igitur bene novit discernere Evangelium a lege, is gratias agat Deo et sciat se esse Theologum.' *In epistolam S. Pauli ad Galatas Commentarius* (1535) WA XL-I, 207.17-18 =LW 26, 115; cf. *Promotionsdisputation des Cyriacus Gerichius* (6 September 1538) WA XXXIX-I, 552.12-13.

Old or in the New Testament. Whatever contains promises is a book of the Gospel; where commandments are found, we have a book of Law. Since, however, in the New Testament promises form the principal content as commandments do in the Old, the one may be designated as Gospel and the other as Law.[90]

This comment is significant for two reasons. In the first instance it reveals that Luther's recognition of Law and Gospel in both testaments was an early development, settled long before the antinomian controversies of the 1530s. Luther would not endorse a neo-Marcionite rejection of the Old Testament on the grounds that it is only Law while the New Testament is only Gospel. There is Law in the New Testament just as there is Gospel in the Old. However, secondly and just as significantly, Luther takes time to explain the sense in which the Old Testament is rightly described as Law and the New as Gospel. In terms of principal content, a function of the historical particularity of the biblical writings and their relation to the advent of Christ, these traditional labels remain appropriate.[91]

In Luther's hands the internal dynamic of Law and Gospel emphasised the profound unity of the entire Scripture. It allowed him to demonstrate a sharper Christological focus to the whole precisely because Christ is both the goal of the Law and the explicit subject of the Gospel.[92] It rendered the traditional method of finding Christ in the Old Testament redundant and made it possible to give attention to the original historical context of Old Testament texts without fear of 'Jewish exegesis'. By identifying the message of a text as Law or

---

[90] 'Es ist keyn buch ynn der Biblien, darynnen sie nicht beyderley sind, gott hatt sie alwege beyeynander gesetzt, beyde, gesetz und zusagung. Denn er leret durchs gesetz, was zu thun ist, und durch die zusagung, wo manß nemen soll. Das aber das newe testament furnemlich Euangelion genent wirtt fur andern buchern, geschicht darumb, das es nach Christus zukunfft geschrieben ist, wilcher die gottliche zusagung erfullet, bracht und offentlich durch mundlich predigt außbreyttet hatt, wilche zuvor vorporgen war ynn der schrifft. Darumb bleyb du auff dießer unterscheyd, und wilcherley buch dyr furkompt, es sey allt odder new testament, das ließ mit solchem unterscheydt, das du auffmerckist, wo zusagunge sind, da ist dasselb buch eyn Euangelionbuch, wo gepott stehen, da ists eyn gesetzbuch. Weyl aber ym newen testament die zusagung mit hauffen stehen, und ym allten die gestetz mit hauffen, nennet man eynß Euangelion, das ander gesetzbuch.' *Adventspostille* (1522) WA X-I/2, 159.7-19.

[91] Cf. *Vorrede auf das Alte Testament* (1523) WADB VIII, 12.9-21 = LW 35, 236-237; Althaus, *Theology*, 86-87.

[92] Regin Prenter, 'The Living Word', in Jaroslav J. Pelikan (ed.), *More About Luther*, II, 70; Lotz, 'Sola Scriptura', 270; Erich W. Gritsch, *Martin — God's Court Jester: Luther in Retrospect*, 93.

Gospel, the interpreter was able to locate it in the context of the whole Bible. In this way even difficult texts, those which might initially seem obscure, could become accessible.[93] It is no surprise then that in *De servo arbitrio* Luther chided Erasmus for misreading the Scripture by neglecting this distinction:

> In these passages, our Diatribe makes no distinction at all between the voices of the law and of the gospel; so blind and ignorant is it that it does not see what the law and the gospel are. Out of the whole of Isaiah it cites no word of the law save this one passage: 'If you are willing'; all the other passages quoted are gospel, by which the afflicted and broken-hearted are summoned to consolation by the word that offers grace. But the Diatribe makes of these, words of the law! Now I ask you, what can a man do in the realm of theology and the sacred writings, if he has not reached the point of knowing what the law and the gospel are, or, if he does know, disdains to observe them? He is bound to mix up everything, heaven with hell and life with death, and will not take the slightest trouble to know about Christ.[94]

Luther was convinced that the inevitable result of neglecting this distinction was a distortion of the message of Scripture. Further, he recognised that such a distortion almost always tended in a particular direction. He warned against this in his comment on Gal. 3:17 from 1535:

---

[93] 'First, if some passage is obscure I consider whether it treats of grace or of law, whether wrath or the forgiveness of sin, and with which of these it agrees better. By this procedure I have oftgen understood themost obscure passages. Either the law or the gospel has made them meaningful, for God divides his teaching into law and gospel. (Primum cum est obscurus aliquis locus, considero, an sit de gratia vel lege, an ira vel remissio peccatorum, wazu es sich am besten reyme. Hac ratione saepe obscurissimos locos intellexi, das es vel lex vel euangelion uns in die hend getriben hat, nam Deus divisit suam doctrinam in legem et euangelion.)' *Tischreden* #312 (Summer 1532) WATr I, 128.5-9 = LW 54, 42.

[94] 'In hic locis Diatribe nostra prorsus nihil discernit inter voces legis et Euangelii, tam scilicet caeca et ignara est, ut, quid lex, quid Euangelion sit, non videat. Ex Esaia enim toto, praeter illum unum locum: Si volueritis, nullum legis verbum affert, reliqui omnes sunt Euangelici, quibus contriti et afflicti verbo gratiae oblatae vocantur ad consolationem. Sed Diatribe verba legis ex ipsis facit. Obsecro autem te, quid ille in re Theologica vel sacris literis efficiat, qui nondum eo pervenit, ut quid Lex, quid Euangelion sit, norit, aut si norit, contemnat tamen observare? Is omnia misceat oportet, coelum, infernum, vitam, mortem ac prorsus nihil de Christo scire laborabit.' *De servo arbitrio* (1525) WA XVIII, 680.23-31 = LW 33, 132.

A Focused Text? 175

> If, then, you want to divide the Word of truth rightly, you must distinguish the promise from the Law as far as possible, both in your attitude and in your whole life. It is not without purpose that Paul urged this argument so diligently; for he saw that in the church this evil would arise, namely, that the Word of God would be confused, which means that the promise would be mixed with the Law and in this way be completely lost. For when the promise is mixed up with the Law, it becomes Law pure and simple.[95]

According to Luther, the human inclination towards hypocritical religiosity ensures that it is the Gospel which is most often lost when the Law/Gospel distinction is ignored. Once all has been resolved into Law the entire fabric of Scripture would begin to unravel, for the Law was never intended to stand on its own without the Gospel. As Luther had remarked in 1532, 'both depend on this distinction'. This was the tragedy of the papacy as Luther saw it: by abandoning the Gospel and fostering 'a faith which was only in the Law', papal religion was also left without the Law as God had revealed it.[96]

The antinomian debates of the 1530s made it necessary for Luther to elaborate further his view of the relation between Law and Gospel.[97] The debates themselves, full of complications such as Luther's sense of personal betrayal at the hands of Johann Agricola and the seldom acknowledged difference between Luther and Melanchthon on the issue, might well have led to a distortion of Luther's earlier teaching. Indeed this is precisely what Agricola alleged. However, what is remarkable is the degree of consistency between the views Luther presented here in the midst of fierce controversy and those worked out during the course of his normal exegetical labours.[98] Luther insisted again that both Law and Gospel were integral to the teaching of Scripture in both testaments. To remove the Law for the sake of the Gospel was as perilous an exercise as that of elevating the Law at the

---

[95] 'Itaque si recte vis secare verbum veritatis, remotissime distinguas quo ad affectum et totam vitam promissionem a lege. Non frustra tam diligenter ursit Paulus hoc argumentum; vidit enim in Ecclesia hoc mali futurum, quod verbum Dei confunderetur, hoc est, promissio misceretur legi, sicque prorsus amitteretur promissio. Quia, cum commiscetur legi promissio, mera lex fit.' *In epistolam S. Pauli ad Galatas Commentarius* (1535) WA XL-I, 469.32-470.14 = LW 26, 302.

[96] *Predigt am Tage der Beschneidung* (1 January 1532) WA XXXVI, 9.6-10.5.

[97] The historical circumstances are outlined in Brecht, *Preservation of the Church*, 147-171.

[98] This remains true despite Luther's own suggestion that different circumstances call for different emphases. *Promotionsdisputation des Cyriacus Gerichius* (1538) WA XXXIX-I, 571.8-574.10.

expense of the Gospel. The Gospel requires the Law as its precondition and context; the Law requires the Gospel as its goal and fulfilment. Both have been revealed by the Holy Spirit, though each with different purposes, and both are necessary for the Christian as well as the unbeliever. One who is always *simul iustus et peccator* remains in constant need of the summons to repentance provided by the Law and the work of Christ which is the fulfilment of the Law. In the light of this it becomes clear that once again it is the Gospel itself which is lost when the preaching of the Law is abandoned. Indeed, Luther saw this as the real crux of the issue. In his *Wider die Antinomer* of 1539 he wrote: 'It is apparent from this that the devil's purpose in this fanaticism is not to remove the Law but to remove Christ, the fulfiller of the Law'.[99]

Luther emphasised that these principles are interwoven throughout the New Testament as well as the Old.[100] Just as both Law and Gospel find their focus in Christ, so too the preaching of Christ contains both Law and Gospel. This is just what Luther believed Agricola and his followers had ignored. As he argued in 1538:

> Even when we say that Christ is set before us as an example or as the Redeemer, we teach the Law. And this is a true preaching of the Law. For if he comes to you as your Redeemer and Saviour, you must have sinned. Redemption itself presupposes sin.[101]

To proclaim the benefits of Christ necessarily implies the need of those benefits.[102] In this way the Gospel itself preaches the Law just as the Law points men and women to the Gospel.

Luther was convinced that the Law/Gospel dynamic could not be extracted from Scripture without doing violence to the purposes of God. The meaning of each biblical text must be related to one pole or

---

[99] 'Aus dem sihet man, das der Teuffel durch diese geisterey, nicht das gesetz meinet weg zu nemen, sondern Christum, den erfuller des gesetzes.' *Wider die Antinomer* (1539) WA L, 471.19-21 = LW 47, 110.

[100] 'All truth, wherever it is, is from the Holy Spirit and to refuse [a place for] the law is to refuse [a place for] the truth of God. (Et omnis veritas, ubicunque est, a Spiritu sancto est, et prohiberi legem est veritatem Dei prohiberi.)' *Die Thesen zu den Disputationen gegen die Antinomer* (1537) WA XXXIX-I, 349.25-26.

[101] 'Secundo hoc ipsum, quod dicimus, Christum esse nobis propositum ut exemplum, ut redemptorem, est docere legem. Et est vera praedicatio legis. Nam si venit tibi redemptor et salvator, necesse est, te habere peccatum et ipsa redemptio includit peccatum.' *Secunda disputatio contra Antinomos* (1538) WA XXXIX-I, 464.12-17.

[102] *Promotionsdisputation des Cyriacus Gerichius* (1538) WA XXXIX-I, 535.12-536.4.

the other and by that very interpretive act another series of relations would be exposed. Fundamental to this conviction is another: that there is a seamless unity to the purposes of God which finds expression in the unity of Holy Scripture. At the centre of both lies the person and work of Jesus Christ.

The Relationship of the Old and New Testaments

The unity of content which Luther found in Scripture had important implications for the traditional questions surrounding the relation of the testaments. If both the Old Testament and the New are fundamentally concerned with Christ, what is the difference between them? If the human predicament and its remedy remains the same in both and if both contain the theological principles of Law and Gospel, is there any sense in which either makes a distinctive contribution to the whole? In what sense is the New Testament new and the Old Testament old?

We have already seen how Luther began to answer such questions in terms of the historical position of each testament and in particular their relation to the incarnation of Christ. The Old Testament looks forward to the Christ to come on the basis of the promise of God. Though its 'chief teaching' or 'principal content' is the Law, that Law is not separated from its relation to the promise without the most dire of consequences. Likewise, the New Testament proclaims the advent of Jesus Christ, the promised one. Its basic character as Gospel does not exclude the integral presence of Law within it.[103] This historical matrix enabled Luther to see the general movement between the testaments as one from promise to fulfilment. This was, of course, hardly innovative. As well as the New Testament precedents, this pattern had been endorsed again and again by the Fathers.[104] However, Luther rigorously applied its implications for both the authority and interpretation of Scripture.

Luther developed Augustine's dictum that 'the New Testament is latent in the Old and the Old Testament is patent in the New'.[105] In the preface to his German translation of the Pentateuch, from 1523, he stressed its foundational role: 'Moses is indeed a well of all wisdom

---

[103] *Adventspostille* (1522) WA X-I/2, 159.7-19; *Vorrede auff das Alte Testament* (1523) WADB VIII, 12.9-21 = LW 35, 236-237.

[104] Geoffrey W. Bromiley, 'The Church Fathers and Holy Scripture', in D. A. Carson and John D. Woodbridge (eds.), *Scripture and Truth*, 212-213.

[105] 'in uetere nouum lateat et in nouo uetus pateat' Augustine, *Quaestionum in Heptateuchum*, II.q.73 (CCSL XXXIII, 106); cf. *De civitate dei contra paganos*, XX.4 (CCSL XLVIII, 703).

and understanding, out of which has sprung all that the prophets knew and said. Moreover even the New Testament flows out of it and is grounded in it'.[106] Luther made much of the promise amidst the curse in Gn. 3:15, which he understood as the origin of a search for the Crusher (*Contritor*) on the part of both the Satan and the woman and her descendants:

> Thus this promise and this threat are very clear, and yet they are also very obscure. They leave the devil in such a state that he suspects all mothers of giving birth to this Seed, although only one woman was to be the mother of this blessed Seed. Thus because God is threatening in general when He says 'her Seed', He is mocking Satan and making him afraid of all women. In the same way the faith of all people was strengthened; from the hour in which the promise was made they waited for the Seed and derived comfort from it against Satan. When Eve had given birth to her first-born son, she hoped that she already had that Crusher. Although she was deceived in this hope, she saw that eventually this Seed would be born from among her descendants, whenever it might be that He would be born. Also so far as human beings were concerned, therefore, this promise was very clear and at the same time very obscure.[107]

This promise so controls the shape of all that follows, and especially of all the other promises which are included in it, that Luther insisted the course of the history of prophetic inspiration ends when this promise finds its fulfilment in Jesus Christ.[108]

---

[106] 'Denn freilich Mose ein Brun ist aller weisheit und verstands, dar aus gequollen ist alles, was alle Propheten gewust und gesagt haben. Dazu auch das newe Testament er aus fleusst und drein gegründet ist' *Vorrede auff das Alte Testament* (1523) WADB VIII, 29.27-29 = LW 35, 247.

[107] 'Ad hunc modum promissio haec et comminatio apertissima est. Sed est eadem quoque obscurissima. Relinquit enim Diabolum in illa suspitione, ut omnes Mulieres suspectas habeat, quae pariunt, ne pariant hoc Semen, cum tamen una tantum Mulier huius benedicti Seminis mater futura esset. Sic, quia in genere minatur, dicens "Semen illius", illuditur Satanae, ut ab omnibus metuat. Et eodem modo etiam omnium hominum fides confirmatur, ut ab illa hora, qua promissio facta est, Semen illud expectarent et se consolarentur contra Satanam. Itaque Heua cum primogenitum suum peperisset, sperabat se iam habere Contritorem illum. Haec spes etsi fallebat eam, tamen vidit ex posteritate sua nasciturum esse tandem hoc Semen, quandocunque nasceretur. Atque ita, quod ad homines quoque attinebat, promissio haec clarissima et simul obscurissima fuit.' *Genesisvorlesung* (1535-45) WA XLII, 144.19-31 = LW 1, 193.

[108] *Vorrede zu Epistolae quaedam piissimae et eruditissimae Iohannis Hus* (1537) WA L, 124.4-6.

A Focused Text?

Luther explored these issues as he expounded 1 Pet. 1:10–12 in 1522. Far from the New Testament rendering the Old Testament superfluous, Luther insisted that 'we must derive from it alone the basis of our faith'. The reason for this is the prophetic role of the Old Testament and its relation to Christ: 'For God sent the prophets to the Jews to bear witness to the Christ who was to come. Consequently, the apostles also convicted the Jews everywhere from their own Scriptures and proved that this was the Christ'. Luther encouraged his readers to follow the apostolic example, to 'go back to the Old Testament and learn to prove the New Testament from the Old'.[109] The fulfilment of what was promised does not do away with the promise itself. Indeed, a proper understanding of the promise is necessary for those who seek to live by faith in the one who fulfils it. This is what Luther understood to be the point of Peter's words in 1 Pet. 1:10–12:

> Here St. Peter refers us to Holy Scripture in order that we may see there how God keeps His promise not because of any merit on our part but out of pure grace. For it is the purpose of all Scripture to tear us away from our works and to bring us to faith. And it is necessary for us to study Scripture well in order to become certain of faith.[110]

Throughout his life Luther emphasised the continuing importance of the Old Testament in these terms. In this he felt he was following the practice of the New Testament. As he read them, both the Gospels and the Epistles sought to explain Christ in the light of the Old Testament and the Old Testament in the light of Christ. In particular, both Christ and his apostles illustrated and supported their teaching by quotation of and allusion to the Old Testament. Here then was a precedent for a truly biblical theology.

However, Luther could also approach the question from the opposite direction. As much as the Old Testament was the authority to which

---

[109] 'Denn Gott hatt die proheten darumb zu den Juden geschickt, das sie von dem zukunfftigen Christo sollten zeugnis geben. Darumb haben die Apostel auch allenthalben die Juden uberweysst und uberwunden auß yhrer eygenen schrifft, das das Christus were.' *Epistel S. Petri gepredigt und ausgelegt* (1523) WA XII, 274.35-275.4 = LW 30, 19; 'Darumb sollten wyr auch also thun, das wyr hynderruck lauffen und das new Testament auß dem alten grunden lernen.' WA XII, 274.27-28 = LW 30, 18.

[110] 'Hie weyset uns S. Petrus zu ruck ynn die heylige schrifft, das wyr darynne sehen, wie uns Gott durch keynes verdiensts willen, sondern auß blosser gnad, hallte das er verheyssen hat. Denn die gantze schrifft ist dahyn gericht, das sie uns von unßern wercken reysse und zum glawben bringe. Und ist nott, das wyr ynn der schrifft wol studieren, auff das wyr des glawbens gewiss werden.' *Epistel S. Petri gepredigt und ausgelegt* (1523) WA XII, 274.14-19 = LW 30, 18.

the New Testament so regularly appealed, the New Testament itself provided the authoritative interpretation of the Old Testament, one which settled any question about the meaning of individual passages within it.[111] In the light of the life, death, and resurrection of Jesus the divinely intended meaning of the Old Testament was clear. Luther explained this aspect of the relation in the *Kirchenpostille*:

> For the New Testament is nothing but a revelation of the Old; it is as if somebody had a sealed letter and later on broke it open. In like manner the Old Testament is a last will and testament of Christ; after his death he had it unsealed and read through the gospel and preached everywhere. This is signified in Revelation 5 where the Lamb of God alone opens the book with the seven seals which, otherwise, nobody could open up, neither in heaven, nor the earth, nor under the earth.[112]

Apart from Christ the Old Testament remained a sealed book: 'We cannot understand the Scripture unless the light shines'.[113] Yet in Christ the light has shone and the purpose of the New Testament is to drive us back into the Old Testament.[114] The Christian can make this move with confidence, Luther suggested, because the Gospel is 'the

---

[111] *Tischreden* #5533 (1543) WATr V, 218.18-20 = LW 54, 446.

[112] '[D]enn das new testament ist nit mehr denn eyn offinbarung des allten, gleych alß wenn yemant tzum ersten eyn beschlossen brieff hette und darnach auffbrech. Alßo ist das alte testament eyn testamentbrieff Christi, wilchen er nach seynem tod hatt auffgethan unnd lassen durchs Euangelium leßen und ubiralle vorkundigen, wie das Apocali. 5. betzeychnet ist durch das lamp gottis, wilchs alleyn auffthett das buch mit den sieben sigillen, das sonst niemant kundt auffthun noch ynn hymel noch auff erden noch unter der erden.' *Kirchenpostille* (1522) WA X-I/1, 181.24-182.5 = LW 52, 41-42. Althaus, *Theology*, 89.

[113] 'Nu wirt die schrifft nit ehe vorstanden, das liecht gehe denn auff.' *Kirchenpostille* (1522) WA X-I/1, 625.17-18 = LW 52, 205.

[114] 'Now the gospels and epistles of the apostles were written for this very purpose. They want themselves to be our guides, to direct us to the writings of the prophets and of Moses in the Old Testament so that we might there read and see for ourselves how Christ is wrapped in swaddling cloths and laid in the manger, that is, how he is comprehended in the writings of the prophets. [Syntemal die Euangeli und Epistel der Apostel darumb geschrieben sind, das sie selb solche zeyger seyn wollen und uns weyßen ynn die schrifft der propheten und Mosi des alten testaments, das wyr alda selbs leßen und sehen sollen, wie Christus ynn die windel thucher gewicklet und yn die krippen gelegt sey, das ist, wie er ynn der schrifft der propheten vorfasset sey.] *Ein Kleyn unterricht, was man ynn den Euangelijs suchen und gewartten soll*. *Kirchenpostille* (1522) WA X-I/1, 15.1-5 = LW 35, 122; cf. *Adventspostille* (1522) WA X-I/2, 34.27-35.1.

exposition of the first commandment', 'the gloss on all the prophets', and even 'the key that unlocks the old Scriptures'.[115] Of course, the New Testament was more than simply an aid to be consulted when the interpreter was faced with *prima facie* obscurity in the Old Testament text. The New Testament was to operate as a control whenever one sought to understand the teaching of the Old. Luther made this clear in the course of his 1535 exposition of Galatians:

> When you read in Scripture, therefore, about the patriarchs, prophets, and kings that they worked righteousness, raised the dead, conquered kingdoms, etc., you should remember that these and similar statements are to be explained according to a new and theological grammar, as the eleventh chapter of the Epistle to the Hebrews explains them: 'By faith they worked righteousness, by faith they raised the dead, by faith they conquered kings and kingdoms …'[116]

There is one other dimension to the relationship between the testaments which Luther explored on a number of occasions. Luther insisted that while the fundamental character of the Old Testament is that of writing or 'Scripture' in the strictest sense, the character of the New Testament is essentially that of proclamation or 'preaching'. As we have already seen, much of Luther's language here arises from his concern to insist on the centrality of preaching in the life of the church and to decry the proliferation of books on theology. 'The Church is a mouth house not a pen house', he protested in 1522.[117] Luther was certainly not attributing less authority to the New Testament than to the Old or suggesting that it was any less the work of God's Spirit. However, he was convinced there is an important distinction to be preserved at this point. While the Old Testament had been written at the command of God, Luther could find no equivalent command in the New Testament: Christ had commissioned his disciples to preach, not

---

[115] 'Euangelium primi praecepti expositio.' *Tischreden* #2792b (1532) WATr II, 663.16; 'Nam euangelium est clarissimum et glossa omnium prophetarum.' *Tischreden* #3789 (1538) WATr III, 616.1-2; 'Euangelium est clavis, quae aperit veterem scripturam.' *Predigt am Ostermontage Nachmittags* (2 April 1526) WA XX, 336.24-25.

[116] 'Itaque cum legis in Scriptura de Patribus, Prophetis, Regibus, quod operati sint iustitiam, suscitaverint mortuos, vicerint regna etc., memineris talia et similia dicta secundum novam et Theologicam Grammaticam exponenda esse, ut Epistola ad Ebr. 11. exponit, nempe sic: Fide operati sunt iustitiam, Fide suscitaverunt mortuos, Fide vicerunt Reges et Regna …' *In epistolam S. Pauli ad Galatas Commentarius* (1535) WA XL-I, 418.21-26 = LW 26, 267.

[117] 'Darumb ist die kirch eyn mundhawß, nit eyn fedderhawß' *Adventspostille* (1522) WA X-I/2, 48.5.

to write.[118] To ignore the oral character of the New Testament left open the possibility of transforming Christ into Moses and writing the new covenant on tablets of stone rather than on human hearts.[119] The fact that we now have the New Testament in a written form does not undermine its essentially oral character:

> Thus the books of Moses and the prophets are also Gospel, since they proclaimed and described in advance what the apostles preached or wrote later about Christ. But there is a difference. For although both have been put on paper word for word, the Gospel, or the New Testament, should really not be written but should be expressed with the living voice which resounds and is heard throughout the world. The fact that it is also written is superfluous. But the Old Testament is only put in writing. Therefore it is called 'a letter'. Thus the apostles call it Scripture; for it only pointed to the Christ who was to come. But the Gospel is a living sermon on the Christ who has come.[120]

The New Testament remains distinct from the Old Testament at precisely this point. Its final written form was an emergency measure of the last days, made necessary by attacks upon the gospel from

---

[118] 'Also Christ himself did not write, nor did he give instructions to write, but to preach orally. Therefore, the apostles are not sent until the Christ, who is [in this sense] a mouth-house, comes: that is, until the time comes to preach orally and the gospel has broken out of the lifeless text and pen into the living voice and mouth. [Auch Christus selbs nichts geschrieben, auch nitt befolhen hatt zu schreyben, ßondern mundlich zu predigen. Alßo sind die Aposteln nit gesand, biß das Christus komen ist gen mundhawß, das ist: biß das es zeytt was, mundlich zu predigen, und das Euangelium auß der todte schrifft und feddern ynn die lebenddige stym unnd mund bracht wort.]' *Adventspostille* (1522) WA x-I/2, 48.9-10.

[119] *Operationes in Psalmos* (1519-21) WA v, 537.17-18.

[120] 'Also sind die bücher Mosi und die propheten auch Euangelium, syntemal sie eben das zuvor verkundiget und beschrieben haben von Christo, das die Apostel hernach gepredigt odder geschrieben haben. Doch ist eyn unterscheyd da zwisschen. Denn wie wol beydes dem buchstaben nach ist auff papyr geschrieben, so soll doch das Euangelion odder das new Testament eygentlich nicht geschrieben, sondern ynn die lebendige stym gefasset werden, die da erschalle und uberal gehört werde ynn der wellt. Das es aber auch geschrieben ist, ist auss uberfluß geschehen. Aber das alte Testament ist nur ynn die schrifft verfasset, und drumb heysst es "ein buchstab", und also nennens die Apostel "die schrifft", denn es hatt alleyn gedeuttet auff den zukunfftigen Christum. Das Euangelion aber ist eyn lebendige predig von Christo, der da kommen ist.' *Epistel Sanct Petri gepredigt und ausgelegt* (1523) WA XII, 275.5-15 = LW 30, 19.

without and by defection from within. Once more it is in the *Kirchenpostille* that Luther makes this clear:

> However, the need to write books was a serious decline and a lack of the Spirit which necessity forced upon us; it is not the manner of the New Testament. For when heretics, false teachers, and all manner of errors arose in the place of pious teachers, giving the flock of Christ poison as pasture, then every last thing that could and needed to be done, had to be attempted, so that at least some sheep might be saved from the wolves. So they began to write in order to lead the flock of Christ as much as possible by Scripture into Scripture.[121]

In this variety of ways Luther was able to stress both the distinctiveness of each testament and their fundamental unity. Their unity is one of origin and content and is focussed on the Christ once promised and now given. Their distinctive contributions to the whole are associated both with their position in the history of God's dealings with his world and with the most basic form which characterises each.

Unity and the Authority of Scripture

When Martin Luther proclaimed his intention to acknowledge the Scripture as the final authority in faith and life he was not, at least in his mind, referring to a disparate, fragmented, or even self-contradictory collection of sacred texts. His affirmations of biblical authority presupposed his convictions concerning the unity of Scripture. He was convinced that Scripture spoke with a single voice in its fundamental testimony to the one long promised and now come in Jesus Christ. It was therefore thoroughly appropriate, as far as he was concerned, to appeal to Scripture in general terms and to speak about the authority of the whole. This is not to say that Luther believed that the unity of Scripture somehow bestowed authority, or additional authority, upon the biblical text. The authority of Scripture always remained the authority of its primary author. However, the conviction that the Holy Spirit stood behind the Scriptures as a whole and not just behind the teaching of isolated texts, and that this guaranteed a

---

[121] 'Das man aber hatt mussen bucher schreyben, ist schon eyn grosser abbruch und eyn geprechen des geystis, das es die nott ertzwungen hatt, und nit die artt ist des newen testaments; denn da an statt der grummen prediger auffstunden ketzer, falsche lere und mangerley yrthum, die den schaffen Christi gifft fur weyde gaben, Da must man das letzt vorsuchen, das tzu thun unnd nott war, auff das doch ettlich schaff fur den wolffen errednet wurden: da fieng man an zu schreyben, und doch durch schrifft, ßo viell es muglich war, die scheffle Christi ynn die schrifft tzu furen und damit vorschaffen' *Kirchenpostille* (1522) WA x-I/1, 627.1-8 = LW 52, 206.

common and profound preoccupation with the purposes of God in Christ, enabled Luther to take his stand with uncommon boldness.[122]

Luther's exposition of the unity of Scripture took him beyond the tradition which he inherited. Certainly some of the directions had been anticipated by those who had come before him. As we have seen, he openly acknowledged his debts to Augustine's explanation of Law and Grace in his *De Spiritu et Littera* and Stapulensis' Christological interpretation in the *Quintuplex Psalterium*. However Luther went further. He discovered a theological unity to the whole of Scripture which was neither superficial nor unidimensional. He explored in fresh ways the connection between the Law/Gospel dynamic and the biblical focus on Christ. Particularly in his later work, he was able to emphasise the Christological reference of Old Testament texts without dismissing the original context as irrelevant or misleading. He recognised points of continuity at the most basic level throughout the Bible: the predicament resulting from the rebellion in the Garden and its only remedy in the Christ who is the object of hope and faith in both the Old Testament and the New. Such developments enabled him to identify the essential message of Scripture which became the first step in allowing the whole Bible to critique Christian doctrine and practice.

Luther's contributions are certainly open to critique. Though he did not admit it himself, his canonical decisions raised questions about the validity of his understanding of the whole of Scripture and the associated claims about its authority. Which is logically prior, a decision about the extent of Scripture or a determination of its essential message? Would the shape of the whole be somewhat different if the Epistle of James had been given an equal place with those of Paul? In addition, Luther's commitment to the centrality of Christ in Scripture sometimes prevents him from being thoroughly consistent in his rejection of allegory and his appreciation of the historical context of biblical texts. Nevertheless, Luther's conviction that Scripture comes to us as a 'seamless robe', which must be appreciated as a whole as well as in its parts, played an important role in his theological and ecclesiastical agenda and would be a significant part of his own legacy to those who came after him.

Unity and the Interpretation of Scripture

Luther's commitment to the unity of Scripture not only reinforced his affirmations of its authority, it also influenced his approach to biblical interpretation. His excursuses on interpretive method together with his own practice of biblical exposition brought together a number of

---

[122] *Rationis Latomianae confutatio* (1521) WA VIII, 61.19-20 = LW 32, 164.

competing insights within the exegetical tradition and at the same time went beyond them. By the time he began to lecture on the Psalms for a second time, in September or October 1518, Luther had not only abandoned the *Quadriga,* he had also given up the traditional expository framework of *glossae* and *scholia.* In stark contrast to the *Dictata* of 1513 to 1515, he provided a continuous commentary on the text of the Psalms which sought to do justice to both their literal meaning in the context of the Hebrew Old Testament and the focus on Christ which he remained convinced was the intention of the Holy Spirit.

While Luther continued to use allegory throughout his life, he discovered that the literal or historical sense could be related to Christ in a better way.[123] The danger with the traditional allegorical methods of interpretation was that, for all the lip-service paid to the priority of the historical sense, such methods almost always undermined it by the emphasis they placed on a variety of spiritual meanings. A search for the spiritual relevance of the biblical text actually led many to miss the relevance *in* the text. Luther explained this tragic paradox in the midst of the Genesis lectures of 1542:

> I urge students of theology to shun this kind of interpretation in the Holy Scriptures. For allegory is pernicious when it does not agree with the history, but especially when it takes the place of the history, from which the church is more correctly instructed about the wonderful administration of God in all stations of life, in the management of a household, in the state, and in the church. Inasmuch as such interpreters overlook these things in the histories, they necessarily transform everything into allegories and a different meaning.[124]

Luther's better way involved two insights closely tied to his convictions concerning the unity of Scripture. The first of these was his insistence that the Old Testament should be interpreted in

---

[123] *Genesisvorlesung* (1535-45) WA XLII, 173.30-36 = LW 1, 232-233; cf. *Tischreden* #335 (1532) WATr I, 136.14-23 = LW 54. 46; *Tischreden* #5285 (1540) WATr V, 45.9-17 = LW 54, 406.

[124] 'Hortor itaque studiosos Theologiae, ut fugiant hoc genus interpretationis in sacris literis. Quia allegoria est perniciosa, quando non congruit cum historia, praecipue vero, quando in locum historiae seccedit, ex qua rectius eruditur Ecclesia de mirabili administratione Dei in omnibus ordinibus vitae, in oeconomia, politia et Ecclesia: quae dum negligunt isti interpretes in historiis, necessario omnia in allegorias et alienum sensum transformant.' *Genesisvorlesung* (1535-45) WA XLIII, 667.4-10 = LW 5, 345; cf. *In epistolam S. Pauli ad Galatas Commentarius* (1535) WA XL-I, 663.12-21 = LW 26, 440.

accordance with the New. This meant that the interpretive questions were often settled by the biblical text itself. In 1521 he told Emser and Murner: 'One must let Aaron be Aaron in the simple sense, unless the Spirit himself interprets him in a new sense, which then would be a new literal sense — as when St. Paul makes Christ out of Aaron for the Hebrews'.[125] Where the New Testament treated an Old Testament character or incident, its interpretation was to be taken as authoritative. Where no such treatment was provided by the New Testament, the simplest sense of the words determined their meaning. As Luther put it to Erasmus in 1525:

> Let us rather take the view that neither an inference nor a trope is admissible in any passage of Scripture, unless it is forced on us by the evident nature of the context and the absurdity of the literal sense as conflicting with one or another of the articles of faith. Instead, we must everywhere stick to the simple, pure, and natural sense of the words that accords with the rules of grammar and the normal use of language as God has created it in man.[126]

Such an approach could act as a brake on the excesses which Luther complained were characteristic of so much of the tradition. It could also endorse connections which might otherwise have appeared implausible.[127]

The interpretation of the Old Testament in accordance with the New also ensured that no text would be interpreted contrary to Christ. Luther made this clear in the Theses concerning Faith and Law from 1535:

> 40. Briefly, Christ is the Lord, not the servant, the Lord of the Sabbath, of law, and of all things.

---

[125] 'Man muß Aaron lassenn schlecht Aaron blehbenn ym einfeltigen sinn, es sei denn das der geist selb auffs new anderß außlege, wilchs als denn einn new schrifftlich sinn ist, wie S. Paulus zu den Hebreern auß Aaron Christum macht.' *Auff das ubirchristlich, ubirgeystlich und urbirkunstlich Buch Bocks Emszers zu Leypczick Antwortt* (1521) WA VII, 650.1-4 = LW 39, 178; cf. WA VII, 652.8-37 = LW 39, 180-181.

[126] 'Sic potius sentiamus, neque sequelam neque tropum in ullo loco scripturae esse admittendum, nisi id cogat circumstantia verborum evidens et absurditas rei manifestae in aliquem fidei articulum peccans; sed ubique inhaerendum est simplici puraeque et naturali significationi verborum, quam grammatica et usus loquendi habet, quem Deus creavit in hominibus.' *De servo arbitrio* (1525) WA XVIII, 700. 31-35 = LW 33, 162; cf. *De captivitate Babylonica ecclesiae praeludium* (1520) WA VI, 509.8-12 = LW 36, 30.

[127] e.g. *Auslegung des 3. und 4. Kapitels Johannes* (1538-40) WA XLVII, 66.9-24 = LW 22, 339.

41. The Scriptures must be understood in favour of Christ, not against him. For that reason they must refer to him or must not be held to be true Scriptures [...]

48. For he is the Head and Leader of righteousness and of life, appointed by God, through and in whom we live and are saved.

49. Therefore, if the adversaries press the Scriptures against Christ, we urge Christ against the Scriptures.

50. We have the Lord, they the servants; we have the Head, they the feet or members, over which the Head necessarily dominates and takes precedence.[128]

Luther was so thoroughly convinced that the entire Bible testified to Christ and the salvation he has wrought and which is received by faith alone, that he refused to countenance any interpretation of a biblical passage which suggested otherwise. It is in this context that Luther made the bold statement of thesis forty-nine.[129] A biblical text abstracted from the whole of Scripture and interpreted against Christ must yield to the Lord of Scripture who is always its proper reference.

Serious questions have been raised about Luther's insistence that the New Testament, and particularly its presentation of Christ, should control the interpretation of the entire Bible. Did Luther really do justice to the particularity of each text? Did he draw the whole around the centre too tightly? Did he correctly locate the centre after all?[130] Luther was certainly less than perfectly consistent, as we have seen. He could insist on the importance of the historical meaning and yet in practice sometimes treat it superficially as he moved on to a reference to Christ or a lesson for the believer. He could become exasperated with texts whose relation to the centre he found difficult to define, such as Esther, or James, or Revelation. Nevertheless, he maintained that he was simply following the practice of the apostles, and in particular Paul. He would have denied any suggestion that he was imposing

---

[128] '40. Summa, Christus est dominus, non servus, Dominus Sabbati, legis et omnium. 41. Et Scriptura est, non contra, sed pro Christo intelligenda, ideo vel ad eum referenda, vel pro vera Scriptura non habenda [...] 48. Ipse enim est caput et dux iustitiae et vitae a Deo constitutus, per et in quo nos vivimus et salvamur. 49. Quod si adversarii scripturam urserint contra Christum, urgemus Christum contra scripturam. 50. Nos dominum habemus, illi servos, Nos caput, illi pedes seu membra, quibus caput oportet dominari et praeferri.' *Die Thesen für die Promotionsdisputation von Hieronymus Weller und Nikolaus Medler* (11 September 1535) WA XXXIX-I, 47.1-4, 47.17-22 = LW 34, 112.

[129] cf. *In epistolam S. Pauli ad Galatas Commentarius* (1535) WA XL-I, 457.16-459.18 = LW 26, 294-295.

[130] Ebeling, 'Hermeneutics II', 326; Stendahl, 'The Word of God', 139.

either a unity or an interpretive grid upon the Scripture from without. He was merely allowing Scripture to be its own interpreter.[131] In 1524 he argued that 'the safest of all methods for discerning the meaning of Scripture is to work for it by drawing together and scrutinising passages'.[132] This could only be legitimate if there was some kind of unity to the entire Scripture.

The second of Luther's insights was the importance of the context for the understanding of any particular text. Luther called for an appropriate attention to the context of biblical statements as early as his debate with Eck in 1519:

> That is not the right way to interpret the Scriptures, to collect statements from different parts of the Bible without any regard for logical order or context. But that is the way it is commonly done; and it leads to nothing but errors. In order not to go wrong, the theologian must therefore keep in mind the whole of Scripture.[133]

He was sure that many of the errors of the heretics could have been avoided by a careful note of the context of each biblical statement. At first glance they might seem to have supported their case with Scripture, but this was only an illusion. They had ignored the rules of a responsible handling of the Scriptures. As Luther explained in the midst of a sermon on Jn. 14:16 in 1537:

> Thus they carp and give instruction. But they are not pious enough to bring the two verses together for a comparison. They pick out one thing here and another thing there; and where they find a word or two, they pounce upon these and hoodwink people, to keep them from seeing what else Scripture has to say about this. Yes if it were fair to take a word or two out of context and to ignore what precedes or follows, or what Scripture says elsewhere, then I, too, could interpret and twist all Holy Scripture and any speech as I chose. But

---

[131] *Assertio omnium articulorum M. Lutheri per bullam Leonis X novissimam damnatorum* (1520) WA VII, 97.23; *Predigt am Jakobstage: Ain Sermon von sant Jacobi dem meereren und hailigen zwölffpotten* (25 July 1522) WA X-III, 238.11. Siggins, 'Word of God', 5.

[132] 'Estque omnium tutissimus modus scrutandi sensus scripturae, si ex locorum collatione et observatione ad illum contendas.' *Vorlesung über das Deuteronomium* (1523-4) WA XIV, 556.28-29 = LW 9, 21.

[133] 'Non est iste modus scripturas divinas feliciter intelligendi vel interpretandi, si ex diversis locis diversa decerpantur dicta nulla habita ratione vel consequentie vel collationis: immo iste est canon errandi vulgatissimus in sacris literis. Oportet ergo theologum, si nolit errare, universam scripturam ob oculos ponere' *Disputatio Johannes Eccii et Martini Lutheri Lipsiae habita* (1519) WA II, 361.16-20.

the rule is: You must look at the entire text, inclusive of the words that follow and those that precede.[134]

In short, to ignore the surrounding context was simply to treat the text with 'brave contempt'.[135] Luther was, in fact, insisting that the form of Holy Scripture should be taken seriously. The Bible is not simply a collection of independent doctrinal statements but an integrated and harmonious collection of documents united both in their origin and their content. In this light, the ultimate context of any passage is the entire Scripture.[136]

This commitment to the unity of Scripture, manifest in an attention to context and a willingness to let the New Testament act as the interpretive control for the Old, did not settle every interpretive question. In particular it still left open the question of address. In this regard Luther did take the original context more seriously than many who preceded him. All of the Scripture might testify to Christ through its theological import as either Law or Gospel, but this did not mean that the instructions and prohibitions of Scripture should be applied directly to Luther or his readers. The student of the Scriptures needs to ask not only what has been spoken but to whom it has been spoken.

---

[134] 'Und wie ers machet und redet, so mus es nicht recht sein, könnens alles taddeln und meistern, Sind aber nicht so from, das sie die sprüche gegen ander hielten, Sondern zwacken hie ein stück und dort ein stück, und wo sie ein wort oder zwey haben, fallen sie darauff, machen damit ein geplerr den leuten fur die augen, das sie nicht sehen sollen, was die Schrifft mehr und weiter sagt, Ja, wenn das solt gelten, das man also ein wort oder zwey aus einem gantzen text reiffen möcht und lassen anstehen, was vor oder nach stehet oder an andern orten der Schrifft gesagt wird, So künde ich auch wol alle Schrifft und rede deuten und leren, wie ich selbs wolt. Es heisst aber also: Sihe diesen Text gantz an beide, mit dem, so nach und vor gehet' *Das 14. und 15. Kapitel S. Johannes gepredigt und ausgelegt* (1538) WA XLV, 555.23-33 = LW 24, 104.

[135] 'It is the habit of all those who elude arguments by means of tropes to show a brave contempt for the the text itself and devote all their energy to picking out some particular word and torturing it by means of tropes, crucifying it on the cross of their own opinion without any regard either for the wider context, or the words that follow and precede, or the intention or motive of the author. (Mos est enim omnium, qui tropis eludunt argumenta, ut textu ipso fortiter contempto hoc solum laborent, ut excerptum vocabulum aliquod tropis torqueant ac suo sensu crucifigant, nullo respectu habito vel circumstantiarum vel sequentium et praecedentium vel intentionis aut caussae authoris.)' *De servo arbitrio* (1525) WA XVIII, 713.3-7 = LW 33, 181.

[136] 'Therefore, the meaning of a word [of Scripture] must be sought from the whole Scripture, and from the context of the events (Ideo verbi intelligentia ex tota scriptura et circumstantia rerum gestarum petenda est)' *Disputatio Johannes Eccii et Martini Lutheri Lipsiae habita* (1519) WA II, 302.1-2.

Luther used 2 Sa. 7:13 as an example. God promised David 'out of you shall come a king'. That does not mean, however, that we can all expect to be the ancestors of kings.[137] 'We must not content ourselves to inquire whether a certain word is of God', Luther explained in 1526, 'but we must also ascertain whether or not this word is intended for us and so apply it to ourselves or not'.[138] The unity of Scripture did not imply a superficial or even identical treatment of each text.

An explanation of Luther's confident approach to Holy Scripture, both in affirming its unique authority and in explaining its meaning, cannot afford to ignore his convictions concerning its fundamental unity. These were much more than the simple statement that the entire Scripture testified to Christ. Nor was Luther content with an affirmation that the whole of Scripture is ultimately ascribed to the Holy Spirit. Rather, through an exploration of first letter and spirit and later Law and Gospel, through reflection on the relation of the testaments, and through the identification of a common human predicament throughout human history which finds its one solution in the person and events which form the very heart of biblical teaching, Luther demonstrated a textured and yet most profound unity of Scripture.

The presupposition of a coherent and focussed text in Holy Scripture enabled Luther to move with ease and confidence between his statements concerning biblical authority and his own expositions of its teaching. Continuing the analogy of previous chapters, here is another part of the conceptual bridge between the two. The authoritative message of Scripture can be identified because for all its diversity it speaks with one voice. There can be no suggestion of competing voices rendering the bold statement 'Scripture says ...' meaningless. At the same time the unity of Scripture ensures that the interpretive task takes a certain shape. The centre must be recognised and the theological dynamic which connects each text to the centre must be properly understood. As far as Luther was concerned, neither atomistic exegesis nor superficial harmonisation are appropriate.

---

[137] *Eyn Unterrichtung wie sich die Christen ynn Mosen sollen schicken* (1525) WA XVI, 385.10-12 = LW 35, 170.

[138] 'Darumb müssen wyr nicht darnach fragen, obs Gotts wort sey, sondern ob uns dasselbige sey gesagt odder nicht, und als denn desselbigen uns annemen odder nicht etce.' *Der Prophet Jona ausgelegt* (1526) WA XIX, 195.10-12 = LW 19, 42.

Chapter 5

An Intelligible Text?

Luther on the Clarity of Holy Scripture

Whenever Martin Luther turned his attention to the Bible, his approach was shaped by a series of basic convictions. He was convinced that the text he was expounding was the product of a unique process of divine inspiration. The sovereign activity of the Holy Spirit had ensured that these human words were in fact the Word of God. He was also convinced that the entire collection of biblical texts could, and should, be seen as a coherent unit. Though each part brought its own particular contribution to the whole, though the original situation and the mode of expression varied throughout the collection, a series of profound theological connections secured a consistent focus on the person and work of Jesus Christ. Nevertheless, convictions such as these cannot fully account for the confidence which characterises Luther's biblical expositions or the boldness with which he claims to teach and act on its authority. Indeed, the convictions themselves are hardly intelligible without the presupposition that the teaching of Scripture, not least its teaching about itself, is clear. It is thus not surprising to find that Luther both affirms and explains *claritas scripturae* on a number of occasions in his theological career.

The clarity of Scripture was, as we have seen, an issue of considerable importance prior to Luther. Once again the basic concerns appear to have been addressed by the biblical writers themselves. Certainly Luther would appeal to the testimony of Scripture concerning its own clarity in his development of the theme.[1] The practice of biblical interpretation by the Church Fathers demonstrates a continued interest in the subject, heightened by the emergence of

---

[1] *De servo arbitrio* (1525) *WA* XVIII, 656.15-18 = *LW* 33, 94-95; cf. Althaus, *Theology*, 78.

heterodox movements within the early church and its interaction with the Graeco-Roman thought-world. In the centuries immediately prior to Luther, the contributions of the biblical scholars associated with the Abbey of Saint Victor in Paris, together with the application of some of the principles of Aristotelian philosophy and a renewed interest in the literal or historical sense of Scripture, also carried important implications for any teaching about the clarity of Scripture. It is, therefore, not only the inner logic of Luther's approach to Scripture which would lead us to expect he would deal with this subject: it also had a significant role in the theological and exegetical tradition to which he was heir.

Modern scholarship has increasingly recognised the importance of *claritas scripturae* in Luther's own theology.[2] However there remains significant disagreement about the details. Some perpetuate the caricature that the medieval church almost universally considered the Bible to be an obscure book which was impenetrable without the authoritative interpretation of the church.[3] Others argue that Luther's doctrine of the clarity of Scripture was 'no more than the consequence of the methodical and, to that extent, scientific Scripture research of

---

[2] Rudolf Hermann, 'Von der Klarheit der Heiligen Schrift. Untersuchungen und Erörterungen über Luthers Lehre von der Schrift in De servo arbitrio', in Horst Beintker *et al.* (eds.), *Studien zur Theologie Luthers und des Luthertums: Gessammelte und nachgelassene Werke*, 170-255; Friedrich Beisser, *Claritas Scripturae bei Martin Luther*; Ernst Wolf, 'Uber "Klarheit der Heiligen Schrift" nach Luthers "De servo arbitrio"', *TLZ* 92 (1967), 721-730; Ulrich Duchrow, 'Die Klarheit der Schrift und die Vernunft', *Kerygma und Dogma*, 15 (1969), 1-17; Otto Kuss, 'Über die Klarheit der Schrift: Historische und hermeneutische Überlegungen zu der Kontroverse des Erasmus und des Luther über den freien oder versklavten Willen', in Josef Ernst (ed.), *Schriftauslegung: Beitrage zur Hermeneutik des Neuen Testamentes und im Neuen Testament*, 89-149; Rudolf Mau, 'Klarheit der Schrift und Evangelium: zum Ausatz des lutherschen Gedankens der claritas scripturae', *Theologische Versuche* 4 (1972), 129-143; Ernst-Wilhelm Kohls, 'Luthers Aussagen über die Mitte, Klarheit un Selbsttätigkeit der Heiligen Schrift', *Luther-Jahrbuch* 40 (1973), 46-75; Peter Neuner and Friedreich Schröger, 'Luthers These von der Klarheit der Schrift', *TGl* 74 (1984), 39-58; Hans-Christian Daniel, 'Luthers Ansatz der claritas scripturae in den Schriften "Assertio omnium articulorum" und "Grund and Ursach aller Artikel" (1520/21)', in Tuomo Mannermaa *et al.* (eds.), *Thesaurus Lutheri: Auf der Suche nach neuen Paradigmen der Luther-Forschung*, 279-290; Bernhard Rothen, *Die Klarheit der Schrift I: Martin Luther. Die wiederentdeckten Grundlagen*; Gregg R. Allison, 'The Protestant Doctrine of the Perspicuity of Scripture: A Reformulation on the Basis of Biblical Teaching', 1-48.

[3] Moisés Silva, *Has the Church Misread the Bible? The History of Interpretation in the Light of Current Issues*, 78.

the Middle Ages'.⁴ Some insist that the idea that Scripture is clear or perspicuous was an innovation of post-Reformation Protestant scholasticism.⁵ Others conclude that it was 'the main contribution of the Protestant Reformers to biblical hermeneutics'.⁶ Most diversity is found on the question of its place in Luther's theology as a whole. Wolfhart Pannenberg speaks for many when he suggests that the clarity of Scripture was a polemical construct which Luther developed in a limited way in his debate with Erasmus in 1525. Only later was it expanded and given prominence by the debates between Luther's successors and Roman Catholic theologians such as Robert Bellarmine.⁷ In contrast, Inge Lønning maintains that 'everything in the universe of Luther's reformation stands or falls with the thesis of the clarity of Holy Scripture'.⁸ It is possible to define a third position which stands in substantial agreement with Alister McGrath's assessment that this idea is characteristic of Luther's early exegetical optimism which was discredited in the face of dissension amongst the Reformers and was replaced by an emphasis on linguistic expertise and the hermeneutical norm of the Protestant catechism.⁹

In this chapter we examine the clarity of Scripture as it was affirmed and explained by Luther himself. An exploration of the contexts in which Luther discusses the idea, his distinctive explanation of its meaning, the place it occupies within his theology, and its relation to other aspects of his approach to Scripture may further illumine the contours of that approach.

The Emergence of the Issue in Luther's writings

Much is sometimes made of the fact that Luther's treatment of the clarity of Scripture always occurs within the context of a discussion of other issues. Friedrich Beisser has suggested that it is remarkable how little Luther talks about the idea itself. He highlighted the fact that even the most extensive treatment of the subject by Luther, in his *De servo arbitrio* of 1525, emerged as a response to the arguments of an

---

[4] Wolfhart Pannenberg, *Basic Questions in Theology*, I, 5.
[5] James Barr, *Holy Scripture: Canon, Authority, Criticism*, 2.
[6] Silva, *Church*, 77.
[7] Wolfhart Pannenberg, *Systematic Theology*, I, 29-30; cf. James P. Callahan, 'Claritas Scripturae: The Role of Perspicuity in Protestant Hermeneutics', *JETS* 39 (1996), 353-372.
[8] Inge Lønning, '"No Other Gospel": Luther's Concept of the "Middle of Scripture" in Its Significance for Ecumenical Communion and Christian Confession Today', in Peter Manns and Harding Meyer (eds.), *Luther's Ecumenical Significance: An Interconfessional Consultation*, 233.
[9] McGrath, *Reformation Thought*, 151-153.

opponent.[10] However, Beisser's surprise is unjustified in the light of two observations. Firstly, a contextual examination of the clarity of Scripture is to be expected in view of the fact that clarity, for Luther, is itself a means to an end. Luther does not value *claritas* as some kind of parallel to the humanist fascination with *eloquentia*.[11] Rather, his treatment of the concept suggests that the clarity of Scripture cannot properly be isolated from the most immediate purpose of Scripture: the direct address of the believer by God himself. As we saw in the last chapter, Luther remained convinced that the central subject of Scripture, and hence Christian theology, is Christ and not itself.[12] Secondly, it is worth noting that Erasmus' work was itself a response, explicitly taking as its point of reference Luther's defence of the propositions condemned by the papal bull of 1520.[13] Luther had thus been speaking about the clarity of Scripture long before Erasmus composed his attack in late 1523 and early 1524. Indeed, it is possible to document Luther's commitment to the concept throughout his teaching career, from the earliest lectures on the Psalms in 1513 to the final lectures on Genesis in 1545. In a variety of contexts, some polemical and others less so, Luther emphasised the reality and comfort of 'a strong and clear saying of Scripture'.[14]

The issue of Scripture's clarity was not treated at length in the *Dictata super Psalterium*. Nevertheless, at a few points the terminology of clarity and obscurity is undeniably present and Luther demonstrated an awareness of how others had taken up the issue in the course of their own exposition of the Psalms. In the *scholia* on Ps. 11:4 he explained the use of the terms 'eyes' and 'eyelids'. He began by referring to the explanation offered by Augustine:

> 'Eyes' and 'eyelids', according to Augustine, here denote certain passages in the Scriptures that are open and closed. The 'eyes' are

---

[10] Beisser, *Claritas Scripturae*, 79.

[11] H. H. Gray, 'Renaissance Humanism: The Pursuit of Eloquence', in P. O. Kristeller and P. F. Wiener (eds.) *Renaissance Essays*, 60-73.

[12] A similar, though not identical observation is made by both Beisser himself and Anthony Thiselton. Beisser, *Claritas Scripturae*, 81; Thiselton, *New Horizons*, 184; cf. Mau: 'Luthers Lehre von der Klarheit der Schrift läßt sich nur im Zusammenhang mit der reformatorischen Erkenntnis des Evangeliums begreifen.' Mau, 'Klarheit', 139.

[13] This is clear from the citation of Luther's *Assertio* on the first page of Erasmus' *De Libero Arbitrio* (*Erasmi Opera*, IX, 997). English translation: *Luther and Erasmus: Free Will and Salvation*, ed. by E. Gordon Rupp and Philip S. Watson (London: SCM, 1969), p. 35.

[14] 'ein starker, klarer spruch der schrifft' *Ein ander Sermon am dinstag nach Invocavit* (1522) *WA* X-III, 23.1 = *LW* 51, 80.

those which are clearly understood, but 'eyelids' are those which are dark.[15]

Actually, Luther did not find this interpretation persuasive, preferring one offered by Cassiodorus. However, what is of note here is Luther's awareness, at the very least simply through reading Augustine's commentary on the Psalms, that the question had been raised. The use made of this terminology later in these lectures suggests that at this early stage Luther saw the distinction between clear and unclear as another way of describing that between the letter and the spirit. In his comment on Ps. 16:7 he drew the connection explicitly: 'in [Scripture] there is a twofold sense, namely, the veil and clarity (*velamen et claritas*), the letter and the spirit, the figure and the truth, the shadow and the form'.[16]

The concept takes a different shape and is decidedly more prominent, in the context of Luther's debate with Rome between the years 1517 and 1521. By June 1520 this debate had taken a decisive turn with the publication of the papal bull *Exsurge Domine*. Two months later Luther issued his *An den christlichen Adel deutscher Nation von des christlichen Standes Besserung*, which presupposed the accessibility of Scripture in its denial of the need for an authoritative papal interpretation.[17] The issue of biblical interpretation became critical as the relationship between Luther and Rome deteriorated. When political pressure was applied to Frederick the Wise over the next few months, he instructed Luther to prepare a thorough explanation of all the articles condemned by the papal bull, and to do so in both Latin and German. It was in the introduction to this work that Luther first took the time to articulate his understanding of the meaning and implications of the clarity of Scripture.[18] The Latin version, *Assertio omnium articulorum*, which was finished first, is a

---

[15] 'Oculi et palpebre secundum Augustinum significant hic aliquos passus in scripturis, apertos et clausos. "Oculi" scil. Ii, qui clare intelliguntur, "palpebre" autem, que obscure sunt.' *Dictata super Psalterium* (1513-15) *WA* LV-II, 112.18-20 = *LW* 10, 99.

[16] *Dictata super Psalterium* (1513-15) *WA* LV-II, 123.20-22 = *LW* 10, 109; cf. *WA* III, 514.32-515.3 = *LW* 10, 458.

[17] *An den christlichen Adel deutscher Nation von des christlichen Standes Besserung* (1520) *WA* VI, 411.8-412.38, 460.20-462.11 = *LW* 44, 133-136, 204-207; cf. McGrath, *Reformation Thought*, 151-152.

[18] *Assertio omnium Articulorum M. Lutheri per Bullam Leonis X. novissimam damnatorum* (1520) *WA* VII, 94-151; *Grund unnd ursach aller Artickel D. Marti. Luther, ßo durch Romische Bulle unrechtlich vordampt seyn* (1521) *WA* VII, 308-457 = *LW* 32, 7-99.

little more extensive than the German. Luther included a straightforward affirmation of Scripture's clarity:

> Or tell me, if you can, who finally decides when two statements of the fathers contradict themselves? Scripture ought to provide this judgement, which cannot be delivered unless we give to Scripture the chief place in everything, that which was acknowledged by the fathers: that is, that it is in and of itself the most certain, the most accessible, the most clear of all, interpreting itself, approving, judging and illuminating all things.[19]

Luther here developed the line of thought we observed in *An den christlichen Adel*. Thanks to the attacks of Cajetan, Prierias, Eck, and others, he had come to realise that his emphasis on the authority of Scripture required an equally bold affirmation of the clarity of Scripture.[20] He was not, of course, suggesting that the patristic legacy was irrelevant in the task of biblical interpretation. Such a task was not undertaken in a vacuum and Luther himself continued to make extensive use of the patristic commentaries. However, he was insisting that the biblical material stands over and above the statements of the Fathers as the self-interpreting norm for Christian faith and practice. The divine words are to be the first principles of Christians with the

---

[19] 'Aut dic, si potes, quo iudice finietur quaestio, si partum dicta sibi pugnaverint. Oportet enim scriptura iudice hic sententiam ferre, quod fieri non potest, nisi scripturae dederimus principem locum in omnibus quae tribuuntur patribus, hoc est, ut sit ipsa per sese certissima, facillima, apertissima, sui ipsius interpres, omnium omnia probans, iudicans et illuminans' *Assertio omnium articulorum M. Lutheri per Bullam Leonis X. novissimam damnatorum* (1520) *WA* VII, 97.19-24; cf. *WA* VII, 317.1-9 = *LW* 32, 11-12.

[20] For example, Luther's written reply to Cajetan, delivered at Augsburg on 17 October 1518: 'Indeed, I did not possess the extraordinary indiscretion so as to discard so many important clear proofs of Scripture on account of a single ambiguous and obscure decretal of a pope who is a mere human being. Much rather I considered it proper that the words of Scripture, in which the saints are described as being deficient in merits, are to be preferred to human words, in which the saints are described to have more merits than they need. For the pope is not above, but under the word of God, according to Gal. 1: "Even if we, or an angel from heaven, should preach to you a gospel contrary to that which you received, let him be accursed". (Ego vero non eram tam insigni temeritate, ut propter unam decretalem pontificis hominis tam ambiguam et obscuram recederem a tot et tantis divinae scripturae testimoniis apertissimis: quin potius arbitrabar quam rectissime, verb scripturae, quibus sancti describuntur deficere in meritis, incomparabiliter praeferenda verbis humanis, quibus scribuntur abundare, cum Papa non super, sed sub verbo dei sit iuxta illud Gal: i. Si angelus de celo aliud vobis euangelisaverit quam accepistis, anathema sit.)' *Acta Augustana* (1518) *WA* II, 10.37-11.4 = *LW* 31, 266-267.

result that 'all human words are conclusions which are deduced from them and must again be brought back to them and approved by them'.[21] As far as Luther was concerned this applied to his own efforts as well:

> I do not desire to be honoured as one who is more learned than all, but Scripture alone to rule: to be interpreted, neither by my spirit nor any human spirit, but understood through itself and by its own spirit.[22]

In 1521 Luther responded to Jerome Emser's attack on the treatise to the German nobility. In this response he described the necessity of his affirmation of the clarity of Scripture:

> I have found out that all who write and intrigue against me have in them a stupid heart and a cowardly conscience. They fear Scripture since they well know that it is unknown to them. That is why they make such a great effort, why they writhe and twist, to avoid the necessity of attacking me with Scripture and of themselves getting beaten with Scripture. So they invent a new lie, discover daggers, spears, and similar tomfoolery, and say that Scripture is so obscure that we cannot understand it without the interpretation of the holy fathers and that therefore we have to follow not the text but the glosses of the fathers.[23]

The Roman insistence on interpreting Scripture through the commentary of the Fathers was based on an assumption that the latter were in fact clearer than the Scriptures themselves. Luther reports Emser's own description of the Roman practice as 'striking not with

---

[21] 'Sint ergo Christianorum prima principia non nisi verba divina, omnium autem hominum verba conclusions hinc educate et rursus illuc reducendae et probandae' *Assertio omnium articulorum M. Lutheri per Bullam Leonis X. novissimam damnatorum* (1520) *WA* VII, 98.4-6.

[22] 'Nolo omnium doctior iactari, sed solam scripturam regnare, nec eam meo spiritu aut ullorum hominum interpretari, sed per seipsam et suo spiritu intelligi volo.' *Assertio omnium articulorum M. Lutheri per Bullam Leonis X. novissimam damnatorum* (1520) *WA* VII, 98.40-99.2.

[23] 'Das hab ich erfarenn, wie alle, die wider mich schreyben unnd treybenn, bringenn mit sich eynn blodiß hertz unnd vortzagt gewissenn, das sie sich fur der schrifft furchten, die sie wol wissen, wie sie yhn unbekant ist; drumb muhen sie sich fast, ringen und winden sich, wie sie mochten dahynn kummen, das nit nott were, mich mit schrifften antzutasten, noch sie mit schrifften geschlagen werdenn: da erdencken sie ein new lugen, finden degen und spieß und der gleychen narrn wreck und sprechen, die schrifft sey ßo finster, das wir sie nit mugen vorstehn on der heyligen vetter außlegung, drumb mussen wyr nit dem text, sondern der vetter glosen folgen' *Auf das überchristlich, übergeistlich und überkünstlich Buch Bocks Emsers zu Leipzig Antwort* (1521) *WA* VII, 638.2-10 = *LW* 39, 163.

the sheath but with the blade'.[24] However, Luther wanted to question the underlying assumption: 'Who told them that the Fathers are clearer than Scripture and not more obscure?'[25] He maintained that it was the commentary of the Fathers and not the Scriptures which are properly viewed as the sheath which blunted the blade. Luther enlisted the practice of the Fathers themselves in his critique of Emser's position:

> Therefore, one must know that Scripture without any glosses is the sun and the whole light from which all teachers receive their light, and not vice versa. This can be seen from the following: when the fathers teach something, they do not trust their own teaching. They are afraid it is too obscure and too uncertain; they run to Scripture and take a clear passage from it to illumine their own point, just as one puts a light into a lantern, as Psalm 18 says, 'Lord, you light my lantern'. In the same way, when they interpret a passage in Scripture they do not do so with their own sense or words (for whenever they do that, as often happens, they generally err). Instead, they add another passage which is clearer and thus illumine and interpret Scripture with Scripture, as my goats would certainly discover if they would read the fathers correctly.[26]

Luther was convinced, not only that his affirmation of the clarity of Scripture stood in perfect continuity with the theology of the Fathers, but that the hermeneutical implication both affirmed and applied by them, namely that Scripture should be interpreted by Scripture, was of particular relevance for the sixteenth century debate. Luther would repeat these arguments, mentioning Emser amongst others, in the

---

[24] 'uud das heysset alhie Emßer nit mit der scheyden sondern mit der schneyden hawen' *Auf das überchristlich, übergeistlich und überkünstslich Buch Bocks Emsers zu Leipzig Antwort* (1521) *WA* VII, 638.10-11 = *LW* 39, 163.

[25] 'wer hat yhn gesagt, das die veter liechter denn die schrifft und nit auch finsterer sein?' *Auf das überchristlich, übergeistlich und überkünstslich Buch Bocks Emsers zu Leipzig Antwort* (1521) *WA* VII, 638.26-28 = *LW* 39, 164.

[26] 'Drumb ist zu wissen, das die schrifft on alle glose ist die sonne und gantzis licht, von wilcher alle lerer yhr licht empfahen, und nit widderumb. Das merckt man da bey: Wo die vetter ettwas leren, ßo trawen sie yhrer lere nit, sorgen, sie sey zu finster und ungewiß, und lauffen yn die schrifft, nemen eynen klaren spruch darauß, damit sie yhr ding erleuchten, gleych wie man licht yn ein laternn setzet, wie ps. 17. 'Herr, du erleuchtist meyn latern'. Desselben gleychen wenn sie eynen ort der schrifft außlegen, ßo thun sie es nit mit yhrem eygen synn odder wortt (Denn wo sie das thun, wie offt geschicht, da yrren sie gemeyniglich), ßondernn bringen eynen andern ort erzu, der klerer ist, und alßo schrifft mit schrifft erleuchten und außlegen, wie das meyne Bocke wol finden wurden, wenn sie die vetter recht leßen wurden.' *Auf das überchristlich, übergeistlich und überkünstslich Buch Bocks Emsers zu Leipzig Antwort* (1521) *WA* VII, 639.1-11 = *LW* 39, 164.

sermon on Psalm 37 which he sent from the Wartburg to 'Christ's little heap in Wittenberg'.[27]

Yet another defence of *claritas scripturae* in the context of the break with Rome was Luther's *Rationis Latomianae confutatio* of June 1521. Latomus had defended the condemnation of Luther by the Universities of Louvain and Cologne, which had been issued in February 1520. He would not allow Luther's simple appeal to the Scriptures since they remain uncertain apart from the authoritative interpretation of the church. Luther took the argument for the clarity of Scripture a step further in his response:

> But doesn't obscure Scripture require explanation? Set aside the obscure and cling to the clear. Further, who has proved that the fathers are not obscure? Are we once again going to have your 'it seems' and their 'they say'? What did the fathers do except seek and present clear and open testimonies of Scripture? Miserable Christians, whose words and faith still depend on the interpretations of men and who expect clarification from them! This is frivolous and ungodly. The Scriptures are common to all, and are clear enough in respect to what is necessary for salvation, and are also obscure enough for inquiring minds. Let everyone search for his portion in the most abundant and universal Word of God, and let us reject the word of man, or else read it with discrimination.[28]

Luther was, of course, developing an argument we have already seen in Augustine.[29] He emphasised the fact that the Scriptures are accessible to all while at the same time admitting that such accessibility involves both sufficient clarity with regard to those things necessary for salvation and sufficient obscurity to provide a challenge for the intellectually gifted. Obscurity, understood in this context, was

---

[27] *Der 36. (37.) Psalm Davids* (1521) *WA* VIII, 236.7-28, 239.16-21.

[28] "'At scriptura obscura indiget explicatione": dimitte eam ubi obscura est, tene ubi clara est. Et quis probavit patres non esse obscuros? Iterum tuum 'videtur' et illorum "dicunt"? Quid enim faciunt et patres, quam ut clarissima et apertissima scripturae testimonia quaerant et proferant? Miseri Christiani, quorum verbum et fides adhuc in hominum glossis pendet et eorum elucidationem expectat. Frivola sunt ista et impia. Scripturae omnibus communes sunt, satis apertae, quantum oportet pro salute, satis etiam obscurae pro contemplatricibus animabus. Quisque suam sortem in abundantissimo et communissimo verbo dei sequatur, et verba hominum aut repudiemus aut cum iudicio legamus. *Rationis Latomianae confutatio* (1521) *WA* VIII, 99.14-23 = *LW* 32, 217.

[29] Augustine, *De doctrina Christiana*, II.6(8) (*CCSL*, XXXII, 36); *Epistulae*, CXXXVII.18 (*CSEL*, XLIV, 122-123).

not in fact a barrier to understanding at all, but the gift of God to stimulate the understanding.

This debate with Rome concerning the clarity of Scripture spilled over into the ostensively non-polemical context of the *Kirchenpostille*. In earlier chapters we have observed how these homilies provide a rich source of evidence for Luther's approach to Holy Scripture. In the sermon for St. James' day, Luther warned of the poison peddled by those who rob God's people of the Scripture and hence of the Gospel:

> However, I must now throw a log on the road, before I take hold of the Gospel. The Gospel leads even our enemy and wants to draw him there, though he is the one who locks the gospel from us and says 'The Gospel and Scripture are dark and obscure, and the one who has them should let them be and not treat them as common property, in order that he might be kept from extracting a wrong understanding from them. Instead, let him hear them as the Pope, Augustine, and the holy fathers interpret them'. In this way we have our deadly poison truly poured out for us while the Scriptures are shoved under the bench![30]

Here was an ancient argument which gained much of its force from the fear of heresy. However, Luther insisted that the Christian's response should be categorical. He who has the Scriptures 'says to himself that he does not believe that the Scripture is dark and one must have the statements of the fathers to illumine it'.[31]

As Emser and others had responded to Luther's appeal to the German nobility, so Erasmus responded to Luther's *Assertio omnium articulorum*. In his *De libero arbitrio ΔΙΑΤΡΙΒΗ sive collatio*, Erasmus took issue with Luther's argument that Scripture could and should be interpreted on its own terms, while at the same time insisting that he was not himself questioning the authority of Scripture:

---

[30] 'Nun müß ich aber ain block auß dem weg stossen, ee ich zu dem Euangelio greiff. Das Euangelium fürn auch unser feind und wöllens dahin ziehen, das sy uns das Euangelium zuschliessen und sagen, das Euangelium und schrifft sey finster und tunckel, der halben sol mans ligen lassen und ain gemainen man nit lassen sesen, das er nit ainn irrigen verstand herauß ziehe, sonder allain hörn laß, wie es der Bapst, Augustinus unnd die hailigen väter außlegen. Also haben sy uns jren gayfer, gifft unnd treüm eingeschenckt und die schrifft under die banck geschoben.' *Predigt am Jakobstage* (1522) *WA* X-III, 236.6-13.

[31] 'Darumb so man euch sagt: die schrifft ist finster unnd man muß der väter sprüch haben die zuerleüchten: das glaubt nit sonder köret das blat umb und sagt, der väter sprüch seyen tunckel und aller menschen leer und bedürffen, das sy durch die geschifft erleücht werden.' *Predigt am Jakobstage* (1522) *WA* X-III, 236.13-17.

An Intelligible Text? 201

I confess that it is right that the sole authority of Holy Scripture should outweigh all the votes of all mortal men. But the authority of the Scripture is not here in dispute (*verum hic de scripturis non est controuersia*). The same Scriptures are acknowledged and venerated by either side. Our battle is about the meaning of Scripture ... I hear the objection, 'What need is there of an interpreter when the Scripture itself is crystal clear (*ubi dilucida est scriptura*)?' But if it is so clear, why have so many outstanding men in so many centuries been blind, and in a matter of such importance, as these would appear? If there is no obscurity (*nihil caliginis*) in Scripture, what was the need of the work of prophecy in the days of the apostles? You say, 'This was the gift of the Spirit'. But I have the suspicion that just as the charismata of healings and tongues ceased, this charisma ceased also. And if it did not cease, then one must ask to whom it has been passed on.[32]

Undoubtedly Luther's most extensive defence of the concept of Scripture's clarity is in his reply to this attack from Erasmus. In *De servo arbitrio* Luther described the clarity of Scripture as 'that first principle of ours'.[33] He even linked this characteristic of the biblical writings to the fact that they have been given to us by God.[34] It is in this treatise that we find Luther distinguishing between two types of clarity with regard to Scripture and insisting on the importance of the Spirit and Christian faith in the process of understanding biblical truth.[35] Here too we find one of his boldest statements on the subject: 'Moreover, against you I say concerning the entire Scripture: I want to call no part of it obscure'.[36]

Luther's convictions concerning the clarity of Scripture also played an important role in the eucharistic debates which occupied so much of his attention in the latter half of the 1520s.[37] Luther had actually published his first work on the Lord's Supper in December 1519.[38] It was one of a trilogy of sermons he had preached earlier in response to

---

[32] Erasmus, *De libero arbitrio* (*Erasmi Opera* IX, 1000) = Rupp and Watson, *Erasmus*, 43, 44.
[33] 'illud ipsum primum principium nostrum' *De servo arbitrio* (1525) *WA* XVIII, 653.33-34 = *LW* 33, 91.
[34] *De servo arbitrio* (1525) *WA* XVIII, 655.25-29 = *LW* 33, 93-94.
[35] *De servo arbitrio* (1525) *WA* XVIII, 609.4-14 = *LW* 33, 28.
[36] 'Deinde contra te de tota scriptura dico, nullam eius partem volo obscuram dici.' *De servo arbitrio* (1525) *WA* XVIII, 656.15-16 = *LW* 33, 94.
[37] Mark D. Thompson, '*Claritas Scripturae* in the eucharistic writings of Martin Luther', *Westminster Theological Journal* 60/1 (1998), 23–41.
[38] *Eyn Sermon von dem Hochwirdigen Sacrament des Heyligen Waren Leychnams Christi* (1519) *WA* II, 742-58 = *LW* 35, 49-73.

requests from friends who were alarmed at the confusion that was already emerging over the sacrament. Some of the characteristic lines of Luther's treatment of the subject can be observed even at that early stage, including his insistence that this meal is 'a sure sign from God himself',[39] his focus on the 'union (*voreynigung*)' between Christ and the believer in the Supper,[40] and his refusal to speculate beyond the promise of God.[41] However, four months later, a Franciscan friar from Leipzig, Augustinus von Alveld, began a series of attacks upon Luther which highlighted a fundamental point of difference between them: Alved's first attack included a call for soundness when it came to the difficult passages in Scripture.[42] *De Captivitate Babylonica Ecclesiae* was in part a response to this attack and contains Luther's appeal to 'the clear Scriptures of God'.[43]

This dimension to the debate over the sacrament remained in focus as Luther began to face opposition from other reformers as well as from the theologians of Rome. During Luther's absence from Wittenberg following the Diet of Worms, Zwilling and Karlstadt had accelerated the process of liturgical change. The resulting confusion and even alarm led Luther to write his next two pieces on the Supper in early 1522: one endorsing the abrogation of private masses,[44] and the other mapping out a restrained program of reform.[45] Here again Luther appealed to 'Christ's certain and faithful word'[46] and 'the pure and clear gospel'.[47] From 1523 almost all of Luther's writing on the Supper centred on his defence of the real presence of Christ against a succession of spiritual interpretations of the words of institution by

---

[39] 'eyn gewiß zeychen von gott selber' *Eyn Sermon von dem Hochwirdigen Sacrament des Heyligen Waren Leychnams Christi* (1519) *WA* II, 744.8-9 = *LW* 35, 52.

[40] *Eyn Sermon von dem Hochwirdigen Sacrament des Heyligen Waren Leychnams Christi* (1519) *WA* II, 748.27-30 = *LW* 35, 59.

[41] *Eyn Sermon von dem Hochwirdigen Sacrament des Heyligen Waren Leychnams Christi* (1519) *WA* II, 750.1-3 = *LW* 35, 60-61.

[42] Augustinus von Alveld, *Super apostolica sede, an videlicet diuina sit iure nec ne* (Leipzig, 1520).

[43] 'evidentes dei scripturae' *De captivitate Babylonica ecclesiae praeludium* (1520) WA VI, 505.24 = *LW* 36, 24.

[44] *De Abroganda Missa Privata* (1521) *WA* VIII, 411-76; *Von mißbrauch der Messen* (1521) *WA* VIII, 482-536 = *LW* 36, 133-230.

[45] *Von beider Gestalt des Sakraments* (1522) *WA* X-II, 11-41 = *LW* 36, 237-267.

[46] 'verbum certum et fidele Christi' *De Abroganda Missa Privata* (1521) *WA* VIII, 412.4-5; 'das mich Christus mit seynem eynigen, gewissen wortt' *Von mißbrauch der Messen* (1521) *WA* VIII, 483.4-5 = *LW* 36, 134.

[47] 'Wyr haben das helle lautter Euangelion' *Von beider Gestalt des Sakraments* (1522) *WA* X-II, 22.24 = *LW* 36, 247.

Karlstadt, Zwingli, Oecolampadius, Schwenckfeld, and others. While there is ample evidence that Luther was aware of the distinctive approaches of each of these opponents, his responses all contained the same basic argument, one that can be found as early as the sermon preached to the Bohemians in April 1523: 'the words stand there clear, unadorned, and plain: "This is my body"'.[48]

The final context for Luther's statements about the clarity of Scripture was his later exegetical work. It must be admitted that the line between Luther's polemical writings and his non-polemical explanations of the teaching of Scripture is an artificial one and that Luther could be just as polemical in his lectures as in various treatises. However, references to the clarity of Scripture occur throughout the later exegetical writings in an almost incidental way and the polemical element, when it is present, is often general rather than particular. So, in the preface to his lectures on Habakkuk from 1526, Luther defended the writings of the prophets from the charge of confusion and obscurity:

> It is indeed very irritating to read a book that observes no order, in which statements are so disconnected that they do not fit together and therefore lack proper coherence. All of that may reasonably be expected of correct and proper speech. Thus the Holy Spirit was accused of an inability to express Himself properly, of talking like a drunkard or a fool, of mixing everything together and of delivering Himself of wild and odd words and statements. But it is we who were at fault; we did not understand the speech, and we were not acquainted with the method of the prophets. For it cannot be otherwise: the Holy Spirit is wise, and He also makes His prophets wise. Now, a wise man must necessarily be able to speak well; this can never fail. But to him who does not hear well or is not sufficiently conversant with a language, to him a speech may seem faulty because he hears or understands hardly half of the words. That has been our experience to date with Scripture. That is why we, too, groped in the dark so, aped others, and often missed the mark and arrived at another meaning. As the saying goes: He who cannot hear well, invents well.[49]

---

[48] 'die wortt helle, durre und klar da stehen: "Das ist meyn leyb".' *Von Anbeten des Sakraments des heiligen Leichnams Christi* (1523) *WA* XI, 435.7-8 = *LW* 36, 280.

[49] 'Nu ists gar unlustig ding, eyn buch lesen, das keine ordnunge helt, da man nicht kan eyns zum andern bringen und an einander hengen, das sichs fein nach enander spünne, wie sichs denn gepürt, wo man recht und wol reden wil. Also hat der heylige geyst mussen die schuld haben, das er nicht wol reden kunde; sondern wie ein trunckenbold odder ein narr redet, so menge ers ynn einander

The charge of confusion and obscurity must fail, Luther insisted, because the character of the Spirit guarantees the propriety of the biblical text. The confusion that many, including Luther himself, had experienced was certainly very real but it was a mistake to locate the source of that confusion in the text. Instead, Luther located such problems in our distance from the world of the text and our ignorance of its mode of expression (elsewhere he would highlight our ignorance of its language forms). Luther took this line of thinking further two years later when, as he explained Is. 29:10, he spoke in general terms of the 'spirit of deep sleep (*spiritum soporis*)', the determined unbelief which keeps both the Jews and the papists from understanding a Scripture so very clear that 'even boys understand it (*eciam pueris cognitae*)'.[50] Similar sentiments can be found in his sermon on Jn. 14:13-14 from 1537 and the lecture on Gn. 48:21 from 1545.[51]

It is evident then that in a variety of polemical contexts, and in some contexts in which the polemical element is at least not the primary concern, Luther affirmed the clarity of Holy Scripture. In chronological terms the references to this concept and the use of associated terminology cover the entire period of Luther's teaching career. Further, while it may well be suggested that the primary context of thought for Luther's *claritas scripturae* was epistemological, this

---

und fure wilde selzame wort und sprüche. Es ist aber unser schuld, die wyr die sprache nicht verstanden noch der Propheten weyse gewust haben. Denn das kan yhe nicht anders sein: Der heylige geyst ist weyse und macht die Propheten auch weyse. Ein weyser aber mus wol reden konnen, das feylet nymer mehr. Wer aber nicht wol höret odder die sprache nicht gnugsam weys, den mags wol duncken, er rede ubel, weil er kaum der wort die helfft höret odder vernympt. Eben so ists uns bis her gangen ynn der schrifft. Darumb haben wyr auch so getappet und nach geomet und gar offt neben hyn gangen und ein anders troffen, wie man sagt: Wer nicht wol höret, der reymet wol.' *Der Prophet Habakuk ausgelegt* (1526) *WA* XIX, 350.15-29 = *LW* 19, 152.

[50] 'As it is not the fault of the book and the letters that a peasant cannot read, but the peasant's, so it is not the fault of the Bible, which is very clear so that even boys understand it, but it is the fault of the ideas and darkness of the papists, who love darkness rather than light. (Sicut non libri et literarum culpa rusticum non legere posse, sed Rustici, ita non culpa Bibiliae lucidissimae, eciam pueris cognitae, sed opinionum et tenebrarum Papisticarum, qui diligunt tenebras plus quam lucem.)' *Vorlesung über Iesaias* (1527-30) *WA* XXXI-II, 176.3, 176.18-19 = *LW* 16, 243.

[51] *Das 14. und 15. Kapitel S. Johannes gepredigt und ausgelegt* (1537-8) *WA* XLV, 544.30-545.2 = *LW* 24, 92; *Genesisvorlesung* (1535-45) *WA* XLIV, 720.3-27 = *LW* 8, 192-193.

spread of evidence suggests a conviction that had more far-reaching implications even for Luther himself.[52]

The Importance of the Clarity of Scripture according to Luther

We have noted the way Luther treats the subject of Scripture's clarity within the context of other issues, especially the unique authority of Scripture, the condition of the human will, or the nature of Christ's presence in the sacrament of the Lord's Supper. The clarity of Scripture seems to function principally as a means to an end. However it does not follow that the concept is therefore unimportant in Luther's thought. At one level that has already been demonstrated by its place in a variety of contexts throughout Luther's teaching career. Yet at a much more profound level it is demonstrated by the connection of this idea to other key themes in Luther's thought. Two of these are particularly noteworthy.

Luther himself drew a connection between the clarity of Scripture and the doctrine of God. Such a connection could be explained in two ways. In the first instance it is the character of God which determines the nature of the Scripture he has given. Luther developed this line of thought in the preface to his Habakkuk lectures quoted above. He argued that the wisdom of the Spirit guarantees an intelligible and edifying Scripture. It simply could not be otherwise.[53] Similar reasoning is evident in *De servo arbitrio,* in particular in Luther's question to Erasmus: 'If Scripture is obscure or ambiguous, what point was there in God's giving it to us?'[54] As far as Luther was concerned, any statement about Scripture entailed a statement about God because the Scripture is, in the final analysis, a gift of God and indeed the self-revelation of God. He suggested, perhaps ironically, that Erasmus may not have understood what was involved in his refusal to acknowledge that Scripture is crystal clear (*dilucida*). Luther himself was in no doubt however: any suggestion that Scripture is obscure is 'impudent

---

[52] Thiselton, *New Horizons,* 182.

[53] 'Denn das kan yhe nicht anders sein: Der heylige geyst ist weyse und macht die Propheten auch weyse. Ein weyser aber mus wol reden konnen, das feylet nymer mehr.' *Der Prophet Habakuk ausgelegt* (1526) *WA* XIX, 350.22-24 = *LW* 19, 152; cf. *Enarratio Psalmi LI.* (1532) *WA* XL-II, 385.35-386.18 = *LW* 12, 351.

[54] 'si scriptura obscura vel ambigua est, quid illam opus fuit nobis divinitus tradi?' *De servo arbitrio* (1525) *WA* XVIII, 655.25-26 = *LW* 33, 93-94; cf. Erling T. Teigen, 'The Clarity of Scripture and Hermeneutical Principles in the Lutheran Confessions', *CTQ,* 46 (1982), 148.

and blasphemous'.[55] It implied God's incompetence in revealing his Word to his people.

Another perspective on this connection emerges when we consider that Luther spoke of God as both hidden (*Deus absconditus*) and revealed (*Deus revelatus*). There is certainly great potential for confusion here, not least because Luther used the expression *Deus absconditus* in more than one way. Sometimes he spoke of God's hiddenness *in* his revelation and at other times of God's hiddenness *behind* his revelation.[56] Nevertheless, what remains constant is that the one God has made himself known and while that self-revelation may and indeed must come under the form of the contrary (*sub specie contraria*), the contrary is not a disguise which may be discarded, but an integral part of the revelation itself.[57] Thus the hiddenness of God and his work in the first sense does not mean that the cross is simply an incidental disguise for the victory of God; rather it reveals the nature of that victory.[58] The donkey and her colt were not merely incidental to Jesus' entry into Jerusalem; they conveyed important information about the kind of kingship he was exercising. Further, the faith that perceives glory hidden under the form of humiliation, mercy hidden under the form of judgement, or life hidden under the form of death, itself depends upon a clear and certain word from God. So, for example, in a sermon from 1533 Luther explained that it is only the word of the prophet Zechariah which enables the believer to see Jesus' entry into Jerusalem for what it is.[59] Even in those cases in which Luther speaks of the hiddenness of God and his work in the second sense, as when he contrasts the 'hidden and awful will of God (*occulta illa et metuenda voluntas Dei*)' in predestination with 'the preached and offered mercy of God (*praedicata et oblata misericordia Dei*)', there is never any suggestion that the latter is a ruse or in some sense less important for our understanding of God than the former. In such contexts Luther maintained that it is not our business to inquire into

---

[55] 'Sed sic obruendum erat impudens et blasphema illa vox, Scripturas esse obscuras' *De servo arbitrio* (1525) *WA* XVIII, 656.6-7 = *LW* 33, 94; cf. Beisser, *Claritas Scripturae*, 87.

[56] Loewenich, *Theology of the Cross*, 27-49; McGrath, *Theology of the Cross*, 164-167.

[57] In a sermon delivered on 24 February 1517, Luther spoke of God's hiddenness as the way he removes pride, which otherwise would be an obstacle to revelation: 'Et quae melior voluntas quam quae sua absconsione nihil aliud facit quam ut impedimenta revelationis tollat, i. e. superbiam?' *Sermo Die S. Matthiae* (1517) *WA* I, 138.13-19.

[58] *Diputatio Heidelbergae habita* (1518) *WA* I, 362.4-19 = *LW* 31, 52-53.

[59] *Predigt am 1. Adventssonntag* (30 November 1533) *WA* XXXVII, 201.2-203.30; David C. Steinmetz, *Luther in Context*, 27-28.

God as he is in his own nature and majesty. Instead our business is with God 'as he is clothed and set forth in his Word'.⁶⁰ It is this Word which Luther insists is clear. In the end, any denial of the clarity of Scripture had serious implications for the *Deus revelatus* which is the only form in which believers can know the living God.

The clarity of Scripture is also of vital significance for Luther's understanding of the Christian life. For Luther the Christian life is responsive and the focus of that response is the Word of God which comes to us in the shape of promises. Luther insisted, 'God does not deal, nor has he ever dealt, with man otherwise than through a word of promise, as I have said. We in turn cannot deal with God otherwise than through faith in the word of his promise'.⁶¹ Luther highlighted the futility and perversity of all attempts to relate to God apart from his promise. On the one hand, the Christian has no sure ground on which to stand if left with merely his or her senses; on the other, the very attempt to engage with God apart from his promise is a proud and empty human work:

> Thus it is not possible that a man, of his own reason and strength, should by works ascend to heaven, anticipating God and moving him to be gracious. On the contrary, God must anticipate all works and thoughts, and make a promise clearly expressed in words, which man then takes and keeps in good, firm faith. Then there follows the Holy Spirit, who is given to man for the sake of this same faith.⁶²

---

[60] 'God must therefore be left to himself in his own majesty, for in this regard we have nothing to do with him, nor has he willed that we should have anything to do with him. But we have something to do with him insofar as he is clothed and set forth in his Word, through which he offers himself to us and which is the beauty and glory with which the psalmist celebrates him as being clothed. (Relinquendus est igitur Deus in maiestate et natura sua, sic enim nihil nos cum illo habemus agere, nec sic voluit a nobis agi cum eo. Sed quatenus indutus et proditus est verbo suo, quo nobis sese obtulit, cum eo agimus, quod est decor et gloria eius, quo Psalmista eum celebrat indutum.)' *De servo arbitrio* (1525) *WA* XVIII, 685.14-17 = *LW* 33, 139.

[61] 'Neque enim deus, ut dixi, aliter cum hominibus unquam egit aut agit quam verbo promissionis. Rursus, nec nos cum deo unquam agere aliter possumus quam fide in verbum promissionis eius.' *De captivitate Babylonica ecclesiae praeludium* (1520) *WA* VI, 516.30-32 = *LW* 36, 42; cf. John Loeschen, 'The Function of Promissio in Luther's Commentary on Romans', *HTR* 60 (1967), 476.

[62] 'alßo das nit muglich ist, das ein mensch auß seyner vornunfft und vormugen solt mit wercken hynauff genn hymel steygen und gott zuvorkummen, yhn bewegen zur gnade, sondern gott muß zuvorkummen alle werck und gedancken, und ein klar außgedruckt zusagen thun mit worten, wilch den der mensch mit eynem rechten, festen glauben ergreyff und behalte, ßo folgt den

Luther was bold enough to describe salvation itself in terms of this dynamic of promise and faith:

> For where there is the Word of the promising God, there must necessarily be the faith of the accepting man. It is plain, therefore, that the beginning of our salvation is a faith which clings to the Word of the promising God, who, without any effort on our part, in free and unmerited mercy, takes the initiative and offers us the word of his promise.[63]

The promise of God is indispensable, but then so too is the clarity of that promise. An obscure promise would be hardly an advance on the ambiguities of nature and history. How could faith be firm when its object is unknown? Without a clear and certain word, faith is merely superstition which can never withstand the assaults of the devil.[64] However, since God has given a clear promise we not only *can* but we *must* trust it, for in trusting the promise we trust the one who promises: 'Faith is nothing else than believing what God promises and says'.[65] Faith is, therefore, both given and demanded. Precisely because its clear meaning makes faith both possible and necessary, the Word of God captures us. This is the language Luther repeatedly used to describe his own experience of the Scriptures. In 1524 he told the Christians at Strasbourg: 'I am a captive and I cannot free myself. The text is too powerfully present, and will not allow itself to be torn from its meaning by mere verbiage'.[66]

Luther did, of course, recognise a time in the past when due to incomplete revelation the promises appeared obscure. Such was the case of the promise-amidst-the-curse in the Garden of Eden, as well as

---

der heylig geyst, der yhm geben wirt umb desselben glaubens willen.' *Ein Sermon von dem neuen Testament, das ist von der heiligen Messe* (1520) *WA* VI, 356.13-19 = *LW* 35, 82-83.

[63] 'Ubi enim est verbum promittentis dei, ibi necessaria est fides acceptantis hominis, ut clarum sit initium salutis nostrae esse fidem, quae pendeat in verbo promittentis dei, qui citra omne nostrum studium gratuita et immerita misericordia nos praevenit et offert promissionis suae verbum.' *De captivitate Babylonica ecclesiae praeludium* (1520) *WA* VI, 514.13-17 = *LW* 36, 39.

[64] *Ein ander Sermon am dinstag nach Invocauit* (11 March 1522) *WA* X-III, 22.11-23.3 = *LW* 51, 80.

[65] 'Fides autem est nihil aliud quam illud, quod deus promittit aut dicit, credere' *Acta Augustana* (1518) *WA* II, 13.18-19 = *LW* 31, 270-271.

[66] 'Aber ich byn gefangen, kan nicht eraus, der text ist zu gewaltig da und will sich mit worten nicht lassen aus dem synn reyssen.' *Ein Brief an die Christen zu Straßburg wider den Schwärmergeist* (1524) *WA* XV, 394.19-20 = *LW* 40, 68;*Verhandlungen mit D. M. Luther auf dem Reichstage zu Worms* (1521) *WA* VII, 838.7-8 = *LW* 32, 112.

the initial promise to Abraham. However, Luther pointed out that in grace God did not allow such obscurity to endure, but he repeatedly enlarged and clarified those promises.[67] By the time we move to the New Testament and stand in the presence of Christ, this clarification is complete. Under the Gospel, then, the dynamic of clear promise and firm faith has its fullest expression.

Luther also saw the clarity of the biblical promises as God's provision in the continuing struggle between Christian faith and a guilty conscience. Such assault was bound to produce acute spiritual turmoil (*Anfechtung*) most typically centring on the disposition of God towards us in view of our continuing sinfulness. This, Luther maintained, was the experience David had described in the Psalms:

> But where there is no faith, there no prayer helps, nor the hearing of many masses. Things can only become worse. As Psalm 23 says, 'Before my eyes you have prepared a table for me against all my affliction'. Is this not a clear verse? What greater affliction is there than sin and the evil conscience which is always afraid of God's anger and never has rest?[68]

In this matter, as in others, Luther was generalising from his own experience of *Anfechtung* to the experience of all Christians in all ages. He did not see himself as uniquely the object of such an attack. The words of David, Paul, and even James, convinced him that he was right to warn all Christians of the danger. Nevertheless, he did recognise a particular relevance of the promise of Christ to his own extraordinary situation:

> I myself experience daily how extremely difficult it is to lay aside a conscience of long standing, one that has been fenced in by man-made ordinances [...] How often did my heart quail, punish me, and reproach me with its single strongest argument: Are you the only wise man? Can it be that all the others are in error and have erred for so long a time? What if you are mistaken and lead so many people into error who might all be eternally damned? Finally, Christ with his clear, unmistakable Word strengthened and confirmed me, so that my heart no longer quails, but resists the arguments of the papists, as

---

[67] *Ein Sermon von dem neuen Testament, das ist von der heiligen Messe* (1520) *WA* VI, 356.20-357.9 = *LW* 35, 83.

[68] 'wo sie aber nit glaubt, da hilfft kein gepet, noch vill meß hören, es muß nur ymer erger werden. Alßo sagt ps. 22. Du hast mir fur mein augen bereyttet eynen tisch widder alle meyne anfechtung. Ist das nit ein clarer spruch? Was ist nu grösser anfechtung denn die sundt und voß gewissen, das gottis zorn altzeyt furcht und nymmer ruge hatt?' *Ein Sermon von dem neuen Testament, das ist von der heiligen Messe* (1520) *WA* VI, 376.30-377.1 = *LW* 35, 109-110.

a stony shore resists the waves, and laughs at their threats and storms!⁶⁹

Ultimately, this resolution of Christian anxiety on the basis of the clear Word of God was simply an extension of Luther's argument about promise and faith as the basic dynamic of the Christian life. To his mind, the promise of God is always the most effective counter to the accusations of the conscience. Yet it is the clarity of that promise which ensures its benefit can be appropriated by the believer.⁷⁰

In the light of this understanding of the Christian life, it is not surprising that Luther maintained that the words of institution are in fact the critical element in the sacrament of the Lord's Supper. They are the clear promise of the one who gives himself for the forgiveness of sins. Without them genuine faith would be impossible. Without them there would be no sacrament:

> Everything depends, therefore, as I have said, upon the words of this sacrament. These are the words of Christ. Truly we should set them in pure gold and precious stones, keeping nothing more diligently before the eyes of our heart, so that faith may thereby be exercised.⁷¹

For Luther, faith in the clear promise of God finds a particular focus in the self-giving of Christ. It is Christ himself who uses the language of 'testament' in connection with the Supper, and the words of institution operate as the words of the testator whose gift is intimately connected to his death.⁷² If they are not clear then the gift cannot be received. Our claim to the gift is based upon the clear words of the testament:

---

[69] 'Ich entpfinde teglich bey myr, wie gar schwer es ist, langwerige gewissen, und mit menschlichen satzungen gefangen, ab tzulegen [...] Wie offt hatt meyn hertz getzappellt, mich gestrafft unnd myr furgeworffen yhr eynick sterckist argument: Du bist alleyn klug? Sollten die andern alle yrren unnd ßo eyn lange tzeytt geyrret haben? Wie, wenn du yrrest und ßo viel leutt ynn yrthum verfurest, wilche all ewiglich verdamnet wurden? Biß ßo lang, das mich Christus mit seynem eynigen gewissen wortt befestiget und bestettiget hat, das meyn gertz nicht mehr tzappellt, ßondern sich widder die argument der Papisten, als eyn steynen uffer widder die wellen, auff lenth, unnd yhr drawen und sturmen verlachet!' *Vom mißbrauch der Messen* (1521) *WA* VIII, 482.27-28, 482.32- 483.8 = *LW* 36, 134.

[70] *Vom mißbrauch der Messen* (1521) *WA* VIII, 483.20-126 = *LW* 36, 134.

[71] 'Drumb hab ich gesagt, es ligt alles an den worten dißes sacraments, die Christus sagt, die man furwar solt mit golt und eytel edel gesteyn fassenn unnd nichts fleyssiger fur den augen des hertzen habenn, den glaubenn dran tzu üben.' *Ein Sermon von dem neuen Testament, das ist von der heiligen Messe* (1520) *WA* VI, 360.29-32 = *LW* 35, 88.

[72] *Ein Sermon von dem neuen Testament, das ist von der heiligen Messe* (1520) *WA* VI, 359.13 = *LW* 35, 86.

Now here stands the text, stating clearly and lucidly that Christ gives his body to eat when he distributes the bread. On this we take our stand, and we also believe and teach that in the Supper we eat and take to ourselves Christ's body truly and physically.[73]

This connection of clear Scripture and the most basic contours of the Christian life helps to explain the emotion which regularly mars Luther's writing on the words of institution. He was convinced that his opponents were challenging the clarity of this promise and that by so doing they were undermining the fundamental structure of life under the Gospel of Christ. Luther explicitly identified the appeal to metaphor by Zwingli, Oecolampadius, and others as a sleight of hand which concealed the devil's long-held strategy of driving a wedge between the believer and the source of faith.[74]

Luther recognised the hand of the devil in any suggestion that Scripture is unclear or that its interpretation is uncertain. If this view was to prevail it would render meaningless any affirmation that the Scriptures represent the authoritative norm in Christian thought and practice.[75] Luther was certain that the devil's real objective was always to ensure 'that no one might be saved and persevere in the Christian truth'.[76] In order to accomplish this, the enemy would do all in his power to distract Christians from their only defence: 'the fortress (*das schlos*) of Scripture'. Whether by promoting preoccupation with external constraint and human tradition or a prolonged quarrelling and dissension over meaning which soon wearies all, Luther was convinced the devil 'resists and hinders at every point'. The only strategy in the face of this unrelenting attack is God himself, and a determined stand upon his promises. The word of God is the only 'sure, impregnable fortress we seek and desire'.[77] That is why all those who practise theology must be careful to support their arguments with

---

[73] 'Da stehet nu der spruch und lautet klar und helle, das Christus seinen leib gibt zu essen, da er das brod reicht. Darauff stehen, gleuben und leren wir auch, das man ym abendmal wahrhafftig und leiblich Christus leib isset und zu sich nymbt.' *Daß diese Worte Christi (Das ist mein Leib etc) noch fest stehen wider die Schwarmgeister* (1527) *WA* XXIII, 87.28-32 = *LW* 37, 28-29.

[74] *Daß diese Worte Christi (Das ist mein Leib etc) noch fest stehen wider die Schwarmgeister* (1527) *WA* XXIII, 64-73 = *LW*, 37, 13-18.

[75] Lønning, 'No Other Gospel', 233; McGrath, *Intellectual Origins*, 151-152.

[76] 'Wie kan er sich da drehen, schleiffen, lencken und wenden auff alle seyten und an allen enden sich sperren und ynn den weg legen, das ja niemand solle selig werden und bey der Christlichen warheit bleiben.' *Daß diese Worte Christi (Das ist mein Leib etc) noch fest stehen wider die Schwarmgeister* (1527) *WA*, XXIII, 65.11-14 = *LW*, 37, 13.

[77] 'Solche gewisse, unbetrieglische festung suchen und begern wyr.' *Vom mißbrauch der Messen* (1521) *WA* VIII, 483.25-26 = *LW* 36, 134.

'clear, sober passages from Scripture which the devil will not overthrow'.[78]

Luther argued that since Scripture is clear, it provides the church with a sure basis for bold and confident action. This connection between biblical teaching and church practice is particularly evident in the preface to Luther's sharp attack on the Roman tradition of whispering the canon of the mass. The lingering opposition in Wittenberg to changes in the practice of communion, in Luther's opinion, was due to a refusal to accept that his exposition was faithful to the clear teaching of Scripture on the matter. Worse still, it betrayed a cavalier attitude to the Scriptures themselves:

> For I fear that people still hold it to be true and do not believe that it is such an abomination as we say, else they would have a different attitude toward doing something about it [...] And I particularly lament that, although it is so clearly written and preached that they could easily read or hear it, yet they simply stop their ears and will neither hear nor see what is intolerable for them.[79]

In contrast, both in theological argument and the transformation of church practices, Luther repeatedly took his stand on the clear teaching of Scripture. He considered this to be the only appropriate response of the Christian. Accordingly, on the matter of distributing the sacrament in both kinds, Luther insisted that no ground could possibly be given to his opponents:

> For in this matter the text of the gospel is so clear that even the papists cannot deny that Christ instituted the sacrament in both kinds and gave them to all of the disciples. Therefore it is your duty, on pain of forfeiting your salvation, to let nobody deny or disfigure it.[80]

---

[78] 'dürre helle sprüche dar legen, die der teuffel nicht soll umbstossen' *Wider die himmlischen Propheten, von den Bildern und Sakrament* (1525) *WA* XVIII, 164.29-30 = *LW* 40, 175.

[79] 'Denn ich besorge, das mans noch fur wort halte, und nicht glewbe, das es eyn solcher grewel sey, wie wyr davon sagen, man würde sonst wol mit anderm ernst dazu thun [...] Nu klag ich das, weyl es so klerlich geschrieben und gepredigt ist, das sie es doch mochten lesen odder hören, sondern schlecht die oren zustopffen, wollens widder hören noch sehen, Wilchs yhn eyn unleydlich ding ist.' *Vom Greuel der stillmesse* (1525) *WA*, XVIII, 22.26-28, 22.31-34 = *LW*, 36, 312.

[80] 'Denn da ist der text des Euangeli ßo klar, das auch die Papisten nicht leucken kunden, das Christus beyder gestalt eynfetzt und gibt allen iungern. Darumb bistu schuldig bey deyner seel selickeyt, solchs nicht zu leucken oder schenden lassen' *Von beider Gestalt des Sakraments zu nehmen* (1522) *WA* X-II, 20.28-21.2 = *LW* 36, 245.

It is evident that Luther's convictions about the clarity of Scripture play an important role in his theology at these two critical points. It is also evident that the theological connections we have considered are pregnant with other associations, some of which Luther developed explicitly and others he simply presupposed without argument. Far from being an isolated and strictly polemical construct, *claritas scripturae* functions as a 'first principle' which could be surrendered only at the cost of the disintegration of his entire theology.[81] The theological significance of this concept might indeed have been highlighted by the arguments of Erasmus, but the evidence of Luther's own theological writing before and after *De servo arbitrio* takes us beyond that immediate context in ways which too often have been overlooked.

What is Clear?

We are now in a position to ask more specific questions about Luther's concept of *claritas scripturae*. The first of these concerns its referent: given that Luther repeatedly affirmed the clarity of Scripture, just what is it about Scripture or in Scripture that he considered clear? Did Luther himself explain what he meant?

Many modern studies of this concept warn against claiming too much under the heading of *claritas scripturae*. They point out that the carefully constructed theological systems of the next century are too easily read back into Luther's language. Inge Lønning presents most forcefully a conclusion endorsed by scholars from a variety of theological positions: Luther predicates clarity, not so much of the words themselves, nor even of the subject matter or meaning which is conveyed by the words in every instance. Rather, Luther has in mind the key teachings of Scripture.[82] This explains why Luther could concede the obscurity of certain parts of Scripture whilst continuing to maintain the clarity of Scripture.

The two sections of *De servo arbitrio* which deal with the clarity of Scripture are regularly cited in support of this conclusion. The first of these occurs early in Luther's review of the preface to *De libero arbitrio*.[83] In that preface Erasmus had argued that some Scripture contains mysteries so deep that pious readers can only echo Paul's doxology in Rom. 11:33. God has not desired that we should penetrate

---

[81] *De servo arbitrio* (1522) *WA* XVIII, 653.33-34 = *LW* 33, 91; Lønning, 'No Other Gospel', 233.

[82] Lønning, 'No Other Gospel', 233-234; Watson, *Let God Be God,* 149; Pannenberg, *Systematic Theology,* I, 29; Silva, *Church,* 81.

[83] *De servo arbitrio* (1525) *WA* XVIII, 606.1-609.14 = *LW* 33, 24-28.

more deeply the Corycian cave of Scripture, and our pious awe compels us to draw back.[84] Luther's response in *De servo arbitrio* was to draw a distinction between God himself, the object of Paul's doxology, and the Scripture:

> God and the Scripture of God are two things, no less than the Creator and the creature are two things. That in God there are many things hidden, of which we are ignorant, no one doubts [...] But that in Scripture some things are abstruse, and everything is not plain — this is an idea put about by the ungodly Sophists, with those lips you also speak here, Erasmus; but they have never produced, nor can they produce, a single article to prove this mad notion of theirs.[85]

Luther's line of argument is easy to follow: God and his ways might be inscrutable, but Scripture is abundantly clear. Our knowledge may not be exhaustive, but what is revealed is clearly known. Any assertion to the contrary was in fact a device of the Satan, whose goal was to frighten Christians from ever approaching the Scripture for themselves. Yet was Luther referring to the text itself, each and every word, or was he speaking more generally of the content of Scripture? Three lines later Luther appears to provide the answer to such questions:

> I admit, of course, that there are many texts in the Scriptures that are obscure and abstruse, not because of the majesty of their subject matter, but because of our ignorance of their vocabulary and grammar; but these texts in no way hinder a knowledge of all the subject matter of Scripture.[86]

Luther's focus was undeniably upon the subject matter of Scripture. 'Truly it is stupid and impious', he said a little later, 'when we know that the subject matter of Scripture has all been placed in the clearest light, to call it obscure on account of a few obscure words'.[87] However,

---

[84] *Erasmi Opera*, IX, 998 = Rupp and Watson, *Erasmus and Luther*, 38.

[85] 'Duae res sunt Deus et Scriptura Dei, non minus quam duae res sunt, Creator et creatura Dei. In Deo esse multa abscondita, quae ignoremus, nemo dubitat [...] Sed esse in scriptura quaedam abstrusa et non omnia exposita, invulgatum est quidem per impios Sophistas, quorum ore et tu loqueris hic Erasme, sed nunquam unum articulum produxerunt, nec producere possunt, quo suam hanc insaniam probarent.' *.De servo arbitrio* (1525) *WA* XVIII, 606.11-13, 606.16-19 = *LW* 33, 25.

[86] 'Hoc sane fateor, esse multa loca in scripturis obscura et abtrusa, non ob maiestatem rerum, sed ob ignorantiam vocabulorum et grammaticae, sed quae nihil impediant scientiam omnium rerum in scripturis.' *De servo arbitrio* (1525) *WA* XVIII, 606.22-24 = *LW* 33, 25.

[87] 'Stultum est vero et impium, scire, res scripturae esse omnes in luce positas clarissima, et propter pauca verba obscura' *De servo arbitrio* (1525) *WA* XVIII, 606.31-33 = *LW* 33, 26.

a number of qualifications must be made at this point. In the first place, the context remains Luther's determined opposition to Erasmus' suggestion that 'in Scripture some things are abstruse and everything is not plain'. Indeed, Luther's tone in this section, with its references to demonic scheming, blasphemous perversity, blindness, and indolence, is inexplicable if all he wished to do was affirm the clarity of the essential content of Scripture. After all, even Erasmus had been willing to concede that just as some parts of Scripture are secret and impenetrable, other parts are plainly evident.[88] If Luther's concern was the basic subject matter of Scripture and not the texts in which this subject matter is conveyed, then why did he oppose Erasmus in such strident terms? Was it simply that one of the subjects Erasmus considered unclear was for Luther 'the real issue' underlying the entire dispute with Rome?[89]

Secondly, when Luther did unambiguously address the details of the biblical texts (*loca in scripturis*), the only kind of obscurity he would admit was that which arises from a lack of familiarity on the part of the reader, not from a defect in the text itself. The illustration he provided, of an illuminated public fountain which is no less illuminated for the fact that it is not visible from a narrow side street, emphasised even further the location of the reader as a significant factor in the interpretive equation. However even here he found no final or insurmountable obstacle, for 'if the words are obscure in one place, they are clear in another'.[90]

Erasmus had sought, by his appeal to Rom. 11:33, to connect the obscurity of Scripture to the glorious inscrutability of God. He for one would not presume to explore the profound mysteries of God, which had, after all, generated so much controversy over the centuries. Luther on the other hand argued that the clarity or otherwise of Scripture has nothing to do with the profundity of the subject matter. Nor does it require that the subject matter be explained in every detail. At some points Scripture simply confesses divine truth without reason or explanation, but when it does so, it does so clearly. Luther cited the very examples Erasmus had used to support his contention that Scripture is obscure:

> Scripture simply confesses the trinity of God and the humanity of Christ and the unforgivable sin, and there is nothing here of

---

[88] Erasmus included amongst the evident portions of Scripture 'the precepts for the good life (*bene uiuendi praecepta*)'. *Erasmi Opera*, IX, 998 = Rupp and Watson, *Erasmus and Luther*, 40.

[89] *De servo arbitrio* (1525) *WA* XVIII, 786.26-27 = *LW* 33, 294.

[90] 'Si uno loco obscura sunt verba, at alio sunt clara.' *De servo arbitrio* (1525) *WA* XVIII, 606.33-34 = *LW* 33, 26.

> obscurity or ambiguity. But *how* these things can be, Scripture does not say (as you imagine), nor is it necessary to know.[91]

It was not the confession of these truths which was unclear, Luther insisted. Rather, it was the scholastic attempt to go beyond this Scriptural confession and to explain the processes involved, which had brought about the dissension Erasmus so deplored and was seeking to avoid.

The second, later passage from *De servo arbitrio* added further depth to Luther's exposition of the clarity of Scripture.[92] Luther began by rehearsing Erasmus' scepticism, and in particular his appeal to learned and godly authorities on both sides of the question they were debating. These authorities, in turn, all seemed to appeal to Scripture. Yet if this was the case, how could one maintain the clarity of the Scriptures and their final authority in issues such as this?

> What, then, are we to do? The Church is hidden, the saints are unknown. What and whom are we to believe? Or, as you very pointedly argue, who gives us certainty? How shall we prove the Spirit? If you look for learning, on both sides there are scholars; if for quality of life, on both sides are sinners; if for Scripture, both sides acknowledge it. But the dispute is not so much about Scripture which may not yet be sufficiently clear, as about the meaning of Scripture; and on both sides are men, of whom neither numbers nor learning nor dignity, much less fewness, ignorance, and humility, have anything to do with the case. The matter therefore remains in doubt and the case is still *sub judice,* so that it looks as if we might be wise to adopt the position of the Sceptics, unless the line you take is best, when you express your uncertainty in such a way as to aver that you are seeking to learn the truth, though in the meantime you incline to the side that asserts free choice, until the truth becomes clear.[93]

---

[91] 'Scriptura simpliciter confitetur trinitatem Dei et humanitatem Christi et peccatum irremissibile. Nihil hic obscuritatis aut ambiguitatis. Quibus vero modis ista habeant, Scriptura non dicit, ut tu fingis, nec opus est nosse.' *De servo arbitrio* (1525) *WA* XVIII, 608.5-8 = *LW* 33, 28.

[92] *De servo arbitrio* (1525) *WA* XVIII, 652.23-659.33 = *LW* 33, 89-100.

[93] 'Quid igitur faciemus? Abscondita est Ecclesia, latent sancti. Quid? Cui credemus? Seu ut tu argutissime disputas: Quis nos certos facit? Unde explorabimus spiritum? Si eruditionem spectes, utrinque sunt Rabini, Sin vitam, utrinque peccatores, Sin scripturam, utrique amplectuntur. Neque adeo de scriptura, quae necdum sit lucida satis, sed de sensu scripturae disputatur, utrinque vero homines, quorum ut neque multitudo, neque eruditio, neque dignitas quicquam facit ad causam, ita multo minus pacucitas, inscitia et humilitas. Relinquitur igitur res in dubio et manet sub iudice lis, ut prudenter

It was Erasmus, rather than Luther, who insisted that their debate was not about Scripture but about the meaning of Scripture. At this point in his treatise Luther was not prepared to endorse the distinction. He listed the passages which speak of Scripture as 'a most certain and evident light'. He cited the practice of Christ and the apostles: their appeal to Old Testament Scripture presupposed its clarity. Yet Luther knew only too well that an affirmation of the clarity of Scripture is meaningless in abstraction. Such clarity makes sense only in relationship to the meaning or subject matter of Scripture. As for the controversies of history and the distribution of learned and godly men on both sides in almost every case, Luther was not at all dismayed:

> It is therefore not astonishing that in divine things men of outstanding talent through so many centuries have been blind. In human things it would be astonishing. In divine things the wonder is rather if there are one or two who are not blind, but it is no wonder if all without exception are blind.[94]

This later section of *De servo arbitrio* provides us with more than simply a repetition of Luther's earlier argument. Luther here introduced two new elements which require attention. The first of these is the relationship between the clarity of Scripture and the purpose of Scripture. Luther's paraphrase of the introduction to *De libero arbitrio* included the claim that Scripture might not yet be 'sufficiently clear'.[95] The line of argument pursued by Erasmus did seem to make a simple affirmation of Scripture's clarity problematic. Are there in fact degrees of *claritas*? If Scripture is clear, is it sufficiently clear to achieve its purpose? Whatever else might be said about Scripture, it was obvious to Erasmus that it was not clear enough to prevent appeal to it by both sides of the debate about free will. Erasmus' challenge enabled Luther to develop his own arguments. Not only does Scripture have a central meaning which is crucial for any affirmation of its clarity, but it also has a purpose which provides other critical parameters for such an

---

facturi vedeamur, si in Scepticorum sententiam concedamus. Nisi quod tu omnium optime facis, qui sic te dubitare dicis, ut veritatem quaerere te et discere testeris, interim in eam partem inclinans, quae liberum arbitrium asserit, donec veritas elucescat.' *De servo arbitrio* (1525) *WA* XVIII, 652.23-34 = *LW* 33, 89.

[94] 'Proinde non est hoc mirum in rebus divinis, quod tot saeculis viri excellentes ingenio caecutiunt, in rebus humanis mirum esset. In rebus divinis mirum potius, si unus et alter non caecutiat; Non mirum vero, si plane omnes caecutiant.' *De servo arbitrio* (1525) *WA* XVIII, 659.3-6 = *LW* 33, 98.

[95] 'de scriptura, quae necdum sit lucida satis' *De servo arbitrio* (1525) *WA* XVIII, 652.27 = *LW* 33, 89.

affirmation. Luther then went on to focus attention on the soteriological purpose of Scripture:

> For it ought above all to be settled and established among Christians that the Holy Scriptures are a spiritual light far brighter than the sun itself, especially in the things that are necessary to salvation.[96]

If the clarity of Scripture could not be considered in isolation from the purpose of Scripture, Luther here suggested that the purpose of Scripture could not be considered apart from 'those things which are necessary to salvation'.[97] The focus of the biblical texts on the person and work of Jesus Christ ensured the prominence of the soteriological dimension of Scripture. For Luther, the most important goal of biblical study and proclamation was an apprehension of what is necessary for salvation and to that end Scripture is perfectly clear, for all genuine Scripture promotes Christ (*Christum treiben*). In Luther's thinking, that which is necessary for salvation is Jesus Christ himself, whom we embrace by faith. The essential task of Scripture, therefore, is to present Christ to us.[98] This is the sense in which Luther had connected the clarity of Scripture and its presentation of Christ earlier in this treatise:

> For what still sublimer thing can remain hidden in the Scriptures, now that the seals have been broken, the stone rolled from the door of the sepulchre, and the supreme mystery brought to light, namely, that Christ the Son of God has been made man, that God is three and one, that Christ has suffered for us and is to reign eternally? Are not these things known and sung even in the highways and byways? Take Christ out of the Scriptures and what will you find left in them?[99]

The Scripture is sufficiently clear to achieve its primary purpose: to point us to Christ.

---

[96] 'Nam id oportet apud Christianos esse imprimis ratum atque firmissimum, Scripturas sanctas esse lucem spiritualem, ipso sole longe clariorem, praesertim in iis quae pertinent ad salutem vel necessitatem. *De servo arbitrio* (1525) *WA* XVIII, 653.28-31 = *LW* 33, 91.

[97] cf. *Rationis Latomianae confutatio* (1521) *WA* VIII, 99.20-21 = *LW* 32, 217.

[98] Beisser, *Claritas Scripturae,* 81.

[99] 'Quid enim potest in scripturis augustius latere reliquum, postquam fractis signaculis et voluto ab hostio sepulchri lapide, illud summum mysterium proditum est, Christum filium Dei factum hominem, Esse Deum trinum et unum, Christum pro nobis passum et regnaturum aeternaliter? Nonne haec etiam in biviis sunt nota et cantata? Tolle Christum e scripturis, quid amplius in illis invenies?' *De servo arbitrio* (1525) *WA* XVIII, 606.24-29 = *LW* 33, 25-26.

The second new element introduced at this point is Luther's own explanation of the role of the church in the task of biblical interpretation. The clarity of Scripture did not imply that everyone was free to 'subject the Scriptures to the interpretation of their own spirit'. Luther alluded to his ongoing battle with the *Phanatici* (*Schwärmer*) on precisely this issue.[100] Their radical individualism had often led to idiosyncratic interpretations of Scripture, and Luther abhorred both the attitude and its result.[101] Instead, Luther argued that all proper interpretation of the Bible and all theological exposition must be aware of its context. Everything was to be tested and two types of judgement were required. The first, an internal judgement, is in fact the discernment of the Holy Spirit given to all who believe. This corresponds to Luther's 'internal clarity of Scripture' and involves a personal consent to the truth.[102] However the second, the external judgement, corresponding to Luther's 'external clarity of Scripture', is that which 'belongs to the public ministry of the Word and to the outward office, and is chiefly the concern of the leaders and the preachers of the Word'.[103] Luther did not consider this a retreat from his trenchant criticism of the Catholic claim that the Church, in the person of the Pope, provided the authoritative interpretation of Scripture. He remained implacably opposed to any suggestion that Scripture stood in need of ecclesiastical sanction or clarification. However, as he had argued back in 1520, 'a Christian lives not in himself, but in Christ and in his neighbour. Otherwise he is not a Christian. He lives in Christ through faith, in his neighbour through love'.[104] This twofold context applies even, perhaps especially, to Christian teaching. Though it might be necessary to oppose the generally accepted teaching on a particular subject, especially if it can

---

[100] 'Nam satis acre mihi bellum isto anno fuit et adhuc est cum istis Phanaticis, qui scripturas suo spiritui subiiciunt interpretandas' *De servo arbitrio* (1525) *WA* XVIII, 653.3-4 = *LW* 33, 90; cf. *Acta Augustana* (1518) *WA* II, 17.5-9 = *LW* 31, 276.

[101] Neuner and Schröger, 'Klarheit', 51, 53-56.

[102] *De servo arbitrio* (1525) *WA* XVIII, 653.14-19 = *LW* 33, 90.

[103] 'Hoc iudicium est publici ministerii in verbo et officii externi et maxime pertinet ad duces et praecones verbi.' *De servo arbitrio* (1525) *WA* XVIII, 653.24-25 = *LW* 33, 91; Hermann, 'Klarheit', 189.

[104] 'Christianum hominem non vivere in seipso, sed in Christo et proximo suo, aut Christianum non esse, in Christo per fidem, in proximo per charitatem' *Tractatus de libertate christiana* (1520) *WA* VII, 69.12-14 = *LW* 31, 371. Compare the German text: 'eyn Christen mensch lebt nit ynn yhm selb, sondern ynn Christo und seynem nehstenn, ynn Christo durch den glauben, ym nehsten durch die liebe. *Von der Freiheit eines Christenmenschen* (1520) *WA* VII, 38.6-8.

be shown to be a deviation from the teaching of Scripture, such a position should never be adopted in a cavalier fashion. Human reflection upon the Scriptures might not be authoritative in the way the Scriptures themselves are, but neither is it totally irrelevant. Luther presented his carefully worded conclusion on this matter to Erasmus: 'all spirits are to be tested by Scripture in the presence of the Church'.[105]

The suggestion that Luther predicates clarity only of the key teachings of Scripture must be modified in the light of this evidence from *De servo arbitrio*. Luther is indeed concerned with the content or subject matter of Scripture but this is not as easy to separate from the text in and by which it is conveyed as many scholars appear to suggest.[106] Further, the purpose of Scripture (to proclaim salvation in Christ) and the role of the church (to operate as the context in which the study of Scripture is properly undertaken) provide important parts of a framework which is necessary to make any affirmation of the clarity of the text itself intelligible.

However, as we have seen, the evidence of *De servo arbitrio* is not the only work in which Luther addresses the issue of Scripture's clarity. A wider exploration of the concept in Luther's writings both confirms and deepens the connection between the content of Scripture and the text of Scripture. It allows us to take seriously Luther's interest in the context, the grammar, and the precise words used, and to encounter his willingness to speak of *claritas scripturae* extending to this level as well.

Luther's earliest use of the terminology of clarity, in the comment we have already examined from the *Dictata,* was used with reference to certain passages in the Scriptures.[107] However, as Luther does not develop the idea any further at this point we must be cautious about inferring too much from this reference. In the midst of the excommunication crisis in 1520, Luther's *Assertio omnium articulorum* spoke of Scripture as the divine words which are themselves the first principles of Christians. He went on to insist that these divine words are 'clearer and more certain than all the words of

---

[105] 'Scriptura iudice omnes spiritus in facie Ecclesiae esse probandos.' *De servo arbitrio* (1525) *WA* XVIII, 653.28 = *LW* 33, 91.

[106] Erling Teigen's distinction between propositions and statements does not solve the problem. What other access is there to the meaning of Scripture than the words of Scripture? Teigen, 'Clarity', 150-151.

[107] '[A]liquos passus in scripturis' *Dictata super Psalterium* (1513-15) *WA* LV-II, 112.18-20 = *LW* 10, 99.

men'.[108] A year later, in his reply to Emser, Luther maintained the clarity of 'the Scripture without any glosses'.[109] That same year he reminded Latomus of 'the most clear and accessible testimonies of Scripture', going on to declare that 'the Scriptures are common to all and clear enough with respect to what is necessary to salvation and also obscure enough for inquiring minds'.[110] However in his sermon on Ps. 37, also from 1521, Luther could say both that 'on earth no clearer book has been written than the Holy Scriptures', and that the same truth which hides behind 'a dark passage of Scripture' inevitably shines out clearly in other places.[111]

These early references to the clarity of Scripture, the latest still four years before the appearance of *De servo arbitrio,* reveal that Luther could speak of the clarity of Scripture in a variety of ways. If on occasion the expression referred in a more general sense to the doctrine taught in Scripture, on others Luther seemed to focus more specifically on the text of Scripture itself. Nevertheless, there is no necessary tension between the two. In fact, in the *Kirchenpostille* Luther himself provided an insight into how these two ways of speaking about Scripture's clarity might be related:

> Prefigurations and interpretations are not enough on which to lay the foundations of the faith; the foundation must be laid by means of clear Scripture, understood according to the sound and meaning of the words. Then, after such words and foundation of faith, such interpretations of the narratives must be built upon the faith, which is nourished and strengthened in this manner.[112]

---

[108] 'verba divina esse apertiora et certiora omnium hominum' *Assertio omnium articulorum M. Lutheri per bullam Leonis X. novissimam damnatorum* (1520) *WA* VII, 98.11.

[109] 'Drumb ist zu wissen, daas die schrifft on alle glose ist die sonne und gantzis licht, von wilcher alle lerer yhr licht empfahen, und nit widderumb.' *Auf das überchristlich, übergeistlich und überkünstlich Buch Emsers zu Leipzig Antwort* (1521) *WA* VII, 639.1-2 = *LW* 39, 164.

[110] 'Quid enim faciunt et patres, quam ut clarissima et apertissima scripturae testimonia quaerant et proferant? [...] Scripturae omnibus communes sunt, satis apertae, quantum oportet pro salute, satis etiam obscurae pro contemplatricibus animabus.' *Rationis Latomianae confutatio* (1521) *WA* VIII, 99.17-18, 99.20-21 = *LW* 32, 217.

[111] 'auff erden keyn klerer buch geschrieben denn die heyligen schrifft [...] Alßo, ist ein tunckel spruch yn der schrifft, ßo zweyffelt nur nit, es ist gewiszlich die selbe warheit dahinden, die am andern ort klar ist, und wer das tunckell nit vorstehen kan, der bleyb bey dem liechten.' *Der 36. (37.) Psalm Davids* (1521) *WA* VIII, 236.9, 239.19-21.

[112] 'Denn figurn und deuttungen sind nit gnug den glawben tzu grunden, er muß tzuuor gegrundett seyn mit klarer schrifft, eynfeltiglich vorstanden nach lautt

The emphasis on the sound (*Laut*) as well as the meaning (*Meinung*) of the words, is instructive. Grasping the meaning of Scripture is undeniably important for Luther; however, it is not possible to arrive at that meaning without the words by which it is conveyed, and the words remain significant even after the meaning has been grasped. Clear Scripture (*klare Schrift*) therefore implies clear words (*klare Worte*). Hence in a sermon from around the same period (25 July 1522), Luther called on his congregation not to believe anything unless it had been proved 'with clear texts from the Bible'.[113]

It is, however, in his treatises and sermons on the Lord's Supper that Luther most directly associated the clarity of Scripture with the concrete form of the biblical text. Over more than ten years Luther repeatedly mounted arguments based upon the precise words, and indeed the order of those words, in particular passages of Scripture.[114] Just as the Word of God comes to us in the shape of promises, so too, Luther insisted, the promises come to us in the form of precise words with which we are not at liberty to tamper. Indeed, some of Luther's strongest invective was reserved for those who deviated 'from the words as they stand' or 'from the order in which they stand'.[115]

An early example is Luther's *De Captivitate Babylonica Ecclesiae* of 1520. In this treatise against the sacramental practice of the church of Rome, Luther pointedly remarked upon the careless attention Alveld had given to the words of 1 Cor. 11 in his defence of communion in one kind only:

> Here again our brilliant distinguisher of kinds, treating the Scriptures with his usual brilliance, teaches that Paul permitted, but did not deliver, the use of both kinds [...] according to a new kind of grammar, 'I have received from the Lord' means the same as 'it is permitted by the Lord', and 'I delivered to you' is the same as 'I have permitted you'. I pray you, mark this well. For by this method

---

und meynung der wortt. Und alsdenn, nach solchen worttenn und grund des glawbens, sind solch deuttung der geschicht auff den glawben zu pawen und yhn damit begiffen und stercken.' *Kirchenpostille* (1522) *WA* X-I/1, 417.12-16 = *LW* 52, 127.

[113] 'Das ist dann sein, wenn sich die schrifft selbs außlegt, darumb glaubt nit und haltet frey für finster was nit beweret wirdt mit klaren sprüchen der Biblien.' *Predigt am Jakobstage* (25 July 1522) *WA* X-III, 238.10-12.

[114] David C. Steinmetz, 'Scripture and the Lord's Supper in Luther's Theology', *Int.* 37 (1983), 253.

[115] 'Wo die heylige schrifft ettwas gründet zu gleuben, da soll man nicht weichen von den worten, wie sie lautten, noch von der ordnunge, wie sie da stehet.' *Wider die himmlischen Propheten, von den Bildern und Sakrament* (1525) *WA* XVIII, 147.23-25 = *LW* 40, 157.

An Intelligible Text? 223

not only the church, but any worthless fellow, will be at liberty, according to this master, to turn all the universal commands, institutions, and ordinances of Christ and the apostles into mere permission.[116]

Luther was convinced that the words of Scripture are not infinitely flexible. Of course their meaning in any particular case was determined to a large extent by their context. However, once placed in such a context, Luther took them to have a definite meaning which could be discerned and must be respected. That is why in a later treatise on this subject he repeatedly spoke of 'clear words (*die hellen wort / die klaren wort*)' as well as 'a lucid, clear text (*ein heller, klarer text*)'.[117] Yet even as early as *De Captivitate* he had spelt out the interpretive principle which follows from this determination to give due weight to the words themselves in their context:

> But there are good grounds for my view, and this above all — no violence is to be done to the words of God, whether by man or angel. They are to be retained in their simplest meaning as far as possible. Unless the context manifestly compels it, they are not to be understood apart from their grammatical and proper sense, lest we give our adversaries occasion to make a mockery of all the Scriptures.[118]

On occasion Luther would contrast the words actually used in a given passage with those which would have been necessary if it really taught the things his opponents claimed. This device was intended to draw attention to the precise words of Scripture, and prevent recourse to a

---

[116] 'Hic iterum noster speciator, sicut ubique scripturas egregie tractans docet, Paulum ibidem permisisse utranque speciem, non tradidisse [...] deinde quod nova grammatica "Accepi a domino" idem sit quod "permissum est a domino", et "tradidi vobis" id est "permisi vobis". Hoc, rogo insigniter nota. Nam hinc non modo Ecclesiae, sed cuilibet passim nebuloni licebit, hoc magistro, permissionem facere ex universis praeceptis, institutis, ordinationibus Christi et Apostolorum.' *De captivitate Babylonica ecclesiae praeludium* (1520) *WA* VI, 500.21-23, 500.28-32 = *LW* 36, 16.

[117] *Daß diese Worte Christi (Das ist mein Leib etc) noch fest stehen wider die Schwarmgeister* (1527) *WA* XXIII, 225.1-18 = *LW* 37, 112-113; cf. *Vom Abendmahl Christi. Bekenntnis.* (1528) *WA* XXVI, 487.12-18 = *LW* 37, 348.

[118] 'Est autem meae sententiae ratio magna, imprimis illa, quod verbis divinis non est ulla facienda vis, neque per hominem neque per angelum, sed quantum fieri potest in simplicissima significatione servanda sunt, et nisi manifesta circumstantia cogat, extra grammaticam et propriam accipienda non sunt, ne detur adversariis occasio universam scripturam eludendi.' *De captivitate Babylonica ecclesiae praeludium* (1520) *WA* VI, 509.8-12 = *LW* 36, 30.

more general exposition. One of the best examples of this kind of argument is found in Luther's treatise against Karlstadt in early 1525:

> Why does [Paul] not put it thus: 'Whoever unworthily eats this bread is guilty of profaning the blood of the Lord. Whoever unworthily drinks of this cup is guilty of profaning the body of the Lord.'? If Dr. Karlstadt's meaning were correct, one of the two would be enough. Indeed, it would be sufficient if he had said, 'Who eats and drinks unworthily is guilty of profaning Christ or the death of Christ', since Dr Karlstadt interprets the sin of unworthy eating to be that one does not rightly honor and observe the suffering and death of Christ. But inasmuch as Paul makes the unworthy drinking of the cup to mean the same as profaning the blood, and the unworthy eating of the bread to mean the same as profaning the body, the clear, natural sense of the words is that the body is in the eating, and the blood is in the drinking. And no one can produce an argument to the contrary which has any show of validity.[119]

Luther insisted that there was a natural reading of the text which ought always to be preferred.[120] He explicitly grounded this approach in the character of God, for he was convinced that it was God who has given us the text of Scripture. He told Emser in 1521 that 'the Holy Spirit is the simplest writer and speaker in heaven and on earth. This is why his words can have no more than the one simplest meaning which we call the written one, or the literal meaning of the tongue'.[121] Later that same year he warned Latomus, 'a man ought not to presume that he speaks

---

[119] 'Warumb setzt ers nicht also: Wer unwirdig isset dis brod, der iest schuldig am blut des HERrn. Wer unwirdig trinckt von diesem kilch, der ist schuldig am leybe des HERrn? Syntemal der beyder eyns were gnug gewesen, das D. Carlstads meynung bestünde. Ja es were gnug gewesen, wenn er hette gesagt, Wer unwirdig isst und trinckt, der ist schuldig an Christo odder am tod Christi, weyl D. Carlstad durchs unwirdige essen die sünde versteht, das man Christus leyden und tod nicht recht ehre und ube x. Nu aber weil Paulus die schuld am blut, so eben auffs unwirdige trincken des kilchs, und die schuld am leybe, auffs unwirdige essen des brods treybt, zwingt die natürlich helle rede, das der leyb ym essen, und das blut ym trincken sey, Und kan niemant dawidder grund auff bringen, der eynigen scheyn habe.' *Wider die himmlischen Propheten, von den Bildern und Sakrament* (1525) *WA* XVIII, 174.36-175.8 = *LW* 40, 184.

[120] Ebeling, *Evangelienauslegung,* 413.

[121] 'Der heilig geist ist der aller einfeltigst schreiber und rether, der inn hymell und erden ist, drumb auch sehne wortt nit mehr denn einen enfeltigsten synn haben kunden, wilchen wir den schrifflichen odder buchstabischen tzungen synn nennen.' *Auf das überchristlich, übergeistlich und überkünstlich Buch Emsers zu Leipzig Antwort* (1521) *WA* VII, 650.21-24 = *LW* 39, 178.

more safely or clearly with his mouth than God spoke with his mouth'.[122]

Luther's affirmation of the clarity of the words of Scripture extended to the order of those words, that is to grammar and syntax. This concern for grammar is evident in the 1527/8 exchange between Luther and Zwingli. In his *Daß diese Worte 'Das ist mein Leib' etc. ewiglich den alten Sinn haben werden etc.*, Zwingli had taken exception to the way Luther translated Jn. 6:63. As we noted in an earlier chapter, Luther had rendered ἡ σὰρξ οὐκ ὠφελεῖ οὐδέν as *Fleisch ist kein nütze* (Flesh is of no avail), omitting the article. Zwingli insisted on the article, and further, he construed it with demonstrative force: 'This very flesh is of no avail'.[123] In this way, according to Zwingli, Christ himself pointed believers away from a physical understanding of eating his flesh and drinking his blood. In *Vom Abendmahl Christi. Bekenntnis, 1528* Luther took up the point:

> Now this spirit must acknowledge that in this passage, 'The flesh is of no avail', there is no pronoun but an article. Yet he makes a pronoun out of it not only in the translation, where he says *das* is equivalent to *eben das,* 'precisely this', but also in his interpretation that in this passage 'the same flesh' is referred to as that of which Christ had previously spoken, 'My flesh is food indeed'. Here, then, he demonstrates that he falsifies the Word of God and treats the common people shamelessly. For an article never refers to an antecedent or to particular objects, as a pronoun does, but merely indicates things in general, which could be equally well understood if the article were omitted, though the style would not be so nice and elegant. Therefore it is impossible according to the rules of grammar that 'flesh' here should mean Christ's flesh in particular, to which he had previously referred. It must mean flesh in general, and we could with perfect propriety speak of it without the article, namely thus: 'Flesh is of no avail'.[124]

---

[122] 'Scripturae enim sinceritas custodienda est, nec praesumat homo suo ore eloqui, aut clarius aut securius, quam deus elocutus est ore suo.' *Rationis Latomianae confutatio* (1521) *WA* VIII, 118.4-5 = *LW* 32, 244.

[123] '"Das fleysch ist ghein nütz" den sinn habend, eben das fleysch, davon die hörenden murretend, ist gar ghein nütz ze essen' Huldrych Zwingli, *Das dise wort Iesu Christi: "Das ist min Lychnam, der für üch hinggeben wirt", ewiglich den alten eynigen sinn haben werdend* (1527) *CR*, XCII, 967.19-22

[124] 'Weil nu dieser geist bekennen mus das hie kein Pronomen sondern ein artickel stehet (Das fleisch ist kein nutze) und er dochein pronomen draus macht nicht allein mit dem Dolmetschen da er spricht (Das) vermuge so viel als (Eben das) sondern auch mit der auslegüng [da er sagt] das an dem ort dasselbige fleisch solle heissen davon Christo droben geredt hat (Mein fleisch ist die rechte

This reference to the rules of grammar was in effect simply another form of the appeal to the plain meaning of the words. It was Luther's answer to the side-stepping of that plain meaning which, he believed, was involved both in the Roman teaching about transubstantiation and the spiritual interpretations of the Supper by the Swiss. He was thoroughly convinced that without constraint by the ordinary rules of grammar there could be no certainty of interpretation. He made precisely this point when he described Alveld as an Aristotelian theologian 'for whom nouns and verbs when interchanged mean the same thing and any thing'.[125] However, Luther also recognised the limitations of grammar, remarking that 'something higher than the rules of grammar must always be present when the grounding of faith is concerned'.[126] Therefore, while it remained important, grammatical detail alone was not enough to establish Christian doctrine.

In the debates with Karlstadt, one of the arguments actually concerned the punctuation of the Greek text. Karlstadt had insisted that the expression 'this is my body' stands independently of the command 'take and eat', the separation being indicated by a period and a capital letter.[127] Luther responded by appealing to the order of the words over and against the human conventions of punctuation marks and capital letters:

> Suppose my book had no periods or capitals and yours had both. Our faith might come to depend on ink and pen, and even on the disposition of writer and printer. That would be a fine foundation! To put it briefly, we must have sober, lucid words and texts which by

---

speise) so bezeuget er hie mit selbs das er Gotts wort verfelsschet und bubisch mit den einfeltigen umbgehet Denn ein artickel nymer mehr von vorigem odder sonderlichem dinge redet wie ein pronomen sondern frey dahin ynn gemein davon redet das mans gleich so wol verstehen kan wo man on artickel davon redet obs gleich nicht so wol und sein lautet. Dar umb ists ummuglich nach der grammatica das hie fleisch muge Christus fleisch ynn sonderheit heissen davon er droben zuvor redet sondern müs ynn gemein hin fleisch heissen also das man davon auchwol on artickel kondte reden nemlich also fleisch ist kein nütze.' *Vom Abendmahl Christi. Bekenntnis* (1528) *WA* XXVI, 363.11-364.7 = *LW* 37, 243.

[125] 'Est enim Theologus Anaxagoricus, immo Aristotelicus, cui nomina et verba transposita eadem et omnia significant.' *De captivitate Babylonica ecclesiae praeludium* (1520) *WA* VI, 500.13-14 = *LW* 36, 16.

[126] 'Es mus alles ettwas höhers seyn, denn regule grammatice sind, was den glauben soll gründen' *Wider die himmlischen Propheten, von den Bildern und Sakrament* (1525) *WA* XVIII, 157.23-24, 157.29-30 = *LW* 40, 167.

[127] Andreas Bodenstein (von Karlstadt), *Dialogus oder ein Gesprächbüchlein von dem greulichen und abgöttischen Missbrauch des hochwürdigen Sakraments Jesu Christi, 1524* (Autographa Reformatorum: Tract. Luther XXXV, p. 147).

reason of their clarity are convincing, regardless of whether they are written with capital or small letters, with or without punctuation. For even if it were true (which it is not) that a period and capital indicated something new, should it follow in regard to Holy Scripture that my faith should rest not on expressions and words alone but on frail periods and capitals which really say or sing nothing? That would indeed be a false foundation.[128]

Luther, obviously, was aware of the secondary nature of the punctuation marks in the original text. In isolation, then, they are a shaky basis for proper interpretation. In contrast, Luther concentrated on the words and the natural grammatical and syntactical relationships between the words.

The evidence will not, therefore, support any suggestion that Luther's concept of *claritas Scripturae* only attaches to 'the essential content of Scripture (*der wesentliche Inhalt der Schrift*)', understood as 'such Christian dogmas or articles of the faith as the Trinity, the incarnation, and the saving work of Christ'.[129] Nor is it true to the evidence to say that Luther believed Scripture is clear only in so far as it affirms Christ,[130] or provides an understanding of the salvific gospel.[131] He was undoubtedly concerned about the doctrinal content of Scripture and he continued to maintain that the determinative centre of Scripture is the person and saving work of Jesus Christ. However, when all of Luther's work is taken into account, it becomes obvious that he also considered the very words of the text, understood naturally and in terms of their context, to be clear (*klar*) and lucid (*hell*). Indeed, Luther was willing to express his commitment to the particularities of the eucharistic texts in the strongest possible terms: 'we want the text

---

[128] 'Wie wenn meyn buch keynen punct noch grossen buchstaben hette, und deyn buch hettes beydes. So höre ich wol, unser glaube stünde auff der dinten und feddern, ja auff dem guten willen der schreyber und drucker, Ey da stünde er feyn, Wyr sagen und wöllens auch kurtz umb haben, Es sollen dürre, helle sprüche und text da seyn, die mit klarem verstand uns zwingen, Gott gebe, es sey mit grossen odder kleynen buchstaben, mit puncten odder on puncten geschrieben, Denn obs gleych bey den menschen den stich hielte, das punct und grosser buchstabe eyn newes mechten (wie es doch nicht thut), sollt drumb ynn der heyligen schrifft auch also meyn glaube on alle sprüche und wort alleyne auff eym ammechtigen punct und buchstaben stehen, der doch nichts saget noch finget? So stünde er ja auff eym peltz ermel.' *Wider die himmlischen Propheten, von den Bildern und Sakrament* (1525) *WA* XVIII, 148.17-149.2 = *LW* 40, 158-59.

[129] Pannenberg, *Systematic Theology*, I, 29-30.

[130] Beisser, *Claritas Scripturae*, 81.

[131] R. F. Surburg, 'The Significance of Luther's Hermeneutics for the Protestant Reformation', *CTM* 24 (1953), 253; Ruokanen, *Doctrina Divinitus*, 104.

of the Supper to be unambiguous, simple, sure, and certain in every word, syllable, and letter'.[132]

Two Types of Clarity

The second important question concerns the meaning of the term 'clarity' itself.[133] What exactly was Luther saying about Scripture? How could an affirmation of its 'clarity' be meaningful in the light of continued disagreement about the meaning of individual texts and the simple observation that not every church-going person was illuminated when they heard Scripture read or preached? In answering these questions it is necessary to develop the comments we have already made concerning Luther's view of the two-fold nature of *claritas scripturae*. While Luther addressed this distinction most directly in *De servo arbitrio*, it involves ideas that can be found elsewhere in his writing as well.

The earlier of the two sections in *De servo arbitrio* which deal directly with the clarity of Scripture includes Luther's programmatic summary: 'To put it briefly, the clarity of Scripture is two-fold, just as its obscurity is two-fold: one external and related to the ministry of the Word, the other located in the understanding of the heart'.[134] The first thing to note here is that Luther does not develop the reference to a two-fold obscurity of Scripture in the explicit way he does his reference to a two-fold clarity. It may indeed be possible to suggest what he had in mind from his comments about the darkened human heart,[135] the absence of the Spirit of God,[136] a lack of familiarity with

---

[132] 'Aber den text ym abendmal wöllen wir eynerley, einfeltig, gewis und sicher haben ynn allen worten, syllaben und buchstaben.' *Vom Abendmahl Christi. Bekenntnis.* (1528) *WA* XXVI, 265.29-30 = *LW*, 37, 167.

[133] Without doubt the most thorough, helpful, and generally reliable exploration of this question is found in Friedrich Beisser's *Claritas Scripturae bei Martin Luther*. However, Beisser's study is marred by an undefended assumption that Luther consistently distinguished between Scripture and the Word of God. At a number of points this leads him to overstate his case. For examples see Beisser, *Claritas Scripturae*, 83, 87, 92.

[134] 'Et ut breviter dicam, Duplex et claritas scripturae, sicut et duplex obscuritas, Una externa in verbi ministerio posita, altera in cordis cognitione sita.' *De servo arbitrio* (1525) *WA* XVIII, 609.4-5 = *LW* 33, 28.

[135] '[O]mnes habent obscuratum cor' *De servo arbitrio* (1525) *WA* XVIII, 609.7 = *LW* 33, 28.

[136] 'nisi qui spiritum Dei habet' *De servo arbitrio* (1525) *WA* XVIII, 609.6-7 = *LW* 33, 28.

An Intelligible Text? 229

the grammar and vocabulary of the text,[137] and the malice of the Satan,[138] but these comments were not drawn together by Luther to form the counterparts to the external and internal clarity of Scripture. His focus was most definitely on clarity rather than obscurity. Nevertheless, it is somewhat striking that nowhere in this treatise does he admit an obscurity pertaining to the text of Scripture as such. The problem always lies elsewhere.

A second observation to be made at this point is that Luther's distinction cannot be explained solely in terms of the objective and subjective elements of human understanding.[139] Nor is it accurate simply to describe the external clarity of Scripture as a natural property of the text and the internal clarity of Scripture as a supernatural work of the Spirit of God.[140] The problem with both of these approaches should be obvious in the light of our findings so far. Both begin with the wrong point of reference. For Luther, the primary point of reference for an analysis of Holy Scripture is God himself. Luther was never comfortable with any approach to the biblical text which viewed it in isolation from its function as the self-expression of God. 'If Scripture is obscure or ambiguous', he asked Erasmus, 'what point was there in God's giving it to us?'[141] Both the external and internal dimensions of *claritas scripturae* are the work of the Spirit of God. In this important sense, therefore, neither is purely a function of human understanding.[142]

It is in connection with the external clarity of Scripture that Luther declared 'nothing at all is left obscure or ambiguous, but everything there is in the Scriptures has been brought forth into the most definite light by the Word, and published to all the world'.[143] Later he repeated this emphasis, defying Erasmus with the words 'I say with respect to

---

[137] 'sed ob ignorantiam vocabulorum et grammaticae' *De servo arbitrio* (1525) *WA* XVIII, 606.23 = *LW* 33, 25.

[138] *De servo arbitrio* (1525) *WA* XVIII, 658.13, 659.22-23, 659.27-33 = *LW* 33, 98, 99, 100.

[139] Köstlin, *Theology*, I, 258; Ruokanen, *Doctrina Divinitus*, 106-107.

[140] Althaus, *Theology*, 78; Kuss, 'Klarheit'. 132; Priscilla Hayden-Roy, 'Hermeneutica gloriae vs hermeneutica crucis: Sebastian Franck and Martin Luther on the Clarity of Scripture', *ARG* 81 (1990), 63-64.

[141] 'si scriptura obscura vel ambigua est, quid illam opus fuit nobis divinitus tradi?' *De servo arbitrio* (1525) *WA* XVIII, 655.25-26 = *LW* 33, 93-94; cf. *Assertio omnium articulorum M Lutheri per Bullam Leonis X. novissimam damnatorum* (1520) *WA* VII, 97.2-3.

[142] Beisser, *Claritas Scripturae*, 95.

[143] 'Nihil prorsus relictum est obscurum aut ambiguum, sed omnia sunt per verbum in lucem producta certissimam et declarata toto orbi quaecunque sunt in scripturis.' *De servo arbitrio* (1525) *WA* XVIII, 609.12-14 = *LW* 33, 28.

the whole Scripture, I will have no part of it called obscure'.[144] Luther insisted that the texts of Scripture could not be divided into the clear and the unclear. He considered the grammatical and semantic clarity of the entire Scripture to be a fundamental 'first principle'. That was not to say that Luther thought of such clarity as simply a natural characteristic of the text. Rather, it is tied to God's gracious choice to express himself within the normal and accessible conventions of human language. If this divine *accommodatio* is accepted, then clarity is necessarily entailed. In this sense external clarity was a necessary, though not a natural, property of the biblical text.[145] Further, the Scriptures can then rightly be described as a public text: 'they have been published to all the world (*declarata toto orbi*)'. Indeed, Luther would later argue that even a heathen, a Jew, or a Turk could explain what the words of institution at the Last Supper mean.[146] In the final analysis, Luther was convinced that the denial of this kind of clarity in the Scriptures made a mockery of the purpose for which they have been given and impugned the character of the God who has given them.[147]

There was, of course, one particular obstacle to be overcome. Luther recognised that an ignorance of the vocabulary and grammar used by the biblical writers could obscure the meaning of a text. However, as far as he was concerned, this was more of an historical accident, albeit compounded by widespread negligence in the matter of education. Our lack of familiarity with the elements of Greek and Hebrew does not alter the character of the text itself. The words used and the constructions which connect them remain clear even though our historical and geographical distance from the writers may present us with peculiar difficulties. It is in just this context that Luther used his illustration of the illuminated public fountain which remains illuminated though those who are elsewhere might not see it.[148] However, Luther did not see this as an insurmountable problem.

---

[144] 'Deinde contra te de tota scriptura dico, nullam eius partem volo obscuram dici.' *De servo arbitrio* (1525) *WA* XVIII, 656.15-16 = *LW* 33, 94.

[145] 'Holy Scripture must necessarily be clearer, simpler, and more reliable than any other writings. (Es muß yhe die heilige schrifft klerer leichter unnd gewisser sein den aller anderer schrifft.)' *Grund unnd ursach aller Artickel D. Marti. Luther, ßo durch Romische Bulle unrechtlich vordampt seyn* (1521) *WA* VII, 317.1-2 = *LW* 32, 11.

[146] 'Wir wissen aber, das diese wort 'Das ist mein leib x.' klar und helle sind, Denn es höre sie gleich ein Christ odder Heide, Jüde odder Türcke, so mus er bekennen, das da werde gered von dem leibe Christi, der ym brod sey' *Vom Abendmahl Christi. Bekenntnis.* (1528) *WA* XXVI, 406.27-29 = *LW* 37, 272.

[147] *De servo arbitrio* (1525) *WA* XVIII, 655.25-26, 656.6-7 = *LW* 33, 93-94.

[148] *De servo arbitrio* (1525) *WA* XVIII, 606.22-39 = *LW* 33, 25-26.

Largely through the efforts of humanists like Reuchlin, Erasmus, and in the Wittenberg context Melanchthon and Aurogallus, a knowledge of the biblical languages was once again possible. Luther himself advocated widespread education in the biblical languages so that none might be prevented from directly engaging with the Scriptures.[149]

Luther's initial definition of external clarity described it as 'related to the ministry of the Word' and as something 'brought out by the Word'.[150] Later in the treatise Luther spoke of the external judgement (*iudicium externum*) which is the duty of 'the public ministry of the Word and the outward office and is chiefly the concern of leaders and preachers of the Word'.[151] Some have taken this as evidence that Luther's version of the 'Scripture principle' has more to do with church structures than appears at first.[152] Others have concluded that 'for Luther the external Word is above all the Word of preaching, surely not the letter of Scripture'.[153] However, neither conclusion is strictly necessary. First of all, this external clarity which is related to the ministry of the Word always remains *claritas scripturae*. Luther did not here transform it into *claritas praedicationis*.[154] The ministry of the Word does not establish the clarity of Scripture; rather, it is made possible by this clarity and openly proclaims that which is clearly taught. Further, the passages of Scripture cited by Luther to support this idea are taken by him to refer to the Scripture itself. It was the Law inscribed by Moses at the command of God which was to regulate life in Israel and settle any questions in dispute. Those holding the office of priest were simply commanded 'to judge according to the law of the Lord'.[155] It was the Old Testament Scriptures to which the apostles appealed for the validation of their gospel, following the pattern of Christ himself who had insisted that those Scriptures bear witness to him.[156] Further still, Luther here distinguished the clear and certain Scriptures from the exposition which is based upon them: 'And what is it that preachers do, to this very day? Do they interpret and expound the Scriptures? Yet if the Scripture they expound is uncertain, who can

---

[149] *An die Ratherren aller Städte deutschen Lands, daß sie christliche Schulen aufrichten und halten sollen* (1524) *WA* XV, 27-53 =*LW* 45, 347-378.

[150] 'Una externa in verbi ministerio posita [...] sed omnia sunt per verbum in lucem producta' *De servo arbitrio* (1525) *WA* XVIII, 609.5, 609.13 = *LW* 33, 28.

[151] 'Hoc iudicium est publici ministerii in verbo et officii externi et maxime pertinet ad duces et praecones verbi.' *De servo arbitrio* (1525) *WA* XVIII, 653.24-25 = *LW* 33, 91.

[152] Neuner and Schröger, 'Klarheit', 51.

[153] Beisser, *Claritas Scripturae*, 83.

[154] *De servo arbitrio* (1525) *WA* XVIII, 609.4, 653.27 = *LW* 33, 28, 91.

[155] *De servo arbitrio* (1525) *WA* XVIII, 654.1-20 = *LW* 33, 93.

[156] *De servo arbitrio* (1525) *WA* XVIII, 655.11-18 = *LW* 33, 93.

assure us that their exposition is certain?'[157] Reference to the exegetical work of the wider church, and especially of those publicly authorised as teachers, may indeed help to check overly individual and idiosyncratic interpretation, yet it is never presented by Luther as an alternative to direct engagement with the clear Scripture: 'all spirits are to be tested by Scripture in the presence of the Church'.[158]

According to Luther, it is this external clarity which makes possible the appeal to Scripture in matters of doctrine and Christian living.[159] In fact, he argued, such clarity is the essential presupposition of Christian discourse. 'Why do you yourself, Erasmus, set out the nature of Christianity for us', Luther asked, 'if the Scriptures are obscure to you?'[160] Here then is the answer both to the Roman insistence on ecclesiastically authorised interpretation and to the novelty Luther associated with the *Schwärmer*. The Scripture has no need of the first and will not permit itself to be distorted into the second. Scripture is to be proclaimed just as God has given it.[161] All that it teaches is 'clear, open, and evident'.[162] The Scriptures are nothing less than the provision of a benevolent God for the strengthening of those who are weak in faith and for the defence of the truth by the refutation of false teaching.[163]

The other side of Luther's distinction was also developed in *De servo arbitrio*. Luther's initial reference to the internal clarity of Scripture alerted his readers to the fact that this dimension more directly explained Erasmus' observation of persistent unbelief and doctrinal disagreement. Although it remains the internal clarity of Holy Scripture (*interior claritas scripturae sanctae*), it 'is located in the understanding of the heart'. Luther explained that left to themselves 'all men have darkened hearts so that even if they can recite everything

---

[157] 'Et quid faciunt, qui adhuc hodie praedicant, Scripturas interpretantur ac declarant? At si obscura est scriptura, quam declarant, Quis nos certos facit, ipsam eorum declarationem esse certam?' *De servo arbitrio* (1525) *WA* XVIII, 655.21-24 = *LW* 33, 93.

[158] 'Scriptura iudice omnes spiritus in facie Ecclesiae esse probandos.' *De servo arbitrio* (1525) *WA* XVIII, 653.28 = *LW* 33, 91.

[159] He saw this as the meaning of ὠφέλιμος in 2 Tim. 3:16. *De servo arbitrio* (1525) *WA* XVIII, 655.28-31 = *LW* 33, 94.

[160] 'Quid et tu nobis, Erasme, praescribis formam Christianismi, si tibi scripturae sunt obscurae?' *De servo arbitrio* (1525) *WA* XVIII, 656.3-4 = *LW* 33, 94.

[161] *De servo arbitrio* (1525) *WA* XVIII, 628.27-29 = *LW* 33, 56; Beisser, *Claritas Scripturae*, 102.

[162] 'Si autem ad Christianos et scripturas pertinet, clarum, apertum et evidens esse debet prorsusque similis caeteris omnibus evidentissimis articulis.' *De servo arbitrio* (1525) *WA* XVIII, 656.24-25 = *LW* 33, 95.

[163] *De servo arbitrio* (1525) *WA* XVIII, 653.26 = *LW* 33, 91.

in Scripture, and know how to quote it, yet they apprehend and truly understand nothing of it'.[164] In other words, the external clarity of Scripture proves insufficient to generate the appropriate response to its teaching because it is faced with the blindness and depravity of the human heart. The same Spirit who inspired the Scripture must make possible its reception. In this sense 'the Spirit is required for the understanding of Scripture, both as a whole and any part of it'.[165]

Luther's explanation of the internal clarity of Scripture thus highlighted the continuing role of the Spirit in relation to the biblical text. The clarity of Scripture is more than just a once and for all accomplishment, more than simply a record of what God has *said*. Rather, as we have repeatedly seen, Luther insists that God still *speaks* this word. Holy Scripture is the word of the God who is present. In the *Dictata*, as he glossed Ps. 71:16, Luther spoke of those moments 'when God breathes directly into a man and teaches him'.[166] The same idea can be found in the opening lines of his commentary on the Magnificat, from 1521: 'No one can correctly understand God or His Word unless he has received such understanding immediately from the Holy Spirit'.[167] The clarity of Scripture retains its character as a gift because of this continuing involvement of the Spirit; it is a spiritual matter, not just a linguistic one. Put another way, 'the burden of signification [always] falls on God'.[168]

It is now evident that more is involved in the internal clarity of Scripture than a human existential decision. Miikka Ruokanen appears to have missed the point when he suggested that the Scripture 'has in itself the power and light to become unambiguously understood by anyone who approaches it in an open and sincere attitude of searching'.[169] Luther was convinced that the internal clarity of

---

[164] 'altera in cordis cognitione sita [...] omnes habent obscuratum cor, ita, ut si etiam dicant et norint proferre omnia scripturae, nihil tamen horum sentiant aut vere cognoscant' *De servo arbitrio* (1525) *WA* XVIII, 609.5, 609.7-9 = *LW* 33, 28; cf. *WA* XVIII, 653.18-19 = *LW* 33, 90.

[165] 'Spiritus enim requiritur ad totam scripturam et ad quamlibet eius partem intelligendam.' *De servo arbitrio* (1525) *WA* XVIII, 609.11-12 = *LW* 33, 28; cf. *Vorlesung über Iesaia* (1527-9) *WA* XXV, 229.37-40 Beisser, *Claritas Scripturae*, 88; Ruokanen, *Doctrina Divinitus*, 106.

[166] 'Quando Deus immediate inspirat et docet hominem, simul dat gratiam et ignem.' *Dictata super Psalterium* (1513-15) *WA* III, 451.26.

[167] 'Denn es mag niemant got noch gottes wort recht vorstehen, er habs denn on mittel von dem heyligen geyst.' *Das Magnificat Vorteutschet und ausßlegt* (1521) *WA* VII, 546.24-25 = *LW* 21, 299. Ebeling, 'Hermeneutics II', 323.

[168] Hayden-Roy, 'Hermeneutica gloriae', 64.

[169] Ruokanen, *Doctrina Divinitus*, 105.

Scripture, just like its external clarity, comes to us *extra se*.[170] It always remains something we have received 'through the Holy Spirit or a special gift of God (*per spiritum vel donum Dei singulare*)'. Nevertheless, personal faith was undoubtedly important in Luther's theology. Indeed, Luther explicitly mentioned the significance of faith when he spoke of the internal clarity of Scripture in the later section of *De servo arbitrio* :

> The spirits are to be tested or proved by two sorts of judgement. One is internal, whereby through the Holy Spirit or a special gift of God, anyone who is enlightened concerning himself and his own salvation, judges and discerns with the greatest certainty the dogmas and opinions of all men. Of this it is said in I Corinthians 1: 'The spiritual man judges all things, but himself is judged by no one'. This belongs to faith and is necessary for every individual Christian. We have called it above 'the internal clarity of Scripture'.[171]

We have already seen how Luther saw saving faith as a work of the Spirit which is itself the appropriate response to the promise of God. In that sense the clarity of the promise always stands outside of and prior to the existence of faith. However, here Luther also emphasised that a transformative understanding of the word of promise does not exist outside of the context of a genuine faith in the one who has spoken the promise. As early as the *Dictata* Luther insisted that 'when Christ is not known it is impossible to have any understanding in Scripture, since he is the sun and truth in Scripture'.[172] Ten years later, as he advised the Teutonic Knights to marry, he spoke of how the Word of God does two opposite things at the same time: it must 'give perfect light and glory to those who believe it, and bring utter blindness and shame upon those who do not believe it'.[173] In this sense faith is prior

---

[170] Hayden-Roy, 'Hermeneutica gloriae', 64.

[171] 'duplici iudicio spiritus esse explorandos seu probandos. Uno interiori, quod per spiritum sanctum vel donum Dei singulare, quilibet pro se suaque solius salute illustratus certissime iudicat et discernit omnium dogmata et sensus, de quo dicitur 1. Corinth. 2: Spiritualis omnia iudicat et a nemine iudicatur. Haec ad fidem pertinet et necessaria est cuilibet etiam privato Christiano. Hanc superius appellavimus interiorem claritatem scripturae sanctae.' *De servo arbitrio* (1525) *WA* XVIII, 653.13-19 = *LW* 33, 90.

[172] Nescito enim Christo impossibile est habere intellectum in Scriptura, cum ipse sit sol et veritas in Scriptura.' *Dictata super Psalterium* (1513-15) *WA* III, 620.5-6 = *LW* 11, 110.

[173] 'Gottis wort mus das wünderlicht ding seyn ynn hymel und erden. Darumb mus es zu gleych beydes thun, auffs höhest erleuchten und ehren, die es glewben, und auffs höhist blenden und schenden die yhm nicht glewben.' *An die Herren*

to understanding and the phenomenon Luther here calls 'the internal clarity of Scripture'. He was convinced that, while not irrational, a true understanding of Scripture is never simply a matter of rational apprehension. It also necessarily involves personal appropriation. In other contexts Luther would speak of the need to be gripped by the text and he would employ the language of experience in a way that is almost indistinguishable from the language of faith.[174] As true understanding cannot finally be isolated from its impact on life, so Luther believed that the internal clarity of Scripture cannot be isolated from genuine faith.[175]

Here then was Luther's answer to Erasmus. This distinction made possible the meaningful affirmation of Scripture's clarity in the face of controversy, heresy, and persistent unbelief. The priority of the external clarity of Scripture, which makes possible the establishment of faith upon the promise of God, does not eliminate the need for the internal clarity of Scripture, that gift of God which takes the believer beyond mere apprehension to appropriation. Luther was able to insist that Scripture needs no external interpretive control (against Rome), that there can be no place for scepticism or agnosticism with regard to those matters treated within Scripture (against Erasmus), and that it is reprehensible to use literary devices or private revelations in a way which avoids the straightforward meaning of the text (against those he called *Phanatici*). The God who has spoken knows how to speak well and his words settle the issues with which they deal.

Clarity and Translation

For Luther the clarity of Scripture cannot be isolated from the words of Scripture. However, this inevitably raised the issue of Holy Scripture as a translated text and questions about the necessity of a knowledge of the languages in which it was originally written. As we have seen, Luther was acutely aware that the Scriptures were not originally written in German or even Latin: the gospel 'came through the medium of the languages'.[176] He often appealed to the meaning of Greek words

---

    deutschs Ordens, daß sie falsche Keuschheit meiden und zur rechten ehelichen Keuschheit greifen, Ermahnung (1523) *WA* XII, 235.35-236.2 = *LW* 45, 146.

[174] *Ein Sermon und Eingang in das erste Buch Mosi* (15 March 1523) *WA* XII, 444.5-12; cf. *Rhapsodia seu Concepta in Librum de loco Iustificationis* (1530) *WA* XXX-II, 673.15-17; *Vom Abendmahl Christi. Bekenntnis.* (1528) *WA* XXXVI, 506.4-5 = *LW* 28, 81; *Tischreden* #448 (1533) *WATr* I, 196.27-28.

[175] Beisser, *Claritas Scripturae*, 85.

[176] 'Denn das konnen wir nicht leucken, das, wie wol das Euangelion alleyn durch den heyligen geyst ist komen und teglich kompt, so ist doch durch mittle der

and the structure of Hebrew idiom. In his 1523 work, *Von Anbeten des Sakraments des heiligen Leichnams Christi*, he stressed the importance of competence in the biblical languages:

> I know for a fact that one who has to preach and expound the Scriptures and has no help from the Latin, Greek, and Hebrew languages, but must do it entirely on the basis of his mother tongue, will make many a pretty mistake. For it has been my experience that the languages are extraordinarily helpful for a clear understanding of the divine Scriptures. This also was the feeling and opinion of St. Augustine; he held that there should be some people in the church who could use Greek and Hebrew before they deal with the Word, because it was in these two languages that the Holy Spirit wrote the Old and New Testaments.[177]

Nevertheless, at least in Luther's mind, recognising that a knowledge of the original languages was indispensable for serious biblical study was in no way inconsistent with an affirmation of the clarity of Scripture.[178] In the first instance Luther distinguished between the 'simple preacher of the faith' and the 'prophets or interpreters' who have a particular responsibility for disputing with those who cite Scripture incorrectly. The former 'has so many clear passages and texts available through translations that he can know and teach Christ, lead a

---

sprachen komen und hat auch dadurch zugenomen, mus auch da durch behalltten werden.' *An die Ratherren aller Städte deutsches Lands* (1524) *WA* XV, 37.3-6 = *LW* 45, 358. This awareness is undeniable despite Luther's comment in 1526: 'Therefore we must build firmly on the words and stand fast in them, and thus we will be able to give a proper answer to the heretics. For these words are expressed in clear enough German. (Derhalben mussen wir uns wol grunden auff die wort und darauff beharren; so konnen wir den ketzern wol antworten. Denn sie sind klar und deutsch genug.')' *Sermon von dem Sakrament des Leibes und Blutes Christi, wider die Schwarmgeister* (1526) *WA* XIX, 508.28-30 = *LW* 36, 351.

[177] 'Ich weyß auch furwar, das, wer die schrifft predigen soll und außlegen und hatt nicht hülffe auß latinischer, Krichischer und Ebreischer sprach unnd solls alleyne auß seyner mutter sprach thun, der wirt gar manchen schonen feylgriff thun. Denn ich erfare, wie die sprachen uber die maß helffen zum lauttern verstandt gotlicher schrifft. Das hatt auch S. Augustinus gefulet und gemeynet, das ynn der kirchen seyn sollen, die auch Kriechisch unnd Ebreisch kunden, tzuvor die das wort handeln sollen, denn der heylig geyst hatt ynn dißen zwo sprachen das allt und new testament geschrieben.' *Von Anbeten des Sakraments des heiligen Leichnams Christi* (1523) *WA* XI, 455.30-456.3 = *LW* 36, 304.

[178] Neither does Luther seem to feel the tension identified by Alister McGrath between the principle of *sola Scriptura* and a robust insistence upon the necessity of the *die Sprechen*. McGrath, *Intellectual Origins*, 138-39.

holy life, and preach to others'. However, the latter task 'cannot be done without the languages'.[179]

Secondly, Luther considered that the purpose of translation was not so much to clarify the original Hebrew or Greek text as to convey in the vernacular its clear meaning. That is why he told Johann Lang in 1521 that there could never be too many translators or translations.[180] Given the widespread ignorance of Hebrew and Greek, he insisted that whenever the Bible was read publicly it should be read in the vernacular of the congregation present.[181] Nevertheless, he was prepared to acknowledge the possibility of error in the process of translation and so argued for a knowledge of the biblical languages which would enable some to dispel any obscurity or confusion that might result.[182] In fact, in his *An die Radherrn aller Stedte deutsches lands*, from 1524, Luther connected the scholastic complaints of obscurity in the Scriptures to their neglect of the languages:

> This is also why the sophists have contended that Scripture is obscure; they have held that God's word by its very nature is obscure and employs a peculiar style of speech. But they fail to realise that the whole trouble lies in the languages. If we understood the languages nothing clearer would ever have been spoken than God's word.[183]

However, one celebrated example seems to call into question this approach to the task of translation. In the September Testament of 1522, Luther translated Rom. 3:28 ($\lambda o\gamma\iota\zeta\acute{o}\mu\epsilon\theta a$ $\gamma\grave{a}\rho$ $\delta\iota\kappa a\iota o\hat{v}\sigma\theta a\iota$ $\pi\acute{\iota}\sigma\tau\epsilon\iota$ $\check{a}\nu\theta\rho\omega\pi o\nu$ $\chi\omega\rho\grave{\iota}\varsigma$ $\check{\epsilon}\rho\gamma\omega\nu$ $\nu\acute{o}\mu o\upsilon$) as *so halten wyrs nu, das der mensch gerechtfertiget werde, on zu thun der werck des gesetzs, alleyn durch den glawben.*[184] Enemies such as Jerome Emser were quick to charge him with inconsistency and adding to the Word of God. In light of the discussion above, we might well also ask whether Luther was seeking to *clarify* Scripture when he inserted the word 'alone (*alleyn*)'?

---

[179] 'das lesset sich on sprachen nicht thun' *An die Ratherren aller Städte deutsches Lands* (1524) *WA* XV, 40.20 = *LW* 45, 363.

[180] Luther an Joh. Lang (18 December 1521) *WABr* II, 413.5-9 = *LW* 48, 356.

[181] *Vorlesung über den 1. Timotheusbrief* (1528) *WA* XXVI, 82.10-15 = *LW* 28, 329.

[182] Amongst many examples of Luther's own criticism of the Vulgate translation is that connected with his exposition of Psalm 51:6. *Enarratio Psalmi LI* (1532) *WA* XL-II, 385.31-387.6 = *LW* 12, 351-352.

[183] 'Der halben haben auch die Sophisten gesagt, Die schrifft sey finster, haben gemeynet, Gottis wort sey von art so finster und rede so seltzam. Aber sie sehen nicht, das aller mangel ligt an den sprachen, sonst were nicht liechters yhe geredt denn Gottis wort, wo wyr die sprachen verstünden.' *An die Ratherren aller Städte deutsches Lands* (1524) *WA* XV, 41.2-5 = *LW* 45, 363-64.

[184] *Das Newe Testament Deutzsch* (1522) *WADB* VII, 38.28-29.

If he was, does this not involve the admission that the text is not, in and of itself, perfectly clear?

Luther defended his translation in his *Ein Sendbrieff D. M. Luthers von Dolmetzschen und Fürbit der heiligenn*, written in 1530. He argued that he had four good reasons for going beyond a word for word correspondence to the original text. The first was the nature of the German language. Luther maintained that the natural way of expressing the kind of contrast Paul has in mind in this verse is to put a negation in one clause and the word *alleyn* in the other. At this point he emphasised that a good and vigorous German translation must take as its guide the common usage of ordinary people, not a literal rendering of the Latin of the Vulgate: 'the literal Latin is a great hindrance to speaking good German'.[185] According to Luther, his use of the word *alleyn* conformed to common usage. The second reason lay in the text which he was translating. Far from going beyond the original text, Luther believed he was accurately rendering that text: 'the text itself and the meaning of St. Paul urgently require and demand it'. The rejection of the works of the Law as a means of justification is so complete, Luther argued, that 'whoever would speak plainly and clearly about this cutting away of works will have to say, "Faith alone justifies us, and not works"'. 'Paul's words are too strong; they admit of no works, none at all.'[186] Luther's third reason was the corroborative precedent of the church fathers: 'I am not the only one, or even the first, to say that faith alone justifies. Ambrose said it before me, and Augustine and many others'.[187] Luther was not importing his own meaning into the text but was faithfully rendering what others before him had seen to be its meaning. The final reason was his own pastoral concern in the face of the continuing temptation facing Christians who had been brought up in the works orientation of medieval Catholicism. Luther concluded, 'for these reasons it is not only right but also highly

---

[185] 'Denn die lateinischen buchstaben hindern aus der massen, seer gut deutsch zu reden.' *Sendbrief vom Dolmetschen* (1530) *WA* XXX-II, 637.34-35 = *LW* 35, 190.

[186] 'Sonder der text und die meinung S. Pauli soddern und erzwingens mit gewallt [...] Wo man aber alle werck so rein abschneit, und da mus ja die meinung sein, das allein der glaube gerecht mache, und wer deutlich und durre von solchem abschneiden der werck reden wil, der mus sagen: Allein der glaube, und nicht die werck machen uns gerecht, das zwinget die sache selbs neben der sprachen art [...] Seine wort sind zu starck, und leiden kein, ja gar kein werck.' *Sendbrief vom Dolmetschen* (1530) *WA* XXX-II, 640.35-6, 641.9-13, 642.29 = *LW* 35, 195, 197.

[187] 'Auch bin ichs nicht allein, noch der erste, der da sagt, Allein der glaube mach gerecht, Es hat fur mir Ambrosius, Aug. und vil andere gesagt.' *Sendbrief vom Dolmetschen* (1530) *WA* XXX-II, 642.26-27 = *LW* 35, 197.

necessary to speak it out as plainly and fully as possible, "Faith alone saves, without works"'.[188] While Luther's defence of his translation may not have settled the matter (then or now), he was himself convinced that he had acted responsibly and without compromise.

Luther was well aware that an accurate translation of a text does not necessarily produce a word for word correspondence to the original. Yet he nevertheless maintained that he was most unwilling to give a single letter a wrong translation intentionally.[189] The principles of translation he adopted were to his mind no more destructive of his commitment to the clarity of Scripture than his lifelong practice of biblical exposition. To explain or unfold the message of a text did not necessarily involve a presupposition of its obscurity. In fact, in Luther's case the evidence actually points in the opposite direction. His passionate commitment to the clear message of the biblical texts as they stand in their contexts led him to a lifetime of both revising his translation and expounding the Scriptures in sermons and lectures.

Clarity and the Authority of Scripture

Luther's commitment to *claritas scripturae* undoubtedly played a critical role in his willingness to make a stand on the basis of its teaching.[190] Whether opposed by the combined might of church and empire, the intellectual sophistication of Desiderius Erasmus, or the apparent intransigence of the more radical reformers, Luther exemplified his own advice from 1522: 'You must rest upon a strong and clear text of Scripture if you would stand the test. If you cannot do that, you will never withstand — the devil will pluck you like a leaf'.[191] It is this conviction that Scripture is clear which precludes us from viewing his stand as simply the imposition of private judgement. Luther saw himself as the servant and captive of Scripture, bound by his oath as a Doctor to defend what Scripture clearly said against all who might oppose it.[192] It was precisely because his writings were

---

[188] 'So ists nit allein recht, sondern auch hoch von nöten, das man auffs aller deutlichst und voligst eraus sage, Allein der glaube on werck macht frum.' *Sendbrief vom Dolmetschen* (1530) *WA* XXX-II, 643.6-8 = *LW* 35, 198.

[189] *Sendbrief vom Dolmetschen* (1530) *WA* XXX-II, 633.19-20 = *LW* 35, 183.

[190] Wood, *Captive,* 135.

[191] 'du must dich gründen auff eynen starcken, klaren spruch der schriefft, da du besteen magst: wenn du den nit hast, so ist es nit müglich, das du bestan kanst, der teüffel reyst dich hinweck wie ein dürre blat.' *Ein ander Sermon D. M. Luthers Am dinstag nach Invocavit* (11 March 1522) *WA* X-III, 22.11-23.3 = *LW* 51, 80.

[192] Siggins, 'Word of God', 7.

based upon the clear teaching of Scripture that he did not feel free to renounce his books when the authorities called upon him to do so.[193]

As we have seen, Luther's commitment to the clarity of Scripture was far from superficial or naive. He faced the questions raised by Erasmus and others, expounding a two-fold clarity of Scripture, and was sensitive to the common experience of Scripture as a translated text. Nevertheless, his statements are remarkably bold, insisting on the clarity of the words as they stand, without gloss or emendation. Indeed, he recognised that only a clear Scripture made possible and meaningful the task of Christian theology.[194] Further, we have observed the significant connections between this perspective on Scripture and other fundamental elements of Luther's own theological position.

Luther had recognised the connection between the clarity and authority of Scripture at least as early as 1517. In his lecture on Heb. 6:4–6 he commented on the use of $\dot{\alpha}\delta\acute{u}\nu\alpha\tau o\nu$ and the attempts within the exegetical tradition to soften its meaning:

> Some think that these words are spoken by the apostle about those who in any way have fallen into sin. And in order to counteract the error of the Novatians they are compelled to distort the word 'impossible' and to declare that it was used instead of the word 'difficult'. But because it is dangerous to twist the clear words of Scripture into a different meaning, one should not readily permit this, except where the context demands it, lest in the end the authority of all Scripture vacillate.[195]

Even at this early stage, Luther demonstrated a sensitivity to such factors as the context in which the words are found. Of course Luther did not always consistently apply such insights, as evidenced by his refusal to accept Zwingli's arguments from the context of the words of institution at the Lord's Supper. However, what is of most significance here is that Luther understood that any suggestion that the words of Scripture are unclear, that they mean something other than what they say or contain some kind of hidden meaning which is not accessible to all, almost inevitably raised questions about their authority.

---

[193] *Luther an die Kurfürsten, Fürsten und Stände des Reichs* (28 April 1521) *WABr* II, 315.18-23.

[194] Kooiman, *Luther*, 103.

[195] 'Aliis videntur haec verba dici ab Apostolo de his, qui quocunque modo lapsi sunt in peccatum. Et hi, ut occurrant Novatianorum errori, coguntur illud 'impossibile' torquere et pro 'difficile' dictum asserere. Sed quia periculosum est aperta verba Scripturae distorquere in alienam significationem, non est facile permittendum, ne totius tandem Scripturae vacillet authoritas, nisi ubi id circumstantia textus exegerit.' *Commentariolus in epistolam divi Pauli Apostoli ad Hebreos* (1517) *WA* LVII-III. 181.9-14 = *LW* 29, 181.

An Intelligible Text?

Conversely, the appeal to the authority Scripture could only be effective if the Scripture to which one appealed was clear. If it was not, then one was left at the mercy of either various degrees of scepticism or the hermeneutical morass exemplified in Catholicism by the *Quadriga*.[196] As we have seen, Luther considered this to be the very real danger posed by the arguments of the Swiss in the eucharistic debates.

It is obvious that the clarity of Scripture provided Luther with a confident basis for action. There can be no place for hesitation or equivocation if God has spoken clearly and decisively.[197] A stand must be made upon the clear words themselves. Nowhere was this more necessary or urgent than in the matter of personal assurance. In the face of the real terror of *die Anfechtungen*, the Christian can and must stand firm because God has made his mind known with utmost clarity. As Luther said of his own experience: 'Christ strengthened and confirmed me with his clear, unmistakeable Word'.[198]

Clarity and the Interpretation of Scripture

Luther's affirmation of the clarity of Scripture did not make redundant the task of biblical interpretation or exposition, nor was this its intention. That task remained necessary and Luther devoted his life to it.[199] However, given the clarity of Scripture, Luther's work of biblical interpretation took on a particular shape. The directions in which he was moving were evident in his concluding comments to the Christmas section of the *Kirchenpostille*:

> And so, my dear Christians, get to it, get to it, and let my exposition and that of all the doctors be no more than a scaffold, an aid for the construction of the true building, so that we may ourselves grasp and taste the pure and simple word of God and abide by it; for there alone God dwells in Zion.[200]

---

[196] Hence Alister McGrath's comment that 'the Reformation principle of *sola scriptura* is rendered either meaningless or unusable without a reliable hermeneutical programme'. McGrath, *Intellectual Origins*, 152.

[197] Thiselton, *New Horizons*, 182, 185.

[198] 'das mich Christus mit seynem eynigen, gewissen wortt befestiget und bestettiget hat' *Vom mißbrauch der Messen* (1521) *WA* VIII, 483.4-5 = *LW* 36, 134.

[199] Silva, *Church*, 84-85; Thiselton, *New Horizons*, 179; Callahan, 'Claritas', 356.

[200] 'Darumb hyneyn, hyneyn, lieben Christen, und last meyn und aller lerer außlegen nur eyn gerust seyn zum rechten baw, das wyr das blosse, lautter gottis wort selbs fassen, schmecken unnd da bleyben; denn da wonet gott alleyn ynn Zion.' *Kirchenpostille* (1522) *WA* X-I/1, 728.18-21 = *LW* 52, 286.

Luther was convinced that the ideal was always a direct and unadorned engagement with the Scriptures themselves. In this sense his own work was strictly dispensable, though it had a place as an unfolding of the message of Scripture for those who were not familiar with it and as a defence against the arguments of those who taught what was contrary to it.[201] As we have seen, Luther argued that the church stood in constant need of those who, familiar with the biblical languages and equipped with a more detailed knowledge of the contents of Scripture, could take on the role of 'prophets or interpreters'.[202]

Luther insisted that the words of the biblical text are not infinitely pliable. When God addresses his people he leaves them in no doubt about what he is saying. In line with this conviction, Luther often expressed a preference for the simplest meaning possible when dealing with the biblical text. In 1523 he had warned the Bohemian Brethren, 'One must not do such violence to the words of God as to give to any word a meaning other than its natural one, unless there is clear and definite Scripture to do that'.[203] Twelve years later, as he discussed the meaning of the expression 'in the beginning' in Gn. 1:1, he remarked, 'So let those who care to do so, trifle with the expression; I prefer what is simplest and can be understood by those with little education'.[204]

This brings us to what is perhaps the chief hermeneutical implication of Luther's doctrine of *claritas scripturae,* namely the principle 'Holy Scripture is its own interpreter (*sacra scriptura sui ipsius interpres*)'. As he told the congregation in Wittenberg on 25 July 1522, 'Scripture is its own light'.[205] Luther was convinced that when a text was properly seen in the light of the whole of Scripture, and more particularly in the light of those other texts which immediately precede and follow it, its meaning was plain. He believed this transformed the task of biblical exposition. The principal responsibility of the biblical scholar is a contextual examination of the text as it stands. Luther explained what he meant in the Galatians

---

[201] Klug, *Luther*, 90.

[202] *An die Ratherren allen Städte deutsches Lands* (1524) *WA* XV, 40.14-20 = *LW* 45, 363.

[203] 'Man muß nicht ßo freveln an gottis wortten, das yemandt on außgedruckte klarre schrifft eym wortt wolt eyn ander deutten geben denn seyn natürlich deutten ist' *Von Anbeten des Sakraments des heiligen Leichnams Christi* (1523) *WA* XI, 434.20-22 = *LW* 36, 279.

[204] 'Quare ludant hic, qui volent, mihi placent, quae simplicissima sunt et a rudioribus possunt intelligi.' *Genesisvorlesung* (1535-45) *WA* XLII, 9.8-9 = *LW* 1, 10.

[205] 'Also ist die schrifft jr selbs ain aigen liecht.' *Predigt am Jakobstage* (25 July 1522) *WA* X-III, 238.10.

commentary, as he argued against those who superimposed their own ideas on the reading of Scripture:

> What they should do is to come to it empty, to derive their ideas from a reading of the sacred words, then to pay careful attention to the words, to compare what precedes with what follows, and to make the effort of grasping the authentic meaning of a particular passage rather than attaching their own notions to words or phrases that they have torn out of context'.[206]

As was suggested in the last chapter, such a careful contextual examination of each text helped to settle the fundamental question of its application. In 1525 Luther wrote, 'You must not only look to see whether this is God's word, whether God has said it; you must also consider to whom it has been spoken, whether it applies to you'.[207] Luther maintained that the text itself would provide the answer. Attention to the text itself reveals that God's command to Abraham that he should sacrifice Isaac was a test and not something required of every believer. Likewise, the promise to David concerning the king from his line who would reign after him was specific to him and is not to be applied to every individual. A careful reading of the text in its context was all that was needed to make the distinction.

In this way the clarity of Scripture was intimately related to the unity of Scripture. Luther resisted any interpretation of an individual text which placed that text in conflict with another part of Scripture: 'the Holy Spirit does not contradict Himself'.[208] This is what Luther meant by his appeal to the articles of faith. As far as he was concerned, the genuine articles of faith are nothing other than distillations of the teaching of Scripture itself. This was the key to his critique of papal

---

[206] 'Sed ita accidit ignavis lectoribus et qui suas cogitationes afferunt lectioni sacrarum literarum, cum vacui accedere deberent et ex literis sacris referre cogitationes, deinde verba dilegenter considerare, praecedentia cum sequentibus conferre et hoc studere, ut integrum sensum alicuius loci caperent, non truncatis vocabulis aut excerptis verbis sua somnia affingerent.' *In epistolam S. Pauli ad Galatas Commentarius* (1535) *WA* XL-II, 36.25-37.8 = *LW* 27, 29.

[207] 'man mus nicht allein ansehen, ob es Gottes wort sey, ob es Gott geredt hab, sondern viel mehr, zu wem es geredt sey, ob es dich treffe oder einen andern.' *Unterrichtung, wie sich die Christen in Mosen sollen schicken* (27 August 1525) *WA* XVI, 385.19-21 = *LW* 35, 170.

[208] 'Ists der HERR, wie Mose schreibet, wie kans Christus sein, wie Paulus schreibt? Nu mussen sie beide recht schreiben, Denn der Heilige geist ist nicht wider sich selbs' *Von den letzten Worten Davids* (1543) *WA* LIV, 66.40-42 = *LW* 15, 313.

primacy.²⁰⁹ Precisely because they were such, these articles could act as controls on interpretive practice without violating the principle *sacra scriptura sui ipsius interpres*. This line of argument played a key role in Luther's defence of the real presence of Christ in 1525:

> This then is our basis. Where Holy Scripture is the ground of faith we are not to deviate from the words as they stand nor from the order in which they stand, unless an express article of faith compels a different interpretation or order. For else what would happen to the Bible? For instance, when the Psalmist says, 'God is my rock', he uses a word which otherwise refers to natural stone. But inasmuch as my faith teaches me that God is not natural stone, I am compelled to give the word 'stone', in this place, another meaning than the natural one. So also in Matt. 16. 'On this rock I will build my church'. In the passage we now are treating no article of faith compels us to sever it and remove it from its place, or to hold that the bread is not the body of Christ. Therefore we must take the words just as they stand, making no change and letting the bread be the body of Christ.²¹⁰

However, Luther also recognised the danger of letting the wider context of Scripture overturn the grammatical meaning of any given text and thus raising again the spectre of obscurity in the Scriptures. Given the more immediate contextual considerations, the words always

---

[209] *Disputatio I. Eccii et M. Lutheri Lipsiae habita* (1519) *WA* II, 279.21-24; *Von dem Papstum zu Rom widder den hochberumpten Romanisten zu Leipzick* (1520) *WA* VI, 322.1-9 = *LW* 39, 101; *Grund und Ursach aller Artikel D Martin Luthers, so durch römische Bulle unrechtlich verdampt sind* (1521) *WA* VII, 455.16-24 = *LW* 32, 98; *De Abroganda Missa Privata* (1521) *WA* VIII, 413.2-414.26 = *LW* 36, 135-137; *Praelectio in psalmum 45* (1532) *WA* XL-II, 592.32-36 = *LW* 12, 287.

[210] 'Darumb ist das unser grund: Wo die heylige schrifft ettwas gündet zu gleuben, da soll man nicht weichen von den worten, wie sie lautten, noch von der ordnunge, wie sie da stehet, Es zwinge denn eynn ausgedruckter artickel des glaubens, die wort anders zu deutten odder zu ordenen, Was wollt sonst die Bibel werden? Als da der Psalter spricht "Gott ist meyn fels", Hie steht das wort fels, das eynen natürlichen steyn sonst heyst. Aber weyl der glaube leret, das Gott keyn natürlich steyn ist, Zwinget er mich, das ich an dem ort mus das wort "fels" anders deutten, denn seyne natürliche deuttunge gibt. Also auch Matt. 16. "Auff diesen fels will ich meyne kirche bawen." Weyl aber hie keyn artickel zwingt, das dis stücklin sey ab zusondern und eraus zu zwacken, odder das das brod nicht Christus leyb sey, soll man schlecht die wort nemen, wie sie lautten und mit nichte endern und lassen das brod Christus leyb seyn.' *Wider die himmlischen Propheten, von den Bildern und Sakrament* (1525) *WA* XVIII, 147.23-35 = *LW* 40, 157-158; cf. *De servo arbitrio* (1525) *WA* XVIII, 656.24-28 = *LW* 33, 95; *WA* XVIII, 700.31-33 = *LW* 33, 162; *Von Abendmahl Christi. Bekenntnis.* (1528) *WA* XXVI, 403.11-13 = *LW* 37, 270.

mean what they say. Almost paradoxically, the strongest expression of this caveat to the importance of context in determining meaning also played an important role in Luther's debate over the words of institution at the Last Supper:

> Indeed, to show how far they miss the truth: not only are they under obligation to prove from Scripture that 'body' is the same as 'sign of the body', and that 'is' is the same as 'represent or signify', but one thing more: even though they should produce such an example in one passage of Scripture (which, however, is impossible), they are still under obligation to prove that it is necessarily so here in the Supper as well, that 'body' is 'sign of the body'. It would not help them at all, even if the entire Scriptures showed nothing but signs of the body in other passages, if they did not show it also at this passage on the Supper. Our present quarrel is not primarily whether somewhere in the Scriptures 'body' means 'sign of the body', but whether in this text of the Supper it has this meaning.[211]

A second hermeneutical implication of the clarity of Scripture was the abandonment of allegorical or spiritual interpretations of the biblical text, at least on the scale which had dominated the tradition particularly since the time of Origen. Luther's own movement away from this method began tentatively in the later sections of the *Dictata* and was clearly in evidence by the time of his exposition of the seven penitential psalms in 1517. In the early Galatians commentary, published in 1519, he maintained 'that four-horse team' is 'not sufficiently supported' by the authority of Scripture, the custom of the fathers, or grammatical principles.[212] Of course Luther would continue to employ allegory as an illustrative tool throughout his teaching career, and he recognised that there was a biblical precedent for

---

[211] 'Ja auff das man sehe, wie gar weit side feylen der warheit, sind sie nicht alleine das schüldig, das sie aus der schrifft beweisen, das "leib" so viel als "leibs zeichen", und das "wesen" so viel als "deuten" sie, sondern noch eines. Wenn sie gleich etwa an einem ort der schrifft solchs auffbrechten, welchs doch nicht müglich ist, so sind sie dennoch auch schuldig zu beweisen, das es hie ym abentmahl auch so müsse sein, das "leib" "leibs zeichen" sey, und hülffe sie gar nichts, wenn gleich die gantze schrifft an andern ortern eitel leibs zeichen auffbrecht und brechts nicht auch an diesem ort ym abentmal auff. Denn wir haddern itzt nicht furnemlich, ob etwa ynn der schrifft "leib" "leibs zeichen" heisse, sondern obs an diesem ort des abendsmal so heisse.' *Das diese Wort Christi 'Das ist mein leib' noch fest stehen* (1527) *WA* XXIII, 97.23-32 = *LW* 37, 34-35.

[212] 'Nam ista quadriga (etsi non reprobem) non scripturae autoritate nec patrum usu nec grammatica satis ratione iuvatur.' *In epistolam Pauli ad Galatas commentarius* (1519) *WA* II, 550.34-35 = *LW* 27, 311.

allegorical interpretation in the writings of Paul. Nevertheless, in lectures, sermons, and over meals he repudiated the wholesale use of spiritual meanings which had even been a feature of his own earliest exegetical work. He argued that these actually obscured the real and intended meaning of Scripture, which otherwise would be perfectly clear. Luther's clearest denunciation of such an approach to biblical interpretation can be found in his later commentary on Galatians:

> Therefore the Jerusalem that is above, that is, the heavenly Jerusalem, is the church here in time. It is not, by anagoge, our fatherland in the life to come or the church triumphant, as the idle and unlettered monks and scholastic doctors imagined. They taught there are four senses of Scripture — the literal, the tropological, the allegorical, and the anagogical — and by means of these they misinterpreted almost every word of Scripture. Thus, according to them, Jerusalem literally signified the city of that name; tropologically, a pure conscience; allegorically, the church militant; and anagogically, our heavenly fatherland or the church triumphant. With these awkward and foolish fables they tore Scripture apart into many meanings and robbed themselves of the ability to give sure instruction to human consciences.[213]

Of course, as we saw in the previous chapter of this study, there were other reasons besides a defence of Scripture's clarity which led Luther to distance himself from the allegorical hermeneutic of many of his predecessors. However, his insistence that the 'the words as they stand' make perfect sense as they stand provides an important new perspective on the celebrated transformation of his own interpretive method.

Against the backdrop of centuries of interest in this topic, Luther affirmed the clarity of Holy Scripture. There can be little doubt that this affirmation was theologically and personally significant for Luther, and indeed he himself claimed that it was the clarity of the

---

[213] 'Quare Hierusalem, quae sursum est, id est, coelestis, est Ecclesia in hoc tempore, non ἀναγωγικῶς futurae vitae patria vel Ecclesia triumphans, ut otiosi et ineruditi Monachi et Scholastici doctores nugati sunt, qui tradereunt quatuor esse sensus scripturae, Literalem, Tropologicum, Allegoricum et Anagogicum, et secundum hos singula fere verba scripturae inepte interpretati sunt; Ut Hierusalem literaliter significabat illis urbem eius nominis, Tropologice conscientiam puram, Allegorice Ecclesiam militantem, Anagogice coelestem patriam seu Ecclesiam triumphantem. His insulsis et nugacibus fabulis, quibus discerpserunt scripturas in tot sententias, fecerunt, ut de nullis rebus conscientiae certo erudiri potuerint.' *In epistolam S. Paul ad Galatas commentarius* (1535) *WA* XL-I, 663.12-21 = *LW* 26, 440; cf. *Vorlesung über Iesaias* (1527-30) *WA* XXXI-II, 97.13-98.8 = *LW* 16, 136-137.

biblical text which enabled him to makes such a bold stand for the Scriptures and against doctrinal and moral error. Undoubtedly, scholarly interest in this facet of Luther's contribution to the theological and exegetical tradition is thoroughly warranted, though some modern studies are marred by insupportable assumptions about Luther's approach to Scripture in general. Inseparable as it is from his statements about the inspiration of Scripture and its coherence or unity, Luther's conviction that the teaching of Scripture is both accessible and intelligible provides perhaps the most critical link in the conceptual bridge between his appeal to the authority of Scripture and his interpretative practice.

Chapter 6

Sola Scriptura?

Luther on the Sufficiency of Holy Scripture

Unless I am convinced by the testimony of the Scriptures or by evident reason — for I can believe neither pope nor councils alone, as it is clear that they have erred repeatedly and contradicted themselves — I consider myself conquered by the Scriptures adduced by me and my conscience is captive to the Word of God.[1]

These famous words from Luther's speech at Worms in 1521 are often taken as the classic statement of the principle *sola scriptura*.[2] His insistence that his theology be evaluated on the basis of Holy Scripture and not simply with reference to patristic or scholastic authorities, or even the decrees of popes and Church Councils, is popularly presented as the heart of the Reformation protest. Yet modern studies, many fuelled by the ecumenical interests of the late twentieth century, have sought a more nuanced approach.[3] Did Luther really dismiss all appeal

---

[1] 'Nisi convictus fuero testimoniis scripturarum aut ratione evidente (nam neque Papae neque conciliis solis credo , cum constet eos et errasse sepius et sibiipsis contradixisse), victus sum scripturis a me adductis et capta conscientia in verbis dei' *Verhandlungen mit D. Martin Luther auf dem Reichstage zu Worms* (1521) *WA* VII, 838.4-7 = *LW* 32, 112.

[2] The actual expression *sola scriptura* is found, amongst other places, in Luther's preface to Melanchthon's notes on Romans: 'Sola scriptura, inquis, legenda est citra commentaria.' *Vorwort zu den Annotationes Philippi Melanchthonis in epistolas Pauli ad Romanos et Corinthios* (1522) *WA* X-II, 310.12-13.

[3] E.g. Gerhard Ebeling, *The Word of God and Tradition: Historical Studies Interpreting the Divisions of Christianity*, 102-147; Theodore S. Liefeld, 'Scripture and Tradition, in Luther and in our Day', in F. W. Meuser and S. D. Schneider (eds.), *Interpreting Luther's Legacy: Essays in Honor of Edward C. Fendt*, 26-38; Heiko A. Oberman, 'Vom Protest zum Bekenntnis. Die

to the tradition of the Church? His own extensive use of the Church Fathers would seem inconsistent with any such blanket repudiation of post-apostolic theology. Did he leave room for the processes of human reason? After all, even at Worms he could speak of being convicted by 'evident reason'. Further, how are we to explain his observation that experience plays a vital role in theological formation?[4] Clearly, Luther's own idea of the sufficiency of Scripture needs more careful exposition in the face of these questions.

Much that we have already considered provides the necessary context for a careful exposition of Luther's affirmation of Scripture's sufficiency. The historical context stretches back to the teaching of Scripture itself, teaching which we saw culminates in Paul's use of $\alpha\rho\tau\iota o\varsigma$ in 2 Tim. 3:17. The patristic period witnessed considerable discussion of the issue, with influential statements by Augustine amongst others.[5] The best minds of the Later Middle Ages addressed the question repeatedly, spurred on by elaborate papal claims, the rise and fall of the conciliar movement, and the embrace of Aristotelian philosophy in many centres of learning. As Luther rose to his feet at the Diet of Worms and insisted that he would only retract his writings if convinced from Holy Scripture that they were in error he was, in one sense at least, simply continuing the debate of previous centuries.[6]

Luther's personal history in the years immediately leading up to the Diet made a further contribution to his famous articulation of this principle. We have already noted his letter to a former teacher in May 1518, in which he attributed his own insistence on the unique authority of the Scriptures to the teaching which he had received in the University of Erfurt.[7] By August that same year a copy of the first official response to Luther's ninety-five theses on indulgences was in his hands in Wittenberg. Its title revealed that a larger issue had been identified right at the very start of the controversy: Sylvester Prierias produced, not *De indulgentiarum virtute dialogus,* but *De potestate papae dialogus.*[8] The third of the four axioms with which Prierias began explicitly denied the sufficiency of Scripture: 'Whoever does

---

Confessio Augustana: Kritischer Maßstab wahrer Ökumene', *Bätter für württembergische Kirchengeschichte,* 80/81 (1980-81), 24-37; Lønning, 'No Other Gospel', 229-245.

[4] E.g. 'Vivendo, immo moriendo et damnando fit theologus, non intelligendo, legendo aut speculando.' *Operationes in Psalmos* (1519-21) *WA* V, 163.28-29.

[5] Augustine, *De Baptismo contra Donatistas,* II.3 (4) (*CSEL,* LI, 178); Augustine, *Contra Epistolam Manicaei Quam vocant Fundamenti,* I.5 (6) (*PL,* XLII, 176); Basil the Great, *De Spiritu sancto,* lxvi (*PG,* XXXII, 188).

[6] McGrath, *Intellectual Origins,* 150.

[7] Luther an Jodokus Trutfetter (9 May 1518) *WABr* I, 171.71-74.

[8] Oberman, *Reformation,* 122-123.

not hold fast to the teachings of the Roman Church and of the Pope as the infallible rule of faith, from which even Holy Scripture draws its strength and authority, is a heretic'.[9] Luther's challenge was to be dealt with at this most fundamental level: a debate about the authority and sufficiency of Scripture. In his reply to Prierias, published before the end of the month, Luther provided his own axioms. He quoted the words of Paul in 1 Thes. 5:21 and Gal. 1:8 and then went on to repeat Augustine's comment to Jerome: 'I have learned to ascribe this honour only to those books which are called canonical, that I most firmly believe that none of their authors have erred. However I do not believe the others to be true, no matter how strong they are in teaching and holiness'.[10] In October, Luther met with Cardinal Cajetan in Augsburg. He would publish an account of their meeting a month later. It is clear from that account that again the function of Scripture was raised as a key area of disagreement. The Cardinal, Luther claimed, 'began to extol the authority of the pope, stating that it is above Church Councils, Scripture, and the entire Church'.[11] Less than a year later, Luther debated perhaps his most formidable opponent, Johann Eck, in the Pleissenberg at Leipzig. The official record of the proceedings for 5 July 1519 reveals the same issue appeared yet again. Luther maintained:

> Neither is it possible for the faithful Christian to be forced beyond Holy Scripture, which is the proper divine law, unless he receives new and proven revelation. Indeed we are prevented by the divine law from believing anything except that which is proven through Divine Scripture or through manifest revelation.[12]

Luther's stand before the Emperor and the representatives of the Roman Church was thus no novelty. Each of the preliminary

---

[9] 'Quicunque non innititur doctrinae Romanae ecclesiae, ac Romani Pontificis, tanquam regulae fidei infallibili, a qua etiam sacra Scriptura robur trahit et autoritatem, haereticus est.' *EA* var. arg. I, 347.

[10] *Ad dialogum Silvestri Prieratis de postestate papae responsio* (1518) *WA* I, 647.17-30.

[11] 'Tunc cepit adversus me potestatem Papae commendare, quoniam supra Concilium, supra scripturam, supra omnia Ecclesiae sit' *Acta Augustana* (1518) *WA* II, 8.10-11 = *LW* 31, 262.

[12] 'Nec potest fidelis Christianus cogi ultra sacram scripturam, que est proprie ius divinum, nisi accesserit nova et probata revelatio: immo ex iure divino prohibemur credere nisi quod sit probatum vel per scripturam divinam vel per manifestam revelationem' *Disputatio I. Eccii et M. Lutheri Lipsiae habita* (1519) *WA* II, 279.23-26.

skirmishes had placed a spotlight on his views about the authority and sufficiency of Holy Scripture.[13]

As well as this historical context, the previous chapters of this study provide a conceptual context for Luther's affirmation of the sufficiency of Scripture. His commitment to the biblical text as the self-expression of the living and present God involved a recognition of its unique status. No purely human text could be treated as a necessary supplement to it without raising serious questions about the character of God or his ability to communicate meaningfully and effectively with his people. Conversely, how could the Scriptures not require supplementation, perhaps even radical correction, if they were nothing more than human reflection upon God and his dealings with the world? Similarly, the particular connectedness of this body of writings, both in terms of origin and in terms of content focussed on Christ, suggested an internal rather than an external hermeneutical principle. If this was merely a disparate collection of religious material, bound together only by some kind of institutional decision, did it make any sense to speak of *sola scriptura*? Finally, Luther's insistence that Scripture is clear, that it is intelligible in terms of its own grammar and context, is a critical part of the conceptual framework which supports his appeal to the sufficiency of Scripture. If the biblical text can only be understood by reference to extra-biblical material, or indeed authorised interpretive structures, the notion of sufficiency is evacuated of almost all meaning.

How then are we to understand Luther's appeal to the sufficiency of Holy Scripture? In this chapter we seek an explanation that goes beyond the rhetoric of subsequent generations. In this search we will need to take seriously both Luther's statements of the principle in their context and the way the principle functioned in his own theological and exegetical work.

Scripture and Tradition

As many have observed, Luther never intended to say anything original.[14] In fact, throughout his life he was deeply suspicious of theological novelty.[15] He was acutely aware that his doctor's oath had installed him as a teacher and as a defender of the truth, not as an

---

[13] Gritsch, *Martin,* 102, 108.
[14] Pelikan, *Obedient Rebels,* 16; Althaus, *Theology,* 3.
[15] *Vermahnung an die Geistlichen, versammelt auf dem Reichstag zu Augsburg* (1530) *WA* XXX-II, 300.15-301.31 = *LW* 34, 27-28; cf. Luther's casual comments about Copernicus which we have already mentioned. *Tischreden* #4638 (4-5 June 1539) *WATr* IV, 412.35-413.3 = *LW* 54, 359.

innovator.[16] His responsibility was to expound the doctrine which God had given and which had been received by the Church. From his perspective, the break with Rome over the years 1517 to 1521 was not something he had initiated in a highly individual search for a new and purer truth, but something thrust upon him by an institution which had abandoned its own inheritance. He would later speak of his three-fold excommunication: first by his religious order, then by the pope, and finally by the emperor.[17] Nevertheless, he did not believe that he had ever ceased to be a member of Christ's Church. He continued to see himself in that 'succession of the faithful in the church', which he had identified in his earliest exposition of Ps. 103.[18] If we are to avoid caricature, full weight must be given to Luther's 'thoroughly dogmatic orthodoxy' as an integral part of his attitude towards tradition.[19]

Long after the decisive breach with Rome, Luther continued to do his theology in conversation with those who had gone before, especially the Church Fathers. He remained true to his early observation that the truth is not a personal possession but something held 'in humility and in common with others'.[20] Thus he often quoted Augustine and Jerome, less often Tertullian, Origen, Cyprian, Ambrose, Gregory the Great, and others. When in the 1520s he was faced with controversy amongst the Reformers over the Lord's Supper, he commissioned friends to gather evidence from the Fathers on the subject and later devoted space in his treatises to an exposition of their opinions and an attack on the use made of them by Karlstadt, Oecolampadius, and Zwingli.[21] However, Luther never felt bound to

---

[16] *Glosse auf das vermeinte kaiserliche Edikt* (1531) *WA* XXX-III, 386.30-34 = *LW* 34, 103; Gerrish, 'Doctor Martin Luther', 2-8.

[17] *Tischreden* #884 (1530) *WATr* I, 442.1-5; Pelikan, *Obedient Rebels*, 16; Oberman, *Luther*, 185-187.

[18] 'successiones fidelium in Ecclesia' *Dictata super Psalterium* (1513-15) *WA* IV, 165.18.

[19] Pelikan, *Obedient Rebels*, 65.

[20] 'Et maledicti declinamus a mandatis dei, qui precepit humiliter et communiter sapere.' *Dictata super Psalterium* (1513-15) *WA* IV, 317.17-18 = *LW* 11, 431.

[21] *Luther an Nikolaus Hausmann* (2 February 1525) *WABr* III, 431.5-15; *Daß diese Worte Christi (Das ist mein Leib etc) noch fest stehen wider die Schwarmgeister* (1527) *WA* XXIII, 208.28-242.23 = *LW* 37, 104-125; *Vom Abendmahl Christi. Bekenntnis* (1528) *WA* XXVI, 322.6-9 = *LW* 37, 211; *WA* XXVI, 362.4-6 = *LW* 37, 242; *WA* XXVI, 432.26-28 = *LW* 37, 288; *WA* XXVI, 471.1-15 = *LW* 37, 328-329. Mention should also be made of the way Luther used his own research into early church history and the canon law in his debate with Eck in 1519. *Luther an Willibald Pirckheimer in Nürnberg* (20 February 1519) *WABr* I, 348.13-22; *Luther an Spalatin* (13 March 1519) *WABr* I, 359.28-

the Fathers' interpretation of the Scriptures. Even as early as the *Dictata* he had been able to side with Cassiodorus against Augustine on the meaning of Ps. 11:4,[22] to describe Jerome's opinion on Ps. 32:1 as 'of no use (*non est utilis*)',[23] and to suggest that Augustine's explanation of one word in Psalm 98.4 is 'true but not necessary for the meaning of the text'.[24] He valued the Fathers as those who had pioneered a Christian exploration of the Scriptures and defended the faith in the face of persecution and heresy, yet he was never prepared to give their writings the same dignity as Holy Scripture. The authority of the Fathers was at best derivative and dependent upon their faithful exposition of the teaching of the Bible.

Luther was absolutely unambiguous about the reasons which compelled him to distinguish so sharply between the writings of the Fathers and the text of Holy Scripture. In the first instance, he recognised only Scripture as the written Word of God, and, as he reminded Eck in Leipzig, 'the Word of God is above all the words of men'.[25] By recognising this distinction, Luther believed he was actually following the practice of the Fathers themselves. He pointed to Augustine as a typical example.[26] However, a second connected reason is much more prominent in Luther's writing on the subject. Luther repeatedly insisted that, unlike Holy Scripture, the Fathers of the Church were susceptible to error. Perhaps his most extended comment on this subject is found in the 1521 treatise on the misuse of the Mass:

> Since the Fathers have often erred, as you yourself confess, who will make us certain as to where they have not erred, assuming their own

---

360.36 = *LW* 48, 114; *Disputatio et excusatio F. Martini Lutheri adversus criminationes D. Iohannis Eccii* (1519) *WA* II, 161.35-38 = *LW* 31, 318.

[22] *Dictata super Psalterium* (1513-15) *WA* LV-II, 112.18-113.7 = *LW* 10, 99.

[23] *Dictata super Psalterium* (1513-15) *WA* III, 175.1 = *LW* 10, 146.

[24] 'Ideo vera est b. Augustini super verbo "Ductilibus" expositio, sed non ad sensum textus necessaria.' *Dictata super Psalterium* (1513-15) *WA* IV, 121.15-16 = *LW* 11, 273.

[25] 'verbum dei super omnia verba hominum est' *Disputatio I. Eccii et M. Lutheri Lipsiae habita* (1519) *WA* II, 263.33-34. That Luther has Scripture in mind is confirmed by the context, in which he insisted that 'Jerome is not so great that on account of him I would forsake Paul (nec tantus est Hieronymus, ut propter eum Paulum deseram)' *WA* II, 263.27-28. Compare Luther's reply to Henry VIII's attack on *De captivitate Babylonica ecclesiae. Contra Henricum Regem Angliae* (1522) *WA* X-II, 214.36-215.8.

[26] *Rationis Latomianae confutatio* (1521) *WA* VIII, 98.27-30 = *LW* 32, 216; Augustine, *Epistulae,* XCIII.x.35-45 (*CSEL*, XXXIV, 480-488); *In epistolam Pauli ad Galatas commentarius* (1519) *WA* II, 447.15-17 = *LW* 27, 156; *Contra Malignvm Iohannis Eccii Ivdicivm svper aliqvot Articvlis a Fratribvs Qvibvsdam ei Svppositis Martini Lvtheri Defensio* (1519) *WA* II, 626.33-39.

Sola Scriptura?

reputation is sufficient and should not be weighed and judged according to the divine Scriptures? They have (you say) also interpreted the Scriptures. What if they erred in their interpretation, as well as in their life and writings? In that way you make gods of all that is human in us, and of men themselves; and the word of men you make equal to the Word of God [...] The saints could err in their writings and sin in their lives, but the Scriptures cannot err, and whoever believes them cannot sin in his life. We accept indeed those saints whose praise comes not from men but from God; not those whom the pope raises up, but those whom God raises up, whose oxen and birds they are, killed and made ready for the marriage feast of Christ, his son; that is, those whose life and teaching the divine Scriptures praise, such as the patriarchs, prophets, and apostles. Them alone and no others can we surely believe and cling to, and thus be preserved.[27]

As far as Luther was concerned, this real and demonstrable fallibility undermined any attempt to build a theology upon the teaching of the Fathers. They might have been great and holy men, men used mightily by God in the history of his church, but in the final analysis they were just like us and erred just like us. They could not simply be discarded as irrelevant to the theological enterprise, for they form part of the context in which that enterprise takes place, but their contribution

---

[27] 'Wer macht uns gewiß, worynne die vetter nicht geyrret, die weyl sie offt geyrret haben, als du selbst bekennest, ßo yhr ansehen gnug ist unnd sollt nit nach gottlicher schrifft gericht und geurteyllt werden? Sie haben (sprichstu) auch die schrifft außgelegt. Wie, wenn sie ßo wol ym außlegen, als yn yhrem leben unnd schreyben geyrret hetten? Mit der weyß machstu alles das unßer menschlich unnd auß den menschen götter, und das wortt der menschen geychestu dem wortt gottis [...] Die heyligen haben in yhrem schreyben yrren und in yhrem leben sundigen künnen: die schrifft kan nit yrren, und wer yhr glewbt, der kan nicht sundigen yn seynem leben. Wyr nemen die heyligen wol an, wilcher lob nit von menschen, ßondern von gott ist, nit die der Bapst erhebet, ßondern die gott erhebt, des ochssen und vogel sie sind, getödt und zu der hochtzeyt Christi, seyns sonß, bereyt, das ist, wilcher leben und lere die gottliche schrifft lobet, als der Patriarchen, Propheten und Aposteln: den alleyn und keynen andern künnen wyr gewißlich glawben, anhangen und alßo erhallten werden.' *Vom Mißbrauch der Messe* (1521) *WA* VIII, 484.24-30, 485.19-27 = *LW* 36, 136, 137; cf. *Grund und Ursach aller Artikel D. Martin Luthers, so durch römische Bulle unrechtlich verdammt sind* (1521) *WA* VII, 315.28-32 =*LW* 32, 11; *Antwort deutsch auf König Heinrichs Buch* (1522) *WA* X-II, 239.26-29 = *LW* 35, 128; *Von Menschenlehre zu meiden und Antwort auf Sprüche* (1522) *WA* X-II, 89.10-13 = *LW* 35, 150; *Genesisvorlesung* (1535-45) *WA* XLII, 91.22-92.5 = *LW* 1, 121; *WA* XLIII, 145.19-25 = *LW* 4, 14; *Auslegung des 1. und 2. Kapitels Johannis* (1537-8) *WA* XLVI, 771.11-19 = *LW* 22, 259.

could never be treated as beyond challenge.[28] Indeed, at points the challenge was internal to the patristic tradition itself. In 1520 Luther asked, 'who is to judge when the Fathers contradict themselves?'[29] In this way a degree of uncertainty always attached to the writings of the saints. Luther therefore considered it absurd to suggest that the teaching of the Fathers was clearer or more certain than that of Scripture.[30]

Luther's use of the Fathers generally accords with the principle he enunciated in 1521:

> This is my answer to all those who accuse me of rejecting all the holy teachers of the Church. I do not reject them. But everyone, indeed, knows that at times they have erred, as men will; therefore I am ready to trust them only when they give me evidence for their opinions from Scripture, which has never erred. This St Paul bids me to do in I Thessalonians 5, where he says, 'Test everything; hold fast to what is good'.[31]

Their testimony was not to be dismissed without a hearing but neither was it to be accepted without a question. It could perform an illustrative or corroborative function, but in the final analysis Christian faith would not survive if it was dependent only upon the teaching of

---

[28] Note the comment to Erasmus we observed in the last chapter: 'All spirits are to be tested by Scripture in the presence of the Church (Scriptura iudice omnes spiritus in facie Ecclesiae esse probandos).' *De servo arbitrio* (1525) *WA* XVIII, 653.28 = *LW* 33, 91.

[29] 'Aut dic, si potes, quo iudice finietur quaestio, si patrum dicta sibi pugnaverint.' *Assertio omnium articulorum M. Lutheri per bullam Leonis X novissimam damnatorum* (1520) *WA* VII, 97.19-20. Note the contrast with his later statement about Scripture: 'It is impossible that Scripture should contradict itself. It only appears so to senseless and obstinate hypocrites (Quanquam impossibile sit Scripturam pugnare nisi apud insensatos et induratos Hypocritas).' *In epistolam S. Pauli ad Galatas Commentarius* (1535) *WA* XL-I, 458.35-36 = *LW* 26, 295.

[30] *Auf das überchristlich, übergeistlich und überkünstlich Buch Bocks Emsers zu Leipzig Antwort* (1521) *WA* VII, 638.26-639.27 = *LW* 39, 164-165.

[31] 'Damit ich auch denen wil antworttet haben, die mir schuld geben, ich vorwerffe alle heylige lerer der kirchen. Ich vorwirff sie nit. Aber die weil yderman wol weysz, das sie zu weilen geyrret haben als menschen, wil ich yhn nit weytter glawben geben den ßo fern sie mir beweysung yhrs vorstands auß der schrifft thun, die noch nie geirret hat. Unnd das heysset mich sanct Pauel i. Tessal. ult. da er sagt: "Pruffet und beweret zuvor alle lere; wilche gut ist, die behaltet".' *Grund und Ursach aller Artikel D. Martin Luthers, so durch römische Bulle unrechtlich verdammt sind* (1521) *WA* VII, 315.28-34 = *LW* 32, 11; cf. *Auf das überchristlich, übergeistlich und überkünstlich Buch Bocks Emsers zu Leipzig Antwort* (1521) *WA* VII, 639.21-23 = *LW* 39, 165.

men.³² Therefore the books of the Fathers, like all human writings, were to be tested by the standard of Holy Scripture. Furthermore, when all the statements of the Fathers had been gathered, it still remained true that a single passage from the Scripture carries more weight than all the books in the world.³³

Though Luther had occasion to be more scathing in his comments about scholastic theology, the same basic principles were operative. These more modern authorities, even William of Occam whose ideas had dominated Luther's own education at the University of Erfurt, were still merely human and thus susceptible to error. Even worse, the impressive intellectual edifices they had constructed, by means of what seemed to Luther an avalanche of written material, could distract Christian people from the one certain source of God's truth. He warned of the danger, which he believed might arise even from his own writings, in his lecture on Genesis 19 from 1539:

> For this reason I myself hate my books and often wish that they would perish, because I fear that they may detain the readers and lead them away from reading Scripture itself, which alone is the fount of all wisdom. Besides, I am frightened by the example of a former age. After those who had devoted themselves to sacred studies had come upon the commentaries of human beings, they not only spent most of their time reading the ancient theologians, but eventually they also busied themselves with Aristotle, Averroes, and others, who later on gave rise to the Thomases, Scotuses, and similar monstrosities.³⁴

---

³² *Von den Konziliis und Kirchen* (1539) *WA* L, 544.2-4 = *LW* 41, 49.

³³ *An die Herren Deutschen Ordens, daß sie falsche Keuschheit meiden* (1532) *WA* XII, 235.17-18 = *LW* 45, 146.

³⁴ 'Nam ego ipse eam ob causam odi meos libros, et saepe opto eos interire, quod metuo, ne morentur lectores, et abducant a lectione ipsius scripturae, quae sola omnis sapientiae fons est: ac terreor exemplo superioris aetatis. Postquam enim in hominum commentarios inciderunt, qui sacris studiis dediti erant, non solum plurimum temporis in lectione veterum Theologorum consumpserunt: sed etiam tandem occupati sunt in Aristotele, Averroe et aliis, ex quibus postea nati sunt Thomae, Scoti et similia portenta.' *Genesisvorlesung* (1535-45) *WA* XLIII, 93.40-94.7 = *LW* 3, 305-306; cf. *An den Christlichen Adel deutscher Nation von des Christlichen standes besserung* (1520) *WA* VI, 460.6-461.23 = *LW* 44, 204-206. Denis R. Janz, *Luther on Thomas Aquinas: The Angelic Doctor in the Thought of the Reformer*, 21.

In an earlier critique, he had posed two questions which revealed the folly of it all: 'How was Christianity taught in the times of the martyrs when this theology did not exist? How did Christ himself teach?'.[35]

Luther had two, more specific, criticisms of the theology of the schools. In the first place, he claimed that their widespread use and development of the patristic concept of multiple senses in Scripture had 'enveloped not only the text of the Bible but also the most beautiful light of the promises in horrible darkness'.[36] In previous chapters we have examined Luther's own movement away from an interpretive method he later considered alien to the biblical text towards one which emphasised more intrinsic factors such as grammar, context and the 'centre' of Scripture. However, once that move had been made, beginning in the later stages of the *Dictata* and almost certainly complete by the time of *Operationes in Psalmos* in October 1518, Luther began to see the widespread use of allegory as not only an imposition upon the text but also a serious obstacle to understanding.

The other criticism he levelled at scholasticism concerned its widespread use of Aristotelian philosophy. As we have seen, such a protest was not without precedent.[37] However, Luther's own protest in the *Disputatio contra scholasticam theologiam* undoubtedly went further than most:

> 43. It is an error to say that no man can become a theologian without Aristotle. This in opposition to common opinion.
> 44. Indeed, no one can become a theologian unless he becomes one without Aristotle [...]
> 50 Briefly, the whole of Aristotle is to theology as darkness is to light.[38]

---

[35] 'Quomodo sunt instituti Christiani tempore martyrum, quando ista philosophia et Theologia non erat? quo modo docuit ipse Christus?' *Rationis Latomianae confutatio* (1521) *WA* VIII, 127.11-12 = *LW* 32, 258.

[36] '[N]on solum Textum Bibliorum, et pulcherrimam lucem promissionum horribili caligine involverunt' *Genesisvorlesung* (1535-45) *WA* XLIV, 772.26-27 = *LW* 8, 263; cf. *Operationes in Psalmos* (1519-21) *WA* V, 644.19-38, 645.34-646.7; *Vorlesung über Jesaja* (1527-30) *WA* XXXI-II, 97.13-98.8 = *LW* 16, 136-137; *In epistolam S. Pauli ad Galatas commentarius* (1535) *WA* XL-I, 663.12-21 = *LW* 26, 440; *Genesisvorlesung* (1535-45) *WA* XLIII, 667.4-10 = *LW* 5, 345.

[37] Bonaventure, *Collationes in Hexaëmeron*, XIX.12 (*Opera Omnia* V, 422); Absalom of St Victor, *Sermon* 4 (*PL*, CCXI, 37D); *Opus epistolarum Erasmi Roterodami*, II, 101.

[38] '43. Error est dicere: sine Aristotele non fit theologus. Contra dictum commune. 44. Immo theologus non fit nisi id fiat sine Aristotele [...] Breviter, Totus

Sola Scriptura?

The evidence of Luther's own correspondence from 1517 suggests that this sweeping dismissal of Aristotle created an early and irreparable breach between Luther and his teachers at Erfurt.[39] Undeterred, Luther repeated his attack in the theses he prepared for the Heidelberg Disputation in April 1518.[40] At the same time he acted on his convictions as he continued the reform of the theological curriculum at the University of Wittenberg.[41]

Luther spoke in such strong terms and acted so decisively because he identified two serious dangers associated with the influence of Aristotle in medieval theology. Firstly, he was convinced that any synthesis of Aristotle's teaching and that of Holy Scripture raised the dangerous prospect of a modification of the teaching of Scripture. He illustrated this with reference to Aristotle's suggestion that the world has existed from eternity, a position he quickly pointed out was irreconcilable with the teaching of Scripture.[42] Yet despite such conflict, Luther was aware of many for whom Aristotle's work had become a necessary supplement or even an alternative to Holy Scripture.[43] Some had even tried to justify this by appeal to an incompleteness in Scripture supposedly suggested by Jn. 21:25.[44] Luther was genuinely appalled by the fact that the universities in general had become places where 'little is taught of the Holy Scriptures and Christian faith, and where only the blind, heathen teacher Aristotle rules'.[45] The end product was thoroughly predictable

---

  Aristoteles ad theologiam est tenebrae ad lucem. Contra schol.' *Disputatio contra scholasticam theologiam* (1517) *WA* I, 226.14-16, 226.26 = *LW* 31, 12.

[39] *Luther an Joh. Lang* (8 February 1517) *WABr* I 88.22-89.29 = *LW* 48, 36-38; *Luther an Jodokus Trutfetter* (9 May 1518) *WABr* I, 171.71-76. Such correspondence renders improbable the suggestion that Luther was simply applying what he had learnt in the anti-Aristotelian environment of Erfurt. Karl-Heinz zur Mühlen, 'Luther and Aristoteles', *Luther-jahrbuch*, 52 (1985), 263-266.

[40] *Disputatio Heidelbergae habita. Conclusiones* (1518) *WA* I, 355.1-25 = *LW* 31, 41-42.

[41] Oberman, *Luther*, 276.

[42] *Disputatio Heidelbergae habita. Conclusiones* (1518) *WA* I, 355.6-7 = *LW* 31, 41; *Kirchenpostille* (1522) *WA* X-I/1, 567.23-24 = *LW* 52, 165; *Wochenpredigten über Joh. 6-8* (1530-32) *WA* XXIII, 91.10-16 = *LW* 37, 30-31.

[43] *Kirchenpostille* (1522) *WA* X-I/1, 387.22-388.5 = *LW* 52, 107-108; *Tischreden* #280 (8 June 1532) *WATr* I, 118.1-3 = *LW* 54, 39.

[44] *Auf das überchristlich, übergeistlich und überkünstlich Buch Bocks Emsers zu Leipzig Antwort* (1521) *WA* VII, 642.23-643.1 = *LW* 39, 168.

[45] 'wenig der heyligen schrifft und Christlicher glaub geleret wirt, und allein der blind heydnischer meyster Aristoteles regiert' *An den Christlichen Adel deutscher Nation von des Christlichen standes besserung* (1520) *WA* VI,

as far as he was concerned: a speculative theology divorced from the reality of faith and the gospel of Christ.[46] In stark contrast, Luther believed that Aristotle's teachings were completely unnecessary for a true understanding of Christian truth: 'We Christians certainly have no need of Aristotle or of human teachings'.[47]

The second danger was really a more specific instance of the first. Luther identified Aristotle as the one who had provided the basic terminology and philosophical substructure for a soteriology he was convinced was Pelagian. The chief problem here was the use medieval theologians had made of Aristotle's *Nichomachean Ethics*. Aristotle's language of 'disposition (ἕξις, *habitus*)' with regard to righteousness, and his assertion that we become just by doing just acts, had reinforced the suggestion that righteousness was something acquired by human effort.[48] Luther recognised here a challenge to the very heart of the gospel, an emphasis on performance which evacuated the cross of its meaning and purpose. This is what motivated him to speak so strongly in 1517: 'Virtually the entire *Ethics* of Aristotle is the worst enemy of grace'.[49]

Luther argued that the Councils of the Church were no more reliable than the Fathers and their successors. It was this confession, with

---

457.33-35 = *LW* 44, 200; cf. *Von der Winkelmesse und Pfaffenweihe* (1533) *WA* XXXVIII, 231.19-20 = *LW* 38, 189.

[46] *Tischreden* #644 (1530) *WATr* I, 302.30 = *LW* 54, 112; cf. *Handbemerkungen Luthers zu den Sentenzen des Petrus Lombardus* (1510-11) *WA* IX, 62.16-24, 65.14-17; *Marburger Gespräch und Marburger Artikel* (1529) *WA* XXX-III, 147.29-35 = *LW* 38, 67; *Disputatio de sententia: Verbum caro factum est* (11 January 1539) *WA* XXXIX-II, 3.1-7 = *LW* 38, 239-242.

[47] 'Auff das man aber sehe, wie gar nichts wyr Christen bedurfften Aristotels odder menschen lere, sondern zu ewigen zeytten gnug ynn der schrifft zu studirn funden, ßo wyr wolten, wollen wyr auch diße zall ubir die vorgesagten wunder der schrifft besehen.' *Kirchenpostille* (1522) *WA* X-I/1, 422.15-19 = *LW* 52, 130; cf. *De captivitate Babylonica ecclesiae praeludium* (1520) *WA* VI, 511.26 = *LW* 36, 34; *Kirchenpostille* (1522) *WA* X-I/1, 592.18-20 = *LW* 52, 183.

[48] Aristotle, *Nichomachean Ethics*, II.1. *Divi Pauli apostoli ad Romanos Epistola* (1515-16) *WA* LVI, 172.9-11 = *LW* 25, 152; *WA* LVI, 395.4-7 = *LW* 25, 385; *WA* LVI, 419.2-6 = *LW* 25, 410; *Sermon D. Martini Luthers geschehen zu Erffurdt am Sontag Quasimodogeniti* (1521) *WA* VII, 810.26-811.7 = *LW* 51, 64; *De votis monasticis Martini Lutheri iudicium* (1521) *WA* VIII, 607.33-36 = *LW* 44, 300; *In epistolam S. Pauli ad Galatas Commentarius* (1535) *WA* XL-I, 370.28-371.17 = *LW* 26, 234; *WA* XL-I, 457.23-29 = *LW* 26, 294; *WA* XL-I, 615.20-23 = *LW* 26, 404.

[49] 'Tota fere Aristotelis Ethica pessima est gratiae inimica. Contra Scholast.' *Disputatio contra scholasticam theologiam* (1517) *WA* I, 226.10 = *LW* 31, 12; cf. *An den Christlichen Adel deutscher Nation von des Christlichen standes besserung* (1520) *WA* VI, 458.14-19 = *LW* 44, 201.

particular reference to the decision of the Council of Constance to condemn all the articles of Jan Hus, which had caused such a stir during the Leipzig Debate of 1519:

> I insist on my Christian freedom and assert that a council may err — as all the teachers of Scripture and the authorities write — and have erred many times, as the histories demonstrate. Even the recent Lateran Council denounced the claims of the Councils of Constance and Basel. Thus the Council of Constance has also erred in its articles. You go ahead and show that it has not erred. On the contrary, one ought more to believe one layman who has Scripture than the Pope and Council without Scripture.[50]

This questioning of the decrees of a General Council was serious because such a council represented the Church itself, and by virtue of this fact laid claim to the leading of the Holy Spirit. Yet Luther was convinced that councils could err and contradict themselves. He never wavered in this conviction. Twenty years after Leipzig he still insisted that councils had no power to create new articles of faith,[51] that their decrees were often compromised by episcopal (especially papal) pretension,[52] contradiction,[53] and subsequent desuetude.[54] Most importantly, he argued that the leading of the Spirit was not to be set over against Holy Scripture.[55] The councils could not supplement Scripture; instead they confessed (*bekennen*) and defended (*verteidigen*) the

---

[50] 'Ehe ich das tu, will ich meiner christlichen Freiheit brauchen und sagen also: Ein Concilium mag irren (wie alle Lehrer der Schrift und Rechten schreiben) und hat etlich Mal geirret, wie die Historien beweisen und das jetzige letzte Römisch anzeigt wider das Costnitzer und Baseler. Also irret in den Artikeln das Costnitzer auch. Ober bewähre du, daß es nit geirret hebe. Sonderlich, so man mehr einem Laien sollt glauben, der Schrift hat, dann dem Papst und Concilio ohne Schrift' *Luther und Karlstadt an Kurfürst Friedrich* (18 August 1519) WABr 1, 472.256-263; cf. *Disputatio I. Ecci et M. Lutheri Lipsiae habita* (1519) *WA* II, 288.34, 399.39-400.14; *Grund und Ursach aller Artikel D. Martin Luthers, so durch römische Bulle unrechtlich verdammt sind* (1521) *WA* VII, 430.9-11 = *LW* 32, 81. The comment about a simple layman armed with Scripture is a quotation from Nicolò de' Tudeschi's *Significasti, de electione et potestate*.

[51] *Von den Konziliis und Kirchen* (1539) *WA* L, 551.24-32, 580.25-581.10, 583.17-18, 591.22-25, 603.15-18, 606.3-7 = *LW* 41, 58-59, 92-93, 96, 105, 118, 121-122. Steinmetz, *Luther in Context*, 89.

[52] *Von den Konziliis und Kirchen* (1539) *WA* L, 576.10-578.13 = *LW* 41, 87-90.

[53] *Von den Konziliis und Kirchen* (1539) *WA* L, 520.11-521.2 = *LW* 41, 20-21; *WA* L, 541.18-19 = *LW* 41, 46.

[54] *Von den Konziliis und Kirchen* (1539) *WA* L, 526.11-528.27 = *LW* 41, 27-30.

[55] *Von den Konziliis und Kirchen* (1539) *WA* L, 604.8-9 = *LW* 41, 119.

teaching of Scripture.[56] 'If they establish anything new with regard to faith or good works', Luther wrote, 'you may rest assured that the Holy Spirit had no hand in it'.[57] Furthermore, he argued that even at their best the councils remained inadequate. None of them had attempted to defend the whole of Christian doctrine as contained in Scripture:

> Put them all together, both Fathers and councils, and you still will not be able to cull from them all the teachings of the Christian faith, even if you culled forever. If it had not been for Holy Scripture, the Church, had it depended on the councils and Fathers, would not have lasted long.[58]

None of this should be taken to imply that Luther had no place at all for councils of the Church. After all, he himself had appealed to a General Council of the Church in November 1518.[59] He continued to maintain throughout his life that the issues raised by him and others were 'sufficiently important and weighty to warrant the summoning of a council', though he despaired of the pope ever allowing such a council to consider the issues without interference.[60] Nevertheless, he always maintained that the decisions of Church Councils should not stand alone. Even the Creeds were only to be accepted because they conformed to the teaching of Scripture.[61] As he put it in 1539, 'we too must have something else and something more reliable for our faith than the councils. That "something else" and "something more" is Holy Scripture'.[62]

---

[56] *Von den Konziliis und Kirchen* (1539) *WA* L, 618.8-14 = *LW* 41, 135-136.

[57] 'Setzen sie aber etwas neues im glauben oder guten wercken, so sey gewis, das der Heilige Geist nicht da sey' *Von den Konziliis und Kirchen* (1539) *WA* L, 606.10-11 = *LW* 41, 122.

[58] 'Und summa, thu sie alle zusamen, beide, Veter und Concilia, so kanstu doch nicht die gantze Lere Christlichen glaubens aus jnen klauben, ob du ewig dran klaubst,, Und wo die Heilige Schrifft nicht gethan und gehalten hette, were die Kirche der Conlilij und Veter halben nicht lange blieben.' *Von den Konziliis und Kirchen* (1539) *WA* L, 546.29-547.3 = *LW* 41, 52.

[59] *Appellatio F. Martini Luther ad Concilium* (1518) *WA* II, 36-40.

[60] 'Demnach hetten wir jtzt zu unser zeit wol sachen, die mehr denn wichtig und werd gnug weren, ein Concilium zu samlen' *WA* L, 619.26-27 = *LW* 41, 137; cf. *Die Schmalkaldischen Artikel* (1537) *WA* L, 195.15-17 = Russell, p. 119; *Wider das Papsttum zu Rom, vom Teuffel gestiftet* (1545) *WA* LIV, 211.13-26 = *LW* 41, 269.

[61] *Rationis Latomianae confutatio* (1521) *WA* VIII, 117.14-118.9 = *LW* 32, 244; *Von Abendmahl Christi. Bekenntnis* (1528) *WA* XXVI, 499.13-500.3 = *LW* 37, 360; *WA* XXVI, 509.19-20 = *LW* 37, 372.

[62] 'So müssen wir auch etwas mehr und gewissers haben fur unsern glauben, weder die Concilia sind, dasselbige, mehr und gewissers, ist die heilige

The principles applied to the writings of the Fathers, the Schoolmen, and the councils were applied also to the pronouncements of the pope. Luther's challenge to this particular element of the tradition was from the earliest days a focal point of his controversy with the Church of Rome. In Rome's first public response to Luther's theses, Sylvester Prierias had challenged the sufficiency of Scripture in precisely these terms, by insisting that the Church experiences the truth of Scripture only in its relationship with the Pope.[63] Luther took up this challenge, identifying the claim that only the pope may interpret Scripture as the second of three walls built by the Roman Church to protect itself from criticism or reform.[64] Yet although Luther's language in his writings against the papacy was often bitter and extreme, even in June 1520, the same month in which the bull *Exsurge Domine* was promulgated, he was still prepared to 'let the pope be pope' and 'help to elevate him as high as they please', provided the pope remained under Christ and let himself be judged by Holy Scripture.[65] Looking back two years later, Luther claimed that in the earliest stages he had thought the papacy was merely 'without the Scriptures (*on schrifft were*)'. As the drama unfolded, however, it became clear to him that the situation was far worse: the papacy itself was actually 'opposed to the Scriptures (*widder die schrifft were*)'.[66]

Luther's dispute with the papacy was certainly fought on a number of fronts, yet repeatedly the sufficiency of Holy Scripture emerged as a key issue. Very early on, Luther maintained that when the pope is above Scripture, Scripture perishes.[67] He included among the errors which provoked the burning of the canon law and papal decrees on 10

Schrifft.' *Von den Konziliis und Kirchen* (1539) *WA* L, 604.24-26 = *LW* 41, 120; cf. *WA* L, 618.30-35 = *LW* 41, 136.

[63] Sylvestri Prierias, *De potestate papae dialogus* (1518) in *EA var. arg.*, I, 344-377. Oberman, *Reformation*, 122-130.

[64] *An den Christlichen Adel deutscher Nation von des Christlichen standes besserung* (1520) *WA* VI, 411.8-412.38 = *LW* 44, 133-136.

[65] 'Wo nw mir diße zwey bleyben, wil ich den Bapst lassenn, ja helffen ßo hoch machen als man ymer wil, wo nit, ßo sol er mir widder bapst, noch Christen seinn.' *Von dem Papstthum zu Rom wider den hochberühmten Romanisten zu Leipzig* (1520) *WA* VI, 321.31-322.22 = *LW* 39, 101-102; cf. *In epistolam Pauli ad Galatas commentarius* (1519) *WA* II, 446.38-447.13 = *LW* 27, 155-156.

[66] 'Nu fur ich mit dem verfluchten grewel am ersten fast senfft unnd leyße und schon, Hette gar gerne das bapstum lassen und helffen etwas seyn. Alleyn die schrifft were, ßondern hiellt es nur, das es on schrifft were, wie andere weltliche uberkeyt durch menschen erhaben.' *Antwort deutsch auf König Heinrichs Buch* (1522) *WA* X-II, 232.13-17.

[67] *Eine Freiheit des Sermons päpistlichen Ablaß und Gnade belangend* (1518) *WA* I, 390.12-28, 391.16-392.11.

December 1520 the claim that only the pope has the right to interpret Scripture.[68] Commenting on Gal. 1:9 in 1535, he declared, 'we are presented here with an example that enables us to know for a certainty that it is an accursed lie that the pope is the arbiter of Scripture or that the Church has authority over Scripture'.[69] Ten years later, in his final treatise against the Roman papacy, Luther thundered his absolute rejection of the notion that the pronouncements of the pope clarified or supplemented the teaching of Scripture: 'He who wants to hear God speak should read Holy Scripture. He who wants to hear the devil speak should read the pope's decretals and bulls'.[70]

An examination of the evidence reveals that Luther's view of tradition, whether represented by the teaching of the Fathers, the theological work of the medieval doctors, the decrees of the Church Councils, or the pronouncements of the popes, was remarkably consistent throughout his ministry. He certainly did not simply jettison fifteen hundred years of exegetical and theological endeavour. He repeatedly testified to his own orthodoxy.[71] Nevertheless, he always insisted that every human word should be tested by Holy Scripture. He himself traced this insistence back to his years at the University of Erfurt and ultimately to the words of Paul in 1 Thes. 5. The change which occurred in the years 1517 to 1521 did not arise from a discovery of the primacy of Scripture, or even of its sufficiency, for his convictions regarding these can be demonstrated in letters, lectures, and sermons prior to this period. Rather, Luther came to realise that, more often than he had ever thought possible, the tradition of the Church failed the test of Scripture. It was when he acted on the basis of that realisation, challenging what he saw as error and proclaiming the truth that he discovered in Scripture, that he drew the fire of Rome.

However, before leaving the subject of tradition, one recent proposal requires consideration. It has been suggested that Luther's commitment to the dignity of the Christian ministry reveals that he did in fact favour the retention of some kind of institutional supplement or

---

[68] *Warum des Papstes und seiner Jünger Bücher von D. Martin Luther verbrannt sind* (1520) *WA* VII, 175.24-176.17 = *LW* 31, 392.

[69] 'Exemplum tamen hich nobis proponitur, quod certe statuere debemus mendacium et Anathema esse sentire, quod Papa sit Arbiter scripturae. Item quod Ecclesia habeat potestatem supra scripturam' *In epistolam S. Pauli ad Galatas Commentarius* (1535) *WA* XL-I, 119.23-25 = *LW* 26, 57.

[70] 'Wer Gott wil hören reden, der lese die heilige Schrifft. Wer den Teufel wil hören reden, der lese des Bapsts Drecket und Bullen.' *Wider das Papstum zu Rom vom Teufel gestiftet* (1545) *WA* LIV, 263.14-16 = *LW* 41, 332.

[71] *Vom Abendmahl Christi. Bekenntnis* (1528) *Die drei Symbola oder Bekenntnis des Glaubens Christi* (1538) *WA* XXVI, 499-509 = *LW* 37, 360-372; *WA* L, 262.5-9 = *LW* 34, 201.

interpretive control, albeit in a modified form. Anthony Lane points to Luther's nervousness about the possibility of interpretive anarchy and concludes that Luther was not in favour of 'the democratisation of theology'.[72] Yet such a conclusion is not warranted by the evidence and it confuses Luther's approach to the exegetical and theological task with his concern for congregational order. In 1523 Luther produced his treatise *De instituendis ministris Ecclesiae*, in which he argued for both the dignity of the public ministry of the Word and a ministry of the Word which is common to all Christians.[73] He methodically worked his way through each of the functions of the priesthood, including the responsibility to judge doctrine, and demonstrated that precisely because the Scriptures teach that each of these belongs to every believer, all Christians are priests. He then proceeded to argue that 'the community rights demand that one, or as many as the community chooses, shall be chosen or approved who, in the name of all with these rights, shall perform these functions publicly'.[74] Luther's concern was that when Christians gather all should be done decently and in order. Therefore only those ordained to the task should teach the congregation. It would be misleading to understand his argument here as a re-installation of the teaching authority of the Church which somehow calls into question the material sufficiency of Scripture.[75]

Scripture and Reason

Luther's attitude towards reason has been an area of continued scholarly interest.[76] Much of the attention has focussed on the

---

[72] Anthony N. S. Lane, 'Sola Scriptura? Making Sense of a Post-Reformation Slogan', in Philip E. Satterthwaite and David F. Wright (eds.), *A Pathway into the Holy Scripture*, 322. Lane refers to the analysis of Nathan Hatch at this point. Nathan O. Hatch, 'Sola Scriptura and Novus Ordo Seclorum', in Nathan O. Hatch and Mark A. Noll (eds.), *The Bible in America*, 61.

[73] *De instituendis ministria Ecclesiae* (1523) *WA* XII, 173.2-6 = *LW* 40, 11; *WA* XII, 180.17-18 = *LW* 40, 21.

[74] 'Verum haec communio iuris cogit, ut unus, aut quotquot placuerint communitati, eligantur vel acceptentur, qui vice et nomine omnium qui idem iuris habent, exequantur officia ista publice' *De instituendis ministria Ecclesiae* (1523) *WA* XII, 189.21-23 = *LW* 40, 34; cf. *Ein Brief D. M. Luthers von den Schleichern und Winkelpredigern* (1532) *WA* XXX-III, 518-527 = *LW* 40, 383-394.

[75] Lane, 'Sola Scriptura?', 318-322.

[76] Among the most important studies are: Kurt-Victor Selge, '"Capta conscientiae in verbis Dei", Luthers Widerrufsverweigerung in Worms', in Fritz Reuter (ed.), *Der Reichstag zu Worms von 1521. Reichspolitik und Luthersache*, 180-

confession at Worms and in particular Luther's insistence that he be convinced 'by the testimony of the Scriptures *or by evident reason* (*ratione evidente*)'.[77] Does this amount to a 'double appeal', with Luther offering to accept the testimony of two distinct, and to some degree independent, authorities? If that were so, should his stand at Worms still be understood as the classic statement of the principle *sola scriptura*? Is Scripture supplemented by 'evident reason'?

Luther himself pointed to the background of this formula in the writings of Augustine. In his reply to Prierias from 1518 and again in the dedication in his early commentary on Galatians (1519), he referred to the words of Augustine's letter to Jerome from AD 405: 'no one should be believed, no matter how greatly he may excel in sanctity and learning (even in the highest degree of sanctity, I believe), unless he convinces you by the divine letters or by acceptable reasoning'.[78] Augustine's meaning is clear when its context is considered. In this same letter Augustine repeatedly argued for the unique status of Scripture. It would make little sense for him to argue such a position and then to insert a comment which allows for two co-ordinate authorities in the matter of theology. Further, his writing elsewhere on the subject confirms that a 'double appeal' is unlikely. In *De doctrina christiana*, he concluded: 'whatever man may have learnt from other sources, if it is hurtful, it is there condemned; if it is useful, it is there contained'.[79] When Augustine speaks of 'acceptable reason (*ratio probabilis*)', then, it is not to be understood as a second, discrete body of knowledge which supplies a lack in the teaching of Scripture. Rather it is the *process* of unfolding the argument of Scripture as a whole. Augustine was counselling a discernment that recognised as authoritative only the actual words of Scripture and the properly argued explanation and co-ordination of those words.

Another commonly recognised source for Luther's thought in this area is the teaching of William of Occam. After all, Luther himself

---

207; Bernhard Lohse, *Ration und Fides. Eine Untersuchung über die ratio in der Theologie Luthers*; Robert H. Fischer, 'A Reasonable Luther', in Franklin H. Littell (ed.), *Reformation Studies: Essays in Honor of R. H. Bainton*, 30-45; Brian A. Gerrish, *Grace and Reason: A Study in the Theology of Luther*, 10-27; Oberman, *Reformation*, 12-18.

[77] *Verhandlungen mit D. Martin Luther auf dem Reichstage zu Worms* (1521) *WA* VII, 838.4.

[78] '[N]isi divinis literis aut ratione probabili persuadeat' Augustine, *Epistulae*, LXXXII.1.3 (*CSEL*, XXXIV, 354). *WA* I, 647.21-24; *WA* II, 447.15-17 = *LW* 27, 156. Heiko Oberman mistakenly suggests that Luther does not cite this passage until 1530 (*WA* XXX-II, 384.1-8). Oberman, *Reformation*, 13 n.16.

[79] 'Nam quicquid homo extra didicerit, si noxium est, ibi damnatur; si utile est, ibi inuenitur' Augustine, *De doctrina christiana*, II.xlii (63) (*CCSL*, XXXII, 76).

identified the Occamist school as that in which he was trained.[80] In the light of this connection, it is significant that Occam had taught a clear separation of the theological and philosophical realms of thought almost two hundred years before the Diet of Worms.[81] While reason is both competent and necessary in the realm of philosophy or worldly experience, revelation reigns supreme in the realm of theology. This distinction is important for a number of reasons, not least because it allowed Occam to give reason a valuable role while still denying any inadequacy or insufficiency in Scripture with respect to the theological realm. Reason could not be treated as a basis for faith for 'it is not necessary to believe what is not contained in the Bible nor deduced by necessary and clear consequence from that which is contained there'.[82]

Luther's inclusion of evident reason in his confession at Worms is undoubtedly made against the background provided by Augustine and Occam. The connection to both is made explicit in Luther's own writing. It gives initial grounds for suspecting that he was not positing a second authority alongside Scripture, but was simply recognising that some biblical truth cannot be established by the production of a single passage of Scripture. For example, there is no one passage which establishes the entire doctrine of the Trinity. Nevertheless, this doctrine exists as an article of faith because it is the good and necessary consequence of a number of passages.

A wider examination of Luther's excursuses on the subject of human reason gives further grounds for this conclusion. It is important to realise that Luther's assessment of human reason was not entirely negative. In the first place, he was prepared to grant the value of logic in the training of a person to preach. While he had little time for Aristotle's metaphysical works, he was prepared to retain the latter's logical works for just this purpose.[83] It was not so much the principles of logic as the application of them which he considered regularly and fundamentally flawed. Indeed, at a number of points Luther criticised the Swiss for their failures in logic.[84]

---

[80] *Responsio Lvtheriana ad Condemnationem Doctrinalem per Magistros Nostros Lovanienses et Colonienses factam* (1520) *WA* VI, 195.4.

[81] Ozment, *Age of Reform*, 61.

[82] 'quod nec in Biblia continetur nec ex solis contentis in Biblia potest consequentia necessaria et manifesta inferri' William of Occam, *Dialogus super Dignitate Papali et Regia*, 411, cf. 415.

[83] *An den christlichen Adel deutscher Nation von des christlichen Standes Besserung* (1520) *WA* VI, 458.26-28 = *LW* 44, 201; cf. *Disputatio de sententia: Verbum caro factum est* (1539) *WA* XXXIX-II, 24.20-26 = *LW* 38, 257.

[84] *Vom Abendmahl Christi. Bekenntnis* (1528) *WA* XXVI, 275.33-34 = *LW* 37, 134; *WA* XXVI, 323.13-327.4 = *LW* 37, 211-214; *WA* XXVI, 437.30-445.17 = *LW* 37, 294-303.

Luther could be extraordinarily positive about the potential of reason, when it was used within its own sphere and in humble dependence upon the God who created it. For example, in the *Disputatio de homine* from 1536, Luther set out the following theses:

> 4. And it is certainly true that reason is the most important and the highest in rank among all things and, in comparison with other things of this life, the best and something divine.
> 5. It is the inventor and mentor of all the arts, medicines, laws, and of whatever wisdom, power, virtue, and glory men possess in this life.
> 6. By virtue of this fact it ought to be named the essential difference by which man is distinguished from the animals and other things.
> 7. Holy Scripture also makes it lord over the earth, birds, fish, and cattle, saying, 'Have dominion'.
> 8. That is, that it is a sun and a kind of god appointed to administer these things in this life.
> 9. Nor did God after the fall of Adam take away this majesty of reason, but rather confirmed it.[85]

Reason itself was not only adequate but sufficient, and indeed divinely intended, for the performance of certain tasks.[86] Luther's use of the language of rule (*gubernatio*) and majesty (*maiestas*) emphasised precisely this divinely given sufficiency. There are certain fields in which reason itself provides all the authority necessary to warrant assent and consequent action. With respect to these it can be said that the Fall has not destroyed or impaired reason in and of itself.[87] Instead, it is the fallen human being who misuses this gift of God, distorting it

---

[85] '4. Et sane verum est, quod ratio omnium rerum res et caput et prae caeteris rebus huius vitae optimum et divinum quiddam sit. 5. Quae est inventrix et gubernatrix omnium Artium, Medicinarum, Iurium, et quidquid in hac vita sapientiae, potentiae, virtutis et gloriae ab hominibus possidetur. 6. Ut hinc merito ipsa vocari debeat differentia essentialis, qua constituatur homo, differre ab animalibus et rebus aliis. 7. Quam et scriptura sancta constituit talem dominam super terram, volucres, pisces, pecora, dicens: Dominamini. 8. Hoc est, ut sit Sol et Numen quoddam ad has res administrandas in hac vita positum. 9. Nec eam Maiestatem Deus post lapsum Adae ademit rationi, sed potius confirmavit.' *Die Disputation de homine* (1536) *WA* XXXIX-I, 175. 9-21 = *LW* 34, 137.

[86] Cf. *Kirchenpostille* (1522) *WA* X-I/1, 527.14-531.4; *Genesisvorlesung* (1535-45) *WA* XLIII, 104.37-39 = *LW* 3, 320; Gerrish, *Grace and Reason*, 12; Althaus, *Theology*, 64.

[87] *In XV Psalmos graduum* (1532-3) *WA* XL-III, 221.10-222.26. Oberman, *Reformation*, 16.

in a way which supports both pride and autonomous action.[88] This misuse includes all attempts to introduce the rule of reason beyond its sphere of competence, especially with respect to the knowledge of God himself. In such cases reason becomes another instrument in the great rebellion led by the devil and as a consequence actually harms those who use it.[89] Since this is the common experience of the race, Luther is able to speak of 'reason prior to faith' as darkness.[90]

Luther spoke positively of reason in another connection, namely when it has been 'illuminated by the Holy Spirit'.[91] This reason arising from faith actually 'promotes' faith.[92] This is the case because the gospel does not do away with the need to think and understand, but provides the context in which that thinking and understanding can be done as God intended it to be done.[93] This context is determinative, allowing Luther to say: 'reason, speech, and all gifts and created things are therefore different in believers and Christians than in unbelievers'.[94] In another piece of *Tischreden* he explained the difference: reason in the context of faith 'takes all its thoughts from the Word'.[95] Indeed, Luther spoke of the possibility that reason might experience 'regeneration through the Word'.[96] In this context, as 'reason captive and in submission to Christ (*ratio capta in obsequium Christi*)', Luther even allows it a place in the interpretive enterprise: 'when illuminated by the Holy Spirit, reason helps to interpret the Holy Scriptures'.[97]

Alongside this positive appraisal of reason as created and reason illuminated by the Holy Spirit, we must acknowledge the numerous

---

[88] *In XV Psalmos graduum* (1532-3) *WA* XL-III, 222.29-223.24.
[89] *Tischreden* #439 (1533) *WATr* I, 191.15-34 = *LW* 54, 71.
[90] 'respondit rationem ante fidem et cognitionem Dei esse tenebras' *Tischreden* #2938b (26-29 January 1533) *WATr* III, 105.14 = *LW* 54, 183.
[91] 'illustrata a Spiritu' *Tischreden* #439 (1533) *WATr* I, 191.25, 191.34 = *LW* 54, 71.
[92] 'ita ratio in piis alia est, cum non pugnat cum fide, sed illam promovet.' *Tischreden* #2938b (26-29 January 1533) *WATr* III, 105.19-20 = *LW* 54, 183.
[93] *Crucigers Sommerpostille* (1544) *WA* XXII, 108.11-18; Gerrish, *Grace and Reason*, 22.
[94] 'Sic ratio, lingua et omnia dona et creaturae sunt aliae in piis et christianis quam in impiis.' *Tischreden* #2938b (26-29 January 1533) *WATr* III, 106.8-10 = *LW* 54, 184.
[95] 'Ratio autem illustrata nimbt alle gedanken vom verbo.' *Tischreden* #439 (1533) *WATr* I, 191.33 = *LW* 54, 71.
[96] 'Atque haec est regeneratio per verbum' *Tischreden* #2938a (26-29 January 1533) *WATr* III, 104.33; *Tischreden* #2938b *WATr* III, 105.24 = *LW* 54, 183.
[97] 'sed illustrata a Spiritu hilfft judicirn die heylig schrifft.' *Tischreden* #439 (1533) *WATr* I, 191.25-26 = *LW* 54, 71.

indisputably negative comments Luther made about reason, including his famous description of it as 'the foremost whore the devil has'.[98] The kind of reason he was attacking was that which transgresses the boundaries of its competence and which, in league with the devil himself, grasps at a knowledge of God apart from his revelation and in defiance of the theology of the cross. Reason in this sense despises faith,[99] finds the truth which gave rise to the formula *simul iustus et peccator* offensive,[100] and cannot persuade us that God gives His Son and loves us.[101] Such is the case, Luther argued, because of 'a kind of neglect of the Word of God'.[102] If reason is to be useful at all, it must be humbled and made submissive to the Word.[103]

Here then is the wider context for an assessment of Luther's well-known confession before the Diet of Worms. Although expressed in a variety of ways, and in some contexts more forcefully than others, there is remarkable consistency in Luther's view of reason — its usefulness, its limits, and its abuse — throughout his life.[104] Most importantly for our purposes, there is no evidence that Luther ever believed reason to be a source of theological truth distinct from Holy Scripture. The only legitimate use of reason in the realm of theology is an instrumental one, applied in the context of faith and the work of the Holy Spirit, and anchored firmly in the text of Scripture itself. In this way it is again clear that Luther's use of the expression *ratio evidens* was completely in line with that of Augustine and Occam. He did not

---

[98] 'Ratio [...] es ist die höchste Hure, die der Teuffel hat' *Predigt am 1 Sonntag nach Epiphaniä* (10 January 1546) *WA* LI, 126.29-32 = *LW* 51, 374.

[99] 'Promissio autem ita est donum, ut nos nihil afferamus ad fidem, quia prius est promissum, et quia ratio aversatur fidem.' *Die Disputation de iustificatione* (1536) *WA* XXXIX-I, 90.23 = *LW* 34, 160; cf. *Von dem Papsttum zu Rom wider den hochberühmten Romanisten zu Leipzig* (1520) *WA* VI, 291.4-18 = *LW* 39, 63; *Predigt über die Passionsgeschichte am Montag nach Invokavit* (6 March 1525) *WA* XVII-I, 68.2-9; *Genesisvorlesung* (1535-45) *WA* XLIII, 374.11 = *LW* 4, 330.

[100] *Die Disputation de iustificatione* (1536) *WA* XXXIX-I, 97.5-13 = *LW* 34, 166; *WA* XXXIX-I, 515.5-8.

[101] 'Ratio videt mortem prae se; das sie da nit sol erschrecken, hoc non potest. Item quod Deus dat suum Filium und sol mich so lieb haben, hoc non potest persuaderi nobis, ut dicamus: Du hast deinen Son nit umbsonst lassen creuzigen. Sunt enim haec supra rationem.' *Tischreden* #388 (30 November 1532) *WATr* I, 168.8-12 = *LW* 54, 60.

[102] 'Hoc ratio non videt. Est enim neglectus quidam verbi Dei' *Die Disputation de iustificatione* (1536) *WA* XXXIX-I, 98.2 = *LW* 34, 167.

[103] This is Luther's explanation of the divine command to circumcise. *Kirchenpostille* (1522) *WA* X-I/1, 505.4-506.9 = *LW* 52, 149-150.

[104] Fischer, 'A Reasonable Luther', 45.

consider it a supplement to Holy Scripture; rather it remained a way of affirming the teaching of the whole Scripture.

Scripture and Experience

Luther emphasised the fundamental importance of experience (*experientia, Erfahrung*) in the process and product of theological reflection. This emphasis is so strong in his preaching and writing that it raises its own questions about any unqualified endorsement of the sufficiency of Holy Scripture. If he believed 'Scripture is not understood unless it is brought home, that is, experienced', then did he hold Christian experience to be a necessary interpretive supplement to Scripture itself?[105]

There can be no doubt that Luther considered Christian experience in general, and the experience of spiritual anguish and despair which he called *Anfechtung* in particular, to be vital if theology was to be of any value. This much is clear in his well-known words from 1519: 'not understanding, reading, or speculation, but living, no, dying and being damned make a theologian'.[106] At table in 1531, he expressed the same idea more succinctly: 'Experience alone makes a theologian'.[107] Luther could even evaluate other theologians on the basis of their awareness of the experiential dimension of theological truth.[108]

Of course Luther was generalising from his own situation. Looking back in 1532 he told of the role experience had played in his theological breakthrough: 'I did not learn my theology all at once. I had to ponder over it ever more deeply, and my spiritual trials were of help to me in this, for one does not learn anything without practice'.[109] Furthermore, the theology which had emerged in the midst of such intense struggle in the years 1514 to 1521, was developed in the context of continuing struggle in the years that followed.[110] Time and

---

[105] 'Die schrifft versteht keiner, sie kome den einem zu haus, id est, experiatur.' *Tischreden* #3097 (n.d.) *WATr* III, 170.1-2.

[106] 'Vivendo, immo moriendo et damnando fit theologus, non intelligendo, legendo aut speculando.' *Operationes in Psalmos* (1519-21) *WA* V, 163.28-29.

[107] 'Sola autem experientia facit theologum.' *Tischreden* #46 (1531) *WATr* I, 16.13 = *LW* 54, 7; cf. *Tischreden* #4777 (1530) *WATr* IV, 490.24-491.1.

[108] *Rationis Latomianae confutatio* (1521) *WA* VIII, 127.18-19 = *LW* 32, 258; *Tischreden* #1351 (January-March 1532) *WATr* II, 64.22-24.

[109] 'Ich hab mein theologiam nit auff ein mal gelernt, sonder hab ymmer tieffer und tieffer grubeln mussen, da haben mich meine tentationes hin bracht, quia sine usu non potest disci.' *Tischreden* #352 (1532) *WATr* I, 146.12-14 = *LW* 54, 50.

[110] John von Rohr, 'Medieval Consolation and the Young Luther's Despair', in Franklin H. Littell (ed.), *Reformation Studies: Essays in Honor of Roland H.*

again Luther referred to his *Anfechtungen,* even explaining the struggles of biblical characters in terms of them.[111]

Nevertheless Luther did not offer experience as the means of gaining a knowledge of God that is not contained in Scripture. On the contrary, experience confirms to the stubborn and rebellious heart the truth that is already taught in Scripture. Luther's comments in the preface to the 1539 edition of his German works made just this point. After agreeing with Augustine about the unique place of the Scriptures, he set out to provide guidelines for 'a correct way of studying theology'. This he proposed to do with reference to three rules presented by David in Ps. 119: prayer (*oratio*), meditation (*meditatio*), and spiritual struggle (*tentatio, Anfechtung*). It is in his explanation of the third of these that he makes the point: 'this is the touchstone which teaches you not only to know and understand, but also to experience how right, how true, how sweet, how lovely, how mighty, how comforting God's Word is, wisdom beyond all wisdom'.[112] Here it is clear that the end result of the spiritual struggle is not an additional or supplementary knowledge of Christian truth. Instead, it is a love for God's word and a seeking for it by those in whom it has already taken root.[113]

The importance of experience comes, then, not from some lack in the Scriptures, but from the nature of the Scriptures as the Word of the living and present God. 'These are not just words for reading', Luther explained in 1530, 'but words for living'.[114] In fact it was not Luther but the Enthusiasts, who proposed experience as an addition to

---

Bainton, 61-74; McGrath, *Theology of the Cross,* 169-175; Oberman, *Luther,* 175-179; Lane, 'Sola Scriptura?', 306.

[111] C. Warren Hovland, 'Anfechtung in Luther's Biblical Exegesis', in Franklin H. Littell (ed.), *Reformation Studies: Essays in Honor of R. H. Bainton,* 46-60. Hovland points to Luther's description of the experiences of Adam and Eve, Cain, Abraham, Jacob, Joseph, Job, the Psalmist, Jonah, Mary, the Canaanite woman in Mt. 15, and Paul.

[112] 'Die ist der Prüfestein, die leret dich nicht allein wissen und verstehen, sondern auch erfaren, wie recht, wie warhafftig, wie süsse, wie lieblich, wie mechtig, wie tröstlich Gottes wort sey, weisheit uber alle weisheit.' *Vorrede zum 1. Bande der Wittenberger Ausgabe* (1539) *WA* L, 660.1-4 = *LW* 34, 286-287.

[113] *Vorrede zum 1. Bande der Wittenberger Ausgabe* (1539) *WA* L, 660.8-10 = *LW* 34, 287.

[114] 'Und es sind doch ja nicht Lesewort, wie sie meinen, Sondern eitel Lebewort drinnen, die nicht zum speculiren und hoch zu tichten sondern zum leben und thun dargesetzt sind.' *Das Schone Consitemini* (1530) *WA* XXXI-I, 67.24-27 = *LW* 14, 46; cf. *Vorlesung über den 1. Timotheusbrief* (1528) *WA* XXVI, 55.35-56.1 = *LW* 28, 290.

Scripture. Luther recognised in this a point of contact between the theology of radicals like Thomas Müntzer and that of the pope:

> In these things, which concern the spoken, external word, it is certain to maintain this: God gives no one his Spirit or grace apart from the external word which goes before. We are thus protected from the enthusiasts, that is the spirits, who boast that they have the Spirit apart from and before contact with the word. They judge the Scriptures or the spoken word accordingly, interpreting and stretching them however it pleases them. Müntzer did this, and there are still many who do this today. They want to be shrewd judges between the spirit and the letter, but they do not know what they say or teach. The papacy is also pure enthusiasm. The pope boasts that 'all laws are in the shrine of his heart' and that what he decides and judges in his churches is supposed to be spirit and law — as if it is equal to or above the Scriptures or the spoken word.[115]

Luther's commitment to engagement with the Scriptures as the Word of the living God, addressed to those who are *simul iustus et peccator,* was crucial to his emphasis on experience in general and *Anfechtung* in particular. The evidence does not support the suggestion that he considered experience to be a supplement to Scripture, nor does it compel us to regard Luther as a proto-existentialist.[116] Instead, it suggests that his insistence on more than speculation and academic detachment when it came to the study of the Scriptures was born of a determination to take the Scriptures themselves seriously. Thus, in the very piece of *Tischreden* in which he spoke of the role of his *Anfechtungen* in his theological development, he went on to say: 'To

---

[115] 'Und jnn diesen stücken, so das mündlich, eusserlich wort betreffen, ist fest darauff zu bleiben, das Gott niemand seinen Geist oder gnade gibt on durch oder mit dem vorgehend eusserlichem wort, Damit wir uns bewaren fur den Enthusiasten, das ist geistern, so sich rhümen, on und vor dem wort den geist zu haben, und darnach die Schrifft oder mündlich wort tichten, deuten und dehnen jres gefallens, wie der Muntzer thet, und noch viel thun heutigs tages, die zwisschen dem Geist und Buchstaben scharfe richter sein wollen, und wissen nicht, was sie sagen oder setzen. Den das Bapstum auch eitel Enthusiasmus ist, darin der Bapst rhümet, alle rechte sind im schrein seines hertzen, Und was er mit seiner Kirchen urteilt und heisst, das sol Geist und Recht sein, wens gleich uber und wider die schrifft oder mündlich wort ist.' *Die Schmalkaldischen Artikel* (1537) *WA* L, 245.1-18 = Russell, p. 145.

[116] Lennart Pinomaa, *Der existentielle Charakter der Theologie Luthers: Das Hervorbrechen der Theologie der Anfechtung und ihre Bedeutung für das Lutherverständnis*. Some of the work of Gerhard Ebeling points in this direction. Ebeling, 'The New Hermeneutics', 45-46; Ebeling, 'Hermeneutics III', 460-464.

be sure, the Holy Scriptures are sufficient in themselves, but God grant that I find the right text'.[117]

Sufficiency and the Purpose of Scripture

Before reflecting on the significance of Luther's affirmation of the sufficiency of Scripture for his statements about its authority and his interpretive method, a brief comment is in order about the purpose of Scripture. As we observed in a previous chapter, any affirmation of sufficiency entails some understanding of purpose. It is always worth asking 'sufficient for what?'

In the first instance, Luther spoke of the sufficiency of Scripture in connection with the articles of faith and the command to good works. In the *Propositiones adversus totam synagogam Sathanae et universas portas inferorum,* prepared in July 1530, he argued:

> 3. All of the articles are sufficiently established in the Holy Scriptures, so that there is no need for them to be established otherwise.
> 4. All of the commandments of good works are sufficiently established in the Holy Scriptures so that there is no need for them to be established otherwise.[118]

Here is the seed of the later Protestant confession that Scripture is sufficient for Christian faith and life. It is Scripture's sufficiency in this respect which dismisses tradition, reason, and experience as necessary supplements to it, while at the same time allowing that each of these may be useful in confirming or aiding the explanation of its teaching. Scripture needs no addition in these areas; indeed, any attempt to provide such could only be seen as unbelief and an assault upon the Scriptures themselves.

More specifically, Luther spoke of the sufficiency of Scripture with regard to its presentation of Christ. In the *Kirchenpostille* he explained why it was necessary for the Magi to come to Herod and to be

---

[117] 'Also ist scriptura sancta auch gewiss gnug, sed Got geb, das ich den rechten spruch erwissche.' *Tischreden* #352 (1532) *WATr* I, 146.25-26 = *LW* 54, 51.

[118] '3. Omnes articuli sufficienter sunt in scripturis sanctis conditi, ut non sit opus ullum praeterea condi. 4. Omnia praecepta bonorum operum sunt in scripturis sanctis sufficienter statuta, ut non sit opus ullum praeterea statui.' *Sequentes propositiones adversus totam synagogam Sathanae & universas portas inferorum* (1530) *WA* XXX-II, 420.11-16; cf. *Grund und Ursach aller Artikel D. Martin Luthers, so durch römische Bulle unrechtlich verdammt sind* (1521) *WA* VII, 453.1-2 = *LW* 32, 96; *Kirchenpostille* (1522) *WA* X-I/1, 627.16-20 = *LW* 52, 206-207; *Die Zirkulardisputation über das Recht des Widerstands gegen den Kaiser* (9 May 1539) *WA* XXXIX-II, 43.20-21. Althaus, p. 5.

Sola Scriptura?

instructed by the chief priests and scribes from the writings of the prophets:

> [Christ] did this to teach us to cling to Scripture and not to follow our own presumptuous ideas or any human teaching. For it was not his desire to give us his Scripture in vain. It is in Scripture and nowhere else, that he permits himself to be found. He who despises Scripture and sets it aside, will never find him.[119]

Since this is the case, there can be no use in proposing alternatives or supplements to Holy Scripture. Luther made the point again in the midst of a sermon on Mt. 16:13 delivered on 29 June 1522: 'Christ will not be known except through his Word'.[120] As the whole Scripture is about Christ and is intended to present him as the object of our faith and hope, and as he is the only one in whom salvation is to be found, Luther is also able to say that Scripture contains all that is necessary for our salvation.[121]

Another explanation of the sufficiency of Scripture which bears on its purpose is Luther's insistence that God has provided in his Word a sure and certain ground for confidence in the face of doubt, a troubled conscience, and the assaults of the devil. In 1521 Luther advised, 'Hold to Scripture and the Word of God. There you will find truth and security — assurance and a faith that is complete, pure, sufficient, and abiding'.[122] The significance of Scripture as a sufficient ground for resisting any attack on Christian faith and hope is obvious in the light of Luther's own continuing experience of *Anfechtung* and his perception of the Christian life as a struggle against the devil.[123]

---

[119] 'Das geschicht darumb, das er uns lere, tzu der schrifft uns hallten, und nit unßerm dunckel noch keyniß menschen lere folgen; denn er wil seyne schrifft nit umbsonst geben haben, da wil er sich finden lassen, und sonst nyrgend; wer die voracht und faren lest, der sol und muß yhn nymmer finden.' *Kirchenpostille* (1522) *WA* X-I/1, 576.6-10 = *LW* 52, 171.

[120] 'Christus wirt nicht erkannt, allain durch sein wort.' *Sermon von Gewalt Sanct Peters* (29 June 1522) *WA* X-III, 210.11-12.

[121] *Vom Mißbrauch der Messe* (1521) *WA* VIII, 491.15-16 = *LW* 36, 144; cf. *Tractatus de libertate christiana* (1520) *WA* VII, 50.33-35; *Rationis Latomianae confutatio* (1521) *WA* VIII, 99.20-21 = *LW* 32, 217; *De servo arbitrio* (1525) *WA* XVIII, 653.28-31 = *LW* 33, 91.

[122] 'Halt dich an die schrifft und gottis wort, da ist die warheyt, da wirstu sicher sein, da ist trew und glawb, gantz, lautter gnugsam und bestendig.' *Grund und Ursach aller Artikel D. Martin Luthers, so durch römische Bulle unrechtlich verdammt sind* (1521) *WA* VII, 455.22-24 = *LW* 32, 98.

[123] For the use of Scripture against the assaults of conscience, see *De abroganda Missa Privata Martini Lutheri Sententia* (1521) *WA* VIII, 412.17-19 = *LW* 36, 134. On the use of Scripture against the assaults of the devil and heretics, see *Praelectio in psalmum 45* (1532) *WA* XL-II, 592.32-37 = *LW* 12, 287.

For Luther, then, the sufficiency of Scripture stands in close relation to its purpose as God's revelation of himself and his purposes focussed in the life and ministry of Jesus Christ. It also affirms the adequacy of God's provision for those who live in the light of that revelation and redemption, yet still in a world where human weakness, sin, and spiritual assault remain undeniable realities.

Sufficiency and the Authority of Scripture

Luther's affirmation of the truth expressed in the slogan *sola scriptura* was first and foremost a statement of the unique authority of Holy Scripture. As we have noted, this was in keeping with his Augustinian and Occamist heritage, and indeed this principle was a feature of his theological work long before the break with Rome. Yet even early on Luther pressed the point with characteristic vigour. In the Dictata he explained that 'the Church does not, like the heretics who teach their own doctrine, have independent breasts with which she feeds milk to the weak, but she is captive to the authority of Scripture and does not teach anything but the Word of God'.[124] Later events would, of course, have an impact on the way in which he expressed this principle. His preparation and conduct of the debate with Eck at Leipzig in 1519, for example, certainly made it necessary for him to unfold its implications. However, right from the start of his career at Wittenberg Luther stressed the unique authority of Scripture which neither requires nor tolerates any supplementation. His statements prior to Leipzig are perfectly consistent with his position in the *Assertio omnium articulorum*: 'nothing but the divine words are to be the first principles of Christians'.[125]

This willingness to be 'captive to the Word of God' entailed a certain freedom with respect to all other authorities. Luther insisted upon this freedom in the debate with Eck: 'it is not possible for the faithful Christian to be forced beyond Holy Scripture, which is the proper divine law, unless he receives new and tested revelation'.[126] He maintained that only God's Word rightly binds the Christian

---

[124] 'Similiter significat, quod Ecclesia ubera, quibus lacte pascit infirmos, non habet discincta sicut Heretici, qui sua docent, sed captiva in auctoritatem Scripture, non docens nisi verbum dei.' *Dictata super Psalterium* (1513-15) *WA* III, 261.13-16 = *LW* 10, 219.

[125] 'Sint ergo Christianorum prima principia non nisi verba divina' *Assertio omnium articulorum M. Lutheri per bullam Leonis X.* (1520) *WA* VII, 98.4.

[126] 'Nec potest fidelis Christianus cogi ultra sacram scripturam, que est proprie ius divinum, nisi accesserit nova et probata revelatio' *Disputatio I. Eccii et M. Lutheri Lipsiae habita* (1519) *WA* II, 279.23-24.

conscience. Although, as he had conceded a year later, other things might be asserted, they may be held only as opinions and need not be believed.[127] Here is an important perspective on Luther's application of the *sola scriptura* principle. Luther, unlike some of his contemporaries and many who came after him, left room for differences of opinion outside the teaching of Scripture. The real problem arises, he observed, when one claims that his extra-biblical opinions are authoritative and ought to be believed by others. This is precisely what Luther considered to be happening amongst the theologians of Rome. Luther argued that this kind of tyranny must be resisted because 'the Scriptures liberate consciences and forbid that they be taken captive by the doctrines of men'.[128] Even Luther himself could refer to the opinions of others with approval, yet there was always a lingering dispensability about the writings of the Fathers, the Schoolmen, the popes, the councils, and the philosophers, which marked them all out as different from the Scriptures. As Luther had maintained in his treatise on Christian freedom from 1520: 'the soul can do without anything except the Word of God'.[129]

However, more was required than merely freedom with respect to extra-biblical authorities. Luther consistently maintained that all putative sources of theological truth outside of Scripture must be tested. Although he could point to a patristic precedent for this insistence,[130] the real impetus came from the Scripture itself, and in particular one verse which he quoted often, especially between 1517 to 1521: 'Test ($\delta o \kappa \iota \mu \acute{a} \zeta \epsilon \tau \epsilon$) everything, hold fast to what is good'.[131] The standard to be applied in this process of testing was nothing less than the teaching of Scripture itself. In a sermon on Jn. 2:23-24, preached on 23 March 1538, Luther explained:

---

[127] 'Nam quod sine scripturis asseritur aut revelatione probata, opinari licet, credi non est necesse.' *De captivitate Babylonica ecclesiae praeludium* (1520) *WA* VI, 508.19-20 = *LW* 36, 29; cf. *Antwort deutsch auf König Heinrichs Buch* (1522) *WA* X-II, 253.10-14.

[128] 'Die schrifft macht die gewissen frey und verpeutt, sie mit menschen leren zu fangen, ßo fangen sie die menschen lere.' *Von Menschenlehre zu meiden und Antwort auf Sprüche* (1522) *WA* X-II, 91.23-25 = *LW* 35, 153.

[129] 'die seele kan allis dings emperen on des worts gottis' *Von der Freiheit eines Christenmenschen* (1520) *WA* VII, 22.9-10 = *LW* 31, 345.

[130] *Auf das überchristlich, übergeistlich und überkünstlich Buch Bocks Emsers zu Leipzig Antwort* (1521) *WA* VII, 640.36-38 = *LW* 39, 166; cf. *Contra malignum I. Eccii iudicium M. Lutheri defensio* (1519) *WA* II, 626.33-39.

[131] 1 Thes. 5:21. The pervasive nature of Luther's appeal to this verse is not often noted.

For even if they are equally holy, you must not for that reason say that they are not able to err or fail, and that we must discuss, trust, and depend on all the Fathers, or take and believe all they have taught as right. Rather, take the touchstone or testing-stone, namely the Divine Word, and test, assess, and judge accordingly all that the Fathers have written, preached and said, as well as the rules and human ordinances made by others. For where one does not do this, he will be easily misled and deceived.[132]

Luther's call to test the statements of the Fathers, and anything else which presented itself as Christian truth, left open the possibility that these things might be approved as consistent with the teaching of Scripture. His own use of extra-biblical material in his theological work makes clear that he viewed this as more than simply a possibility. The Fathers were not always wrong, and the principles of logic were not faulty in and of themselves. When they accorded with the teaching of Scripture it was perfectly appropriate to use them as corroborative or illustrative material. Nevertheless, it is also clear that only Scripture itself operated as an authority for him in the strict sense of the term, for it was only Scripture which he felt constrained to believe without reservation and without reference to some external validating principle. The authority of Scripture is absolute, arising from within itself and related to its origin and character as the Word of God. The authority of all other theological writing depends upon its agreement with what is contained in Scripture. Thus Luther did not use the language of sufficiency as a device for avoiding all engagement with the thoughts of others. Instead he used it to demonstrate the unique character of Scripture which justifies the claims made for it and undergirds his approach to biblical interpretation. He put it this way in the *Acta Augustana* of 1518: 'The truth of Scripture comes first. After that is accepted, one may determine whether the words of men can be

---

[132] 'denn ob sie gleich heilig sind, so must du darumb nicht sagen, das sie nicht jrren und feilen köndten, und das man auff alle der Veter rede trawen und bawen solte, item, alles fur recht annemen und gleuben, was sie geleret hetten, sondern nim den Streichstein oder Probirstein fur die hand, nemlich das Göttliche Wort, und probire, urteile und richte darnach alle das jenige, was die Veter geschrieben, gepredigt und geredet haben, auch sonst von Regeln, Meschen satzungen und anderm gemacht haben, denn wo man diss nicht thut, so wird man lidderlich verfüret und betrogen. *Auslegung des ersten und zweiten Kaptiels des Johannesevangeliums* (1538) *WA* XLVI, 767.7-15 = *LW* 22, 254.

accepted as true'.[133] Holy Scripture is the only sure rock on which we can stand.[134]

In polemical contexts Luther could, of course, speak in stronger terms. Here the call to test all other writings gave way to descriptions which left little room for anything but their complete rejection. In 1521, in his treatise on the misuse of the mass, he could say both that 'all that occurs outside the Scriptures, whether it is done by angels or men, is and ought to be suspect', and that 'whatever does not have its origin in the Scripture is surely from the devil himself'.[135] At the other end of his teaching career, in his reply to the thirty-two articles of the Louvain theologians in 1545, Luther insisted: 'whatever is taught in the Church of God without the Word is a godless lie'.[136] Yet even in the very treatises in which such remarks were made, Luther continued to use extra-biblical material in his argument, albeit in a carefully circumscribed way.[137]

Sufficiency and the Interpretation of Scripture

The sufficiency of Scripture would mean little if the biblical text could not be interpreted, or if it could only be interpreted with reference to

---

[133] 'prior est veritas scripturae, et post hoc, si hominis verba vera esse possunt, videndum.' *Acta Augustana* (1518) *WA* II, 21.5-6 = *LW* 31, 282.

[134] 'But that even many decretals are inconsistent with the sense of the Gospel is clearer than light, so that actual necessity itself compels us to flee for refuge to the most solid rock of Divine Scripture and not to believe rashly any, whoever they may be, who speak, decide, or act contrary to its authority. (Sed et multas decretales esse a sensu euangelico alienas, luce clarius est, ita ut necessitas ipsa rerum nos cogat ad divinae scripturae solidissimam petram confugere nec temere credere ullis, quicunque sint, qui citra illius autoritatem loquuntur, statuunt aut faciunt.)' *In epistolam Pauli ad Galatas commentarius* (1519) *WA* II, 447.11 = *LW* 27, 156; cf. *Predigt am Pfingstdienstag* (10 June 1522) *WA* X-III, 172.19-28.

[135] 'unnd alles, was ausserhalb der schrifft geschiet, es thun engel odder menschen, das ist und soll verdechtig seyn'; 'Denn was seyn ankunfft auß der schrifft nicht hatt, das ist gewißlich vom teuffel selbst.' *Vom Mißbrauch der Messe* (1521) *WA* VIII, 531. 29-31, 491.14-15 = *LW* 36, 191, 144.

[136] 'Quicquid in Ecclesia Dei docetur sine Verbo, mendatium & impietas est.' *Contra XXXII articulos Lovaniensium theologistarum* (1545) *WA* LIV, 425.2 = *LW* 34, 354.

[137] *Vom Mißbrauch der Messe* (1521) *WA* VIII, 503.4-6 = *LW* 36, 158; *WA* VIII, 510.7-8 = *LW* 36, 167; *WA* VIII, 547.35-548.2 = *LW* 36, 211; *Contra XXXII articulos Lovaniensium theologistarum* (1545) *WA* LIV, 427.3-4 = *LW* 34, 355-356.

extra-biblical material.[138] However, Luther's own statements, and his interpretive practice over thirty years of lecturing and writing, demonstrate that he did not believe this to be the case. Indeed, some of his most strident defences of the sufficiency of Scripture occur precisely in the context of a discussion about the interpretation of Scripture. A prime example is his claim in the *Assertio omnium articulorum* that Scripture is 'in and of itself most certain, simple, clear, its own interpreter, testing, judging and illuminating everything else'.[139] Here he was explicitly rejecting the Roman insistence that Holy Scripture could not be understood properly without the Fathers or the pope.

Luther's interpretive practice involved, as we have seen, the corroborative and illustrative use of all sorts of extra-biblical material. His lectures were full of references to the Fathers, to church history, and to the events of his own time. He could also criticise the interpretations of others for failures in elementary logic. Yet in all of this there could be no doubt that Scripture reigned supreme. The most useful tool he brought to his interpretation of any passage was his impressive knowledge of the Bible as a whole. He was quick to recognise allusions and parallels to other parts of Scripture, and remained determined to demonstrate the Christ-centredness of the whole Bible. Most importantly, it was the biblical text itself which remained the focus of Luther's attention, rather than the extra-biblical material he had introduced to illustrate or corroborate what was being said. All else could be accepted or rejected, yet Scripture must be heard because it is the Word of God.[140] While Luther obviously valued some writers above others, none were beyond criticism. An opinion of Augustine could just as readily be dismissed as that of Thomas Aquinas or Huldrych Zwingli. With remarkable consistency, though not always convincingly, he sought to explain the biblical text on its own terms, and called on others to do the same. Lecturing on Gn.

---

[138] Althaus, *Theology*, 76; R. W. Doermann, 'Luther's Principles of Biblical Interpretation', in F. W. Meuser and S. D. Schneider (eds.), *Interpreting Luther's Legacy: Essays in Honor of Edward C. Fendt*, 14; McGrath, *Theology of the Cross*, 76.

[139] 'scriptura [...] sit ipsa per sese certissima, facillima, apertissima, sui ipsius interpres, omnium omnia probans, iudicans et illuminans' *Assertio omnium articulorum M. Lutheri per bullam Leonis X novissimam damnatorum* (1520) *WA* VII, 97.23-24.

[140] Note Luther's comment on Jonah, from 1526: 'Who would believe this story and not regard it a lie and a fairy tale if it were not recorded in Scripture? (Wer wolts auch gleuben und nicht fur eine lügen und meerlin halten, wo es nicht ynn der schrifft stünde?)' *Der Prophet Jona ausgelegt* (1526) *WA* XIX, 219.26-27 = *LW* 19, 68.

24:1-4 in 1540, Luther considered the range of explanations available for the practice of making a vow with one hand under a thigh and then went on to conclude:

> One might have these thoughts if this custom had been handed down and adopted by the Fathers; but because Holy Scripture is altogether silent, it is not our business to make any assertions or denials. What Holy Scripture teaches, denies, or affirms, that we can safely imitate and teach.[141]

It is worth noticing once again that the concepts we have been examining in Luther's approach to Scripture reinforce one another. The sufficiency of Scripture requires the clarity of Scripture in order to be meaningful just as the clarity of Scripture could not properly be understood in isolation from its unity and coherence. Luther's conviction that the Bible has its origin in the benevolent purposes of God further strengthens his argument for each of its other characteristics. If his claims about the unique and sufficient authority of the biblical text were to be reflected in his interpretive practice, then much else would be entailed. Our investigation has revealed that much else was indeed entailed.

Modern studies have been correct to insist that in Luther's own practice *sola scriptura* did not equate with *nuda scriptura*. Luther proclaimed the unique and unassailable authority of Scripture, yet he did not simply leap over fifteen centuries to get back to the text and its time.[142] His approach to Scripture ought not therefore to be caricatured as an obscurantist refusal to listen to those who were engaged in the interpretive task before him or beside him. Yet we cannot avoid the conclusion that Luther meant much more by the sufficiency of Scripture than some would have him mean. A redefinition of *sola scriptura* in terms of 'the hermeneutical situation in which the reader is not so much the interpreter as the interpreted',[143] or as a metaphor pointing to the truth that the gospel is of God's making,[144] fails to do justice to the evidence. Luther's affirmation of the sufficiency of Scripture concerned both its authority and its interpretation. It forms another important part of the conceptual bridge we have been

---

[141] 'Haec cogitare licet, si fuisset is mos a patribus traditus et acceptus, sed quia scriptura sancta prorsus tacet, nostrum non est quicquam asserere aut negare. Quod scriptura sancta docet, negat aut affirmat, id tuto imitari et docere possumus.' *Genesisvorlesung* (1535-45) *WA* XLIII, 301.8-12 = *LW* 4, 230.

[142] Peter Stuhlmacher, *Historical Criticism and Theological Interpretation of Scripture*, 35.

[143] Gerald L. Bruns, *Hermeneutics Ancient and Modern*, 146.

[144] John Barton, *People of the Book? The Authority of the Bible in Christianity*, 86.

examining between these two dimensions of Luther's approach to Scripture. Late in life Luther reiterated its significance:

> I am content with this gift which I have, Holy Scripture, which abundantly teaches and supplies all things necessary both for this life and also for the life to come.[145]

---

[145] 'Contentus enim sum hoc dono, quod habeo scripturam sanctam, quae abunde docet et suppeditat omnia, quae sunt necessaria cum ad hanc, tum ad futuram vitam.' *Genesisvorlesung* (1535-45) *WA* XLIV, 246.12-14 = *LW* 6, 329.

Conclusion

Luther's Confidence in Scripture as the Authoritative Word of God

This study has provided a fresh examination of the evidence for Luther's approach to Holy Scripture. It has sought a more reliable interpretation of this aspect of Luther's thought through an appreciation of the exegetical and theological tradition which formed his pre-understanding and a careful, contextually-sensitive examination of his own statements. Above all else, it has pursued Luther's own words and his own connections of thought. Too often twentieth-century categories and twentieth-century interests have prevented us from properly understanding the contribution of this man who lived and taught in a very different world.

We have discovered a remarkable continuity in Luther's thought on the subject of Scripture from the years prior to the indulgence controversy to the end of his life. Undoubtedly he changed his mind on certain points. His use of such methods as the *Quadriga* began to give way to a greater stress on the grammatical sense of the biblical text and its historical situation even while he delivered his first series of lectures on the Psalms between the years 1513 and 1515. The 'letter and spirit' distinction which he first saw in Scripture was more often expressed in terms of 'law and gospel' after 1519. His views on particular biblical books would change as well, as witnessed by his revision of the early prefaces to Hebrews and Revelation. However his commitment to the authority of Scripture, and the basic lines of his understanding of its origin, nature, and use were given expression very early in his teaching career and remained constant throughout. The young Luther and the old Luther, Luther the controversialist and the Luther the pastor and teacher to the congregation in the *Schloßkirche* at Wittenberg, this complex and dynamic figure was both driven and energised by an approach to Holy Scripture which he considered thoroughly orthodox.[1] It is thus possible to recognise the true nature of the transformation which took place during those critical years between 1517 and 1521: it was not so much Luther's view of Scripture that changed as his perspective on the teaching of the Roman church. That which he once assumed was fundamentally in accord with Scripture he came to see as tragically opposed to its own life-source.

It has been shown that Luther's approach to Scripture drew significantly upon his exegetical and theological inheritance. This is not to deny the freshness and importance of his own contribution. However, when he discussed the origin of Scripture he used the language of divine and human authorship which can be found in the Fathers and many of the theologians of the medieval period. He built upon Augustine's distinction between law and grace when he discussed the unity of Scripture as well as adding a new dimension to the well-established practice of Christological exegesis. His strong insistence upon the clarity of Scripture had a distinctive character; nevertheless the question and its implications had featured in Christian thought since the time of the New Testament. Even his arguments for the sufficiency of Scripture have precedents in earlier mainstream Christian writing. The language of Worms is properly understood as a reflection of that found in the writings of Augustine and Occam.

We have also been able to demonstrate that Luther's assertions about the origin, nature, and use of Holy Scripture are profoundly connected to other major themes in his theology. His views on the nature of Scripture are closely related to his teaching on the incarnation of the Word and the theology of the cross. He was convinced that one could not tamper with the Scriptures without tampering with God. One could not describe the Scriptures as obscure without blaspheming God. Further, he insisted that the Scriptures had a vital role in what he saw as the basic structure of the Christian life: God addresses his people in human words and calls upon them to believe the words that he has spoken. These words are the Christian's only certain refuge in the face of the reality of suffering and trial (*die Anfechtungen*). To these connections could be added the nature of the Church as a creation of the word God has spoken and the human predicament which is both made known and itself addressed in the promises of Scripture. This evidence suggests that Luther's approach to Scripture is more integral to his entire theology than some modern studies have suggested.

In contrast to much modern Luther scholarship, the evidence we have examined establishes beyond doubt that Luther was concerned

---

[1] E. Gordon Rupp, '*Miles Emeritus?* Continuity and Discontinuity between the Young and the Old Luther', in George Yule (ed.), *Luther: Theologian for Catholics and Protestants*, 75-86.

with the actual words of Scripture. He understood the influence of the Holy Spirit to extend to 'the words and the order of the words'. He was willing to identify the text of Scripture as the Word of God repeatedly and without qualification, though in other places he used the same expression of Christ and insisted that only one form of the Word was *substantialiter Deus*. He spoke of the importance of languages, grammar, and assertions without denying the role of the Holy Spirit in the process of understanding as well as that of production. He emphasised the choice of words, the context in which they were used, and the intention of the author. When he affirmed the clarity of Scripture it was not simply the clarity of its essential doctrinal content with which he was concerned, but also the concrete form in which that doctrine is expressed. He even exhorted his congregations to build their understanding upon the foundation of clear Scripture 'understood according to the sound and meaning of the words'. Finally, it was the biblical text itself which he sought to defend and to which he considered himself a captive.

Most important of all, this study has shown the lines of connection between Luther's statements about biblical authority and his own interpretative method. We have used the image of a conceptual bridge which is made up of a series of basic convictions and which enables Luther to move between these two poles in his approach to Scripture. For the purposes of analysis four broad areas have been identified, though in Luther's own work these often occur together and are mutually dependent. In the first place, Luther could argue that Holy Scripture has supreme authority in matters of doctrine and life because he believed it to be the Word of God. These human words are God's self-expression and carry his authority. Thus they hold together by the very fact of their common primary authorship. Their origin in the purposes of the God who has turned towards us in Christ also generates an expectation that they are both accessible and intelligible, for it is inconceivable that God might fail to communicate effectively. Further, when God himself has spoken, all other speaking is immediately relativised. Here too is a reason for Luther's confidence as he approached the task of biblical interpretation. Luther could not approach the text with hesitation or indifference precisely because he knew this to be the Word of God which testifies to Christ. Careful attention to the text is the only appropriate course for one who is convinced that this is what God says.

Luther could also argue for the authority of Scripture because he believed that this collection of texts, in both its unity and diversity, points the believer to Christ, the one to whom God has given all authority and power. Luther's approach is clearly vulnerable at this point, especially in the light of his canonical decisions. He could certainly be charged with constructing an artificial unity in Scripture by marginalising those texts which did not seem to fit the pattern he had identified as the central thrust of Scripture. His ongoing struggle with the Epistle of James is a case in point here. Nevertheless, Luther's commitment to an entity he described as 'the whole Scripture' featured prominently in both his affirmations of biblical authority and his interpretive method. The whole Scripture was attributed to God and thus carried his authority. Likewise the whole Scripture circumscribed the interpretive task: *sacra scriptura sui ipsius interpres*. The identification of larger patterns of thought within the Bible itself (such as the law/gospel distinction) enabled Luther to break free from external interpretive structures such as the *Quadriga*. In this way Luther's appeal to the unity of Scripture reinforced his claims about its clarity. A difficult passage might become clear when it was seen in its immediate context or in the context of the Bible as a whole. Luther's regular practice of illustrating the thought of one passage with the teaching of another operates on just such a presupposition.

In similar ways, Luther's convictions about the clarity of Scripture support both his claims about its authority and his practice of biblical interpretation. Luther recognised that an appeal to the authority of Scripture could only be effective if the Scripture to which he appealed was clear. Yet precisely because God's choice to reveal himself and his purposes is always an effective one, Luther felt free to call on all people everywhere to submit to the teaching of Scripture. For the same reason he insisted that Christians are able to approach the biblical text with confidence rather than with scepticism. 'The Holy Spirit is no sceptic' was his aphoristic response to Erasmus.[2] He maintained that the clarity of Scripture is exactly what one would expect given the inspiration of the Scriptures by the God of the gospel. Clarity is essential to the purpose of the Scriptures, which is to testify in each and every place to Christ. It also means that the text can be approached directly, without glosses or commentary.

One further span of the conceptual bridge between Luther's doctrine of Scripture and his hermeneutic is his affirmation of *sola scriptura*. This affirmation was first and foremost a statement of the unique authority of Scripture. The Word of God always stands over and above the words of men. Yet it was at the same time a statement that Scripture could be interpreted on its own terms and did not require an external interpretive formula. Luther certainly did not jettison almost fifteen centuries of Christian reflection upon the text of Scripture, but he did consider himself free to disagree with the conclusions of the

---

[2] 'Spiritus sanctus non est Scepticus' *De servo arbitrio* (1525) *WA* XVIII, 605.32 = *LW* 33, 24.

Church Fathers and medieval doctors. He believed that to insist upon reading the Scriptures through the commentary of later writers was also to concede that Scripture was at best ambiguous and at worst unintelligible without them. This he would not do. Luther's commitment to the clarity of Scripture thus reinforced his affirmation of the sufficiency of Scripture.

It remains true that Luther did not provide a full-length treatise on the origin, nature and use of Holy Scripture. It is also true that the network of connections we have explored in Luther's scattered comments on the subject did not ensure he was always thoroughly consistent in his approach to Scripture. Yet the points of tension identified in the course of our study, arising from his determination to find Christ in every part of Scripture, or the arguments presented by opponents in the heat of controversy, or even his personal frustration with the challenge that James 2 appeared to present to his understanding of justification by faith, should not be allowed to obscure the way these connections operated in the bulk of his theological work. Further, these are tensions which later generations have seen in Luther's approach. Luther himself saw no inconsistency between his principles and his practice.

As we noted at the very beginning of this study, Luther used the word 'boldness (*Kühnheit*)' or 'confidence (*confidentia*)' in connection with a Christian's possession and use of Holy Scripture. Such boldness characterised his own statements concerning the authority of Scripture and his own interpretative practice. Luther did not hesitate to place himself and all men under the scrutiny of Scripture. He would accept no attempt at evasion, whether through an appeal to ecclesiastical authority, autonomous human reason, or private revelations of the Spirit. Nor did he hesitate to proclaim what he saw to be the teaching of Scripture. He insisted that God has spoken and it is both possible and necessary for his people to understand what he has said. This study helps to explain Luther's boldness when it came to the Bible. Luther approached Holy Scripture as the inspired Word of God, which find its focus in the person and work of Jesus Christ, of whom it speaks both clearly and sufficiently. It is this understanding which led him to write to the Elector Frederick on 27 March 1519:

> I cannot help loving those about whom I hear that they love the Holy Scriptures, and hating those who distort and despise them.[3]

---

[3] 'Nescio enim qui fiat, ut quoscunque sacrarum literarum amantes audio, non possim non diligere, rursum perversores et contemptores earum non odisse' *Operationes in Psalmos* (1519) *WA* v, 22.11-13 = *LW* 14, 284.

Bibliography

Allison, G.R., 'The Protestant Doctrine of the Perspicuity of Scripture: A Reformulation on the Basis of Biblical Teaching' (unpublished doctoral dissertation, Trinity Evangelical Divinity School, 1995).
Althaus, P., 'Autorität und Freiheit in Luthers Stellung zur Heiligen Schrift', *Luther* 33 (1962), 41-51.
— 'Die Bedeutung der Theologie Luthers für die theologische Arbeit', *Lutherjahrbuch* 28 (1961), 13–29.
— *The Theology of Martin Luther* (trans. Robert C. Schultz; Philadelphia: Fortress, 1966) [Original: *Die Theologie Martin Luthers* (Gerd: Gütersloher, 1962).]
Anderson, M.W., *The Battle for the Gospel: the Bible and the Reformation 1444-1589* (Grand Rapids: Baker, 1978).
Atkinson, J., *Martin Luther and the Birth of Protestantism* (London: Marshall, Morgan & Scott, 1968).
— *Martin Luther: Prophet to the Church Catholic* (Exeter: Paternoster, 1983).
Augustijn, C., 'Hyperaspistes I, Erasmus en Luther's leer van de claritas scripturae', *Vox Theologica* 39 (1969), 93-104.
Bainton, R.H., *Studies on the Reformation* (Boston: Beacon, 1963).
— 'The Bible in the Reformation', in S. L. Greenslade (ed.), *Cambridge History of the Bible: The West from the Reformation to the Present Day* (Cambridge: Cambridge University Press, 1963), 1-37.
Barr, J., *Holy Scripture: Canon, Authority, Criticism* (Oxford: Clarendon, 1983).
— 'Luther and Biblical Chronology', *Bulletin of the John Rylands University Library of Manchester* 72 (1990), 51-67.
Barth, K. , *Church Dogmatics*, 4 vols in 14 half-vols. (trans. G. Thomson, Harold Knight, *et al.*; Edinburgh: T. & T. Clark, 1956-74) [Original: *Die Kirchliche Dogmatik*, 4 vols in 14 half-volumes (Zollikon: Evangelischer, 1932-1967)].
— 'Das Schriftprinzip der reformierten Kirche', *Zwischen den Zeiten* 3 (1925), 215-245.
— *Die Schrift und die Kirche* (Theologische Studien 22; Zürich: Zollikon, 1947).
Barton, J., 'Verbal Inspiration', in R. J. Coggins and J. L. Houlden (eds.), *A Dictionary of Biblical Interpretation* (London: SCM Press, 1990), 719-722.
— *People of the Book? The Authority of the Bible in Christianity* (London: SPCK, 1988).
Bauer, K., *Die Wittenberger Universitätstheologie und die Anfänge der deutschen Reformation* (Tübingen: Mohr, 1928).
Bauer-Wabnegg, W. und Hiebel, H.H., 'Das "sola sancta scriptura" und die Mittel der Schrift', in Heinz L. Arnold (ed.), *Martin Luther* (Text und Kritik

Sonderband; München, 1983), 33-58.

Baur, J., 'Sola Scriptura: historisches Erbe und bleibende Bedeutung', in *Luther und seine klassischen Erben: theologische Aufsätze und Forschungen* (Tübingen: Mohr, 1993), 46-113.

Bea, A., *De Scripturae Inspiratione. Quaestiones Historicae et Dogmaticae* (Rome: Pontificum Institutum Biblicum, 1935).

— 'Deus auctor Sacrae Scripturae: Herkunft und Bedeutung der Formel', *Angelicum* 20 (1943), 16-31.

— *De Inspiratione et Inerrantia Sacrae Scripturae* (Rome: Pontificum Institutum Biblicum, 1947).

Becke, U., 'Eine hinterlassene psychiatrische Studie Paul Johann Reiters über Luther', *Zeitschrift für Kirchengeschichte*, 90 (1979), 85-95.

Becker, J., *Annäherungen: zur urchristlichen Theologiegeschichte und zum Umgang mit ihren Quellen* (Beihefte zur Zeitschrift für die neutestamentliche Wissenschaft 76; ed. Ulrich Mell; Berlin: de Gruyter, 1995).

Beinert, W.A., 'The Patristic Background of Luther's Theology', *Lutheran Quarterly* 9/3 (1995), 263-279.

Beintker, H., 'Verbum Domini manet in Aeternum: eine Skizze zum Schriftverständnis der Reformation', *Theologische Literaturzeitung* 107 (1982), 161-176.

Beisser, F., *Claritas Scripturae bei Martin Luther* (Forschungen zur Kirchen- und Dogmengeschichte 18; Göttingen: Vandenhoeck & Ruprecht, 1966).

— 'Luthers Schriftverständnis', in Peter Manns (ed.), *Martin Luther, Reformator und Vater im Glauben* (Stuttgart: Steiner, 1985), 25-37.

— 'Wort Gottes und Heilige Schrift bei Luther', in *Schrift und Schriftauslegung* (Veröffentlichungen der Luther-Akademie Ratzeburg 10; ed. Heinrich Kraft; Erlangen: Martin Luther, 1987), 15-29.

Benoit, A., *Saint Irénée: Introduction à l'Étude de sa Théologie* (Études d'Histoire et de Philosophie Religieuses; ed. R. Mehl; Paris: Presses Universitaires de France, 1960).

Bentley, J.H., *Humanists and Holy Writ: New Testament Scholarship in the Renaissance* (Princeton, N.J: Princeton University Press, 1983).

Beumer, J., 'Das katholische Schriftprinzip in der theologischen Literatur der Scholastik bis zur Reformation', *Scholastik* 16 (1941), 24-52.

Beutel, A., *In dem Anfang war das Wort: Studien zu Luthers Sprachverständnis* (Hermeneutische Untersuchungen zur Theologie 27; Tübingen: Mohr, 1991).

— '"Scriptura ita loquitur, cur non nos?": Sprache des Glaubens bei Luther', *Kerygma und Dogma* 40/3 (1994), 184-202.

Bielfeldt, D., 'Luther, Metaphor, and Theological Language', *Modern Theology* 6 (1989), 121-135.

— 'Luther on Language', *Lutheran Quarterly* 26 (2002), 195-220.

Blocher, H., 'Luther et la Bible', *La Revue réformée* 138 (1984), 41-55.

Bluhm, H., *Martin Luther Creative Translator* (St Louis: Concordia, 1965).

Bodamer, W., 'Luthers Stellung zur Lehre von der Verbalinspiration',

Theologische Quartalschrift (Hg. von der Ev-Luth Synod von Wisconsin) 33 (1936), 241-266; 34 (1937), 171-200.

Bornkamm, H., 'Iustitia Dei beim jungen Luther', in Bernhard Lohse (ed.), *Der Durchbruch der reformatorischen Erkenntnis bei Luther* (Darmstadt: Wissenschaftliche Buchgesellschaft, 1968), 289-383.

— *Luther and the Old Testament* (ed. Eric W. and Ruth C. Gritsch; Philadelphia: Fortress, 1969) [Original: *Luther und das Alte Testament* (Tübingen: Mohr, 1948).]

— 'Luther und sein Vater: Bemerkungen zu Erik H. Erikson, *Young Man Luther*', *Zeitschrift für Theologie und Kirche* 66 (1969), 38-61.

Braaten, C.E., 'Can we still hold the principle of "Sola Scriptura"?', *Dialog* 20 (1981), 189-194.

Brecht, M., 'Luthers Bibelübersetzung', in *Martin Luther: Leistung und Erbe* (ed. Horst Bartel *et al.*; Berlin: Akademie, 1986), 118-125.

— *Martin Luther: His Road to Reformation 1483-1521* (trans. James L. Schaaf; Philadelphia: Fortress, 1985) [Original: *Martin Luther: Sein Weg zur Reformation 1483-1521* (Stuttgart: Calwer, 1981).]

— *Martin Luther: Shaping and Defining the Reformation 1521-1532* (trans. James L. Schaaf; Minneapolis: Fortress, 1990) [Original: *Martin Luther: Zweiter Band: Ordnung und Abgrenzung der Reformation, 1521-1532* (Stuttgart: Calwer, 1986).]

— *Martin Luther: The Preservation of the Church 1532-1546* (trans. James L. Schaaf; Minneapolis: Fortress, 1993) [Original: *Martin Luther: Dritte Band: Die Erhaltung der Kirche, 1532-1546* (Stuttgart: Calwer, 1987).]

— 'Zu Luthers Schriftverständnis', in Karl Kertelge (ed.), *Die Autorität der Schrift im ökumenischen Gespräch* (Frankfurt: Lembeck, 1985), 9-29.

— 'Zu Typologie in Luthers Schriftauslegung. Kurt Aland zum 70. Geburtstag', in Heinrich Kraft (ed.), *Schrift und Schriftauslegung* (Erlangen: Luther, 1987), 55-68.

Bring, R., *Luthers Anschauung von der Bibel* (Berlin: Lutherisches, 1951).

Brink, J.A.B. van den, 'Bible and Biblical Theology in the Early Reformation I', *Scottish Journal of Theology* 14 (1961), 337-352.

— 'Bible and Biblical Theology in the Early Reformation II', *Scottish Journal of Theology* 15 (1962), 50-65.

Bromiley, G.W., 'The Church Fathers and Holy Scripture', in D. A. Carson and John D. Woodbridge (eds.), *Scripture and Truth* (Leicester: IVP, 1983), 195-220.

Bruns, G.L., *Hermeneutics Ancient and Modern* (New Haven: Yale University Press, 1992).

Buchholz, A. *Schrift Gottes im Lehrstreit: Luthers Schriftverständnis und Schriftauslegung in seinen drei grossen Lehrstreitigkeiten der Jahre 1521-28* (Frankfurt: Lang, 1993).

Callahan, J., 'Claritas Scripturae: The Role of Perspicuity in Protestant Hermeneutics', *Journal of the Evangelical Theological Society* 39/3 (1996),

353-372.

Callan, C.J., 'The Bible in the Summa Theologica of St. Thomas Aquinas', *Catholic Biblical Quarterly* 9/1 (1947), 33-47.

Campenhausen, H.F. von, *Die Entstehung der Christlichen Bibel* (Beiträge zur Historischen Theologie 39; ed. Gerhard Ebeling; Tübingen: Mohr, 1968).

Carlson, E.M., *The Reinterpretation of Luther* (Philadelphia: Muhlenberg, 1948).

Carson, D.A., 'Is the doctrine of "claritas scripturae" still relevant today?', in E. Hahn and H.-W. Neudorfer (eds.), *Dein Wort ist die Wahrheit: Beiträge zu einer schriftgemäßen Theologie* (Brennen: Brockhaus, 1997), 97-111.

Carter, C.S., *The Reformers and Holy Scripture: A Historical Investigation* (London: Thynne & Jarvis, 1928).

Chau, W.-S., *The Letter and the Spirit: A History of Interpretation from Origen to Luther* (American University Studies VII, 167; New York: Lang, 1995).

Childs, B.S., 'The Sensus Literalis of Scripture: An Ancient and Modern Problem', in H. Donner *et al.* (eds.), *Beiträge zur Alttestamentlichen Theologie* (Göttingen: Vandenhoeck & Ruprecht, 1977), 80-93.

Countryman, W., *Biblical Authority or Biblical Tyranny? Scripture and the Christian Pilgrimage* (Philadelphia: Fortress, 1981).

d'Étaples, J.L., *Quincuplex Psalterium: Fac-similé de l'édition de 1513* (Travaux d'Humanisme et Renaissance 170; Geneva: Droz, 1979).

Daniel, H.-C., 'Luthers Ansatz der claritas scripturae in den Schriften "Assertio omnium articulorum" und "Grund and Ursach aller Artikel" (1520/21)', in Tuomo Mannermaa *et al.* (eds.), *Thesaurus Lutheri: Auf der Suche nach neuen Paradigmen der Luther-Forschung* (Helsinki: Luther-Agricola Gesellschaft, 1986), 279-290.

Davies, R.E., *The Problem of Authority in the Continental Reformers: A Study in Luther, Zwingli and Calvin* (London: Epworth Press, 1946).

Denzinger, H. und Schönmetzer, A. (eds.), *Enchiridion Symbolorum: Definitionum et Declarationum de Rebus Fidei et Morum* (Rome: Herder, 33rd edn 1965).

Dillenberger, J., *God Hidden and Revealed: The Interpretation of Luther's Deus Absconditus and Its Significance for Religious Thought* (Philadelphia: Muhlenberg, 1953).

Dockery, D.S., 'Martin Luther's Christological Hermeneutics', *Grace Theological Journal* 4.2 (1983), 189-203.

Doermann, R.W., 'Luther's Principles of Biblical Interpretation', in F. W. Meuser and S. D. Schneider (eds.), *Interpreting Luther's Legacy: Essays in Honor of Edward C. Fendt* (Minneapolis: Augsburg, 1969), 14-25.

Duchrow, U., 'Die Klarheit der Schrift und die Vernunft', *Kerygma und Dogma*, 15 (1969), 1-17.

Dunbar, D.G., 'The Biblical Canon', in D. A. Carson and John D. Woodbridge (eds.), *Hermeneutics, Authority, and Canon* (Grand Rapids: Zondervan, 1986), 299-360.

Ebeling, G., 'The Beginnings of Luther's Hermeneutics I', trans. by Richard B. Steele, *Lutheran Quarterly* 7.2 (1993), 129-158.

— 'The Beginnings of Luther's Hermeneutics II', trans. by Richard B. Steele, *Lutheran Quarterly* 7.3 (1993), 315-338.

— 'The Beginnings of Luther's Hermeneutics III', trans. by Richard B. Steele, *Lutheran Quarterly* 7.4 (1993), 451-468 [Original: 'Die Anfänge von Luthers Hermeneutik', *Zeitschrift für Theologie und Kirche* 48 (1951), 172-230.]

— 'The New Hermeneutics and the Early Luther', *Theology Today* 21 (1964), 34-46.

— *Evangelische Evangelienauslegung: Eine Untersuchung zu Luthers Hermeneutik* (Darmstadt: Wissenschaftliche Buchgesellschaft, 2nd edn 1962).

— *Luther: An Introduction to his Thought* (trans. R. A. Wilson; London: Collins, 1970).

— *The Word of God and Tradition: Historical Studies Interpreting the Divisions of Christianity* (trans. S. H. Hooke; London: Collins, 1968).

Eckermann, W., 'Die Aristoteleskritik Luthers: Ihre Bedeutung für seine Theologie, *Catholica* 32 (1978), 114-130.

Ellingsen, M., 'Luther as Narrative Exegete', *Journal of Religion* 63 (1983), 394-413.

Erikson, E.H., *Young Man Luther: A Study in Psychoanalysis and History* (New York: Norton, 1958).

Evans, G.R., *Augustine on Evil* (Cambridge: Cambridge University Press, 1982).

— *Philosophy and Theology in the Middle Ages* (London: Routledge, 1993).

— *Problems of Authority in the Reformation Debates* (Cambridge: Cambridge University Press, 1992).

— *The Language and Logic of the Bible: The Earlier Middle Ages* (Cambridge: Cambridge University Press, 1984).

— *The Language and Logic of the Bible: The Road to Reformation* (Cambridge: Cambridge University Press, 1985).

Farkasfalvy, D., 'Theology of Scripture in Irenaeus', *Revue bénédictine* 78 (1968), 319-333.

Feld, H., *Die Anfänge der Modernen Biblischen Hermeneutik in der Spätmittelalterlichen Theologie* (Institut für Europäische Geschichte Mainz Vorträge 66; Wiesbaden: Steiner, 1977).

Ferguson, S.B., 'How does the Bible look at itself?', in Harvie M. Conn (ed.), *Inerrancy and Hermeneutic: A Tradition, A Challenge, A Debate* (Grand Rapids: Baker, 1988), 47-66.

Ferry, P., 'Martin Luther on Preaching: Promises and Problems of the Sermon as a Source of Reformation History and as an Instrument of Reformation', *Concordia Theological Quarterly* 54.4 (1990), 265-280.

Fischer, D.H., *Historian's Fallacies: Toward a Logic of Historical Thought* (London: Routledge & Kegan Paul, 1971).

Fischer, R.H., 'A Reasonable Luther', in Franklin H. Littell (ed.), *Reformation Studies: Essays in Honor of R. H. Bainton* (Richmond: Knox, 1962), 30-45.

Forde, G.O., 'Infallibility Language and the Early Lutheran Tradition', in Paul C. Empie *et al.* (eds.), *Teaching Authority and Infallibility in the Church*

(Minneapolis: Augsburg, 1980), 120-137.
— 'Law and Gospel in Luther's Hermeneutic', *Interpretation* 37 (1983), 240-252.
Frame, J.M., 'Scripture speaks for Itself', in John W. Montgomery (ed.), *God's Inerrant Word* (Minneapolis: Bethany, 1974), 178-200.
Frank, I., *Der Sinn der Kanonbildung: Eine Historisch-Theologische Untersuchung der Zeit vom 1. Clemensbrief bis Irenäus von Lyon* (Freiburger Theologische Studien 90; ed. Johannes Vincke et al.; Freiburg: Herder, 1971).
Froehlich, K., '"Always to Keep the Literal Sense in Holy Scripture means to Kill One's Soul": The State of Biblical Hermeneutics at the Beginning of the Fifteenth Century', in Earl Miner (ed.), *The Literary Uses of Typology from the Late Middle Ages to the Present* (Princeton, N.J.: Princeton University Press, 1977), 20-48.
Frost, R.N., 'Aristotle's *Ethics:* The *Real* Reason for Luther's Reformation?', *Trinity Journal* 18 ns (1997), 223-241.
Führer, W., *Das Wort Gottes in Luthers Theologie* (Göttinger Theologische Arbeiten 30; ed. Georg Strecker; Göttingen: Vandenhoeck & Ruprecht, 1984).
Gaffin, R.B., 'The New Testament as Canon', in Harvie M. Conn (ed.), *Inerrancy and Hermeneutic: A Tradition, A Challenge, A Debate* (Grand Rapids: Baker, 1988), 165-183.
Gerrish, B.A., 'Biblical Authority and the Continental Reformation', *Scottish Journal of Theology* 10 (1957), 337-360.
— 'Doctor Martin Luther: Subjectivity and Doctrine in the Lutheran Reformation', in P.N. Brooks (ed.), *Seven-Headed Luther: Essays in Commemoration of a Quincentenary 1483-1983* (Oxford: Clarendon Press, 1983), 2-24.
— *Grace and Reason: A Study in the Theology of Luther* (Oxford: Clarendon Press, 1962).
— 'The Word of God and the Words of Scripture: Luther and Calvin on Biblical Authority', in *The Old Protestantism and the New: Essays on the Reformation Heritage* (Edinburgh: T. & T. Clark, 1982), 51-68.
Godfrey, W.R., 'Biblical Authority in the Sixteenth and Seventeenth Centuries: A Question of Transition', in D.A. Carson and John D. Woodbridge (eds.), *Scripture and Truth* (Leicester: IVP, 1983), 221-243.
Goeser, R., 'Luther: Word of God, Language, and Art', *Currents in Theology and Mission* 18.1 (1991), 6-11.
Gogarten, F., *Luthers Theologie* (Tübingen: Mohr, 1967).
Goldingay, J., 'Luther and the Bible', *Scottish Journal of Theology* 35 (1982), 33-58.
Gougaud, L., *Devotional and Ascetic Practices in the Middle Ages* (London: Burns, Oates, & Washbourne, 1927).
Graham, W.A., *Beyond the Written Word: Oral Aspects of Scripture in the History of Religion* (Cambridge: Cambridge University Press, 1987).
Grant, R.M. and Tracy, D., *A Short History of the Interpretation of the Bible* (Philadelphia: Fortress, 2nd edn 1984).
Gray, H.H., 'Renaissance Humanism: The Pursuit of Eloquence', in P.O. Kristeller

and P.F. Wiener (eds.), *Renaissance Essays* (New York: Harper & Row, 1968), 60-73.

Gritsch, E.W., 'Luther's Humor as a Tool for Interpreting Scripture', in Mark S. Burrows and Paul Rorem (eds.), *Biblical Hermeneutics in Historical Perspective: Studies in Honor of Karlfried Froehlich on His Sixtieth Birthday* (Grand Rapids: Eerdmans, 1991), 187-197.

— *Martin — God's Court Jester: Luther in Retrospect* (Philadelphia: Fortress, 1983).

— 'The Cultural Context of Luther's Interpretation', *Interpretation* 37 (1983), 266-277.

Grudem, W.A., 'Scripture's Self-Attestation and the Problem of Formulating a Doctrine of Scripture', in D.A. Carson and John D. Woodbridge (eds.), *Scripture and Truth* (Leicester: IVP, 1983), 19-59.

Gruenagel, F., *Was ist Wort Gottes? Eine Antwort von Luthers Schriftverständnis* (Stuttgart: Calwer, 1962).

Hagen, K., *Luther's Approach to Scripture as seen in his 'Commentaries' on Galatians 1519-1538* (Tübingen: Mohr, 1993).

Hägglund, B., *History of Theology* (trans. Gene J. Lund; St. Louis: Concordia, 3rd edn 1968) [Original: *Theologins Historia* (Lund: Gleerup, 1966).]

— 'Om "Skriftens klarhet" reformations bortglömda grundprincip', *Svensk teologisk kvartalskrift* 65 (1989), 162-168.

Hahn, F., 'Die Heilige Schrift als Problem der Auslegung bei Luther', *Evangelische Theologie* 9 (1950/1), 407-424.

— 'Faber Stapulensis und Luther', *Zeitschrift für Kirchengeschichte* 57 (1938), 356-432.

— 'Luthers Auslegungsgrundsätze und ihre theologischen Voraussetzungen', *Zeitschrift für systematische Theologie* 12 (1934/5), 165-218.

Hamilton, B., *Religion in the Medieval West* (London: Arnold, 1986).

Hammann, G., 'Clarté et Autorité de L'Écriture: Luther en Débat avec Zwingli et Érasme', *Études Théologiques et Religieuses* 71/2 (1996), 175-206.

Hannah, J.D., 'The Meaning of Saving Faith: Luther's Interpretation of Romans 3:28', *Bibliotheca Sacra* 140 (1983), 322-334.

Hanson, R.P.C., *Allegory and Event: A Study of the Sources and Significance of Origen's Interpretation of Scripture* (Richmond: Knox, 1959).

Harnack, A. von, *History of Dogma*, 7 vols (trans. N. Buchanan; London: Williams & Norgate, 1899), VII.

Hatch, N.O., 'Sola Scriptura and Novus Ordo Seclorum', in Nathan O. Hatch and Mark A. Noll (eds.), *The Bible in America* (New York: Oxford University Press, 1982), 59-78.

Hayden-Roy, P., 'Hermeneutica gloriae vs hermeneutica crucis: Sebastian Franck and Martin Luther on the Clarity of Scripture', *Archiv für Reformationsgeschichte*, 81 (1990), 50-67.

Hendrix, S.H., 'American Luther Research in the Twentieth Century', *Lutheran Quarterly* 15/1 (2001), 1-23.

— 'Luther against the Background of the History of Biblical Interpretation', *Interpretation* 37 (1983), 229-239.

Hermann, R., 'Von der Klarheit der Heiligen Schrift. Untersuchungen und Erörterungen über Luthers Lehre von der Schrift in De servo arbitrio', in Horst Beintker *et al.* (eds.), *Studien zur Theologie Luthers und des Luthertums: Gessammelte und nachgelassene Werke* (Göttingen: Vandenhoeck & Ruprecht, 1981), 170-255.

Hirsch, E., 'Initium theologiae Lutheri', in *Lutherstudien*, 2 vols (Gütersloh: Bertelsmann, 1954), II, 9-35.

Holl, K., 'Luthers Bedeutung für den Fortschritt der Auslegungskunst', in *Gesammelte Aufsätze zur Kirchengeschichte I (Luther)* (Tübingen: Mohr, 7th edn 1948), 544-582.

— 'Luthers Urteile über sich selbst', in *Gesammelte Aufsätze zur Kirchengeschichte I (Luther)* (Tübingen: Mohr, 7th edn 1948), 381-419 [E.T.: 'Martin Luther on Luther', in Jaroslav Pelikan (ed.), *Interpreters of Luther: Essays in Honor of Wilhelm Pauck* (trans. H. C. Erik Midelfort; Philadelphia: Fortress, 1968), 9-34.]

Hovland, C.W., 'Anfechtung in Luther's Biblical Exegesis', in Franklin H. Littell (ed.), *Reformation Studies: Essays in Honor of R.H. Bainton* (Richmond: Knox, 1962), 46-60.

Janz, D.R., *Luther on Thomas Aquinas: The Angelic Doctor in the Thought of the Reformer* (Veröffentlichungen des Instituts für Europäische Geschichte Mainz 140: Abteilung für Abendländische Religionsgeschichte; ed. Peter Manns; Stuttgart: Steiner, 1989).

Jensen, P.F., 'Luther for Today - With Special Reference to Scripture', *Tyndale Papers* 28 (1983), 1-9.

Johansen, J.H. 'Martin Luther on Scripture and Authority and the Church, Ministry and Sacraments', *Scottish Journal of Theology* 15 (1962), 350-368.

Johnson, J.F., 'Biblical Authority and Scholastic Theology', in John D. Hannah (ed.), *Inerrancy and the Church* (Chicago: Moody, 1984), 67-97.

Josefson, R., 'Christus und die Heilige Schrift', in Vilmos Vajta (ed.), *Lutherforschung Heute: Referate und Berichte des 1. Internationalen Lutherforschungskongresses Aarhus, 18.-23. August 1956* (Berlin: Lutherisches Verlaghaus, 1958), 57-63.

Kelly, J.N.D., *Early Christian Doctrines* (London: Black, 5th edn 1977).

Klug, E.F., *From Luther to Chemnitz: On Scripture and the Word* (Grand Rapids: Eerdmans, 1971).

— 'Word and Scripture in Luther Studies since World War II', *Trinity Journal* 5 ns (1984), 3-46.

Knox, D.B., 'Authority and the Word of God', *Reformed Theological Review* 9.2 (1950), 13-18.

Kohls, E.-W., 'Luthers Aussagen über die Mitte, Klarheit und Selbsttätigkeit der Heiligen Schrift', *Luther-Jahrbuch* 40 (1973), 46-75.

— 'Die Lutherforschung in deutschen Sprachbereich seits 1970', *Luther-Jahrbuch*

44 (1977), 28-56.
Kooiman, W.J., *Luther and the Bible* (trans. John Schmidt; Philadelphia: Muhlenberg, 1961).
Köstlin, J., *The Theology of Luther in its Historical Development and Inner Harmony*, 2 vols (St. Louis: Concordia, 1986).
Kramm, H.H.W., *The Theology of Martin Luther* (London: James Clarke, 1947).
Kropatscheck, F., *Das Schriftprinzip der lutherischen Kirche, geschichtliche und dogmatische Untersuchungen: I. Die Vorgeschichte; Das Erbe des Mittelalters* (Leipzig: Deichert, 1904).
Kuss, O., 'Über die Klarheit der Schrift: Historische und hermeneutische Überlegungen zu der Kontroverse des Erasmus und des Luther über den freien oder versklavten Willen', in Josef Ernst (ed.), *Schriftauslegung: Beitrage zur Hermeneutik des Neuen Testamentes und im Neuen Testament* (München: Schöningh, 1972), 89-149.
Lamparter, H., 'Martin Luthers Stellung zur Heiligen Schrift', in Waltraud Herbstrith (ed.), *Teresa Avila — Martin Luther: große Gestalten kirchlicher Reform* (München: Kaffke, 1983), 112-119.
Lane, A.N.S., 'Sola Scriptura? Making Sense of a Post-Reformation Slogan', in Philip E. Satterthwaite and David F. Wright (eds.), *A Pathway into the Holy Scripture* (Grand Rapids: Eerdmans, 1994), 297-327.
Lawson, J., *The Biblical Theology of St. Irenaeus* (London: Epworth Press, 1948).
Lazareth, W.H., 'Luther's "Sola Scriptura": Traditions of the Gospel for Norming Christian Righteousness', in R.J. Neuhaus (ed.), *Biblical Interpretation in Crisis: The Ratzinger Conference on Bible and Church* (Grand Rapids: Eerdmans, 1989), 50-73.
Lenk, W., 'Martin Luther und die Macht des Wortes', in Joachim Schildt (ed.), *Luthers Sprachschaffen*, 2 vols (Berlin: Akademie der Wissenschaften der DDR, 1984), I, 134-153.
Liebling, H., 'Sola Scriptura — die reformatorische Antwort auf das Problem der Tradition', in Wolfgang Bienert and Wolfgang Hage (eds.), *Humanismus — Reformation — Konfession* (Marburg: Elwert, 1986), 26-38.
Liefeld, T.S., 'Scripture and Tradition, in Luther and in our Day', in F.W. Meuser and S.D. Schneider (eds.), *Interpreting Luther's Legacy: Essays in Honor of Edward C. Fendt* (Minneapolis: Augsburg, 1969), 26-38.
Lienhard, M., *Luther: Witness to Jesus Christ: Stages and Themes of the Reformer's Christology* (trans. Edwin H. Robertson; Minneapolis: Augsburg, 1982).
Loeschen, J., 'The Function of Promisio in Luther's Commentary on Romans', *Harvard Theological Review* 60 (1967), 476-482.
Loewenich, W. von, *Luther's Theology of the Cross* (trans. Herbert J. A. Bouman; Minneapolis: Augsburg, 1976) [Original: *Luthers Theologia Crucis* (Wittenberg: Luther, 5th edn 1967).]
— *Martin Luther: The Man and His Work* (trans. Lawrence W. Denef; Minneapolis: Augsburg, 1986) [Original: *Martin Luther: Der Mann und das*

Werk (München: List, 1982).]
Lohse, B., 'Conscience and Authority in Luther', in Heiko A. Oberman (ed.), *Luther and the Dawn of the Modern Era: Papers for the Fourth International Congress for Luther Research* (trans. Herbert J. A. Bouman; Leiden: Brill, 1974), 158-183.
— *Luthers Theologie in ihrer historischen Entwicklung und in ihrem systematischen Zusammenhang* (Göttingen: Vandenhoeck & Ruprecht, 1995).
— *Ratio und Fides. Eine Untersuchung über die ratio in der Theologie Luthers* (Göttingen, Vandenhoeck & Ruprecht, 1958).
Longenecker, R.N., *Biblical Exegesis in the Apostolic Period* (Grand Rapids: Eerdmans, 1975).
Lønning, I., *Kanon im Kanon: zum dogmatischen Grundlagenproblem des neutestamentlichen Kanons* (Forschungen zur Geschichte und Lehre des Protestantismus 43; ed. Ernst Wolf; München: Kaiser, 1972).
— '"No Other Gospel": Luther's Concept of the "Middle of Scripture" in Its Significance for Ecumenical Communion and Christian Confession Today', in Peter Manns and Harding Meyer (eds.), *Luther's Ecumenical Significance: An Interconfessional Consultation* (trans. Patricia M. Williams and Harry McSorley; Philadelphia: Fortress, 1984), 229-245.
Loofs, F., *Leitfaden zum Studien der Dogmengeschichte: I. und 2. Teil: Alte Kirche Mittelalter und Katholizismus bis zur Gegenwart* (ed. Kurt Aland; Tübingen: Niemeyer, 6th edn 1959).
Lortz, J. *The Reformation: A Problem for Today* (Westminster: Newman, 1964).
Lotz, D.W., 'Sola Scriptura: Luther on Biblical Authority', *Interpretation* 35 (1981), 258-273.
Lubac, H. de, *Exégèse Médiévale: les Quatre Sens de l'Écriture*, 4 vols (Paris: Aubier, 1959-63).
Lüpke, J. von, 'Theologie als "Grammatik zur Sprache der heiligen Schrift": Eine Studie zu Luthers Theologieverständnis', *Neue Zeitschrift für systematische Theologie und Religionsphilosophie* 34/3 (1992), 227-250.
McGrath, A.E., *Luther's Theology of the Cross: Martin Luther's Theological Breakthrough* (Oxford: Blackwell, 1985).
— *Reformation Thought: An Introduction* (Oxford: Blackwell, 2nd edn 1993).
— *The Intellectual Origins of the European Reformation* (Oxford: Blackwell, 1987).
McSorley, H.J., *Luther: Right or Wrong? An Ecumenical-Theological Study of Luther's Major Work, The Bondage of the Will* (New York: Newman, 1969).
Mallard, W., 'John Wyclif and the Tradition of Biblical Authority', *Church History* 30 (1961), 50-60.
Marhold, H., 'Was war für Luther Gottes Wort?', *Freies Christentum* 14 (1962), 113-116.
Marshall, R.F., 'Luther's Two Factor Hermeneutic', *Lutheran Quarterly* 28 (1976), 54-69.
Maschke, T., 'Contemporaneity: A Hermeneutical Perspective in Martin Luther's

Work', in Timothy Maschke, Franz Posset, and Joan Skocir (eds.), *Ad fontes Lutheri: Toward the Recovery of the Real Luther, Essays in Honor of Kenneth Hagen's Sixty-Fifth Birthday* (Milwaukee: Marquette University Press, 2001), 165-182.

Mau, R., 'Klarheit der Schrift und Evangelium: zum Ausatz des lutherschen Gedankens der claritas scripturae', *Theologische Versuche* 4 (1972), 129-143.

Maurer, W., 'Luthers Verständnis des neutestamentlichen Kanons', in Ernst-Wilhelm Kohl and Gerhard Müller (eds.), *Kirche und Geschichte*, 2 vols (Göttingen: Vandenhoeck & Ruprecht, 1970), I, 134-158.

Metzger, B.M., *The Canon of the New Testament* (Oxford: Oxford University Press, 1987).

Montgomery, J.W., 'Lessons from Luther on the Inerrancy of Holy Writ', in John W. Montgomery (ed.), *God's Inerrant Word: An International Symposium on the Trustworthiness of Scripture* (Minneapolis: Bethany, 1974), 63-94.

Mostert, W., 'Scriptura sacra sui ipsius interpres: Bemerkungen zum Verständnis der Heiligen Schrift durch Luther', *Luther-Jahrbuch* 46 (1979), 60-96.

Mühlen, K.-H. zur, 'Der Begriff sensus in der Exegese der Reformationszeit' (Paper to the Oxford-Bonn Conference 1995, Oxford, 1995).

— 'Luther and Aristoteles', *Luther-Jahrbuch* 52 (1985), 263-266.

Muller, R.A., 'Biblical Interpretation in the Era of the Reformation: The View from the Middle Ages', in Richard A. Muller and John L. Thompson (eds.), *Biblical Interpretation in the Era of the Reformation* (Grand Rapids: Eerdmans, 1996), 3-22.

— *Post-Reformation Reformed Dogmatics: Volume 2. Holy Scripture: The Cognitive Foundation of Theology* (Grand Rapids: Baker, 1993).

— *The Unaccommodated Calvin: Studies in the Foundation of a Theological Tradition* (Oxford Studies in Historical Theology; New York/Oxford: Oxford University Press, 2000).

Muller, R.A. and Thompson, J.L., 'The Significance of Precritical Exegesis: Retrospect and Prospect', in Richard A. Muller and John L. Thompson (eds.), *Biblical Interpretation in the Era of the Reformation* (Grand Rapids: Eerdmans, 1996), 335-345.

Murray, J., 'The Attestation of Scripture', in Paul Woolley and Ned B. Stonehouse (eds.), *The Infallible Word* (Phildadelphia: Presbyterian & Reformed, 1967), 1-54.

Neuner, P. und Schröger, F., 'Luthers These von der Klarheit der Schrift', *Theologie und Glaube* 74.1 (1984), 39-58.

Oberman, H.A., *Forerunners of the Reformation: The Shape of Late Medieval Thought Illustrated by Key Documents* (London: Lutterworth, 1966).

— *Luther: Man between God and the Devil* (trans. Eileen Walliser-Schwarzbart; New Haven: Yale University Press, 1989).

— *The Harvest of Medieval Theology: Gabriel Biel and Later Medieval Nominalism* (Cambridge, Mass.: Harvard University Press, 1963).

— *The Reformation: Roots and Ramifications* (Edinburgh: T. & T. Clark, 1994).

— 'Vom Protest zum Bekenntnis. Die Confessio Augustana : Kritischer Maßstab wahrer Ökumene', *Bätter für württembergische Kirchengeschichte* 80/81 (1980-81), 24-37.

Ocker, C. 'Medieval Exegesis and the Origin of Hermeneutics', *Scottish Journal of Theology* 52/3 (1999), 328-45.

Oesch, W.M., 'Luther zur Inspiration der Heiligen Schrift', *Lutherische Rundblick* 13 (1965), 66-73, 114-135.

Ohly, F., 'Die Typologie in Luthers Schriftauslegung', in *Gesetz und Evangelium zur Typologie bei Luther und Lucas Cranach, zum Blutstrahl der Gnade in der Kunst* (Munster: Aschendorff, 1985), 1-15.

Østergaard-Nielsen, H., *Scriptura Sacra et Viva Vox: Eine Lutherstudie* (Forschungen zur Geschichte und Lehre des Protestantismus X; ed. Ernst Wolf; München: Kaiser, 1957).

Ozment, S.E., *The Age of Reform 1250-1550: An Intellectual and Religious History of Late Medieval and Reformation Europe* (New Haven: Yale University Press, 1980).

Pannenberg, W., *Basic Questions in Theology*, 3 vols (trans. George H. Kehm; London: SCM Press, 1970), I.

— *Systematic Theology*, 3 vols (trans. Geoffrey W. Bromiley; Edinburgh: T. & T. Clark, 1991), I.

Pauck, W., *The Heritage of the Reformation* (Glencoe, Ill.: Beacon, 1950).

Pelikan, J., *Luther the Expositor: Introduction to the Reformer's Exegetical Writings* (Companion Volume to Luther's Works; St. Louis: Concordia, 1959).

— *Obedient Rebels: Catholic Substance and Protestant Principle in Luther's Reformation* (London: SCM Press, 1964).

— *Reformation of Church and Dogma (1300-1700)* (The Christian Tradition: A History of the Development of Doctrine 4; Chicago: University of Chicago, 1984).

— *The Emergence of the Catholic Tradition (100-600)* (The Catholic Tradition: A History of the Development of Doctrine 1; Chicago: University of Chicago Press, 1971).

Pesch, C., *De inspiratione sacrae scripturae* (Freiburg: Herder, 1906).

Pfitzner, V.C., 'Luther as Interpreter of John's Gospel: With Special Reference to his Sermons on the Gospel of John', *Lutheran Theological Journal* 18 (1984), 65-73.

Pilch, J.J., 'Luther's Hermeneutical Shift', *Harvard Theological Review* 63 (1970), 445-448.

Pinomaa, L., *Der existentielle Charakter der Theologie Luthers: Das Hervorbrechen der Theologie der Anfechtung und ihre Bedeutung für das Lutherverständnis* (Annales Academiae scientiarum Fennicae, Ser. B. 47, 3; Helsinki: Finnische Akademie der Wissenschaften, 1940).

Polman, A.D.R., *The Word of God According to St. Augustine* (London: Hodder and Stoughton, 1961) [Original: *De Theologie van Augustinus het Woord Gods bij Augustinus* (Kampden: Kok, 1955).]

Prenter, R., *Spiritus Creator* (Forschungen zur Geschichte und Lehre des Protestantismus 6; ed. Ernst Wolf; München: Kaiser, 1954).
— 'The Living Word', in Jaroslav J. Pelikan *et al.* (eds.), *More About Luther*, 2 vols (Decorah, Iowa: Luther College, 1958), II, 65-80.
— *The Word and the Spirit: Essays on Inspiration of the Scriptures* (trans. Harris E. Kaasa; Minneapolis: Augsburg, 1965).
Preus, J.S., 'From Promise to Presence: The Christ in Luther's Old Testament', in Eric W. Gritsch (ed.), *Encounters with Luther: Lectures, Discussions and Sermons at the Martin Luther Colloquia*, 2 vols (Gettysburg: Lutheran Theological Seminary, 1980), I, 109-119.
— *From Shadow to Promise: Old Testament Interpretation from Augustine to the Young Luther* (Cambridge, Mass.: Harvard University Press, 1969).
— 'Old Testament Promissio and Luther's New Hermeneutic', *Harvard Theological Review* 60 (1967), 145-161.
Preus, R.D., 'Luther and Biblical Infallibility', in John D. Hannah (ed.), *Inerrancy and the Church* (Chicago: Moody, 1984), 99-142.
— 'Luther: Word, Doctrine, and Confession', *Concordia Theological Quarterly* 60.3 (1996), 175-228.
— 'The Unity of Scripture', *Concordia Theological Quarterly* 54 (1990), 1-23.
— 'The View of the Bible Held by the Church: The Early Church through Luther', in Norman L. Geisler (ed.), *Inerrancy* (Grand Rapids: Zondervan, 1980), 355-382.
Quanbeck, W.A., 'Luther's Early Exegesis', in Roland Bainton *et al.* (eds.), *Luther Today: Martin Luther Lectures* (Decorah, Io.: Luther College, 1957), I, 35-103.
Raeder, S., 'Luther als Ausleger und Übersetzer der Heiligen Schrift', in Helmar Junghans (ed.), *Leben und Werk Martin Luthers von 1526 bis 1546: Festgabe zu seinem 500. Geburtstag*, 2 vols (Göttingen: Vandenhoeck & Ruprecht, 1983), I, 253-278.
Reardon, B.M.G., *Religious Thought in the Reformation* (London: Longman, 2nd edn 1995).
Reid, J.K.S., *The Authority of Scripture: A Study of the Reformation and Post-Reformation Understanding of the Bible* (London: Methuen, 1957).
Reinke, D.R., 'From Allegory to Metaphor: More Notes on Luther's Hermeneutical Shift', *Harvard Theological Review* 66 (1973), 386-395.
Reiter, P., *Luthers Umwelt und Persönlichkeit*, 2 vols (Copenhagen: Levin und Munsgaard, 1937-1941).
Reu, M., *Luther and the Scriptures* (Columbus, Ohio: Wartburg, 1944).
— *Luther's German Bible* (Columbus, Ohio: Lutheran Book Concern, 1934).
Reventlow, H.G., *The Authority of the Bible and the Rise of the Modern World* (London: SCM Press, 1984).
Ritschl, A., 'Über die beiden Prinzipien des Protestantismus', *Zeitschrift für Kirchengeschichte* 1 (1876), 397-413.
Rogers, J.B. and McKim, D.K., *The Authority and Interpretation of the Bible: An Historical Approach* (San Francisco: Harper & Row, 1979).

Rohnert, W., *Was lehrt Luther von der Inspiration der Heiligen Schrift?* (Leipzig: Bohme, 1890).
Rohr, J. von, 'Medieval Consolation and the Young Luther's Despair', in Franklin H. Littell (ed.), *Reformation Studies: Essays in Honor of Roland H. Bainton*, (Richmond: Knox, 1962), 61-74.
Rosato, L., 'Ioannis Duns Scoti Doctrina de Scriptura et Traditione', in Charles Balic (ed.), *De Scriptura et Tradition* (Rome: Pontificia Mariana Internationalis, 1963), 233-252.
Rosin, W.H., 'In Response to Bergt Hägglund: The Importance of Epistemology for Luther's and Melanchthon's Theology', *Concordia Theological Quarterly* 44 (1980), 134-140.
Rothen, B., *Die Klarheit der Schrift I: Martin Luther. Die wiederentdeckten Grundlagen* (Göttingen: Vandenhoeck & Ruprecht, 1990).
Runia, K., 'The Hermeneutics of the Reformers', *Calvin Theological Journal* 19 (1984), 129-132.
Ruokanen, M., 'Does Luther have a theory of Biblical Inspiration?', *Modern Theology* 4.1 (1987), 1-16.
— *Doctrina Divinitus Inspirata: Martin Luther's position in the ecumenical problem of biblical inspiration* (Publications of the Luther-Agricola Society B 14; Helsinki: Luther-Agricola Society, 1985).
Rupp, E.G. and Watson P.S. (eds.), *Luther and Erasmus: Free Will and Salvation* (London: SCM Press, 1969).
Rupp, E.G., '*Miles Emeritus?* Continuity and Discontinuity between the Young and the Old Luther', in George Yule (ed.), *Luther: Theologian for Catholics and Protestants* (Edinburgh: T. & T. Clark, 1985), 75-86.
— 'The Bible in the Age of the Reformation', in Dennis E. Nineham (ed.), *The Church's Use of the Bible* (London: SPCK, 1963), 73-87.
— *The Righeousness of God: Luther Studies* (London: Hodder & Stoughton, 1953).
— 'Word and Spirit in the Early Years of the Reformation', *Archiv für Reformationsgeschichte* 49 (1958), 13-26.
Russell, W.R., *Luther's Theological Testament: The Schmalkald Articles* (Minneapolis: Fortress, 1995).
Saarinen, R., 'The Word of God in Luther's Theology', *Lutheran Quarterly* 4 (1990), 31-44.
Sandin, R.T., 'The Clarity of Scripture', in Morris Inch and Ronald Youngblood (eds.), *The Living and Active Word of God: Studies in Honor of Samuel J. Schultz* (Winona Lake, Ind.: Eisenbrauns, 1983), 237-253.
Sasse, H., 'Luther and the Word of God', in Heino O. Kadai (ed.), *Accents in Luther's Theology: Essays in Commemoration of the 450th Anniversary of the Reformation* (St. Louis: Concordia, 1967), 47-97.
— 'Sacra Scriptura: Observations on Augustine's Doctrine of Inspiration', *Reformed Theological Review* 14.3 (1955), 65-80.
— 'The Rise of the Dogma of Holy Scripture in the Middle Ages', *Reformed*

Theological Review 18.2 (1959), 45-54.

— 'Was sagt uns Luther über die Irrtumslosigkeit der Heiligen Schrift?', in Friedrich Wilhelm Hopf (ed.), *Sacra Scriptura: Studien zur Lehre von der Heiligen Schrift* (Erlangen: Evang.-Luth. Mission, 1981), 291-320.

Scheel, J.O.E.I. (ed.), *Dokumente zu Luthers Entwicklung (bis 1519)* (Tübingen: Mohr, 2nd edn 1929).

Schempp, P., 'Luthers Stellung zur Heiligen Schrift', in Richard Widemann (ed.), *Theologische Entwürfe* (München: Kaiser, 1973), 10-74.

Schild, M., 'On Luther's Understanding of the Word and History', *Reformed Theological Review* 28 (1969), 90-99.

Schloemann, M., 'Die Mitte der Schrift: Luther Notabene', in Wolfgang E. Müller and Hartmut H. R. Schultz (eds.), *Theologie und Aufklärung: Festschrift für Gottfried Hornig zum 65. Geburtstag* (Würtzburg: Königshausen und Neumann, 1992), 29-40.

Schlüssler, H., 'Sacred Doctrine and the Authority of Scripture in Canonistic Thought on the Eve of the Reformation', in Guy F. Lytle (ed.), *Reform and Authority in the Mediaeval and Reformation Church* (Washington: Catholic University of America Press, 1981), 55-68.

Schwiebert, E.G., *Luther and his times: The Reformation from a New Perspective* (Saint Louis: Concordia, 1950).

Seeberg, E., 'Die Anfänge der Theologie Luthers', *Zeitschrift für Kirchengeschichte* 53 (1934), 229-241.

Seeberg, R., *Text-book of the History of Doctrines*, 2 vols (trans. Charles E. Hay; Grand Rapids: Baker, 1952).

Selge, K.-V., '"Capta conscientia in verbis Dei", Luthers Widerrufsverweigerung in Worms', in Fritz Reuter (ed.), *Der Reichstag zu Worms von 1521. Reichspolitik und Luthersache*, (Worms: publisher, 1971), 180-207.

Seppänen, L., 'Das innere und äußere Wort Luthers', *Zeitschrift für Germanistik* 5 (1984), 133-143.

Siggins, I.D.K., 'Luther on the Word of God and Scripture', *Tyndale Papers* (1960).

Silva, M., *Has the Church Misread the Bible? The History of Interpretation in the Light of Current Issues* (Foundations of Contemporary Interpretation 1; Moisés Silva (ed.); Grand Rapids: Zondervan, 1987).

Smalley, B., *Studies in Medieval Thought and Learning from Abelard to Wyclif* (London: Hambledon, 1981).

— *The Study of the Bible in the Middle Ages* (Oxford: Blackwell, 3rd edn 1983).

Smart, J.D., *The Strange Silence of the Bible in the Church: A Study in Hermeneutics* (London: SCM Press, 1970).

Spitz, L.W., 'Luther's Sola Scriptura', *Concordia Theological Monthly* 31 (1960), 740-745.

Steinlein, H., *Luthers Doktorat: Zum 400 jährigen Jubiläum desselben (18./19. Oktober 1912)* (Leipzig: Deichert, 1912).

Steinmetz, D.C., 'Hermeneutic and Old Testament Interpretation in Staupitz and

the young Martin Luther', *Archiv für Reformationsgeschichte* 70 (1979), 24-58.
— *Luther and Staupitz: An Essay in the Intellectual Origins of the Protestant Reformation* (Duke Monographs in Medieval and Renaissance Studies 4; Durham: Duke University Press, 1980).
— *Luther in Context* (Bloomington: Indiana University Press, 1986).
— 'Scripture and the Lord's Supper in Luther's Theology', *Interpretation* 37 (1983), 253-265.
— 'The Superiority of Pre-Critical Exegesis', *Theology Today* 37.1 (1980), 27-38.
Stendahl, K., 'The Apostle Paul and the Introspective Conscience of the West', *Harvard Theological Review* 56 (1963), 199-215.
— 'The Word of God and the Words of Luther', in M.J. Harran (ed.), *Luther and Learning: The Wittenberg University Luther Symposium* (Selinsgrove: Susquehanna University Press, 1985), 133-141.
Stock, U., 'Spes Exercens Conscientia: Sprache und Affekt in Luthers Auslegung des 6. Psalms in den Operationes in Psalmos', in Gerhard Hammer and Karl-Heinz zur Mühlen (eds.), *Lutheriana: Zum 500 Geburtstag Martin Luthers von den Mitarbeitern der Weimarer Ausgabe* (Cologne/Vienna: Böhlau, 1984), 229-243.
Strecker, G., 'Die Bibel lesen und verstehen: Luther als Übersetzer und Auslegere der Heiligen Schrift', *Lutherische Monatshefte* 22 (1983), 556-559.
Stuhlmacher, P., *Historical Criticism and Theological Interpretation of Scripture* (trans. Roy A. Harrisville; London: SPCK, 1977).
Surburg, R.F., 'The Significance of Luther's Hermeneutics for the Protestant Reformation', *Concordia Theological Monthly* 24 (1953), 241-161.
Teigen, E.T., 'The Clarity of Scripture and Hermeneutical Principles in the Lutheran Confessions', *Concordia Theological Quarterly* 46 (1982), 147-166.
Thiselton, A.C., *New Horizons in Hermeneutics* (Grand Rapids: Zondervan, 1992).
Thomas, T.C., 'Luther's Canon: Christ Againts Scripture', *Word and World* 8 (1988), 141-149.
Thompson, M.D., '*Claritas Scripturae* in the eucharistic writings of Martin Luther', *Westminster Theological Journal* 60/1 (1998), 23-41.
Tierney, B., *Origins of Papal Infallibility 1150-1350: A Study on the Concepts of Infallibility, Sovereignty, and Tradition in the Middle Ages* (Studies in the History of Christian Thought 6; ed. Heiko A. Oberman; Leiden: Brill, 1972).
Torjesen, K.J., *Hermeneutical Procedure und Theological Method in Origen's Exegesis* (Patristische Texte und Studien 28; Berlin: de Gruyter, 1986).
Torrance, T.F., 'The Eschatology of Faith: Martin Luther', in *Kingdom and Church: A Study in the Theology of the Reformation* (Edinburgh: Oliver & Boyd, 1956), 7-72.
Tracy, J.D., '*Ad Fontes*: The Humanist Understanding of Scripture as Nourishment for the Soul', in Jill Raitt (ed.), *Christian Spirituality: High Middle Ages and Reformation* (London: Routledge & Kegan Paul, 1987), 252-267.
Tregelles, S.P., *Canon Muratorianus* (Oxford: Oxford University Press, 1867).
Trueman, C.R., 'Pathway to Reformation: William Tyndale and the Importance of

the Scriptures', in Philip E. Satterthwaite and David F. Wright (eds.), *A Pathway into the Holy Scripture* (Grand Rapids: Eerdmans, 1994), 11-29.
Vawter, B., *Biblical Inspiration* (Theological Resources; ed. John P. Whalen and Jaroslav Pelikan; London: Hutchinson, 1972).
Verhoef, P.A., 'Luther and Calvin's Exegetical Library', *Calvin Theological Journal* 3 (1968), 5-20.
Vogel, H.J., *Vogel's Cross Reference and Index to the Contents of Luther's Works: A Cross Reference between the American Edition and the St. Louis, Weimar and Erlangen Editions of Luther's Works* (Milwaukee: Northwestern, 1983).
Vogelsang, E., *Die Anfänge von Luthers Christologie nach der ersten Psalmenvorlesung* (Arbeiten zur Kirchengeschichte 15; Berlin, 1929).
Wachler, G., *Die Inspiration und Irrtumslosigkeit der Schrift: Eine dogmengeschichtliche und dogmatische Untersuchung zu H. Sasse, Sacra Scriptura* (Biblicums Skriftserie 4; Uppsala: Stiftelsen Biblicum, 1984).
Watson, P.S., *Let God Be God! An Interpretation of the Theology of Martin Luther* (London: Epworth Press, 1947).
Weier, R., 'Luthers "sola scriptura" in dogmatischer Sicht', *Trierer Theologische Zeitschrift* 80 (1971), 43-55.
Wendorf, J., 'Der Durchbruch der neuen Erkenntnis Luthers im Lichte der handschriftlichen Überlieferung', *Historische Vierteljahrschrift* 27 (1932), 124-144, 285-324.
Wiener, P.F., *Martin Luther: Hitler's Spiritual Ancestor* (London: Hutchinson, 1945).
Williams, A.L., *Adversus Judaeos: A Bird's Eye View of Christian Apologiae until the Renaissance* (Cambridge: Cambridge University Press, 1935).
Williams, R. 'The Bible', in *Early Christianity: Origins and Evolution to AD 600* (ed. Ian Hazlett; London: SPCK, 1991), 81-91.
Wolf, E., 'Über "Klarheit der Heiligen Schrift" nach Luthers "De servo arbitrio"', *Theologische Literaturzeitung* 92/10 (1967), 721-730.
Wolterstorff, N., *Divine Discourse: Philosophical reflections on the claim that God speaks* (Cambridge: Cambridge University Press, 1995).
Wood, A.S., *Captive to the Word: Martin Luther, Doctor of Sacred Scripture* (Exeter: Paternoster, 1969).
— 'Luther's Concept of Revelation', *Evangelical Quarterly* 35 (1963), 149-159.
— *Luther's Principles of Biblical Intepretation* (London: Tyndale, 1960).
— *The Principles of Biblical Interpretation as Enunciated by Irenaeus, Origen, Augustine, Luther, and Calvin* (Grand Rapids: Zondervan, 1967).
Zim, R., 'The Reformation: The Trial of God's Word', in Stephen Prickett (ed.), *Reading the Text: Biblical Criticism and Literary Theory* (Oxford: Blackwell, 1991), 64-135.

Alphabetical Index of Luther's Works Cited

Acta F. Martini Luther Augustiniani apud D. Legatum Apostolicum Augustae (Proceedings at Augsburg between Luther and Cajetan at Augsburg), 54, 196, 208, 219, 251, 279

Ad dialogum Silvestri Prieratis de potestate papae responsio (Response to the Dialogue of Silvester Prierias), 117, 140, 251

Ad librum eximii magistri nostri Mag. Ambrosii Cartharini, defensoris Silv. Prieratis acerrimi, responsio (Answer to the Book of our Esteemed Master Ambrosius, Keen Defender of Sylvester Prierias), 123

Adventspostille, 75, 89, 148, 173, 177, 180, 181, 182

An den christlichen Adel deutscher Nation von des christlichen Standes Besserung (To the Christian Nobility of the German Nation Concerning the Reform of the Christian Estate), 195, 257, 259, 260, 263, 267

An die Herren deutschs Ordens, daß sie falsche Keuschheit meiden und zur rechten ehelichen Keuschheit greifen, Ermahnung (An Exhortation to the Knights of the Teutonic Order that They Lay Aside False Chastity and Assume the True Chastity of Marriage), 234–5, 257

An die Ratherren aller Städte deutsches Lands, daß sie christliche Schulen aufrichten und halten sollen (To the Councilmen of All Cities in Germany That they Establish and Maintain Christian Schools), 81, 101, 114, 115, 143, 144, 231, 235–6, 237, 242

Antwort deutsch auf König Heinrichs Buch (German Answer to King Henry's Book), 255, 263, 277

Apellatio F. Martini Luther ad Concilium (Martin Luther's Appeal to a Council), 262

Assertio omnium articulorum M. Lutheri per bullam Leonis X novissimam damnatorum (Declaration of all the Articles of Martin Luther Newly Condemned by the Bull of Pope Leo X), 145, 188, 195, 196, 197, 199, 220, 221, 229, 256, 276, 280

Auff das übirchristlich, übirgeystlich und übirkunstlich Buch Bocks Emsers zu Leypczick Antwortt (Answer to the Hyperchristian, Hyperspiritual, and Hyperlearned Book by Goat Emser in Leipzig), 58, 145, 169, 186, 197, 198, 221, 224, 256, 259, 277

Auslegung des 118. Psalms (An Exposition of Psalm 118), 148

Auslegung des dritten und vierten Kapitels Johannis (Exposition of John 3 and 4), 60, 122, 142, 161, 186

Auslegung des ersten und zweiten Kapitels Johannis (Exposition of John 1 and 2), 73, 82, 99, 127, 139, 141, 145, 255, 278

Auslegung das XIV und XV Kapitel S. Johannis (Exposition of John 14 and 15), 54, 61, 87, 189, 204

Briefe (Letters)

   Luther an die Kurfürsten, Fürsten und Stände des Reichs 1521 (to the Electors, Princes and Diet of the Empire), 240

   Luther an Jodokus Trutfetter in Erfurt 1518 (to Jodokus Trutfetter), 7, 53, 120, 250, 259

   Luther an Joh. Lang 1517 (to Johann Lang), 259

   Luther an Joh. Lang 1521 (to Johann Lang), 237

   Luther an Nikolaus Hausmann 1525 (to Nicholas Hausmann) 253

   Luther an Spalatin 1516 (to George Spalatin), 154

   Luther an Spalatin 1519 (to George Spalatin), 253

   Luther an Willibald Pirckheimer in Nürnberg 1519 (to Willibald Pirckheimer), 253

   Luther und Karlstadt an Kurfürst Friedrich 1519 (Luther and Karlstadt to the Elector Frederick), 261

Commentariolus in epistolam divi Pauli Apostoli ad Hebreos (Commentary on the Epistle to the Hebrews), 62, 105, 142, 148, 151, 240

Contra Henricum Regem Angliae (Against Henry, King of England), 254

Contra Malignvm Iohannis Eccii Ivdicivm svper aliqvot Articvlis a Fratribvs Qvibvsdam ei Svppositis Martini Lvtheri Defensio (Defence against the Malicious Judgment of Eck over a few Articles which were Ascribed to him by Certain Monks), 254, 277

Contra XXXII articulos Lovaniensium theologistarum (Against the Thirty-two Articles of the Louvain Theologians), 279

Crucigers Sommerpostille, 269

Das fünfte, sechste und siebente Kapitel Matthaei gepredigt und ausgelegt (Sermons on the Sermon on the Mount), 131

Das Magnificat Vorteutschet und ausßlegt (Translation and Exposition of the Magnificat), 233

Das Neue Testament. Vorrede (Preface to the New Testament 1546), 132

Das Newe Testament Deutzsch. Vorrede (Preface to the New Testament 1522), 131, 133, 237

Das Schone Consitemini (An Exposition of Psalm 118), 272

Daß diese Wort Christi "Das ist mein leib" noch fest stehen wider die Schwarmgeister (That these words of Christ 'This is my body' still hold against the Fanatics), 137, 152, 211, 223, 245, 253

De captivitate Babylonica ecclesiae praeludium (Prelude concerning the Babylonian Captivity of the Church), 78, 186, 202, 207, 208, 223, 226, 260, 277

De instituendis ministria Ecclesiae (Concerning the Ministry), 265

Alphabetical Index of Luther's Works Cited 309

De potestate leges ferendi in ecclesia (Concerning the authority the laws carry in the Church), 121

De servo arbitrio (On the Bondage of the Will), 8, 84, 91, 99, 106, 112, 143, 148, 162, 174, 186, 189, 191, 201, 205, 206, 207, 213, 214, 215, 216, 217, 218, 219, 220, 228, 229, 230, 231, 232, 233, 234, 244, 256, 275, 286

De votis monasticis Martini Lutheri iudicium (The Judgment of Martin Luther on Monastic Vows), 113, 260

Decem praecepta Wittenbergensi praedicata populo (Ten Injunctions preached to the People of Wittenberg), 169

Der 111. Psalm ausgelegt (Exposition of Psalm 111), 141

Der 112. Psalm Davids gepredigt (Sermon on Psalm 12), 141

Der 36. (37.) Psalm Davids (Exposition of Psalm 37), 199, 221

Der 82. Psalm ausgelegt (Exposition of Psalm 82), 4

Der Prophet Habakuk ausgelegt (Exposition of the Prophet Habakkuk), 58, 203–4, 205

Der Prophet Jona ausgelegt (Exposition of the Prophet Jonah), 190, 280

Deuteronomion Mosi cum annotationibus (The Deuteronomy of Moses with Annotations), 63, 100–101, 105, 188

Deutsche Auslegung des 67 Psalmes (German Exposition of Psalm 67), 142

Dictata super Psalterium (First Series of Psalm Lectures), 61, 71, 75, 83, 94, 95–6, 102, 104, 116, 143, 148, 153, 154, 155–6, 156, 157, 158, 167, 168, 169, 170, 195, 220, 233, 234, 253, 254, 276

Die Abroganda Missa Privata Martini Lutheri Sententia (The Abrogation of the Secret Mass) See *Vom mißbrauch der Messen*, 122–3, 202, 244, 275

Die andere Epistel S. Petri und eine S. Judas gepredigt und ausgelegt (Expositions of 2 Peter and Jude), 148

Die Disputation de homine (The Disputation concerning Man), 268

Die Disputation de iustificatione (The Disputation concerning Justification), 270

Die Disputation de potestate concilii (The Disputation concerning the power of a Council), 98, 99

Die Disputation über Daniel 4:24 (The Disputation on Daniel 4:24), 165

Die drei Symbola oder Bekenntnis des Glaubens Christi (The Three Symbols or Creeds of the Christian Faith), 79, 104, 264

Die funf und viertzigste Predigt, am Sonnabendt nach dem tage Timothej (Sermon on John 3:32), 103

Die Promotionsdisputation des Cyriacus Gerichius (The Licentiate Examination of Cyriacus Gerichius), 172, 175, 176

Die Promotionsdisputation von Heinrich Schmedenstede (The Licentiate Examination of Heinrich Schmedenstede), 136

Die Promotionsdisputation von Johannes Macchabäus Scotus (The Licentiate Examination of Johann Maccabeus Scotus), 166

Die Promotionsdisputation von Palladius und Tilemann (The Licentiate Examination of Peter Palladius and Tilemann), 137

Die Prophet Sacharja ausgelegt (Exposition of the Prophecy of Zachariah), 138–9

Die Schmalkaldischen Artikel (The Schmalkaldic Articles), 47, 171, 262, 273

Die Thesen für die Promotionsdisputation von Hieronymus Weller und Nikolaus Medler (Theses for the Licentiate Examination of Jerome Weller and Nicholas Medler), 187

Die Thesen zu den Disputationen gegen die Antinomer (The theses for the Disputation against the Antinomians), 176

Die Zirkulardisputation über das Recht des Widerstands gegen den Kaiser (The Rotating Disputation on the right to opposing the Emperor), 274

Disputatio contra scholasticam theologiam (Disputation against Scholastic Theology), 53, 258–9, 260

Disputatio de sententia: Verbum caro factum est (Disputation on the statement: The word became flesh), 260, 267

Disputatio et excusatio F. Martini Lutheri adversus criminations D. Iohannis Eccii (Disputation and Defense of Martin Luther against the accusations of Johann Eck), 254

Disputatio Heidelbergae habita (The Heidelberg Disputation), 109, 206, 259

Disputatio I. Eccii et M. Lutheri Lipsiae habita (The Leipzig Disputation), 8, 62, 188, 189, 244, 251, 254, 261, 276

Disputatio pro declaratione virtutis indulgentiarum (95 Theses), 53

Divi Pauli apostoli ad Romanos Epistola (Commentary on Romans), 56, 70, 83, 110, 117, 118, 133, 142, 150, 163, 169, 171, 171–2, 260

Ein ander Sermon am dinstag nach Invocavit (The Third Invocavit Sermon 1522), 194, 208, 239

Ein Brief D. M. Luters von den Schleichern und Winkelpredigern (On Infiltrating and Clandestine Preachers), 4, 265

Ein Sermon und Eingang in das erste Buch Mosi (A Sermon and Introduction to Genesis), 120, 235

Ein Sermon von dem neuen Testament, das ist von der heiligen Messe (A Sermon on the New Testament, that is, on the the Holy Mass), 208, 209, 210

Eine Freiheit des Sermons päpistlichen Ablaß und Gnade belangend (Concerning the Freedom of the Sermon on Papal Indulgences and Grace), 263

Enarratio Psalmi LI (Exposition of Psalm 51), 59, 118, 148, 205, 237

Enarratio psalmi XC (Exposition of Psalm 90), 122

Enarrationes epistolarum et euangeliorum, quas postillas vocant (Reflections on the Epistles and Gospels), 172

Alphabetical Index of Luther's Works Cited 311

Epistel Sanct Petri gepredigt und ausgelegt (Sermons on 1 Peter), 66, 80, 118, 162, 179, 182

Eyn brief an die Christen zu Straspurg wider den schwermer geyst (A Letter to the Christians at Strasburg against the Fanatical Spirit), 5, 114, 208

Eyn kleyn unterricht, was man ynn den Euangelijs suchen und gewartten soll (A Brief Instruction on what to Look for and Expect in the Gospels), 76, 148, 159, 180

Eyn Sermon von dem Hochwirdigen Sacrament des Heyligen Waren Leychnams Christi (The Blessed Sacrament of the Holy and True Body of Christ), 201, 202

Eyn Unterrichtung wie sich die Christen ynn Mosen sollen schicken (How Christians Should Regard Moses), 7, 57, 166, 190, 243

Fastenpostille, 127, 130, 145

Genesisvorlesung (Genesis Lectures), 59, 60, 66, 67, 70, 73–4, 85, 87, 88, 91, 93, 101, 107–8, 116, 117, 121, 128, 129, 130, 135, 142, 149, 178, 185, 204, 242, 255, 257, 258, 266, 270, 281, 282

Glosse auf das vermeinte Kaiserliche Edikt (Commentary on the Alleged Imperial Edict), 4, 47, 253

Grund und Ursach aller Artikel D. Martin Luthers, βo durch Romische Bulle unrechtlich vordampt seyn (Defense and Explanation of all the Articles of Martin Luther, unfairly condemned by the Roman Bull), 85, 195, 230, 244, 255, 256, 261, 274, 275

Handbemerkungen Luthers zu den Sentenzen des Petrus Lombardus (Notes on Peter Lombard's Sentences), 260

Hauspostille, 161

In epistolam Pauli ad Galatas commentarius (First Galatians Commentary), 8, 122, 148, 155, 245, 254, 263, 279

In epistolam S. Pauli ad Galatas Commentarius (Great Galatians Commentary), 7, 58, 59, 60, 64, 65, 72, 85, 93, 98, 113, 116, 118, 125, 130, 141, 148, 149, 162, 172, 175, 181, 185, 187, 243, 246, 256, 258, 260, 264

In Quindecim Psalmos Graduum (On the Fifteen Psalms of Ascent), 119, 137, 268, 269

In sieben Bußpsalmen (On the Seven Penitential Psalms), 148

Kirchenpostille, 76, 86, 97, 98, 107, 117, 148, 159, 183, 221–2, 241, 259, 260, 268, 270, 274, 275

Kurtz bekentnis D. Mart. Luthers, vom heiligen Sacrament (A Short Confession concerning the Holy Sacrament), 152

Marburger Gespräch und Marburger Artikel (Marburg Colloquy and Articles), 260

Operationes in Psalmos (Second Series of Psalms Lectures), 64, 75, 91, 142, 164, 169, 182, 250, 258, 271, 287

Praelectio in librum Iudicum (Lectures on Judges), 7, 55, 121

Praelectio in psalmum 45 (Lectures on Psalm 45), 59, 84, 95, 102–3, 116, 141, 142, 244, 275

Praelectiones in Malachiam (Lectures on Malachi), 74

Praelectiones in prophetas minores (Lectures on the Minor Prophets), 99, 100

Predigt am 1 Sonntag nach Epiphaniä (Sermon on First Sunday after Epiphany), 270

Predigt am 1. Adventssonntag (Sermon on the First Sunday of Advent 1533), 206

Predigt am 11 Sonntag nach Trinitatis, nachmittags (Afternoon Sermon on the Eleventh Sundary after Trinity 1532), 82

Predigt am 8 Sonntag nach Trinitatis (Sermon on the Eighth Sunday after Trinity 1532), 74–5

Predigt am Jakobstage (Sermon on St James' Day 1522), 188, 200, 222, 242

Predigt am Ostermontage Nachmittags (Afternoon Sermon on Easter Monday 1526), 181

Predigt am Ostertag (Sermon on Easter Day 1525), 127

Predigt am Pfingstdienstag (Sermon on Pentecost Tuesday 1522), 117, 279

Predigt am Sonntag Bocem Jocunditatis (Sermon on John 16:24), 136

Predigt am Stephanstage (Sermon on St Stephen's Day 1523), 163

Predigt am Tage der Beschneidung (Sermon on Day of Christ's Circumcision 1532), 175

Predigt über den 110 Psalm (Sermon on Psalm 110), 141

Predigt über die Passionsgeschichte am Montag nach Invocavit (Sermon concerning the Passion Narrative on the Monday after Invocavit 1525), 270

Predigten über das 2 Buch Mose (Sermon on Exodus), 8, 111

Rationis Latomianae confutatio (Against Latomus), 56, 120, 164, 184, 199, 218, 221, 225, 254, 258, 262, 271, 275

Resolutiones disputationum de indulgentiarum virtute (Explanations of the Ninety-Five Theses), 143

Responsio ad condemnationem doctrinalem per Magistros Nostros Lovanienses at Colonienses factam (Response to the condemnation by the Faculty of Louvain and Cologne), 54, 267

Rhapsodia seu Concepta in Librum de loco Iustificationis (Recitation on the Place of Justification), 235

Secunda disputatio contra Antinomos (Second Dispuation against the Antinomians), 176

Sendbrief vom Dolmetschen (Open Letter on Translation), 238, 239

Sequentes propositiones adversus totam synagogam Sathanae & universas portas inferorum (Propositions against all the synagogue of Satan and the entire Gates of Hell), 274

Sermo de Mt. 23:34 (Sermon on Matthew 23:34), 97

Sermo de propria sapientia et voluntate (Sermon on the right wisdom and will), 71

Sermo Die S. Matthiae (Sermon on St Matthew's Day 1517), 206

Sermon am 1. Sonntag nach Epiphania (Sermon on the First Sunday after Epiphany 1523), 160

Sermon D. Martini Luthers geschehen zu Erffurdt am Sontag Quasimodogeniti (Sermon

Preached at Erfurt on the way to Worms 1521), 260
Sermon von dem Sakrament des Leibes und Blutes Christi, wider die Schwarmgeister (Sermon on the Sacrament of the Body and Blood of Christ against the Fanatical Spirit), 236
Sermon von Gewalt Sanct Peters (Sermon on the Authority of St Peter), 275
Sermon von sant Jacob dem meereren und hailigen zwolffpotten (Sermon on Matthew 20:20–23 from 1522), 145
Sommerpostille, 140
Sprüche aus dem Alten Testament (Sayings from the Old Testament), 83, 105
Supputatio annorum mundi (Reckoning of the Age of the World), 126, 127, 128
Tischreden (Table Talk Fragments):
   #46, 271
   #116, 12
   #280, 259
   #291, 101
   #312, 174
   #335, 185
   #352, 271
   #352d, 274
   #388, 270
   #439, 269
   #448, 235
   #475, 64
   #644, 260
   #884, 253
   #1351, 271
   #1610, 139
   #1839, 124
   #1877, 12
   #2383, 161
   #2777, 124
   #2792b, 181
   #2844a, 123
   #2938a, 269
   #2938b, 85, 269
   #3097, 271
   #3292a, 135
   #3789, 181
   #4638, 140, 252
   #4777, 271
   #4964, 124
   #5002, 116
   #5177, 72, 106
   #5285, 185
   #5443, 136
   #5533, 180
   #5854, 136
   #5974, 136
Tractatus de libertate Christiana (Treatise concerning Christian Liberty) See *Von der Freiheit eines Christenmenschen*, 76, 219, 275
Über das 1 Buch Mose. Predigten (Sermons on Genesis), 140
Verhandlungen mit D. Martin Luther auf dem Reichstage zu Worms (Luther at the Diet of Worms), 5, 8, 113, 208, 249, 266
Vermahnung an die Geistlichen, versammelt auf dem Reichstag zu Augsburg (Exhortation to All Clergy Assembled at Augsburg), 252
Vier tröstliche Psalmen an die Königin zu Ungarn (Four Psalms of Consolation to the Queen of Hungary), 88
Vom Abendmahl Christi. Bekenntnis (Confession Concerning Christ's Supper), 79, 115, 116, 117, 121, 141, 223, 225–6, 228, 230, 235, 244, 253, 262, 264, 267

Vom Greuel der stillmesse (The Abomination of the Secret Mass), 212

Vom mißbrauch der Messen (The Misuse of the Mass) See *Die Abroganda Missa Privata Martini Lutheri Sententia*, 3, 202, 210, 211, 241, 255, 275, 279

Von Anbeten des Sakraments des heiligen Leichnams Christi (The Adoration of the Sacrament of the Holy Body of Christ), 114, 143, 203, 236, 242

Von beider Gestalt des Sakraments zu nehmen (Receiving Both Kinds in the Sacrament), 202, 212

Von dem Papstthum zu Rom wider den hochberühmten Romanisten zu Leipzig (On the Papacy in Rome, Against the Most Celebrated Romanist in Leipzig), 5, 58, 84, 244, 263, 270

Von den Konziliis und Kirchen (On the Councils and the Churches), 257, 261, 262, 262-3

Von den letzten worten Davids (On the Last Words of David), 59, 96, 151, 243

Von der Freiheit eines Christenmenschen (On the Freedom of a Christian) See *Tractatus de libertate Christiana*, 172, 219, 277

Von der Winkelmesse und Pfaffenweihe (On the Private Mass and the Consecration of Priests), 260

Von Menschenlehre zu meiden und Antwort auf Sprüche (Avoiding the Doctrines of Men and A Reply to Texts), 63, 68, 88, 100, 255, 277

Von Ordnung Gottesdiensts in der Gemeine (Concerning the Order of Public Worship), 148

Vorlesung über das Hohelied (Lectures on the Song of Songs), 91

Vorlesung über den 1 Brief des Johannes (Lectures on 1 John), 60, 77, 122

Vorlesung über den 1. Timotheusbrief (Lectures on 1 Timothy), 141, 237, 272

Vorlesung über die Briefe an Titus und Philemon (Lectures on Titus and Philemon), 121

Vorlesung über Iesaia (Lectures on Isaiah), 86, 87, 93, 204, 233, 246, 258

Vorrede auf den Prediger Salomonis (Preface to Ecclesiastes), 124

Vorrede auf den Propheten Iesaja (Preface to the Prophecy of Isaiah), 124

Vorrede auf den Propheten Joel (Preface to the Prophecy of Joel), 67

Vorrede auf die Epistel an die Hebräer (Preface to the Epistle to the Hebrews), 132, 133

Vorrede auf die Epistel an die Hebräer (Preface to the Epistle to the Hebrews), 133

Vorrede auf die Episteln S. Jacobi und Judas (Preface to the Epistles of James and Jude 1522), 124, 125, 134

Vorrede auf die Episteln S. Jacobi und Jude (Preface to the Epistles of James and Jude 1546), 133, 148, 162

Vorrede auf die Offenbarung S. Johannis (Preface to the Book of Revelation), 125

Vorrede auff das Alte Testament (Preface to the Old Testament 1523), 160, 173, 177, 178
Vorrede auff das Alte Testament (Preface to the Old Testament 1545) 162
Vorrede auff die offenbarung S. Johannis (Preface to the Book of Revelation), 133
Vorrede über den Propheten Hosea (Preface to the Propecy of Hosea), 12, 124
Vorrede über den Propheten Jeremia (Preface to the Prophecy of Jeremiah), 12, 124
Vorrede zu Epistolae quaedam piissimae et eruditissimae Iohannis Hus (Preface to the letters of a certain godly and learned Jan Hus), 178
Vorrede zum 1. Bande der Wittenberger Ausgabe der deutschen Schriften (Preface to Volume 1 of the Wittenberg Edition of Luther's German Works), 55, 120, 144, 149, 272
Vorwort zu den Annotationes Philippi Melanchthonis in epistolas Pauli ad Romanos et Corinthios (Forward to Philip Melanchthon's Annotations of Paul's Epistles to the Romans and the Corinthians), 8, 249

Warum des Papstes und seiner Jünger Bücher von D. Martin Luther verbrannt sind (Why the Books of the Pope and his Disciples were Burnt by Martin Luther), 264
Wider das Papstum zu Rom, vom Teufel gestifft (Against the Roman Papacy, an Institution of the Devil), 57, 148, 163, 262, 264
Wider den falsch genannten geistlichen Stand des Papsts und der Bischöfe (Against the Spiritual Estate of the Pope and the Bishops, Falsely So Called), 78
Wider die Antinomer (Against the Antinomians), 176
Wider die himmlischen Propheten, von den Bildern und Sakrament (Against the Heavenly Prophets in the Matter of Images and Sacraments), 212, 222, 224, 226, 227, 244
Wochenpredigten über Joh. 6–8 (Midweek sermons on John 6–8), 76, 77, 120, 121, 148, 259
Wochenpredigten über Joh. 16–20 (Midweek sermons on John 16–20), 127, 145
Wochenpredigten über Matth. 5–7 (Midweek sermons on the Sermon on the Mount), 81

Chronological Index of Luther's Works Cited

1510
Handbemerkungen Luthers zu den Sentenzen des Petrus Lombardus (Notes on Peter Lombard's Sentences), 260

1513
Dictata super Psalterium (First Series of Psalm Lectures), 61, 71, 75, 83, 94, 95–6, 102, 104, 116, 143, 148, 153, 154, 155–6, 156, 157, 158, 167, 168, 169, 170, 195, 220, 233, 234, 253, 254, 276

1514
Sermo de Mt. 23:34 (Sermon on Matthew 23:34), 97
Sermo de propria sapientia et voluntate (Sermon on the right wisdom and will), 71

1515
Divi Pauli apostoli ad Romanos Epistola (Commentary on Romans), 56, 70, 83, 110, 117, 118, 133, 142, 150, 163, 169, 171, 171–2, 260

1516
Luther an Spalatin (to George Spalatin), 154
Praelectio in librum Iudicum (Lectures on Judges), 7, 55, 121

1517
Luther an Joh. Lang (to Johann Lang), 259
Commentariolus in epistolam divi Pauli Apostoli ad Hebreos (Commentary on the Epistle to the Hebrews), 62, 105, 142, 148, 151, 240

Disputatio contra scholasticam theologiam (Disputation against Scholastic Theology), 53, 258–9, 260
Disputatio pro declaratione virtutis indulgentiarum (95 Theses), 53
Sermo Die S. Matthiae (Sermon on St Matthew's Day), 206

1518
Acta F. Martini Luther Augustiniani apud D. Legatum Apostolicum Augustae (Proceedings at Augsburg between Luther and Cajetan at Augsburg), 54, 196, 208, 219, 251, 279
Ad dialogum Silvestri Prieratis de potestate papae responsio (Response to the Dialogue of Silvester Prierias), 117, 140, 251
Apellatio F. Martini Luther ad Concilium (Martin Luther's Appeal to a Council), 262
Luther an Jodokus Trutfetter in Erfurt (to Jodokus Trutfetter), 7, 53, 120, 250, 259
Decem praecepta Wittenbergensi praedicata populo (Ten Injunctions preached to the People of Wittenberg), 169
Disputatio Heidelbergae habita (The Heidelberg Disputation), 109, 206, 259
Eine Freiheit des Sermons päpistlichen Ablaß und Gnade belangend (Concerning the Freedom of the Sermon on Papal Indulgences and Grace), 263

Resolutiones disputationum de indulgentiarum virtute (Explanations of the Ninety-Five Theses), 143

1519

Luther an Spalatin (to George Spalatin), 253

Luther an Willibald Pirckheimer in Nürnberg (to Willibald Pirckheimer), 253

Luther und Karlstadt an Kurfürst Friedrich (Luther and Karlstadt to the Elector Frederick), 261

Contra Malignvm Iohannis Eccii Ivdicivm svper aliqvot Articvlis a Fratribvs Qvibvsdam ei Svppositis Martini Lvtheri Defensio (Defence against the Malicious Judgment of Eck over a few Articles which were Ascribed to him by Certain Monks), 254, 277

Disputatio et excusatio F. Martini Lutheri adversus criminations D. Iohannis Eccii (Disputation and Defense of Martin Luther against the accusations of Johann Eck), 254

Disputatio I. Eccii et M. Lutheri Lipsiae habita (The Leipzig Disputation), 8, 62, 188, 189, 244, 251, 254, 261, 276

Eyn Sermon von dem Hochwirdigen Sacrament des Heyligen Waren Leychnams Christi (The Blessed Sacrament of the Holy and True Body of Christ) 201, 202

In epistolam Pauli ad Galatas commentarius (First Galatians Commentary), 8, 122, 148, 155, 245, 254, 263, 279

Operationes in Psalmos (Second Series of Psalms Lectures), 64, 75, 91, 142, 164, 169, 182, 250, 258, 271, 287

1520

An den christlichen Adel deutscher Nation von des christlichen Standes Besserung (To the Christian Nobility of the German Nation Concerning the Reform of the Christian Estate), 195, 257, 259, 260, 263, 267

Assertio omnium articulorum M. Lutheri per bullam Leonis X novissimam damnatorum (Declaration of all the Articles of Martin Luther Newly Condemned by the Bull of Pope Leo X), 145, 188, 195, 196, 197, 199, 220, 221, 229, 256, 276, 280

De captivitate Babylonica ecclesiae praeludium (Prelude concerning the Babylonian Captivity of the Church), 78, 186, 202, 207, 208, 223, 226, 260, 277

Ein Sermon von dem neuen Testament, das ist von der heiligen Messe (A Sermon on the New Testament, that is, on the the Holy Mass), 208, 209, 210

Responsio ad condemnationem doctrinalem per Magistros Nostros Lovanienses at Colonienses factam (Response to the condemnation by the Faculty of Louvain and Cologne), 54, 267

Tractatus de libertate Christiana (Treatise concerning Christian Liberty) See *Von der Freiheit eines Christenmenschen*, 76, 219, 275

Von dem Papstthum zu Rom wider den hochberühmten Romanisten zu Leipzig (On the Papacy in

Chronological Index of Luther's Works Cited 319

Rome, Against the Most Celebrated Romanist in Leipzig), 5, 58, 84, 244, 263, 270

Von der Freiheit eines Christenmenschen (On the Freedom of a Christian) *See Tractatus de libertate Christiana*, 172, 219, 277

Warum des Papstes und seiner Jünger Bücher von D. Martin Luther verbrannt sind (Why the Books of the Pope and his Disciples were Burnt by Martin Luther), 264

1521

Ad librum eximii magistri nostri Mag. Ambrosii Cartharini, defensoris Silv. Prieratis acerrimi, responsio (Answer to the Book of our Esteemed Master Ambrosius, Keen Defender of Sylvester Prierias), 123

Auff das übirchristlich, übirgeystlich und übirkunstlich Buch Bocks Emsers zu Leypczick Antwortt (Answer to the Hyperchristian, Hyperspiritual, and Hyperlearned Book by Goat Emser in Leipzig), 58, 145, 169, 186, 197, 198, 221, 224, 256, 259, 277

Luther an die Kurfürsten, Fürsten und Stände des Reichs (to the Electors, Princes and Diet of the Empire), 240

Luther an Joh. Lang (to Johann Lang), 237

Das Magnificat Vorteutschet und ausßlegt (Translation and Exposition of the Magnificat), 233

De votis monasticis Martini Lutheri iudicium (The Judgment of Martin Luther on Monastic Vows), 113, 260

Der 36. (37.) Psalm Davids (Exposition of Psalm 37), 199, 221

Deutsche Auslegung des 67 Psalmes (German Exposition of Psalm 67), 142

Die Abroganda Missa Privata Martini Lutheri Sententia (The Abrogation of the Secret Mass) *See Vom mißbrauch der Messen*, 122–3, 202, 244, 275

Enarrationes epistolarum et euangeliorum, quas postillas vocant (Reflections on the Epistles and Gospels), 172

Grund und Ursach aller Artikel D. Martin Luthers, ßo durch Romische Bulle unrechtlich vordampt seyn (Defense and Explanation of all the Articles of Martin Luther, unfairly condemned by the Roman Bull), 85, 195, 230, 244, 255, 256, 261, 274, 275

Rationis Latomianae confutatio (Against Latomus), 56, 120, 164, 184, 199, 218, 221, 225, 254, 258, 262, 271, 275

Sermon D. Martini Luthers geschehen zu Erffurdt am Sontag Quasimodogeniti (Sermon Preached at Erfurt on the way to Worms), 260

Verhandlungen mit D. Martin Luther auf dem Reichstage zu Worms (Luther at the Diet of Worms), 5, 8, 113, 208, 249, 266

Vom mißbrauch der Messen (The Misuse of the Mass) *See Die Abroganda Missa Privata Martini Lutheri Sententia*, 3,

202, 210, 211, 241, 255, 275, 279
1522
Adventspostille, 75, 89, 148, 173, 177, 180, 181, 182
Antwort deutsch auf König Heinrichs Buch (German Answer to King Henry's Book), 255, 263, 277
Contra Henricum Regem Angliae (Against Henry, King of England), 254
Das Newe Testament Deutzsch. Vorrede (Preface to the New Testament), 131, 133, 237
Ein ander Sermon am dinstag nach Invocavit (The Third Invocavit Sermon), 194, 208, 239
Epistel Sanct Petri gepredigt und ausgelegt (Sermons on 1 Peter), 66, 80, 118, 162, 179, 182
Eyn kleyn unterricht, was man ynn den Euangelijs suchen und gewartten soll (A Brief Instruction on what to Look for and Expect in the Gospels), 76, 148, 159, 180
Kirchenpostille, 76, 86, 97, 98, 107, 117, 148, 159, 183, 221–2, 241, 259, 260, 268, 270, 274, 275
Predigt am Jakobstage (Sermon on St James' Day), 188, 200, 222, 242
Predigt am Pfingstdienstag (Sermon on Pentecost Tuesday), 117, 279
Sermon von Gewalt Sanct Peters (Sermon on the Authority of St Peter), 275
Sermon von sant Jacob dem meereren und hailigen zwolffpotten (Sermon on Matthew 20:20–23), 145
Von beider Gestalt des Sakraments zu nehmen (Receiving Both Kinds in the Sacrament), 202, 212
Von Menschenlehre zu meiden und Antwort auf Sprüche (Avoiding the Doctrines of Men and A Reply to Texts), 63, 68, 88, 100, 255, 277
Vorrede auf die Epistel an die Hebräer (Preface to the Epistle to the Hebrews), 132, 133
Vorrede auf die Episteln S. Jacobi und Judas (Preface to the Epistles of James and Jude), 124, 125, 134
Vorrede auf die Offenbarung S. Johannis (Preface to the Book of Revelation), 125
Vorwort zu den Annotationes Philippi Melanchthonis in epistolas Pauli ad Romanos et Corinthios (Forward to Philip Melanchthon's Annotations of Paul's Epistles to the Romans and the Corinthians), 8, 249
Wider den falsch genannten geistlichen Stand des Papsts und der Bischöfe (Against the Spiritual Estate of the Pope and the Bishops, Falsely So Called), 78
1523
An die Herren deutschs Ordens, daß sie falsche Keuschheit meiden und zur rechten ehelichen Keuschheit greifen, Ermahnung (An Exhortation to the Knights of the Teutonic Order that They Lay Aside False Chastity and Assume the True Chastity of Marriage), 234–5, 257
De instituendis ministria Ecclesiae (Concerning the Ministry), 265
Die andere Epistel S. Petri und eine S. Judas gepredigt und ausgelegt

(Expositions of 2 Peter and Jude), 148
Ein Sermon und Eingang in das erste Buch Mosi (A Sermon and Introduction to Genesis), 120, 235
Predigt am Stephanstage (Sermon on St Stephen's Day), 163
Sermon am 1. Sonntag nach Epiphania (Sermon on the First Sunday after Epiphany), 160
Von Anbeten des Sakraments des heiligen Leichnams Christi (The Adoration of the Sacrament of the Holy Body of Christ), 114, 143, 203, 236, 242
Von Ordnung Gottesdiensts in der Gemeine (Concerning the Order of Public Worship), 148
Vorrede auff das Alte Testament (Preface to the Old Testament), 160, 173, 177, 178

1524

An die Ratherren aller Städte deutsches Lands, daß sie christliche Schulen aufrichten und halten sollen (To the Councilmen of All Cities in Germany That they Establish and Maintain Christian Schools), 81, 101, 114, 115, 143, 144, 231, 235–6, 237, 242
Eyn brief an die Christen zu Straspurg wider den schwermer geyst (A Letter to the Christians at Strasburg against the Fanatical Spirit), 5, 114, 208
Praelectiones in prophetas minores (Lectures on the Minor Prophets), 99, 100
Predigten über das 2 Buch Mose (Sermon on Exodus), 8, 111

Vorrede auf den Prediger Salomonis (Preface to Ecclesiastes), 124

1525

Luther an Nikolaus Hausmann (to Nicholas Hausmann), 253
De servo arbitrio (On the Bondage of the Will), 8, 84, 91, 99, 106, 112, 143, 148, 162, 174, 186, 189, 191, 201, 205, 206, 207, 213, 214, 215, 216, 217, 218, 219, 220, 228, 229, 230, 231, 232, 233, 234, 244, 256, 275, 286
Deuteronomion Mosi cum annotationibus (The Deuteronomy of Moses with Annotations), 63, 100–101, 105, 188
Eyn Unterrichtung wie sich die Christen ynn Mosen sollen schicken (How Christians Should Regard Moses), 7, 57, 166, 190, 243
Fastenpostille, 127, 130, 145
In sieben Bußpsalmen (On the Seven Penitential Psalms), 148
Predigt am Ostertag (Sermon on Easter Day), 127
Predigt über die Passionsgeschichte am Montag nach Invocavit (Sermon concerning the Passion Narrative on the Monday after Invocavit), 270
Sommerpostille, 140
Vom Greuel der stillmesse (The Abomination of the Secret Mass), 212
Wider die himmlischen Propheten, von den Bildern und Sakrament (Against the Heavenly Prophets in the Matter of Images and Sacraments), 212, 222, 224, 226, 227, 244

1526

Der 112. Psalm Davids gepredigt (Sermon on Psalm 12), 141

Der Prophet Habakuk ausgelegt (Exposition of the Prophet Habakkuk), 58, 203–4, 205

Der Prophet Jona ausgelegt (Exposition of the Prophet Jonah), 190, 280

Praelectiones in Malachiam (Lectures on Malachi), 74

Predigt am Ostermontage Nachmittags (Afternoon Sermon on Easter Monday), 181

Sermon von dem Sakrament des Leibes und Blutes Christi, wider die Schwarmgeister (Sermon on the Sacrament of the Body and Blood of Christ against the Fanatical Spirit), 236

Vier tröstliche Psalmen an die Königin zu Ungarn (Four Psalms of Consolation to the Queen of Hungary), 88

1527

Daß diese Wort Christi "Das ist mein leib" noch fest stehen wider die Schwarmgeister (That these words of Christ 'This is my body' still hold against the Fanatics), 137, 152, 211, 223, 245, 253

Die Prophet Sacharja ausgelegt (Exposition of the Prophecy of Zachariah), 138–9

Über das 1 Buch Mose. Predigten (Sermons on Genesis), 140

Vorlesung über den 1 Brief des Johannes (Lectures on 1 John), 60, 77, 122

Vorlesung über die Briefe an Titus und Philemon (Lectures on Titus and Philemon), 121

Vorlesung über Iesaia (Lectures on Isaiah), 86, 87, 204, 233, 246, 258

1528

Vom Abendmahl Christi. Bekenntnis (Confession Concerning Christ's Supper), 79, 115, 116, 117, 121, 141, 223, 225–6, 228, 230, 235, 244, 253, 262, 264, 267

Vorlesung über den 1. Timotheusbrief (Lectures on 1 Timothy), 141, 237, 272

Wochenpredigten über Joh. 16–20 (Midweek sermons on John 16–20), 127, 145

1529

Auslegung des 118. Psalms (An Exposition of Psalm 118), 148

Marburger Gespräch und Marburger Artikel (Marburg Colloquy and Articles), 260

1530

Das Schone Consitemini (Exposition of Psalm 118), 272

De potestate leges ferendi in ecclesia (Concerning the authority the laws carry in the Church), 121

Der 111. Psalm ausgelegt (An Exposition of Psalm 111), 141

Der 82. Psalm ausgelegt (An Exposition of Psalm 82), 4

Rhapsodia seu Concepta in Librum de loco Iustificationis (Recitation on the Place of Justification), 235

Sendbrief vom Dolmetschen (Open Letter on Translation), 238, 239

Sequentes propositiones adversus totam synagogam Sathanae & universas portas inferorum (Propositions against all the synagogue of Satan and the entire Gates of Hell), 274

Chronological Index of Luther's Works Cited 323

Tischreden #644, 260
Tischreden #884, 253
Tischreden #4777, 271
Vermahnung an die Geistlichen, versammelt auf dem Reichstag zu Augsburg (Exhortation to All Clergy Assembled at Augsburg), 252
Vorlesung über das Hohelied (Lectures on the Song of Songs), 91
Wochenpredigten über Joh. 6–8 (Midweek sermons on John 6–8), 76, 77, 120, 121, 148, 259

1531
Glosse auf das vermeinte kaiserliche Edikt (Commentary on the Alleged Imperial Edict), 4, 47, 253
Predigt am Sonntag Bocem Jocunditatis (Sermon on John 16:24), 136
Tischreden #46, 271
Tischreden #116, 12

1532
Das fünfte, sechste und siebente Kapitel Matthaei gepredigt und ausgelegt (Sermons on the Sermon on the Mount), 131
Ein Brief D. M. Luters von den Schleichern und Winkelpredigern (A Sermon on Infiltrating and Clandestine Preachers), 4, 265
Enarratio Psalmi LI (Exposition of Psalm 51), 59, 118, 148, 205, 237
In Quindecim Psalmos Graduum (On the Fifteen Psalms of Ascent), 119, 137, 268, 269
Praelectio in psalmum 45 (Lectures on Psalm 45), 59, 84, 95, 102–3, 116, 141, 142, 244, 275

Predigt am 11 Sonntag nach Trinitatis, nachmittags (Afternoon Sermon on the Eleventh Sunday after Trinity), 82
Predigt am 8 Sonntag nach Trinitatis (Sermon on the Eighth Sunday after Trinity), 74–5
Predigt am Tage der Beschneidung (Sermon on Day of Christ's Circumcision), 175
Tischreden #280, 259
Tischreden #291, 101
Tischreden #312, 174
Tischreden #335, 185
Tischreden #352, 271
Tischreden #352d, 274
Tischreden #388, 270
Tischreden #1351, 271
Tischreden #1610, 139
Tischreden #1839, 124
Tischreden #1877, 12
Tischreden #2383, 161
Tischreden #2777, 124
Tischreden #2792b, 181
Tischreden #2844a, 123
Tischreden #3292a, 135
Vorlesung über Iesaia (Lectures on Isaiah), 93
Vorrede auf den Propheten Joel (Preface to the Prophecy of Joel), 67
Vorrede über den Propheten Hosea (Preface to the Propecy of Hosea), 12, 124
Wochenpredigten über Matth. 5–7 (Midweek sermons on the Sermon on the Mount), 81

1533
Predigt am 1. Adventssonntag (Sermon on the First Sunday of Advent), 206
Tischreden #439, 269
Tischreden #448, 235

Tischreden #475, 64
Tischreden #2938b, 85
Tischreden #3097, 271
Tischreden 2938a, 269
Tischreden 2938b, 269
Von der Winkelmesse und Pfaffenweihe (On the Private Mass and the Consecration of Priests), 260
1534
Enarratio psalmi XC (Exposition of Psalm 90), 122
1535
Die Disputation über Daniel 4:24 (The Disputation on Daniel 4:24), 165
Die Thesen für die Promotionsdisputation von Hieronymus Weller und Nikolaus Medler (Theses for the Licentiate Examination of Jerome Weller and Nicholas Medler), 187
Genesisvorlesung (The Genesis Lectures), 59, 60, 66, 67, 70, 73–4, 85, 87, 88, 91, 93, 101, 107–8, 116, 117, 121, 128, 129, 130, 135, 142, 149, 178, 185, 204, 242, 255, 257, 258, 266, 270, 281, 282
In epistolam S. Pauli ad Galatas Commentarius (Great Galatians Commentary), 7, 58, 59, 60, 64, 65, 72, 85, 93, 98, 113, 116, 118, 125, 130, 141, 148, 149, 162, 172, 175, 181, 185, 187, 243, 246, 256, 258, 260, 264
Predigt über den 110 Psalm (Sermon on Psalm 110), 141
1536
Die Disputation de homine (The Disputation concerning Man), 268

Die Disputation de iustificatione (The Disputation concerning Justification), 270
Die Disputation de potestate concilii (The Disputation concerning the power of a Council), 98, 99
1537
Auslegung des ersten und zweiten Kapitels Johannis (Exposition of John 1 and 2), 73, 82, 99, 127, 139, 141, 145, 255, 278
Auslegung das XIV und XV Kapitel S. Johannis (Exposition of John 14 and 15), 54, 61, 87, 189, 204
Die Promotionsdisputation von Palladius und Tilemann (The Licentiate Examination of Peter Palladius and Tilemann), 137
Die Schmalkaldischen Artikel (The Schmalkaldic Articles), 47, 171, 262, 273
Die Thesen zu den Disputationen gegen die Antinomer (The theses for the Disputation against the Antinomians), 176
Vorrede zu Epistolae quaedam piissimae et eruditissimae Iohannis Hus (Preface to the letters of a certain godly and learned Jan Hus), 178
1538
Auslegung des dritten und vierten Kapitels Johannis (Exposition of John 3 and 4), 60, 122, 142, 161, 186
Die drei Symbola oder Bekenntnis des Glaubens Christi (The Three Symbols or Creeds of the Christian Faith), 79, 104, 264
Die Promotionsdisputation des Cyriacus Gerichius (The Licentiate Examination of

Cyriacus Gerichius), 172, 175, 176
Secunda disputatio contra Antinomos (Second Dispuation against the Antinomians), 176
Tischreden #3789, 181

1539
Die funf und viertzigste Predigt, am Sonnabendt nach dem tage Timothej (Sermon on John 3:32), 103
Die Zirkulardisputation über das Recht des Widerstands gegen den Kaiser (The Rotating Disputation on the right of opposing the Emperor), 274
Disputatio de sententia: Verbum caro factum est (Disputation on the statement: The word became flesh), 260, 267
Tischreden #4638, 140, 252
Von den Konziliis und Kirchen (On the Councils and the Churches), 257, 261, 262, 262–3
Vorrede zum 1. Bande der Wittenberger Ausgabe der deutschen Schriften (Preface to Volume 1 of the Wittenberg Edition of Luther's German Works), 55, 120, 144, 149, 272
Wider die Antinomer (Against the Antinomians), 176

1540
Tischreden #4964, 124
Tischreden #5002, 116
Tischreden #5177, 72, 106
Tischreden #5285, 185

1541
Sprüche aus dem Alten Testament (Sayings from the Old Testament), 83, 105
Supputatio annorum mundi (Reckoning of the Age of the World), 126, 127, 128

1542
Die Promotionsdisputation von Heinrich Schmedenstede (The Licentiate Examination of Heinrich Schmedenstede), 136
Die Promotionsdisputation von Johannes Macchabäus Scotus (The Licentiate Examination of Johann Maccabeus Scotus), 166
Tischreden #5443, 136

1543
Tischreden #5533, 180
Tischreden #5854, 136
Tischreden #5974, 136
Von den letzten worten Davids (On the Last Words of David), 59, 96, 151, 243

1544
Crucigers Sommerpostille, 269
Kurtz bekentnis D. Mart. Luthers, vom heiligen Sacrament (A Short Confession concerning the Holy Sacrament), 152

1545
Contra XXXII articulos Lovaniensium theologistarum (Against the Thirty-two Articles of the Louvain Theologians), 279
Hauspostille, 161
Vorrede auf den Propheten Iesaja (Preface to the Prophecy of Isaiah), 124
Vorrede auff das Alte Testament (Preface to the Old Testament), 162
Vorrede über den Propheten Jeremia (Preface to the Prophecy of Jeremiah), 12, 124
Wider das Papstum zu Rom, vom Teufel gestifft (Against the Roman Papacy, an Institution of the Devil), 57, 148, 163, 262, 264

1546

Das Neue Testament. Vorrede (Preface to the New Testament), 132

Predigt am 1 Sonntag nach Epiphaniä (Sermon on First Sunday after Epiphany), 270

Vorrede auf die Epistel an die Hebräer (Preface to the Epistle to the Hebrews), 133

Vorrede auf die Episteln S. Jacobi und Jude (Preface to the Epistles of James and Jude), 133, 148, 162

Vorrede auff die offenbarung S. Johannis (Preface to the Book of Revelation), 133

Scripture Index

Genesis
1	65, 73, 120
1:1	242
1:14	87
1:26	116
2:27	87
3:15	178
11–12	127
12	59, 101, 128
15:6	13
19	257
19:23–25	85
22:12	135
24:1–4	280–1
42:33	67
48:21	204

Exodus
2	110
24:4	13
24:7	13
24:27	13

Deuteronomy
1:3	100
12:32	13
13:1	13
17:18	13
30:11	13
30:14	13

2 Samuel
7:13	190
23	96, 155
23:1	154
23:1–4	95
23:1-7	151

2 Kings
8:26	126

2 Chronicles
22:2	126

Psalms
1	163-164
4	94
4:1	155
11:4	194, 254
16:5	168
16:7	195
18	198
23	209
32:1	254
37	199, 221
45	101
45:1	71, 104, 169
45:6	84
45:11	116
51:10	118
71:16	233
72	157–8
77:1	157
82	4
98:4	254
101	156
101:5	156
102:2	170
103	253
110:2	141
112	157
119	156, 272
119:17	170
119:105	13
127	118
130	13
143	157

Isaiah
8:1	13

29:10	204
29:14	86
30:8	13
51	93
66:2b	13

Jeremiah

23:22	13
30:1–2	13
36:1–32	13

Daniel

4:24	165
4:27	165

Malachi

2:7	74, 150

Joel

2:28	99

Zechariah

11:12–13	138–9

Matthew

1:18	19
2:1–12	85
5–7	81
7:15	74
11	172
11:2–10	172
16	162–3, 244
16:13	275
17:5	15
23	96
23:34	71
27:9	138–9

Mark

1:15	13
12:1–12	24

Luke

2	160
2:33–40	98
24:25–27	14
24:33–40	117
24:44	14

John

1	73
1:3	99
1:1–18	14
1:14–18	14
2	139
2:23–24	277
3:14	161
3:23	142
4:4	150
5:39	83
5:39–47	14
6:45–46	76
6:63	115, 225
14:13–14	204
14:16	188
14:25–26	15
15:5	54
16:2–15	15
16:20	13
17:8	15
17:18	15
17:20-21	15
21:25	259
26:26	78

Acts

1:8	15
4	130
4:8	15
4:31	15
7	127–8
7:2	128
7:55–56	15
9:1–22	15
13:9	15

Romans

1:2	14
3	151
3:21–22	56
3:22	150
3:28	237
7:6	142

10:4	14	Ch 5	264
10:15	171	5:21	251
10:17	13	5:27	15
11:33	213–6	**2 Thessalonians**	
12:1–2	110	2:15	15
12:2	109	**1 Timothy**	
12:6	130	1:11	140
15:4	88	4:1–3	113
1 Corinthians		**2 Timothy**	
2:6–13	15	3:3–5	17
3:7	102	3:13	16, 17
7:9	21	3:15	16
9:9–10	24	3:16	93, 150
11	222	3:16–17	16, 53, 91
14:37	15	3:17	250
15	82	**Hebrews**	
2 Corinthians		1:1–3	14
1:20	14	1:1–4	14
3:2	103	4:12	15
3:6	26, 167	6	133
4	164, 165	6:4–6	240
5:18–21	15	9:23–24	24
Galatians		10	133
1	196 n.20	10:5	151
1:8	251	11	166
1:9	264	11:7	142
1:11–24	15	13:8	166
2:6	58	**James**	
2:17	162	2	287
3	165	**1 Peter**	
3:14	60	1	130
3:17	174	1:10–12	179
3:23–4:7	14	1:23	15
4:24	24	3:15	80
5:2	98	3:21	24
5:6	65	**2 Peter**	
Colossians		1	71
4:16	15	1:16–19	15
1 Thessalonians		1:19	84
2:13	15	1:20–21	15
4:2	15		

1:21	99, 151
3:2	15
3:15–16	15

Revelation

19:3	14

Subject Index

accommodation 106, 107–108, 109, 111
Agricola, Johannes 175, 176
allegory 3, 24–27, 38–41, 65, 110, 147, 160, 184, 185, 245, 258
anagogy 27, 246
antinomianism 173, 175-176
Aquinas, Thomas 32, 33, 35, 36, 39, 40, 42, 147, 257, 280
Aristotle 43–44, 257, 258–260, 267
Augustine 17, 19, 23–24, 26–27, 28–29, 30, 31, 34, 39, 43, 44, 106, 114, 140, 167, 169, 171, 177, 184, 194–195, 199, 200, 236, 238, 250, 251, 253, 254, 266, 267, 272, 280, 284
authorial intention 41–42, 44, 127, 129, 144
biblical chronology 125–129
Cajetan, Thomas 54, 132, 196, 251
canonicity 19, 29, 30, 124–125, 132–138, 149, 184, 285–286
Chrysostom, John 19, 106, 124
clarity 5, 7, 8, 13, 18, 20–21, 25–27, 35, 45, 106, 142–143, 148, 191–247, 252, 281, 284, 286
    and the character of God 205–207, 224–225, 229–300, 284
    and the Christian life 207–212, 232, 284
    and the mystery of God 215–216
    internal clarity 232–235
    external clarity 219, 228, 229–232

confidence 7, 111, 191, 211–212, 275, 285, 286, 287
creation 65–66, 73, 87, 120, 139
dating of biblical books 101, 123–124, 132–138
doctors of the church 11
Duns Scotus, Johannes 36, 257
early church 11, 17–31, 32, 42, 142, 177, 190–191, 196, 198, 199, 254, 284
Eck, Johannes 62, 188, 254, 276Epistle of James
Erasmus, Desiderius 43, 45, 84, 106, 112, 132, 142, 143, 162, 174, 186, 193, 194, 200–201, 205, 213–217, 220, 229, 231, 232, 235, 239, 240, 286
error in the Bible 125–129, 130, 138–141
experience 271–274
faith 13, 94–95, 99, 103, 104, 111, 130, 139, 150, 151, 152, 204, 207–210, 219, 227, 234–235, 269
Gospel 29, 74, 75–76, 131–132, 133–135, 170–177, 184, 200, 283
Gregory the Great 17, 23, 102, 106, 253
Holy Scripture
    authority of 5, 29, 32, 36, 119–123, 125, 131, 137, 139, 184, 190, 196, 239–241, 252, 276–279, 285, 286
    authorship of books 123–124
    divine origin of 15–17, 32, 42

hierarchy of books within 131–132
human origin of 96, 97, 98, 101, 102
preservation of 101
purpose of 274–276
humanism 3, 7, 44–46, 231
illumination 43, 269
inerrancy 51, 92, 140–141
inspiration 7, 8, 16, 22-24, 32, 91-146, 147, 150-152, 191, 247
prophetic pattern of 95–103, 104
analogy with incarnation 103–112
of doctrinal content of Scripture 112–113, 286
of Scriptural text 113–119, 139, 143–145, 285–286
interpretive method 20–21, 141–146, 184–190, 241–246, 252, 279–282, 285–286
Israel 13
Jesus Christ 14, 15
as the centre of the Bible 17–18, 20, 24, 40–41, 124–125, 130, 131–132, 152–163, 168, 172, 184, 185–187, 194, 218, 227, 252, 280, 284, 285, 287
cross of 14
incarnation 14
justification by faith 2, 65, 133, 134, 136, 165, 237–239
language 31–32, 114–117, 143–144, 225–227, 230–231, 235–239
Law 13, 14, 26, 141, 170–177, 184, 283
Leipzig debate (1519) 62, 188, 196, 251, 254, 261, 276
letter and spirit 167–171, 283
literal and historical sense 25, 38–43, 145, 155–156, 158, 184, 185, 225–227

Lord's Supper 78–79, 115–116, 117, 201–203, 210–212, 224–228, 240, 244–245, 253
Luther, Martin
change in his views 5–6, 133, 157, 169–170, 245–246, 283, 284
consistency in his views 5–6, 158–159, 175, 194, 204, 264, 280, 283
interest in the doctrine of Scripture 4–5
modern images of 1–2, 6, 68–70, 91–94, 119, 122, 123, 192–194, 213, 220, 227, 247, 249–250, 264–265, 281, 283
monastic training 11, 12, 167, 250, 257, 259, 264
opponents of 132, 137, 140, 188, 193–194, 195–196, 197–199, 220–221, 223–224, 237, 250–251, 254, 263
the man 1, 3, 6, 9, 11, 113, 152, 250, 252–253, 257, 283
Lyra, Nicholas of 40, 43, 126, 147, 156–157, 161–162
Melanchthon, Philip 175, 231
New Testament 14–17, 18–20, 24, 97–100, 138–139, 153–154, 159, 162, 165–166, 172–173, 176, 177–183, 185–186, 189, 217
Occam, William of 37, 49, 54, 257, 267, 270, 276, 284
Oecolampadius, Johannes 211, 253, 203
Old Testament 13, 15, 17–18, 19, 23, 24, 39, 40, 95–98, 101, 138–139, 152–154, 159–162, 165–166, 168, 172–173, 176, 177–183, 185-186, 189, 217
Prierias, Sylvester 177, 140, 196, 250. 251, 263, 266
prophets/prophecy 13, 14, 15, 130, 153, 158, 178–179, 201

Quadriga 27, 33–34, 38, 42, 45, 110, 155, 167, 169, 170–171, 185, 241, 283, 286

radicals 141, 170–171, 219, 224, 226–227, 232, 239, 253, 272–273

reason 94–95, 111, 265–271

scholasticism 7, 31–44, 45, 193, 257–260

sin, noetic effects of 107–108, 228–229, 268–270

sola scriptura 8, 249–282, 286

Spirit 14, 15, 16, 19, 27, 32, 33, 41, 94–95, 96, 98–99, 101, 102, 103, 104, 111, 112, 113, 116, 118, 121, 128, 130, 139, 141, 142, 151, 152, 164, 201, 219, 233–234, 273, 286

Staupitz, Johannes von 12

sufficiency 7, 8, 13, 17, 24, 30, 249–282, 284, 286–287

theology of the cross 109–112, 170, 206–207

tradition 28–31, 36–38, 119, 122, 197–200, 219–220, 231–232, 249–251, 252–265, 276–279, 280, 281, 284, 286–287

tropology 27, 41, 157–158, 246

unity of Scripture 7, 8, 41, 147–190, 243–244, 247, 252, 284

Victorines 3–4, 34–35, 38, 39–41, 42, 147, 192

Word of God
  Jesus Christ as 72–73, 82–83
  spoken 13, 15, 72, 74–77, 104–105, 121, 181–183
  threefold manner of 68–89, 104, 122, 285
  written and read 13, 15, 76–89 104–105, 119–121, 145, 181–183, 285–286

Zwingli, Huldrych 78, 115–116, 117, 203, 211, 225, 240, 253, 280

Author Index

Allison, G. R., 196
Althaus, P., 5, 50, 94, 154, 176, 183, 195, 234, 272, 284

Bainton, R. H., 51
Barr, J., 128, 197
Barth, K., 51, 89, 123
Barton, J., 286
Bauer, K., 171
Becke, U., 3
Beisser, F., 5, 49, 58, 94, 196, 198, 210, 223, 232, 233, 234, 236, 237, 238, 240
Benoit, A., 19
Bodamer, W., 51
Bornkamm, H., 3, 94, 160
Brecht, M., 11, 54, 140, 142, 174, 178
Bromiley, G. W., 180
Bruns, G. L., 285
Burdach, K., 57

Callahan, J. P., 197, 246
Calov, A., 94
Campenhausen, H. F. von, 19
Carter, C. S., 48

Daniel, H.-C., 196
Dockery, D. S., 48, 68, 155
Doermann, R. W., 284
Duchrow, U., 196
Dunbar, D. G., 18

Ebeling, G., 2, 49, 69, 94, 107, 155, 158, 159, 160, 169, 171, 172, 190, 229, 238, 253, 277
Ellingsen, M., 172
Erikson, E. H., 3
Evans, G. R., 26, 27, 32, 35, 37, 39, 42, 43, 44, 150

Farkasfalvy, D., 19

Feld, H., 155
Fischer, D. H., 13
Fischer, R. H., 270, 274

Gerrish, B. A., 4, 37, 52, 126, 257, 270, 272, 273
Godfrey, W. R., 106, 126
Goeser, R., 90
Gougaud, L., 35
Graham, W. A., 49, 56, 57
Grant, R. M., 26
Gray, H. H., 198
Gritsch, E. W., 176, 256

Hagen, K., 10
Hägglund, B., 149
Hamilton, B., 32, 33
Hanson, R. P. C., 25
Harnack, C. G. A. von, 50
Hatch, N., 269
Hayden-Roy, P., 234, 238
Hendrix, S., 2
Hermann, R., 94, 196, 224
Herrmann, W., 94
Hirsch, E., 159
Holl, K., 94, 134, 159
Hollaz, D., 94
Hovland, C. W., 276

Janz, D. R., 261
Jensen, P. F., 115
Johansen, J. H., 66

Kelly, J. N. D., 22
Klug, E. F., 2, 52, 61, 69, 70, 106, 247
Knox, D. B., 123
Kohls, E.-W., 1, 196
Kooiman, W. J., 50, 111, 245
Köstlin, J., 61, 234
Kropatscheck, F., 32
Kuss, O., 196, 234

Lane, A. N. S., 269, 276
Lawson, J., 149
Lazareth, W. H., 162
Liefeld, T. S., 253
Lienhard, M., 154, 160
Loeschen, J., 212
Loewenich, W. von, 2, 11, 210
Lohse, B., 69, 270
Lønning, I., 124, 197, 216, 217, 218, 254
Lotz, D. W., 50, 121, 124
Lubac, H. de, 33

Maschke, T., 168
Mau, R., 196, 198
Maurer, W., 94
McGrath, A. E., 36, 45, 70, 146, 155, 159, 160, 197, 199, 210, 216, 241, 246, 254, 276, 284
McKim, D. K., 2, 106, 109
Metzger, B. M., 18
Montgomery, J. W., 2, 94
Mühlen, K.-H. zur, 159, 263
Muller, R. A., 1, 12, 71, 124

Neuner, P., 196, 223, 236

Oberman, H. A., 2, 11, 36, 38, 70, 123, 140, 155, 253, 254, 257, 263, 267, 270, 273, 276
Ozment, S. E., 40, 271

Pannenberg, W., 197, 218, 232
Pauck, W., 50
Pelikan, J., 17, 18, 47, 70, 134, 256, 257
Pfitzner, V. C., 160
Pieper, F., 94
Pilch, J. J., 98, 159
Pinomaa, L., 2, 277
Polman, A. D. R., 19, 23
Prenter, R., 70, 176
Preus, J. S., 98, 154, 158

Quanbeck, W. A., 49
Quenstedt, J., 94

Reid, J. K. S., 49, 69

Reinke, D. R., 98, 159
Reiter, P., 3
Reu, M., 52, 135
Ritschl, A., 94
Rogers, J. B., 2, 106, 109
Rohnert, W., 52, 94
Rohr, J. von, 276
Rosato, L., 37
Rothen, B., 196
Ruokanen, M., 48, 69, 93, 94, 95, 96, 101, 106, 111, 114, 232, 234, 238
Rupp, E. G., 288

Sasse, H., 94, 150
Scheel, O., 94
Schempp, P., 51, 94
Schröger, F., 196, 223, 236
Seeberg, R., 48, 94, 125
Selge, K.-V., 269
Siggins, I. D. K., 114, 190, 244
Silva, M., 197, 218, 246
Smalley, B., 26, 34, 35, 37, 38, 39, 40, 42, 43, 44
Spitz, L. W., 3, 61, 126
Steinmetz, D., 2, 12, 211, 227, 265
Stendahl, K., 49, 190
Stuhlmacher, P., 285
Surburg, R. F., 232

Teigen, E. T., 210, 225
Thiselton, A., 25, 198, 209, 246
Thompson, J. L., 12
Thompson, M. D., 206
Tierney, B., 37
Torrance, T. F., 70
Tracy, D., 26
Tregelles, S. P., 20

Vawter, B., 22
Vogelsang, E., 159

Watson, P. S., 49, 69, 218
Wendorf, J., 160
Wiener, P. F., 1
Williams, A. L., 18
Wolf, E., 196
Wood, A. S., 52, 93, 106, 108, 151, 244

Studies in Christian History and Thought

(All titles uniform with this volume)
Dates in bold are of projected publication

David Bebbington
Holiness in Nineteenth-Century England

David Bebbington stresses the relationship of movements of spirituality to changes in their cultural setting, especially the legacies of the Enlightenment and Romanticism. He shows that these broad shifts in ideological mood had a profound effect on the ways in which piety was conceptualized and practised. Holiness was intimately bound up with the spirit of the age.

2000 / 0-85364-981-2 / viii + 98pp

J. William Black
Reformation Pastors
Richard Baxter and the Ideal of the Reformed Pastor

This work examines Richard Baxter's *Gildas Salvianus, The Reformed Pastor* (1656) and explores each aspect of his pastoral strategy in light of his own concern for 'reformation' and in the broader context of Edwardian, Elizabethan and early Stuart pastoral ideals and practice.

2003 / 1-84227-190-3 / xxii + 308pp

James Bruce
Prophecy, Miracles, Angels, *and* Heavenly Light?
The Eschatology, Pneumatology and Missiology of Adomnán's Life of Columba

This book surveys approaches to the marvellous in hagiography, providing the first critique of Plummer's hypothesis of Irish saga origin. It then analyses the uniquely systematized phenomena in the *Life of Columba* from Adomnán's seventh-century theological perspective, identifying the coming of the eschatological Kingdom as the key to understanding.

2004 / 1-84227-227-6 / xviii + 286pp

Colin J. Bulley
The Priesthood of Some Believers
Developments from the General to the Special Priesthood in the Christian Literature of the First Three Centuries

The first in-depth treatment of early Christian texts on the priesthood of all believers shows that the developing priesthood of the ordained related closely to the division between laity and clergy and had deleterious effects on the practice of the general priesthood.

2000 / 1-84227-034-6 / xii + 336pp

November 2004

Anthony R. Cross (ed.)
Ecumenism and History
Studies in Honour of John H.Y. Briggs

This collection of essays examines the inter-relationships between the two fields in which Professor Briggs has contributed so much: history—particularly Baptist and Nonconformist—and the ecumenical movement. With contributions from colleagues and former research students from Britain, Europe and North America, *Ecumenism and History* provides wide-ranging studies in important aspects of Christian history, theology and ecumenical studies.

2002 / 1-84227-135-0 / xx + 362pp

Maggi Dawn
Confessions of an Inquiring Spirit
Form as Constitutive of Meaning in S.T. Coleridge's Theological Writing

This study of Coleridge's *Confessions* focuses on its confessional, epistolary and fragmentary form, suggesting that attention to these features significantly affects its interpretation. Bringing a close study of these three literary forms, the author suggests ways in which they nuance the text with particular understandings of the Trinity, and of a kenotic christology. Some parallels are drawn between Romantic and postmodern dilemmas concerning the authority of the biblical text.

2006 / 1-84227-255-1 / approx. 224 pp

Ruth Gouldbourne
The Flesh and the Feminine
Gender and Theology in the Writings of Caspar Schwenckfeld

Caspar Schwenckfeld and his movement exemplify one of the radical communities of the sixteenth century. Challenging theological and liturgical norms, they also found themselves challenging social and particularly gender assumptions. In this book, the issues of the relationship between radical theology and the understanding of gender are considered.

2005 / 1-84227-048-6 / approx. 304pp

Galen K. Johnson
Prisoner of Conscience
John Bunyan on Self, Community and Christian Faith

This is an interdisciplinary study of John Bunyan's understanding of conscience across his autobiographical, theological and fictional writings, investigating whether conscience always deserves fidelity, and how Bunyan's view of conscience affects his relationship both to modern Western individualism and historic Christianity.

2003 / 1-84227- 151-2 / xvi + 236pp

R.T. Kendall
Calvin and English Calvinism to 1649
The author's thesis is that those who formed the Westminster Confession of Faith, which is regarded as Calvinism, in fact departed from John Calvin on two points: (1) the extent of the atonement and (2) the ground of assurance of salvation.
1997 / 0-85364-827-1 / xii + 264pp

Byung-Ho Moon
Lex Dei Regula Vivendi et Vivificandi
Calvin's Christological Understanding of the Law in the Light of his Concept of Christus Mediator Legis
This book explores the coherence between Christology and soteriology in Calvin's theology of the law, examining its intellectual origins and his position on the concept and extent of Christ's mediation of the law. A comparative study between Calvin and contemporary Reformers—Luther, Bucer, Melancthon and Bullinger—and his opponent Michael Servetus is made for the purpose of pointing out the unique feature of Calvin's Christological understanding of the law.
2005 / 1-84227-318-3 / approx. 370pp

John Eifion Morgan-Wynne
Holy Spirit and Religious Experience in Christian Writings, c.AD90–200
This study examines how far Christians in the third to fifth generations (c.AD90–200) attributed their sense of encounter with the divine presence, their sense of illumination in the truth or guidance in decision-making, and their sense of ethical empowerment to the activity of the Holy Spirit in their lives.
2005 / 1-84227-319-1 / approx. 274pp

James I. Packer
The Redemption and Restoration of Man in the Thought of Richard Baxter
James I. Packer provides a full and sympathetic exposition of Richard Baxter's doctrine of humanity, created and fallen; its redemption by Christ Jesus; and its restoration in the image of God through the obedience of faith by the power of the Holy Spirit.
2002 / 1-84227-147-4 / 432pp

November 2004

Andrew Partington,
Church and State
The Contribution of the Church of England Bishops to the House of Lords during the Thatcher Years

In *Church and State*, Andrew Partington argues that the contribution of the Church of England bishops to the House of Lords during the Thatcher years was overwhelmingly critical of the government; failed to have a significant influence in the public realm; was inefficient, being undertaken by a minority of those eligible to sit on the Bench of Bishops; and was insufficiently moral and spiritual in its content to be distinctive. On the basis of this, and the likely reduction of the number of places available for Church of England bishops in a fully reformed Second Chamber, the author argues for an evolution in the Church of England's approach to the service of its bishops in the House of Lords. He proposes the Church of England works to overcome the genuine obstacles which hinder busy diocesan bishops from contributing to the debates of the House of Lords and to its life more informally.

2005 / 1-84227-334-5 / approx. 324pp

Alan P.F. Sell
Enlightenment, Ecumenism, Evangel
Theological Themes and Thinkers 1550–2000

This book consists of papers in which such interlocking topics as the Enlightenment, the problem of authority, the development of doctrine, spirituality, ecumenism, theological method and the heart of the gospel are discussed. Issues of significance to the church at large are explored with special reference to writers from the Reformed and Dissenting traditions.

2005 / 1-84227330-2 / xviii + 422pp

Alan P.F. Sell
Hinterland Theology
Some Reformed and Dissenting Adjustments

Many books have been written on theology's 'giants' and significant trends, but what of those lesser-known writers who adjusted to them? In this book some hinterland theologians of the British Reformed and Dissenting traditions, who followed in the wake of toleration, the Evangelical Revival, the rise of modern biblical criticism and Karl Barth, are allowed to have their say. They include Thomas Ridgley, Ralph Wardlaw, T.V. Tymms and N.H.G. Robinson.

2006 / 1-84227-331-0

Alan P.F. Sell and Anthony R. Cross (eds)
Protestant Nonconformity in the Twentieth Century
In this collection of essays scholars representative of a number of Nonconformist traditions reflect thematically on Nonconformists' life and witness during the twentieth century. Among the subjects reviewed are biblical studies, theology, worship, evangelism and spirituality, and ecumenism. Over and above its immediate interest, this collection provides a marker to future scholars and others wishing to know how some of their forebears assessed Nonconformity's contribution to a variety of fields during the century leading up to Christianity's third millennium.
2003 / 1-84227-221-7 / x + 398pp

Mark Smith
Religion in Industrial Society
Oldham and Saddleworth 1740–1865
This book analyses the way British churches sought to meet the challenge of industrialization and urbanization during the period 1740–1865. Working from a case-study of Oldham and Saddleworth, Mark Smith challenges the received view that the Anglican Church in the eighteenth century was characterized by complacency and inertia, and reveals Anglicanism's vigorous and creative response to the new conditions. He reassesses the significance of the centrally directed church reforms of the mid-nineteenth century, and emphasizes the importance of local energy and enthusiasm. Charting the growth of denominational pluralism in Oldham and Saddleworth, Dr Smith compares the strengths and weaknesses of the various Anglican and Nonconformist approaches to promoting church growth. He also demonstrates the extent to which all the churches participated in a common culture shaped by the influence of evangelicalism, and shows that active co-operation between the churches rather than denominational conflict dominated. This revised and updated edition of Dr Smith's challenging and original study makes an important contribution both to the social history of religion and to urban studies.
2005 / 1-84227-335-3 / approx. 300pp

Martin Sutherland
Peace, Toleration and Decay
The Ecclesiology of Later Stuart Dissent
This fresh analysis brings to light the complexity and fragility of the later Stuart Nonconformist consensus. Recent findings on wider seventeenth-century thought are incorporated into a new picture of the dynamics of Dissent and the roots of evangelicalism.
2003 / 1-84227-152-0 / xxii + 216pp

G. Michael Thomas
The Extent of the Atonement
A Dilemma for Reformed Theology from Calvin to the Consensus
A study of the way Reformed theology addressed the question, 'Did Christ die for all, or for the elect only?', commencing with John Calvin, and including debates with Lutheranism, the Synod of Dort and the teaching of Moïse Amyraut.
1997 / 0-85364-828-X / x + 278pp

Mark D. Thompson
A Sure Ground on which to Stand
The Relation of Authority and Interpretive Method of Luther's Approach to Scripture
The best interpreter of Luther is Luther himself. Unfortunately many modern studies have superimposed contemporary agendas upon this sixteenth-century Reformer's writings. This fresh study examines Luther's own words to find an explanation for his robust confidence in the Scriptures, a confidence that generated the famous 'stand' at Worms in 1521.
2004 / 1-84227-145-8 / xvi + 322pp

Carl R. Trueman and R.S. Clark (eds)
Protestant Scholasticism
Essays in Reassessment
Traditionally Protestant theology, between Luther's early reforming career and the dawn of the Enlightenment, has been seen in terms of decline and fall into the wastelands of rationalism and scholastic speculation. In this volume a number of scholars question such an interpretation. The editors argue that the development of post-Reformation Protestantism can only be understood when a proper historical model of doctrinal change is adopted. This historical concern underlies the subsequent studies of theologians such as Calvin, Beza, Olevian, Baxter, and the two Turrentini. The result is a significantly different reading of the development of Protestant Orthodoxy, one which both challenges the older scholarly interpretations and clichés about the relationship of Protestantism to, among other things, scholasticism and rationalism, and which demonstrates the fruitfulness of the new, historical approach.
1999 / 0-85364-853-0 / xx + 344pp

Shawn D. Wright
Our Sovereign Refuge
The Pastoral Theology of Theodore Beza

Our Sovereign Refuge is a study of the pastoral theology of the Protestant reformer who inherited the mantle of leadership in the Reformed church from John Calvin. Countering a common view of Beza as supremely a 'scholastic' theologian who deviated from Calvin's biblical focus, Wright uncovers a new portrait. He was not a cold and rigid academic theologian obsessed with probing the eternal decrees of God. Rather, by placing him in his pastoral context and by noting his concerns in his pastoral and biblical treatises, Wright shows that Beza was fundamentally a committed Christian who was troubled by the vicissitudes of life in the second half of the sixteenth century. He believed that the biblical truth of the supreme sovereignty of God alone could support Christians on their earthly pilgrimage to heaven. This pastoral and personal portrait forms the heart of Wright's argument.

2004 / 1-84227-252-7 / xviii + 308pp

Paternoster
9 Holdom Avenue
Bletchley
Milton Keynes MK1 1QR
United Kingdom

Web: www.authenticmedia.co.uk/paternoster

www.ingramcontent.com/pod-product-compliance
Lightning Source LLC
Chambersburg PA
CBHW050614300426
44112CB00012B/1496